13 Ideas That Are Transforming the Community College World

13 Ideas That Are Transforming the Community College World

Edited by Terry U. O'Banion

AMERICAN
ASSOCIATION OF
COMMUNITY
COLLEGES

ROWMAN & LITTLEFIELD
Lanham • Boulder • New York • London

Published by Rowman & Littlefield
An imprint of The Rowman & Littlefield Publishing Group, Inc.
4501 Forbes Boulevard, Suite 200, Lanham, Maryland 20706
www.rowman.com

Unit A, Whitacre Mews, 26-34 Stannary Street, London SE11 4AB

British Library Cataloguing in Publication Information Available

Library of Congress Cataloging-in-Publication Data

Names: O'Banion, Terry, 1936–
Title: 13 ideas that are transforming the community college world / Terry U. O'Banion.
Description: Lanham : Rowman & Littlefield, [2019] | Includes bibliographical references and index.
Identifiers: LCCN 2018047776 (print) | LCCN 2018048454 (ebook) | ISBN 9781475844917 (Electronic) | ISBN 9781475844894 (cloth : alk. paper) | ISBN 9781475844900 (pbk. : alk. paper)
Subjects: LCSH: Community colleges—United States. | Community colleges—United States—Administration.
Classification: LCC LB2328.15.U6 (ebook) | LCC LB2328.15.U6 O32 2019 (print) | DDC 378.1/5430973—dc23
LC record available at https://lccn.loc.gov/2018047776

∞™ The paper used in this publication meets the minimum requirements of American
National Standard for Information Sciences Permanence of Paper for Printed Library
Materials, ANSI/NISO Z39.48-1992.

Printed in the United States of America

For my good friend, K. Patricia Cross, endowed professor emerita at both Harvard and Berkeley, who has contributed more to higher education—especially community colleges—than any other leader of her generation.

Contents

Foreword

Walter Bumphus

In fundamental ways, community colleges are a reflection of America itself. They are egalitarian, complex, and ever-changing. Small wonder, then, that they are sometimes also ill-defined or misunderstood. Throughout their 117-year history, community colleges have been willing—even eager—to innovate to serve the needs of a highly diverse student population and disparate communities. Ironically, their very uniqueness, as evolving institutions that consciously and continually reinvent themselves, can become a vulnerability.

Fortunately, the majority of those who actually benefit from community colleges face no such quandary. A recent study by the think tank New America indicates that 83 percent of those polled had a positive opinion of community colleges. Still, the question "What is a community college?" elicits a range of responses depending on widely varying personal experiences. I addressed this topic in a recent *Community College Daily* commentary.

Clarity about the important role of today's community colleges and the deep and lasting value they bring to individuals and society is crucial. That is why I am so enthusiastic about this new book edited by Terry O'Banion, *13 Ideas That Are Transforming the Community College World*.

Few individuals are as qualified to identify, analyze, and put into context the key concepts that drive the contemporary community college as is O'Banion. As CEO of the League for Innovation for twenty-three years, a prolific author of seminal works for the two-year sector, and an engaged and engaging presenter, O'Banion has few equals. He has been a recognized thought leader and a passionate defender of community colleges for more than six decades.

This book aims to reboot the intellectual and operational concepts energizing today's community college, and its publication couldn't be timelier or more relevant. O'Banion has assembled an impressive "bench" of expert chapter authors (twenty-three national leaders representing twelve national organizations) who are both seasoned and forward thinking. Each brings realistic, informed, and clear-eyed thinking to ideas that have had a major impact on community colleges over the last two decades. These are ideas that continue to evolve to meet changing academic and cultural needs at the institutions and for the communities they serve.

Some of the ideas presented in the chapters have been part of the community college lexicon for many years but continue to exert considerable influence: the learning college, the completion agenda, institutional effectiveness. Other chapters address broad topics such as workforce development and developmental learning, part of the bedrock of the community college mission but now undergoing major reforms. Several chapters focus on more recent efforts to strengthen the educational continuum: better transition from high school to community college to baccalaureate institutions. Appropriate focus is given to the exciting and still expanding Community College Promise movement, intended "to make a community college education as accessible, free, and universal as the American high school has been for nearly a century!"

I was particularly pleased to see a chapter by Kay McClenney on the Guided Pathways Project, a multiyear effort led by the American Association of Community Colleges (AACC) that involves seven national partners. The project is aimed at helping community colleges design and implement structured academic and career pathways at scale. Pathways has been under way for just a few years, but the principles guiding its work have long been proven to improve student outcomes and persistence.

Adding substantially to the impact of *13 Ideas* is fresh thinking on overarching concepts related to college governance and transformative leadership. In our knowledge economy, technology infuses every facet of the learning enterprise, and its multiple effects are given new scrutiny in this work.

Awareness of these driving forces is crucial at all levels of community college operations, but it is especially so for a new generation of leaders. It is they who must understand the community college mission, advocate for its advancement, and fiercely guard the integrity of its values. With a virtual tsunami of leadership turnover now engulfing community colleges, every sitting and aspiring leader should be thoroughly grounded in the concepts *13 Ideas* presents: their genesis, how they evolved, and why they matter.

The AACC Board and I spend a good deal of our time pondering how to better prepare future community college leaders for the role of a lifetime. Working with staff, we devise programs and enlist topic experts who share their knowledge and experiences. Many of the authors contributing to *13 Ideas* have been frequent participants in AACC's multilevel Leadership Suite and other association programs, as well as contributors to the development and ongoing refinement of the AACC Leadership Competencies.

At a time when discourse is too often measured in 140 characters, and analysis can be more ephemeral than cogent, this new publication presents a much-needed and substantive reexamination of enduring and transformative learning concepts specific to two-year institutions. In a powerful, highly readable work, O'Banion and his colleagues have effectively synthesized many of the "big" ideas that will guide community colleges to continued progress and greater, more impactful service to students.

Preface

Terry U. O'Banion

In the past fifteen to twenty years most books on the community college have examined very generic topics, such as workforce education, leadership, teaching and learning, and diversity, or very specific topics, such as black male success, civic responsibility, college suicide, benchmarking, critical thinking, and media relations. Of the seventy-three community college titles listed since 1992 under "Jossey-Bass—Higher and Adult Education," only Cohen and Brawer's seminal work *The American Community College* provides a broad view of the community college.

One other exception is *Redesigning America's Community Colleges* by Tom Bailey and colleagues, published by Harvard University Press. The titles in the New Directions series at Jossey-Bass are all targeted at a specific topic aimed at a very limited audience. Of the twenty-one community college titles listed for Stylus Publishing, most books are designed for audiences interested in the same limited topics: gun violence, baccalaureate degrees, faculty learning communities, GED completers, fundraising, racism, and so forth.

Community college educators and their supporters need a more refreshing book that provides a broad framework for ideas or issues that undergird the community college. Moreover, with the glut of information available today, readers will find very useful a book that summarizes the primary ideas that animate the contemporary community college. The purpose of *13 Ideas That Are Transforming the Community College World* is to expand the field by engaging a broad audience of community college educators and stakeholders in a discussion of the most significant issues facing this institution.

This book will be of great interest to the more than fifteen hundred presidents and chancellors and the more than forty-five hundred vice presidents of community colleges as a primer on the ideas they have had to implement but may never have had an opportunity to fully understand. The book will be very attractive as a text for community college leadership and higher education programs because of its content range and the quality of the authors of the chapters. The more than sixty-five hundred community college trustees who are members of the Association of Community College Trustees will find this book a very handy guide to better understand the ideas and issues for which they bear governance responsibility.

Faculty leaders and new faculty participating in required orientation programs constitute a defined audience. Policy makers, legislators, and foundation officers may find this book quite useful for themselves and their staffs. There may be an international audience because of the increasing interest in community colleges around the world. This book should definitely become a standard for professional development programs in which colleges purchase multiple copies for their administrators, full- and part-time faculty, trustees, foundation boards, and local partners.

The thirteen ideas were created by surveying the opinions of a group of national community college leaders about which ideas should be included and who is best qualified to write a chapter on each one. I asked that the ideas be "contemporary," meaning an idea that has emerged during the last twenty years or so and is still evolving and being embedded in community college culture. Total Quality Management and the Common Core of General Education, for example, are significant ideas that had a great impact at one time on the community college but are no longer considered "contemporary."

Some of the ideas included, such as developmental education and workforce education, are programs that have been well established in the community college for many decades, but they are going through major reforms that make them more significant and more contemporary than ever. Some topics, such as entrepreneurial college, sustainability, and globalization—suggested by national leaders—are still in the early stages of development and may not have a sufficient history to have a broad impact compared to the topics included.

The twenty-three authors of the chapters in this volume may constitute the most significant and substantive list of authors ever to participate in an edited book on the community college. Each author is a nationally recognized authority on the topic he or she writes about. Some are seasoned by fifty or more years in their special fields; others bring new energy and new ideas to the table. All have played major roles as leaders of national organizations.

I am deeply honored that each author accepted my invitation to be a colleague in this effort and urge readers to read their brief biographies. My colleagues and I invite you to immerse yourself in these thirteen ideas that are transforming the community college and then engage your colleagues in rich and courageous discussions to expand and improve opportunities for our students to make a good living and live a good life.

Introduction

The Continuing Evolution of the American Community College

Terry U. O'Banion

When William Rainey Harper, president of the University of Chicago, and J. Stanley Brown, superintendent of Joliet Township High School in Illinois, roomed together at Baptist conventions, they often talked late into the evening about their students. They were equally concerned about quality and opportunity.

Brown went to Joliet in 1893 as the principal of Joliet High School and became a strong advocate of encouraging low-performing students to consider attending college. He transformed the local high school into one of the best in the region, employing a faculty and creating a curriculum that impressed area universities. As early as 1894 Brown included courses with college-level content, and several universities, including the University of Illinois and the University of Michigan, accepted these credits for transfer.

On June 2, 1896, Professor Francis W. Kelsey of the University of Michigan wrote to Brown: "I am much pleased to learn that you have taken your students over more than the required preparatory work. If you will kindly give to those who come to the University of Michigan a certificate to the effect that the extra work has been well done, I will see that advanced credit is given for it" (Sterling, 2001, para. 5).

Harper went to the University of Chicago in 1891 as the first president, at the invitation of founding philanthropist John D. Rockefeller. Harper was a distinguished professor of religion, one of the great innovators of his time, and an organizational genius. President at the age of thirty-five, he was known as a "young man in a hurry." He was indefatigable in his efforts to

1

make the University of Chicago the prototype of the great American university, and he succeeded.

Through their Baptist connections and roles as educational leaders in Illinois, Brown and Harper began to discuss how their institutions could work together to help underprepared students attend college—a value they both strongly championed. Their collaboration led to the creation of Joliet Junior College in 1901, housed in Joliet High School. The first class enrolled six students and soon became a feeder institution to the University of Chicago. It was a simple model, in which Joliet Junior College would serve as a junior academy to the University of Chicago's senior academy.

Brown and Harper had not planned for their idea to become one of the most important and substantive ideas in the history of higher education—an idea that has been evolving for 117 years and that will likely continue to change for decades to come.

WHAT IS THIS THING, THIS COMMUNITY COLLEGE IDEA?

In a February 1, 2018, speech to a Republican congressional retreat in West Virginia, President Donald Trump said, "A lot of people don't know what a community college means or represents." He elaborated on his views "And I think the word 'vocational' is a much better word than, in many cases, a community college. You learn mechanical, you learn bricklaying and carpentry, and all of these things. We don't have that very much anymore."

Trump was right about a lot of people not knowing what a community college means or represents, because as a dynamic institution it has been changing for decades. Advocates and critics alike have tried to pin it down and tag it with a name; these names appear briefly in the literature until the next new one comes along. Here are some perspectives on what a community college is, culled by the author from a variety of sources:

- A handmaiden to the university, a junior academy serving the senior academy, a bridge between high school and the university, an institution to catch the overflow when universities are full.
- A high school with ashtrays, a college for the dumb rich and the bright poor, a part-time college for part-time students taught by part-time faculty, a holding place to keep students off the street.
- A technical college, a vocational college, an occupational college.
- A junior college, a two-year college, a community-junior college.
- A second-chance college, all things to all people, the nexus of the community.
- The workforce engine of the nation, a college for remediation, a college for general education.

- The teaching college, the learning college, the institution of student access, the institution of student success.
- The innovation college, the flexible college, the responsive college, an entrepreneurial college.
- The people's college, democracy's college, tomorrow's college, the comprehensive community college.

In 2019 and for several years to come, the most ubiquitous and most accepted name for this institution is likely to be "community college." The name avoids the pejorative and the hyperbolic and is generic enough to include a variety of values, missions, purposes, programs, policies, and practices under its "big tent." However, with the rapid changes in American society fueled by advances in technology, pharmacology, social justice, economic justice, demographics, climate change, global issues, science, and so forth, nothing about the future is guaranteed.

The community college, responsive to its local community and increasingly to the global community, will continue to change rapidly. It will mutate into new forms, grow appendages to respond to special interests and needs, lose energy because of political gridlock, and be attacked because it does not deliver on its promises.

In the worst-case scenario, the community college could fall into the hands of fascists and become a tool of the state to train followers. In the best-case scenario, the community college will continue to evolve into an "ism-free" force that serves all the people with its key goal intact: helping students make a good living and live a good life.

THIRTEEN IDEAS THAT ARE TRANSFORMING THE COMMUNITY COLLEGE WORLD

The editor and authors of this book are strong advocates of the best-case scenario and believe that the community college's best days are still ahead. The thirteen ideas presented here by national leaders are all very positive ones that are transforming the community college world; they will shape the future of the community college and determine what it will become and what it will be called.

National leaders determined these thirteen ideas and also suggested the authors, who were invited to follow a set of guidelines in preparing their chapters. In the following sections each of the thirteen ideas is summarized for the reader by the editor, along with his own perspectives on each idea. For a more complete review of the ideas, readers are encouraged to review the chapters in which they have special interest.

In the epilogue the editor suggests that the curriculum is the elephant in the room, overlooked by current reformers as one of the most important ideas that could transform the community college world, and he proposes an approach to the creation of a new curriculum he calls an "essential education" that will help students make a good living and live a good life (O'Banion, 2016).

Chapter 1, The Learning Paradigm

Institutions of higher education in the United States have achieved worldwide recognition in pursuit of three key missions: research, teaching, and service—missions valued by their stakeholders primarily in that order. The great centers of university research have produced breakthroughs in every field of science that have made American universities the envy of the world. Because of their success, "research" has become embedded as one of the cardinal values and purposes of higher education.

Leading four-year colleges and community colleges have established "teaching" as a second cardinal value, as many four-year colleges provide ideal residential communities for selected groups of students, and community colleges provide innovative approaches to assist great numbers of underprepared students in achieving success. All levels of institutions ascribe to "service" as an expression of their core values as they work to improve society at the local, state, national, and international levels. Research, teaching, and service have provided a rich harvest from the higher education enterprise for American society and the world.

At the end of the twentieth century another key mission or purpose—a corollary of research, teaching, and service—began to sprout in the landscape of higher education. The new mission was not new at all, but it had not been as visible as research, teaching, and service in the policies, programs, and practices of institutions. Awakened from its dormancy, it began to claim territory that could establish it as more than a graft or a mutation of the historical missions rooted for decades.

At the beginning of the twenty-first century it became increasingly clear that "learning" had broken through the traditional hardpan of higher education and had established its own patch in the groves of academe. For some who toil in the vineyards of higher education, "learning" will be no more than an upstart, an inconsequential sprout destined to wither and die. For others "learning" is the core business of all educational institutions—a transcendent value that arches over research, teaching, and service—providing a sharply focused perspective that will greatly enrich the work of the educational community.

As a newly articulated mission of higher education, "learning" has been cited by several leaders as part of the triumvirate of traditional missions. In a letter to the editor of *Change* magazine, James Bess, professor of higher education at New York University, said, "Institutions of higher education must maintain their unique roles in society—as extraordinary places where *teaching, learning, and research* (italics added) can unfold, unfettered by the crass, short-term expectations of profit" (2000, p. 6).

Two years later, in the lead article of the Association of Governing Board's newsletter, Berberet and McMillin (2002, p. 1) stated, "It doesn't take a Ph.D. to know that a college or university fulfills its multiple missions—*student learning, discovery of new knowledge, and community engagement* (italics added)—chiefly through its faculty." It is noteworthy that "learning" is now reflected in key mission statements by major universities and national organizations.

In the last twenty years a learning revolution has spread rapidly across all levels of American higher education. George Boggs and his colleagues at Palomar College in California were among the first champions who launched the idea that the learning paradigm is the overarching purpose of all higher education. In 1994 the cover of *Business Week* declared a learning revolution to be in progress; in 1995, a special section in *Time* magazine announced the developing learning revolution. In 1996 the first national conference on the learning paradigm, sponsored by Palomar College, was held in San Diego, California, and the Association of Community College Trustees released a special issue of the *Trustee Quarterly*, "The Learning Revolution: A Guide for Community College Trustees."

In 1997 the American Council on Education and the American Association of Community Colleges (AACC) jointly published *A Learning College for the 21st Century* by Terry O'Banion, which for the first time outlined the principles and practices of a learning college. In 1997 and 1998 the League for Innovation and the Public Broadcasting Service (PBS) sponsored three national teleconferences on the learning revolution and the learning college. In a few short years the learning revolution has taken American higher education by storm and has found community colleges to be particularly committed to implementing it (O'Banion & Wilson, 2010, p. 4).

Of all the thirteen ideas in this book, the learning paradigm/learning revolution/learning college may have had more impact than any of the others because it has played a major role, not only in its impact on transforming the community college, but also in transforming four-year colleges, universities, and aspects of American secondary education.

Chapter 2, Community Colleges and the Ladder of Student Success

The purpose of the Access Agenda is to make it easy for students to enroll in college. The purpose of the Student Success Agenda is to assist students in meeting their individual education and career goals. The Completion Agenda is a part of the Student Success Agenda with a more targeted goal of doubling the number of students in the next decade who complete a certificate or associate degree or who transfer and complete their credential at another college or university. (O'Banion, 2013, p. 1)

This statement from *Access, Success, and Completion: A Primer for Community College Faculty, Administrators, Staff, and Trustees* sets the context for this chapter by two of the key players in the student success/completion agenda. Suzanne Walsh and Mark Milliron, working with their colleagues at the Bill & Melinda Gates Foundation, were the architects of the Completion by Design initiative, which is helping to change policies and practices about student success. Creating policies, programs, and practices and engaging personnel in initiatives to improve and expand student success is not an easy task:

The barriers to student success are clear: low credit enrollment, poorly designed and delivered remedial education, overwhelming and unclear choices, and a system out of touch with the needs of students who must often balance work and family with their coursework. The result is a system of higher education that costs too much, takes too long, and graduates too few. (Completecollege.org)

But the student success movement is well under way and making progress in spite of these and other barriers. Never in the history of the community college have so many foundations provided so many funds to support student success. Never in the history of the community college has there been so much research on what works to improve and expand student learning. Never in the history of the community college have so many stakeholders in community colleges, states, and the nation been so deeply engaged in this very focused agenda. Increasing student success has become the overarching mission of the nation's community colleges.

In chapter 2 of this book on the student success agenda, the authors provide a new gestalt, a new framework for bringing all the pieces together to better understand the foundation that will lead community colleges to achieve the goals of the student success/completion agenda. Walsh and Milliron propose a *student success ladder* that includes four key steps, about which they say:

The access step remains essential to allow for any kind of advancement for students, of course. Yes, it is a century-old work in progress, but it is still in need of expansion and even repair. The learning step has always mattered but has received significantly more attention over the last twenty-five years. Focused and sometimes frenzied construction on the completion step has been the work of the last decade, however, and is still galvanizing the higher education practice and policy world in compelling ways.

The coming together over the last five years of work on the access, learning, and completion steps is showing the powerful potential of the concept of the student success ladder. Given that the larger higher education field is diving deep into more of these multistep, comprehensive student success efforts, examples of this work are a major focus here. However, the need to begin more intense work on the last step, postgraduation outcomes, is also explored.

Each of the key steps is placed in historical context by the authors and linked to national initiatives and actions by national organizations. The authors also include another framework created by the Gates Foundation, the loss/momentum framework, which allows colleges to determine at what points on their journeys students lose momentum. Students begin in this framework at connection and move through entry and progress, to completion.

This is a more detailed framework that undergirds the student success ladder and has been used by nine colleges in three states participating in the Gates Foundation Completion by Design initiative. These concepts of ladders, frameworks, and initiatives are providing the conceptual foundations for student success and completion for millions of community college students.

Chapter 3, The College Promise: Transforming the Lives of Community College Students

In April 2017 candidate for president Senator Bernie Sanders introduced a bill with support from Elizabeth Warren, Keith Ellison, and other members of Congress that had the potential to transform higher education. The College for All Act was designed to eliminate tuition and fees at public four-year colleges and universities for students from families that make up to $125,000 per year. The bill would have made community college tuition free for all income levels.

Hilary Clinton, former president Barack Obama, and many progressive leaders and organizations supported the bill, which did not become law. But the bill was the tip of an iceberg that had been floating in the seas of higher education for decades. While it did not catch hold this time, it motivated many other efforts to create tuition-free colleges, led by the idea of the College Promise, reviewed in chapter 3 by the current leaders (Martha Kanter and Andra Armstrong) of the national College Promise Campaign.

California is a case study in the history of free and low tuition for community college students. When Fresno High School opened its collegiate division in 1910 as the first such effort in the state, courses were free to residents of the school district; nonresidents paid a tuition charge of $4.00 a month (Witt, Wattenbarger, Gollattscheck, & Supinger, 1994, pp. 37 & 38). In 1984 California authorized its first-ever per-unit fee for community college students. Fees were initially set at $5.00 per credit unit, with a maximum cap of $50.00 for twelve credits or more. Although the 1960 master plan called for tuition-free public higher education in California, the precedent was set to charge students for taking classes—even if the charges were called fees instead of tuition (Boggs, in press).

The College Promise, building on past efforts, is the major attempt today to finally make college tuition and related expenses free to community college students. As the authors note:

> The College Promise is based on the proposition that a community college or technical education should be as universal, free, and accessible as high school has been since 1929. . . .
>
> A growing number of four-year colleges and universities are also launching the College Promise, many in partnership with community colleges and others on their own or as required by state legislation. But community colleges are dominant in this dramatic expansion of College Promise programs. [Today,] more than two hundred [are] under way in forty-four states, with twenty-three established at the statewide level.

The authors review the history of efforts to secure free tuition and feature some of the most outstanding state efforts that lead the way today. They include references to the initial support from President Obama and Jill Biden, wife of Vice President Joe Biden, who made a strong case that the College Promise would help fulfill the American dream by addressing issues of social and economic justice. National, state, and community leaders have also become advocates because they understand how the College Promise will improve and expand the local and regional economy, provide opportunity for underserved students, and contribute to the general welfare of the nation.

Chapter 4, Guided Pathways to College Completion and Equity

Counseling and advising students on which courses to take and which services to use has been a hallmark of community colleges for many decades. In the early days, community colleges and high schools created articulation agreements to ensure that students would have clear markers to follow on which courses to take. The idea became more focused in the college tech prep program in 1990, supported by the Carl D. Perkins Vocational and Applied Technology Act, a federally funded program. College tech prep is a high school through college program with a seamless, rigorous sequence of academic and technical coursework culminating in postsecondary degrees and/or industry-recognized credentials.

Career pathways emerged from the work on tech prep and were defined as "a coherent, articulated sequence of rigorous academic and career courses that embed the knowledge and skills necessary to prepare learners to pursue a wide range of career opportunities" (*Significant Discussions*, 2010, p. 52). At the same time that the concept of the career pathway was gaining acceptance, the Bill & Melinda Gates Foundation (Pennington & Milliron, 2010) and the Community College Research Center (Jenkins, 2011) began to champion the student success pathway (SSP) for all students. Even the American Association of Colleges and Universities weighed in on the value of the SSP:

> After many years of research on enhancing student engagement and success, higher education now has explicit articulations of what is needed to support student success as well as a roadmap for getting there. . . . [S]tudents need a "compass" or a clearly delineated pathway to support their success, and the academy itself has needed such a thoughtful and documented pathway for supporting students. (2011, para. 18)

At the beginning of this decade all the key organizations committed to student success through various pathways converged on a key idea: the pathway is not a jungle through which students hack their own trail; it is a roadmap students can count on for direction. The organizations also agreed to champion the term *guided pathways*, suggested by Tom Bailey and his colleagues at the Community College Research Center:

> We argue that to improve outcomes, colleges need to move away from the prevailing cafeteria-style model. Instead, they need to engage faculty and student services professionals in creating more clearly structured, educationally coherent program pathways that lead to students' end goals, and in rethinking instruction and student support services in ways that facilitate students' learning and success as they progress along these paths. In short, to maximize both access *and* success, a fundamental redesign is necessary. We refer to the resulting strategy as the *guided pathways model*. (Bailey, Jaggars, & Jenkins, 2015, p. 3)

Kay McClenney has played a key role in shaping the model of the guided pathway and has been engaged with her colleagues at AACC in implementing a national project to test out the model in thirty community colleges. The project goals reflect the recommendations set forth in the report of the 21st Century Commission on the Future of Community Colleges, *Reclaiming the American Dream* (2012). In particular, the commission report emphasized the imperative for community colleges to fundamentally redesign students' educational experiences, and it identified a specific implementation strategy that became the foundation for AACC's Guided Pathways Project: "Construct coherent, structured pathways to certificate and degree completion. This strategy should aim to incorporate high-impact, evidence-based practices; integrate student support with instruction; promote implementation at scale; rigorously evaluate the effectiveness of programs and services for students; and courageously end ineffective practices" (AACC, 2012, p. 16).

In chapter 4 McClenney notes that by mid-2018, over 250 community colleges across the country were implementing guided pathways. Leading and supporting the work is a network of national organizations, scholars, state officials, state-based student success centers, and institutional leaders at all levels who have the vision and courage to undertake transformational change in the interest of students. With this many colleges, organizations, officials, and national leaders involved—including foundations supporting projects with millions of dollars—the concept of the guided pathway is well positioned to become one of the most transforming ideas of this generation.

Chapter 5, The Community College Baccalaureate Movement: Evolutionary and Revolutionary

For almost eighty years after the community college was founded, no leaders talked or wrote about the idea of adding a bachelor's degree to the community college mission. Two years was the absolute parameter for community college programs accepted by legislators, accrediting associations, foundations, policy makers, and community college leaders. A few two-year institutions dreamed about becoming four-year institutions—and a few did, but this was a very limited movement. The idea of adding a bachelor's degree to the mission was soundly criticized as "mission creep" when the idea finally emerged; James Wattenbarger, state director of community colleges in Florida, known as the "Father of the Florida community college system," was a major critic who was concerned that adding the bachelor's degree would destroy the idea of the two-year college.

But it was an idea whose time had come, according to Deborah Floyd and Michael Skolnik, authors of this chapter:

> The original CCB idea was to add a new function to the mission of the community college: offering four-year bachelor's degree programs in applied fields of study for which there was a demand from industry. According to its proponents, the CCB was intended as an *addition* to other community college functions, not a replacement for them.

In the 1980s the first such program was established at Parkersburg Community College in West Virginia, and the growth over the next few decades has confirmed the CCB to be an idea whose time has come. Today there are 957 CCB programs offered by 136 institutions; twenty-four states allow community colleges to award baccalaureate degrees, and several more have recently proposed legislation.

Florida was one of the first states to adopt the CCB idea as a statewide effort, and today twenty-seven of Florida's twenty-eight community colleges offer the applied baccalaureate. The degree is available in teacher education, organizational management, applied health sciences, nursing, supervision and management, dental hygiene, information technology, cybersecurity, business and management, paralegal studies, orthotics and prosthetics, health services administration, energy technology management, emergency management, electrical and computer technology, radiologic and imaging sciences, cardiopulmonary sciences, and international businesses and trades.

The CCB has been successful because it filled a gap and a need. Universities near community colleges did not offer four-year degrees in the applied sciences, so students with a two-year degree in information technology or cybersecurity could not transfer to an area university to continue their education. Many students could not afford to attend universities even if they did offer such programs because of the costs and travel that may have been required.

Business and industry increasingly needed workers who had earned a higher than two-year degree. Community colleges could build on existing applied programs to create four-year degrees, and they had faculty who could teach at this level. The community college baccalaureate is an idea totally compatible with community college philosophy and values, and its time has come.

Chapter 6, Institutional Effectiveness: From Intuition to Evidence

For decades institutional effectiveness (IE) was caught in a web of compliance with regulations issued by the federal and state governments. Effectiveness was measured in terms of how efficient and timely a college could be in meeting the always expanding set of regulations. And when institutions failed to meet the regulations, they could be punished with fines, delays in service, and public embarrassment.

It was not until the culture in higher education changed to focus on student success as the overarching goal and a culture of evidence provided the means that a new perspective emerged on the meaning and role of institutional effectiveness. Today, all regional accrediting agencies have made institutional effectiveness their central goal, as Barbara Gellman-Danley and Eric Martin note in chapter 6. And that means all institutions of higher education have made IE a central goal as well. That does not mean that all institutions of higher education agree on a definition of institutional effectiveness.

In a survey of community colleges holding membership in the Higher Learning Commission, conducted just for chapter 6, the authors found that only 20 percent of respondents agreed that IE "has been appropriately defined." Forty-two percent indicated that IE "has not been appropriately defined." Colleges in the survey had different perceptions about the definition:

- [Institutional effectiveness is] meeting the mission of the institution and serving the needs of students and the broader community (Front Range Community College, CO).
- Institutional effectiveness supports a culture of inquiry, evidence, accountability, and continuous improvement related to all college functions and activities (Gateway Technical College, WI).
- Institutional effectiveness is the degree to which the organization is achieving its mission-based objectives (Jackson College, MI).
- An organization's effectiveness is a product of its collective self-awareness, its propensity for self-evaluation and self-reflection, and its obsession with achieving excellent results. For an institution to be truly effective, every single employee needs to be actively involved in improving performance (Kankakee Community College, IL).
- When you measure everything, how do you know what really matters? And how do all these measures lead to improvement for the individual student? (Lamar Community College, CO).
- Institutional effectiveness is the result of the college reaching or exceeding its measurable goals and objectives as defined and informed by the college's mission and vision and external legal and accreditation expectations (Northwest Arkansas Community College, AR).
- With decreased state funding of community colleges, as is seen in Illinois, an effective institution would be one that just stays open (Sauk Valley Community College, IL).

Seymour and Bourgeois (2018, p. 11), in the *Institutional Effectiveness Field Book*, provide an explanation for these various definitions:

> The challenge of defining institutional effectiveness is largely due to its not being a smaller, more circumscribed idea. Instead, IE is a boundary-buster that infringes on organizational turf and defies the pigeonholing that makes organization life easier for many individuals. But that more robust, cross-functional aspect is also what makes it a powerful force for creating coherence and driving positive change.

Recognizing the challenge of creating a universal definition for institutional effectiveness, the chapter's authors nevertheless note its central value to improving colleges and universities with assistance from the regional accrediting agencies. In addition, they recommend six strategies colleges should follow to support and embed IE into institutional culture:

1. Work collaboratively across the institution to agree upon a definition of institutional effectiveness and how it will be measured.
2. Be certain that institutional effectiveness is a priority for the CEO and governing board.

3. Integrate IE into all strategic plans, including those of the institution, each department, and for individual employees.
4. Educate everyone at the institution about accreditation standards, criteria, and expectations, both regional and specialized, when appropriate.
5. Identify organizational structures to elevate IE as a priority.
6. Participate in national initiatives and research available to strengthen IE for community colleges.

Chapter 7, Recognition, Reform, and Convergence in Developmental Education

Remedial has become such a pejorative word in the community college world that it has been shunned by leaders, practitioners, and policy makers. The rejection has something to do with perceptions that remediation is not an appropriate function for college-level work. Some colleges show their rejection by assigning the remedial courses to adjunct and new faculty. The rejection also has something to do with the fact that remedial education has been a constant thorn in the side of the community college for decades, reminding community college leaders of their failure to "remediate" students.

So community college leaders and practitioners agreed to change the term to *developmental*, which suggests a process of maturing and is more acceptable as a function of college over the idea of fixing something that had failed. The problem, however, is that in the new "developmental education" programs these same leaders and practitioners continued to do the same thing they had been doing for decades in the "remedial education" programs. That is, entering students were still assessed primarily with one national examination and, based on these scores, were placed in developmental math, writing, and English with very little additional support.

Nothing changed except the term used to label the students and the programs. Anywhere from 60 to 70 percent of students were placed in these programs, and there was no increase in completion of these developmental courses and no increase in completion of college-level courses, for which the developmental courses supposedly prepared students.

Finally, several decades ago bold leaders, fed up with the failures of traditional developmental education, began to experiment with different models. Byron McClenney and his staff at the Community College of Denver experimented with accelerating students through these courses by placing them in college-level courses and providing supplemental instruction, tutors, and technology supports; they also made extensive use of open-entry, open-exit, and self-paced instruction.

Research on these new models indicated that students in the accelerated programs, compared with students in traditional developmental programs, completed the developmental courses earlier, completed college-level courses at a higher rate, and earned more credits. The Community College of Denver was on its way to closing the achievement gap between students of color and white students.

The success at the Community College of Denver was soon reflected in a number of other community colleges experimenting with a variety of models: Community College of Baltimore County (MD), Los Medanos College and Chabot College (CA), and the I-Best program in Washington State, where the contextual learning model of combining a developmental course with a college-level technical course proved effective. These programs and others have been subjects in a variety of national studies that have triggered a revolution in developmental education.

In chapter 7, by Bruce Vandal, the research that has moved the needle on developmental education is reviewed in detail. Vandal concludes this chapter by noting there is an emerging consensus on how developmental education can be successful:

> New evidence is proving that access can be achieved and quality learning can be maintained through a fundamental recognition that the problems of student success were never about the lack of academic readiness of students or the inability of faculty to maintain high academic standards in diverse classrooms. By merely recognizing the learning students demonstrated in high school and focusing instruction on students passing gateway courses, colleges can see dramatic improvements in gateway course success and ultimately greater college completion rates.

Vandal summarizes where the field is today in developmental education by listing the key principles from a joint statement issued by six of the leading national organizations engaged in this work:

1. Every student's postsecondary education begins with an intake process to choose an academic direction and identify the support needed to pass relevant credit-bearing gateway courses in the first year.
2. Enrollment in college-level math and English courses or course sequences aligned with the student's program of study is the default placement for the vast majority of students.
3. Academic and nonacademic support is provided in conjunction with gateway courses in the student's academic or career area of interest through corequisite or other models with evidence of success in which supports are embedded in curricula and instructional strategies.
4. Students for whom the default college-level course placement is not appropriate, even with additional mandatory support, are enrolled in rigorous, streamlined remediation options that align with the knowl-

edge and skills required for success in gateway courses in their academic or career area of interest.

5. Every student is engaged with content of required gateway courses that is aligned with his or her academic program of study—especially in math.

6. Every student is supported to stay on track to a college credential, from intake forward, through the institution's use of effective mechanisms to generate, share, and act on academic performance and progression data.

Oddly, the joint statement uses the word *remediation* in its title: *Core Principles for Transforming Remediation within a Comprehensive Student Success Strategy: A JOINT STATEMENT.*

Chapter 8, The Evolving Mission of Workforce Development in the Community College

Anthony Carnevale reminds us, "The inescapable reality is that ours is a society based on work. It's hard to live fully in your time if you are living under a bridge" (2014, p. xii). Work is so basic to human survival that it is hardly necessary to make a case for workforce education as a social and economic necessity. As Melvin Barlow says, "The most respected—and respectable—word in the American language is 'work'" (1976, p. 65).

Some leaders have argued that the community college has become the primary purveyor of workforce education in the nation. According to Paul Fain, "Because of their geographic accessibility and affordability, community colleges have routinely—and rightly—been identified as the U.S. higher education institution most capable of and responsible for our country's economic and employment rebound" (2014, para. 22). James Jacobs notes, "If there is one common mission identified with community colleges, it is workforce education" (2009, para. 1).

In a period of one hundred years, workforce education in the United States has evolved through a number of movements: apprenticeship training, manual training, trade schools, industrial education, home economics, agricultural education, vocational education, and career and technical education. Barlow notes, "By 1926, vocational education was beginning to make its mark upon the educational purposes of the nation" (1976, p. 58).

With federal funding and the need to keep the United States globally competitive, vocational education became so dominant in community colleges that in 2003–2004, 46 percent of associate degrees were conferred on students in the arts and sciences or general education, and 54 percent on students in occupational curricula (Cohen & Brawer, 2008).

According to the Association for Career and Technical Education, from 1997 to 2007, there was a 58.4 percent increase in less-than-one-year certificates awarded at two-year institutions, a 28.5 percent increase in certificates that take at least one year but less than two years, and an 18.7 percent increase in associate degrees (n.d., para. 7). As Jamie Merisotis, president of the Lumina Foundation, said, "[T]o deny that job skills development is one of the key purposes of higher education is increasingly untenable" (as cited in Altschuler, 2014, para. 5).

In chapter 8, James Jacobs and Jennifer Worth describe the evolving mission of workforce development in the community college, noting that the history of workforce education parallels the history of the community college itself. Historically, community colleges were designed to serve a specific geographical area such as a city or a county or several counties; workforce development programs were also limited to serving the needs of students and business and industry in the defined area. Over time the workforce function began to expand to serve regions beyond the local geographical area, then states, then the entire nation; a number of community colleges even served an international market. This expansion created new challenges as well as new opportunities for collaborative efforts, new partnerships, and new sources of funding.

Workforce development will continue to be a significant function of the comprehensive community college, constantly transforming the community college itself as it continues to evolve to serve the nation's economic and social interests.

Chapter 9, Eliminating the Gap between High School and College: What the Next Generation of Transition Programs Must Do

The first American schools in the thirteen original colonies opened in the seventeenth century. The Boston Latin School was founded in 1635 and is both the first public school and the oldest existing school in the United States. American high schools had evolved through 266 years of development before there was a two-year college.

Joliet Junior College, the first junior college in the United States, established in 1901, was housed in a high school: Joliet Township High School in Joliet, Illinois. It must have taken numerous meetings and much planning between the leaders of the junior college and the high school to create this historical alliance. And certainly there must have been many discussions about what the junior college curriculum would be and how it would articulate with the high school curriculum. There must have been many discussions about who was qualified to teach the junior college courses. There had to be discussions about admission to the junior college, assessment of students, academic advising, course loads, recruitment, staff development, accreditation, and a host of other issues. Discussions about how to govern and manage the junior college operating in a high school must have been at the top of the agenda for many meetings.

An artifact of those early discussions about governance and management is still visible today in California community colleges, in which the title used for the CEO of districts is "superintendent/president." There is no philosophical reason to use the designation "superintendent," which is a term historically used for administrators in secondary schools, but the artifact persists. (See George Boggs's title: superintendent/president emeritus, Palomar College.) Another artifact of the high school/community college connection continued to exist into the 1960s, when presidents of community colleges in Florida were required to report to the county school superintendents.

These early connections between high schools and community colleges persisted for many decades, and one would have thought those connections would have blossomed into many effective programs and practices to help high school students move successfully into the community colleges. Unfortunately that did not happen, for a number of reasons. One primary reason was the need for community colleges to establish themselves as part of higher education and not be seen as part of secondary education. Community colleges were defensive about being seen as "high schools with ashtrays."

Between the 1950s and 1970s there was a continuing discussion about whether community colleges should be viewed as secondary education or higher education. This issue was the topic of many articles and convention programs and finally settled into a resolution that community colleges would find comfort with the designation "postsecondary education." This designation was not totally satisfactory because it still connects to "secondary," something akin to designating community colleges as "pre-higher education."

Fortunately, this controversy is long forgotten by today's leaders, and the community college is universally accepted as part of higher education. Community colleges have built strong and effective alliances with high schools as the need to increase student success has become the overarching mission of both institutions. As the authors of chapter 9 note:

> Now there is a growing appetite on both sides for collaborating to increase college success and arguably a movement toward intertwined missions: high schools have been pushed to expand their goals to include ensuring that their students are prepared for college and career, and community colleges have been pushed to think more about developing the pipeline of students transitioning into their institutions.

Joel Vargas and his colleagues at Jobs for the Future (JFF), with their extensive experience in creating, implementing, and evaluating transition programs between high schools and community colleges, have documented what does and does not work in chapter 9. These authors review the impact and status of dual enrollment, the common core, early college high schools, early assessment, career pathways, and guided pathways as the primary initiatives currently in practice to help students make transitions successfully.

The authors also caution community college leaders about depending on one or two of these strategies as the solution to eliminating the gap between high school and community colleges:

> The early success of these individual strategies has ironically put them at risk of being adopted as stand-alone (even symbolic) solutions rather than as strategies integral to larger systemic change goals, including authentic alignment and partnerships with K–12 systems, credentialing paths that maximize short-term income outcomes and also provide opportunities for further education, and guided pathways that create a more coherent and structured educational experience so that more students reach key educational milestones and careers. This is the next generation of work surrounding collaborative high school to college efforts, if these efforts are to contribute in a meaningful way to the equitable and large-scale success of community college students.

Chapter 10, Demography as Opportunity

No African American students attended Central Florida Junior College (CFJC) in Ocala, Florida, in 1965, even though Ocala was a very diverse community. African American students attended another junior college for students of color across town: Hampton Junior College (HJC), named for a local dentist who had championed the education of minorities. Both junior colleges were created in 1958; HJC was created as a "separate but equal" college, which reflected the culture of the state of Florida at that time. There were twelve junior colleges for African American students in Florida in the 1960s, referred to as the "Magnificent Twelve" (Smith, 1994). The establishment of these colleges was not Florida's finest hour:

> Professor James Wattenbarger, the "Father of Florida's Community College System" noted: "The establishment of the twelve predominantly Black junior colleges was an undesirable but necessary action in Florida. What was believed to be undesirable in 1957 did have some positive result in terms of long-term values in the 1990s." The products of these colleges have been "the total development of Florida's political, social and economic growth for thousands of Florida's citizens." (Yglesias, 1996)

Hampton Junior College merged with Central Florida Junior College in 1966, the last of Florida's black junior colleges to merge with their local counterparts. The reason for recalling this brief history is to underscore the fact that segregated facilities in community colleges existed not too long ago.

Facilities are now more or less equal; policies, programs, practices, and personnel still have a long way to go.

Nikki Edgecombe, in chapter 10, proposes a provocative idea:

> *Demography as opportunity* is a simple idea grounded in a commitment to affirm the worth of the students who attend community colleges by being responsive to their life circumstances.
>
> As the demography of the nation changes—the United States is predicted to be majority minority by 2045 (Frey, 2018)—human capital investment in students from racial and ethnic groups, many of whom are first-generation college goers and low income, is critical to the nation's vitality. This idea is optimistic in that it views diversity as an asset and community college graduates as central actors in equitable economic growth.

Edgecombe cobbles together the important data on the growth of minority enrollment from numerous research studies:

- In fall 2015 roughly 44 percent of all undergraduate students were nonwhite: 19 percent were Hispanic, 14 percent were black, and 7 percent were Asian/Pacific Islander.
- Between 2015 and 2026, postsecondary enrollment rates of nonwhite Hispanic, black, and Asian/Pacific Islander students were expected to increase by 26 percent, 20 percent, and 12 percent, respectively, compared to 1 percent for white students.
- Fifty-six percent of all Hispanic undergraduates attend community colleges; the comparable figure for black undergraduates is 44 percent.

Edgecombe urges leaders not to see the increasing numbers of minorities attending community colleges as a *deficit* (with its historical baggage of negative perspectives) but as an *opportunity* to increase inclusivity and social and economic justice. Furthermore, she offers basic principles for community colleges to follow if these goals are to be reached:

- Know your students.
- Understand the obstacles to their success.
- Adopt and adapt responsive policy and practice.
- Scale and institutionalize continuous improvement.

As an underresourced sector of higher education, community colleges struggle to consistently implement these principles, which are applicable to all students but especially to minority students. Edgecombe ends her chapter by citing examples of policies and practices that have been enormously successful in increasing student success.

Chapter 11, Catching the Waves: Technology and the Community College

Of all the topics discussed in this book, technology, because of its power and its promise, may be one of the most effective forces that has transformed and will continue to transform the community college world. The pace of change with technology is breathtaking compared to that of the other twelve ideas. As the authors note, "In the year 2000 GPS was still science fiction for most, smartphones did not exist, social media sites were years away, and the internet was dominated by technology devotees who spoke in a shorthand language most did not understand."

In less than two decades these technological innovations have become ubiquitous in almost all world societies, with four-year olds sometimes being more knowledgeable than their parents about how to use them. For many users there is still a lack of understanding of the shorthand language created by the age of technology.

Mark Milliron (cofounder of Civitas Learning) and John O'Brien (president of EDUCAUSE) bring their formidable backgrounds to chapter 11 to explain the impact of technology on the nation's community colleges. They posit four waves of technology, linking the waves to access and success, which are the twin pillars of community college philosophy.

Regarding wave 1, access and efficiency, the authors review the importance of creating a new kind of access to higher education, which in itself served to transform the community college world. Never in the history of the world has a society experimented with the idea that every person would have the opportunity to attend the first two years of college. The idea is not yet fully implemented, but recent efforts, a number of them discussed in this book, will bring the idea to full fruition, barring cataclysmic changes.

The technology that addresses the concept of access is a basic technology designed to do more efficiently what is already being done. There have been improved systems to make more efficient course schedules, registration, performance tracking, financial aid, admissions, and many business operations. No president, dean of students, division chair, foundation director, registrar, or business officer could function today without an understanding and use of these early applications of technology.

In wave 2, access and learning, the focus shifted from becoming more efficient at helping students to enter college and began to link the idea that technology could play a major role in improving and expanding learning itself. This wave complemented the learning paradigm/learning college/learning revolution movement in the community college (see chapter 1 in this book). This movement raised two key questions for educators: Does this action improve and expand student learning? How do we know this action improves and expands student learning? Technology plays a significant role in the answers to these two key questions.

Focused more on how technology supports learning, the authors cite examples of learning materials and learning spaces. They also review major innovations designed to improve and expand learning: online learning, blended learning, e-portfolios, competency-based education, and open education systems, among others.

Discussing wave 3, access and success, the authors pick up on the first question: How do we know this action improves and expands student learning?

> Then technology tools to capture in-class learning progression and mastery began taking shape.
>
> Learning outcomes assessment became a tool set available to colleges that needed to map and document learning mastery for accreditation, licensure, and professional certification. As discussed in *Learning Outcomes for the 21st Century*, leveraging technology to help answer the how-do-we-know questions at this level was vital if learning-centered innovations were to expand. However, these conversations were in some ways eclipsed as the completion agenda exploded on the scene in 2009–2010.

Analytics became the next "hot" tool in the kit of technology, as the authors note: "[A]nalytics held the potential to move the needle on student success." At the same time that colleges were beginning to address the issue of organizing and analyzing data, the completion agenda almost overnight began to dominate reform efforts, with its emphasis on creating a "culture of evidence" (see chapter 2 in this volume).

In the last ten to fifteen years the completion agenda has become the overarching agenda of the American community college and a number of other sectors of education. Where education will place its priorities next is not altogether clear, but Milliron and O'Brien have created a student success transformation matrix that could become a roadmap for the future of the current emphasis on learning and student success.

The authors use the matrix in discussing wave 4, access and transformation, to suggest what is possible for the future:

> The good news is that the upper right quadrant is becoming more crowded as it becomes more common for student success leaders to expand and improve their capacity through advanced analytics and qualitative explorations. This insight is then coupled with skill and will in change management to measurably move the needle on student success work. Most exciting is that the deep work in this quadrant also holds the potential to bring more of the access, efficiency, learning, and success innovation together for students. Indeed, it may be the key to community colleges making the most of the next wave: access and transformation.

This transformation might come to a fuller fruition if leaders will heed the implications regarding institutional capacity and the importance embedded in the matrix. To gain better understanding of the role transformational leadership will play in this roadmap to the future, see chapter 12 in this book.

As community colleges continue to evolve, it is hoped that the optimism of the authors noted in the conclusion to this chapter will be shared by the great majority of community college stakeholders, and that they will also have the will and the skills to make the next decade a "golden age of learning":

> An exciting time is at hand. Community college faculty are poised to have more tools, techniques, and technologies at their fingertips than ever before to help students access learning, succeed on their learning journeys, and ready themselves for productive careers and lives. [It's been called] the coming "golden age of learning," when key players are able to try, test, tune, and learn together all in a collective effort to watch students make the most of their time in the nation's community colleges.

Chapter 12, Transformative Leadership Wanted: Making Good on the Promise of the Open Door

Most species of animals have formed hierarchies of power, seen especially in primates and canines, among whom the alpha male dominates as the leader. Sometimes, but not often, there are alpha females, such as those among the bonobo chimpanzees, who dominate as leaders. These traits have been passed on to humans through evolution, and the Neanderthals and later *Homo sapiens,* who emerged about forty thousand years ago, inherited these various patterns of dominance that undergird leadership styles.

Unfortunately, although there are a few examples of animal groups that are not dependent on the alpha male for leadership, there are more examples in the animal world and the world of human beings that do depend on the alpha male as the model for leadership. In the world of humans there have been too many models of the alpha male as leader. The behaviors of alpha males dominate literature, churches, movies, corporations, and every level of politics. In the twenty-first century there is an increasing interest in and return to the alpha male as leader, with Putin and Trump as exemplars.

Contemporary human beings have continued to evolve, to the point that they have created frameworks of leadership based on scientific studies of the behavior of leaders and followers. While there are many such frameworks and theories, one common way to identify various leadership styles is as *transactional leadership, laissez-faire leadership*, or *transformational leadership.* Transactional leadership focuses on rewards and punishment to achieve compliance from followers. Laissez-faire leadership allows followers to fend for themselves, with no direction from the leader. Transformational leaders take charge, create a vision for the work of the organization, engage followers as full and respected partners, and focus on achieving agreed-upon goals.

In chapter 12 Margaretta Mathis and John Roueche examine and illustrate the core characteristics of transformational leadership as it has been applied in higher education, especially in community colleges. After providing an overview of some of the challenges community colleges face and the need for new leadership styles to address these challenges, they raise key questions that will stimulate the reader to consider what follows:

> *Toward what* are colleges leading? In their many deliberations, do leaders pause to consider, "*So what?*" before eliciting the many constituents in expensive and time-consuming propositions? What about the context makes an undertaking *ripe* for introduction and successful implementation? What is it about a vision that *propels* an institution (and country) forward, and what is the magic elixir that keeps stakeholders engaged and committed to the work while naysayers inevitably hover, preparing to pounce and provoke? Do community college leaders consider the *how* of introducing and fostering transformation as they look toward a desired and often illusive outcome?

They answer these questions with examples of the behaviors of transformational leaders from some of the flagship community colleges in the nation. They also use a framework based on the Community College Leadership Program at National American University, which they direct, to illustrate how transformational leaders can be prepared. As they say:

> No one person can "do it all." It is the astute leader who involves internal and external institutional stakeholders in developing a culture that builds toward a desired future, rather than being mired in the many daily operational challenges that arise. A culture of excellence and execution requires that these noble men and women look beyond "self" and wisely prepare the next generation of leaders to foster an institutional culture that is responsive to economic and societal shifts.

Mathis and Roueche draw from the literature and their extensive experience working with community college leaders to create a list of the primary characteristics of transformational leadership:

Shared Vision, Values, and Involvement—As the Bible records, "Without a vision the people will perish." It is the same for religious zealots, a nation, and a college. Educators come to their work already deeply dedicated to making a difference in the lives of their students and their communities. When leaders tap into this commitment and involve a community of colleagues who share core values reflected in a common mission, they can disturb the universe that is and create the dream in which they all wish to be involved.

Courage, Candor, and Collaboration—If there is to be substantial and lasting change in college culture, leaders must have the courage to address the established culture and the long-held views of many of the faculty and administrators, as well as the stamina to withstand the backlash that will come. Leaders must be transparent and speak with candor to all members of the college staff about the challenges revealed by data and examination. At the same time that leaders are creating some chaos in the established order, they must figure out ways to ensure that all members of the college are kept informed and that there is sufficient collaboration to move forward.

Commitment—Change is difficult for many people, especially for leaders who have spent years creating and managing systems for which they have responsibility. When a new leader suggests a new vision or a leader on the job for years discovers a new approach, those on the firing line feel that their judgment and performance are being questioned. Transformational leaders understand these dynamics and realize the college must be in the reform effort for the long haul. They support and take care of the faculty and staff under stress, and they commit to staying around long enough to see the efforts succeed.

Getting Important Things Done—Leaders establish big goals and high expectations because they believe anything less sells their colleagues short. Leaders know that quality faculty and administrators like to work in an environment where leaders focus on the important things and accomplish important things. Instead of being bogged down by the details of daily management, a college with transformational leaders will hum with excitement and creativity. Leaders intuitively understand the common adage "Management is doing things right, but leadership is doing the right thing."

Persistence, Purpose, and People—Change requires commitment, but it also requires persistence linked to a clear purpose. Transformational leaders have "grit," recognized even by grandmothers as a powerful incentive for getting the job done:

> It is the power of a person to become a leader, armed with principles and rising above self-interest narrowly conceived, that invests that person with power and may ultimately transform both leaders and followers into persons who jointly adhere to moral values and end-values. A person, whether leader or follower, girded with moral purpose is a tiny principality of power. (Burns, 1978, p. 457)

Performance, Preparation, and the Courage to Lead—As the authors note, "[P]urposeful and passionate leaders are unyielding in their pursuit of effective and sustainable solutions that will transform institutions—without overwhelming the very stakeholders who are needed to implement them. It is a compelling goal and remarkable achievement for any college leader to so transform the culture of his or her institution that when the college addresses its most challenging teaching and learning issues, the quality of the decisions can be judged by how closely they match up to its collective goals, hopes, and dreams."

Chapter 13, Using Data to Monitor What Matters: A New Role for Trustees

The community college and the lay board are both American social inventions that illustrate democracy in action. The community college is an expression of access and opportunity; the lay board is an expression of citizen responsibility for oversight and representation. They are symbiotic concepts, in which the lay board is charged with assuring the community college carries out its mission and goals. Each depends on the other for its success (O'Banion, 2009, p. 9).

In the United States, community colleges are governed by boards of trustees, either elected or appointed. According to data compiled by the Association of Community College Trustees and reported by Smith, Piland, and Boggs (2001, p. 3), locally elected boards are the norm in thirteen states; boards appointed by the governor, by local leaders, or by a mix of the two are the norm in nineteen states. In four states boards are selected by a mix of appointees and elected officials. In all other states the trustees are advisory, or colleges are governed by a statewide entity. There are approximately sixty-five hundred trustees serving over six hundred community colleges that have either locally elected or appointed boards (Mellow & Heelan, 2008, p. 83).

Most of these trustees are exceptional community leaders, elected and appointed to champion the community college mission for the community and students they represent. These local trustees, serving as the guardians of their local community colleges, have helped create the most dynamic and innovative system of colleges in the world.

As the author of the chapter on a new role for trustees, Byron McClenney notes: "As with governing boards in other sectors of higher education, community college boards have historically been focused on buildings, budgets, and bonds. Much more attention has been focused on an annual financial audit than on a report from an accreditor."

In the late 1990s forces such as a call for accountability and institutional effectiveness and the impact of the learning revolution led to the creation of a number of national initiatives such as Achieving the Dream and Completion by Design. The purpose of these initiatives was to create programs and practices that would lead to increases in retention and graduation rates. From about 2005 to the present, the student success/completion agenda became the overarching mission of the nation's community colleges. Never before had community colleges had so much financial support from foundations, so much relevant research to underscore programs and practices, and so much agreement from all key groups on the value and importance of the agenda.

Byron McClenney and his colleagues at The University of Texas, the Association of Community College Trustees, and the AACC had championed the student success/completion agenda and came to realize that if the goals of the agenda were to be realized, trustees would have to play a major role. In 2007 McClenney and his colleagues created the Board of Trustees Institute (BOTI) to train trustees in how to analyze data on student success in their colleges and how to monitor those data to improve and expand student success. These efforts have proved to be a revolutionary episode in the role of trustees and in the continuing evolution of the student success/completion agenda. In the past ten years additional initiatives to involve more trustees in monitoring data on student success and failure have become one of the transforming forces on the community college world.

SO, WHAT IS THIS THING, THIS COMMUNITY COLLEGE IDEA?

At the beginning of this chapter, the author noted that a lot of people do not know what a community college means or represents because it is a dynamic institution that has been changing for decades. As an experiment in democracy, the community college is still evolving, but after 118 years some of its basic challenges have begun to be resolved:

1. *Access and success*, the twin pillars of the community college philosophy, have often been pitched as ideas in opposition to each other, with *access* dominating for almost one hundred years and *success* now rising to dominance, driven by the completion agenda. While each might still end up on the opposite end of a continuum, leaders now pretty much agree that both access and success carry equal weight and are more like a coin, with access on one side and success on the other. They are forever bonded as the foundation of the community college.
2. The "community" in community college has had a rough ride, evolving from "junior" and now disappearing where some colleges are offering baccalaureate degrees. Originally interpreted to mean a local geographical area such as a city, county, or region—and in earlier times sometimes confined by practice or law to serving only that area—it is a dynamic institution that cannot be confined. Today, community colleges serve their state and the nation; many now serve the

global community. "How're you going to keep them down on the farm once they've seen Gay Paree?"

3. The "college" in community college has also had its ups and down. At first comfortably "junior college"—an institution not quite a college—it morphed into postsecondary education, still defined by its connection to secondary education. As the community college evolved, it demanded a seat at the table of higher education, where it is now pretty much an accepted and respected colleague of four-year colleges and universities.

4. The community college is now also accepted and respected by US presidents, federal and state agencies, legislators, business and industry, and foundations as a key player in the nation's march to improve and expand economic and social justice. Community colleges, "made in America," are now exported to other countries around the world.

5. The community college is the only institution in the history of the world to open its doors to all citizens—and even noncitizens. It is still an evolving social experiment that promises a better life for those who accept the invitation to come through the "open door." It is strongly committed to diversity and leveling the playing field for those who are "different." Equality is a much thornier issue that has not been resolved by the nation, much less the community college.

So, what is this thing, this community college idea? In 2019, here is a definition that most leaders would agree reflects consensus: *The primary purpose of the community college is to ensure that students are prepared to make a good living and live a good life. It is an open-door institution that accepts all who can benefit from its programs and services. It is a comprehensive institution that offers a variety of programs and opportunities to meet the needs of its diverse population. It is grounded in its local community but serves national and global needs when opportunities arise. It is Democracy's College, ever evolving.*

Rick Smyre, president of the Center for Communities of the Future, has said: "Institutions that have existed for over 100 years are in the process of declining, and most will soon disappear from our society and economy" (2018, p. 5). If this observation is true, what will become of the community college of the future, which is now 119 years old?

The community college is so embedded in American culture that it is not likely to disappear anytime soon, and there is no evidence to date that it is in the process of declining. What is clear is that the community college will continue to evolve, and its future will be marked by the thirteen ideas in this book, which will become common practice. While the community college we know today may cease to exist, the community college we dream of for the future will prosper and grow, enriched by these thirteen ideas that are transforming the community college world.

REFERENCES

Altschuler, G. (2014, May 15). A defense of liberal learning. *Inside Higher Ed*. Retrieved from https://insidehighered.com/views/2014/05/15/essay-new-book-beyond-university

American Association of Colleges and Universities. (2011). *College learning for the new global century: An executive summary of the LEAP report*. Washington, DC: AAC&U.

American Association of Community Colleges. (2012). *Reclaiming the American dream: Community colleges and the nation's future*. Washington, DC: AACC.

Association of Career and Technical Education. (n.d.). para 7.

Bailey, T., Jaggars, S., & Jenkins, D. (2015). *Redesigning America's community colleges*. Cambridge, MA: Harvard University Press.

Barlow, M. (1976, May). The vocational age emerges, 1876–1926. *American Vocational Education*, *51*(5), 45–58.

Berberet, J., & McMillin, L. (2002). The American professoriate in transition. *AGB Priorities*, *18*(Spring), 1–15.

Bess, J. (2000, May). Letter to the editor. *Change: The Magazine of Higher Learning*, *32*(3), 6

Boggs, G. (in press). *A history of California community colleges*.

Burns, J. M. (1978). *Leadership*. New York: Harper & Row.

Carnevale, A. (2014). Foreword. In G. Mellow & C. Heelan (Eds.), *Minding the dream: The process and practice of the American community college* (2nd ed., p. xii). Blue Ridge Summit, PA: Rowman & Littlefield Publishers.

Cohen, A. M., & Brawer, F. B. (2008). *The American community college* (5th ed.). San Francisco, CA: Jossey-Bass.

Fain, P. (2014, June 17). Open access and inequity. *Inside Higher Ed*. Retrieved from https://www.insidehighered.com/news/2014/06/17/new-book-says-community-colleges-should-tighten-their-admissions-policies

Frey, W. H. (2018, March 14). The US will become "minority white" in 2045, Census projects [The Avenue blog]. Washington, DC: The Brookings Institution. Retrieved from https://www.brookings.edu/blog/the-avenue/2018/03/14/the-us-will-become-minority-white-in-2045-census-projects/

Jacobs, J. (2009). Meeting new challenges and demands for workforce education. In G. Myran (Ed.), *Reinventing the open door: Transformational strategies for community colleges*. Washington, DC: Community College Press.

Jenkins, D. (2011). *Redesigning community colleges for completion: Lessons from research on high-performance organizations* (CCRC Working Paper No. 24, Assessment of Evidence Series). New York: Community College Research Center, Teachers College, Columbia University.

Mellow, G., & Heelan, C. (2008). *Minding the dream: The process and practice of the American community college*. Lanham, MD: Rowman & Littlefield Publishers.

O'Banion, T. (2009). *The rogue trustee: The elephant in the room*. Chandler, AZ: The League for Innovation in the Community College.

O'Banion, T. (2013). *Access, success, and completion: A primer for community college faculty, administrators, staff, and trustees*. Chandler, AZ: The League for Innovation in the Community College.

O'Banion, T. (2016). *Bread and roses: Helping students make a good living and live a good life*. Chandler, AZ: The League for Innovation in the Community College.

O'Banion, T., & Wilson, C. (Eds.). (2010). *Focus on learning: A learning college reader*. Phoenix, AZ: The League for Innovation in the Community College.

Pennington, H., & Milliron, M. (2010). *Completion by design: Final concept paper—an initiative of the postsecondary success team*. Seattle, WA: Bill & Melinda Gates Foundation.

Seymour, D., & Bourgeois, M. (2018). *Institutional effectiveness field book: Creating coherence in colleges and universities*. Santa Barbara, CA: Olive Press Publishing.

Significant discussions: A guide for secondary and postsecondary curriculum alignment. (2010). Phoenix, AZ: The League for Innovation in the Community College.

Smith, C., Piland, B., & Boggs, G. (2001). *The political nature of community college trusteeship*. Washington, DC: Association of Community College Trustees.

Smith, W. (1994). *The magnificent twelve: Florida's black junior colleges*. Winter Park, FL: Four-G Publishers.

Smyre, R. (2018). *Redesigning education for constant change: The emergence of a future forward college*. Unpublished manuscript.

Sterling, R. E. (2001). *A pictorial history of America's oldest public community college*. St. Louis, MO: C. Bradley Publishing.

Trump, D. (2018, February 1). Remarks by President Trump at the 2018 House and Senate Republican Member Conference. The Greenbriar, White Sulphur Springs, WV.

Witt, A. A., Wattenbarger, J. L., Gollattscheck, J. F., & Suppinger, J. E. (1994). *America's community colleges: The first century*. Washington, DC: American Association of Community Colleges.

Yglesias, K. (1996, October). Book review: *The magnificent twelve: Florida's black junior colleges*. *Black Issues in Higher Education*, *13*(17).

Part I

Ideas as National Initiatives

While most of the ideas in this section reflect some need or activity inside community colleges, they soon emerged as national initiatives or "movements" that took on a life of their own. The community college baccalaureate (CCB) spawned its own national association. College Promise became a "movement" with numerous networks that engaged states to create opportunities for free tuition. Guided Pathways was grounded in research primarily from the Community College Research Center. The learning paradigm expanded with the support of strong advocates who sponsored national conferences and authored books. The student success/completion agenda struck a chord in every community college in the nation and became the primary mission of all community colleges and most universities.

All of these national initiatives were supported by grants from major foundations to refine their models and to field-test their efficacy. Books, articles, toolkits, and guides were created for all five. National organizations and projects developed around these initiatives to ensure sustainability. All have emerged in recent years.

Although some community colleges have elected not to engage in some of these initiatives, such as the CCB and the learning paradigm, the great majority of community colleges have been deeply influenced by these ideas. As the ideas continue to evolve, more and more community colleges are likely to join in these efforts and others that are transforming the community college world.

Chapter One

The Learning Paradigm

George Boggs

In 1991, a revolutionary concept emerged from a community college in California. It was a new way of thinking about the mission of community colleges. The concept became a movement that continues to influence all of higher education: how it is held accountable, how it is organized, and how it is funded. It was a shift away from identification with processes to identification with results or outcomes, and its consequences are still being debated.

Because it was a new way of thinking about the world of higher education, the leaders of the movement labeled it a new paradigm for education and called it the learning paradigm, differentiating it from the instruction paradigm that was dominant at the time and that to a great extent still exists. The ideas emerged from Palomar College, a community college in California, in the last decade of the twentieth century. The language in the foreword to the Palomar College vision statement that was released in 1991 provides the basis for understanding the transformation:

> Readers of these statements will note that they reflect perhaps a subtle but nonetheless profound shift in how we think of the college and what we do. We have shifted from an identification with process to an identification with results. We are no longer content with merely providing quality instruction. We will judge ourselves henceforth on the quality of student learning we produce, And further, we will judge ourselves by our ability to produce ever greater and more sophisticated student learning and meaningful educational success with each passing year, each exiting student, and each graduating class. To do this we must ourselves continually experiment, discover, grow, and learn. Consequently, we see ourselves as a learning institution in both our object and our method. (Boggs, 1991)

The learning paradigm as it was proposed by Palomar College identified four tenets:

- The mission of colleges and universities should be student learning rather than teaching or instruction.
- Institutions should accept responsibility for student learning.
- Supporting and promoting student learning should be everyone's job and should guide institutional decisions.
- Institutions should judge their effectiveness and be evaluated on student learning outcomes rather than on resources or processes (Boggs, 1999a, 1999b).

Terry O'Banion began to call the institutions that were pioneering the learning paradigm "learning colleges"; his 1997 book *A Learning College for the 21st Century* served as a guide for college leaders who embraced a mission based on student learning (O'Banion, 1997a). O'Banion defined the learning college as an institution that "places learning first and provides educational experiences for learners anyway, anyplace, and anytime" (1997a, p. 47). He outlined six principles on which the learning college is based:

1. The learning college creates substantive change in individual learners.
2. The learning college engages learners as full partners in the learning process, with learners assuming responsibility for their own choices.
3. The learning college creates and offers as many options for learning as possible.
4. The learning college assists learners to form and participate on collaborative learning activities.
5. The learning college defines the roles of learning facilitators by the needs of the learners.
6. The learning college and its learning facilitators succeed only when improved and expanded learning can be documented for its learners (O'Banion, 1997a, p. 47).

THE ACCESS MISSION IS NOT ENOUGH

From the beginning of the community college movement, the colleges have focused on increasing access to higher education and training. This mission has been reinforced many times over the years, perhaps most notably in the 1947 and 1948 reports of the President's Commission on Higher Education, also known as the Truman Commission. The rapid expansion of open-admission community colleges has provided opportunities for millions of students to go to college. Today, community colleges are located within commuting distance of over 90 percent of the population of the United States, and the colleges have further increased access through distance education. Today more than twelve million students, or about 41 percent of all college students, are enrolled in community colleges.

In the early 1900s many proponents of what were then called junior colleges were university leaders who wanted to limit access to their institutions to students who had demonstrated their academic abilities. They saw junior colleges as the way to provide an opportunity for high school graduates to complete their first two years of college. Only the best of the junior college students would be able to enter the selective "senior college" at the university. That way, the universities could focus on research and related scholarly activities.

The junior college mission expanded over the years from just screening students and preparing some to transfer to include workforce, developmental, adult, and community education, and most are identified today as community colleges. The growth of the junior colleges in the 1950s and 1960s made it politically possible for universities to become more exclusive in their admissions practices (Brint & Karabel, 1989, p. 90). Although most universities chose not to limit their mission to upper division and graduate curricula, most of them became even more focused on the missions of research and scholarly publication; service and teaching were lower priority functions.

Community colleges were not established as centers for research or the creation of knowledge. Because teaching loads are much higher in community colleges, most faculty members are not engaged in research or scholarly publication. Instead, they focus on teaching. Most community college faculty members constantly strive to improve their teaching. They get the greatest reward when their students learn and when their former students are successful. However, institutional barriers often act as obstacles to their ideas and innovations to help students learn.

The problem is that the institutions that employ the faculty were designed to provide access to instruction, not necessarily to promote and support student learning and success. A common philosophy in the 1960s was "students have a right to fail," meaning colleges should give students a chance, but institutions have no responsibility for their success or failure—that is up to the students. To make up for the loss of students who drop out, colleges work to recruit others. As late as 1992, Robert Barr, director of research and planning at Palomar College, found no focus on learning in any of the mission statements of California's 107 community colleges (Barr, 1995). In the few instances where the word *learning* was even mentioned, it was almost always bundled in the phrase "teaching and learning."

The colleges were organized to recruit and admit students and then to provide them with instruction. Classroom design had not changed much in almost a hundred years. Processes for scheduling classes and registering students were inflexible. Budget allocations were often not aligned with any thought about student learning and success. Faculty who wanted to increase student interaction, to start a learning community, or to experiment with self-paced classes were usually discouraged by institutional architecture and bureaucracy.

The world is now very different from the one in which colleges and universities evolved, and the students who attend them today do not have much in common with the students of the early 1900s. Technology has transformed the way people do business, the way they live, and the way they learn. Every year the student population is becoming more diverse, bringing into question whether traditional instructional methods work—if they ever did. Many students have part-time or even full-time jobs. Many have family responsibilities, often as single heads of households, and are trying to improve their lives through education. Many students are returning to study after some time away from an academic environment and may feel ill at ease attending classes with younger students. Unfortunately, many community college students are not academically prepared to succeed in college level classes.

However, it is not just the fact that the student population has changed that matters; social and political pressures are also mounting. State legislators and governors across the nation have responded to fiscal exigency by reducing funding support to higher education. There is a constant call for institutions to "do more with less," to improve efficiency and effectiveness, and to be more accountable. Employers complain that the country's workforce is inadequately trained, and corporations spend billions of dollars on employee training.

In its 1993 report *An American Imperative: Higher Expectations for Higher Education,* The Wingspread Group pointed to a disturbing and dangerous mismatch that exists between what American society needs from higher education and what it is receiving. Nowhere was the mismatch more obvious than in the quality of undergraduate education provided on many campuses. The report declared that institutional efforts that should be focused on the needs of students are instead channeled toward other institutional interests, often for the convenience or special interests of educators.

THE VISION OF THE LEARNING MISSION COMES INTO FOCUS

The pressures on the mission of community colleges were becoming clear by the mid-1980s. The president of Palomar College, George Boggs, served as chair of the Commission on Research for the California Association of Community Colleges (CACC) from 1987 through 1989. Serving with him was Director of Institutional Research and Planning Robert Barr. Institutional effectiveness was a major focus of the commission in those years. In 1988 CACC published a report by the commission, *Indicators and Measures of Successful Community Colleges*, and in 1989 it published *Criteria and Measures of Institutional Effectiveness*. Although the commission members were determined to develop methods to document college effectiveness, they did not focus on learning outcomes.

At the national level, the American Association of Community and Junior Colleges had just issued, in 1988, the report of its Commission on the Future of Community Colleges, *Building Communities: A Vision for a New Century*. The report called on colleges to expand access, to improve retention of students, to form new partnerships and alliances, to develop a core of common learning, and to build a climate of community. The report labeled community colleges the nation's premier teaching institutions and declared that quality instruction was the hallmark of the movement.

It was in this environment that the president of Palomar College convened and chaired the college's Vision Task Force. The charge of the group was to develop a proposed vision statement for the college and to envision what the college should be fifteen years in the future. As the research and discussions progressed, the task force began to see a link between the success of the college and the success of its students. The members decided that the college needed to take responsibility for the learning of its students. Teaching was seen as an essential process, but it was not the desired outcome. And student learning was not just the responsibility of the teachers; it was everyone's responsibility. Everyone, from the groundskeeper to the teacher to the librarian to the president to the student, was there for one purpose: student learning.

As a result of the work of the Vision Task Force, the college had a new mission statement that defined its purpose as student learning. Catalogs, publications, hiring criteria, employee orientations, and job descriptions were changed. For example, the job description of the instructional deans was revised to include responsibility for creating effective learning environments for students. Student service deans were now expected to develop and evaluate the performance of assigned personnel in terms of their contributions to student learning and success. By 1991–1992, Palomar College had aligned its educational master plan and college goals with its new vision statement.

SHARING THE VISION OF STUDENT LEARNING

Starting in 1993, Palomar College staff members began to write about the learning paradigm and to present their ideas at conferences. In May 1993 George Boggs made the first national presentation contrasting the learning and instruction paradigms at the annual conference of the National Institute for Staff and Organizational Development (NISOD) (Boggs, 1993). Robert Barr and George Boggs made presentations at several state and national conferences, including two national videoconferences, between 1993 and 1995.

As chair of the board of the American Association of Community Colleges (AACC) in 1993–1994 and past chair in 1994–1995, Boggs wrote and spoke extensively about the need to focus on student learning and success (Boggs, 1993–1994, 1995a, 1995b, 1995c). In 1995 John Tagg, a member of the English faculty and fellow member of the Vision Task Force, joined Barr in writing what would become the most widely cited article in the history of *Change* magazine, "From Teaching to Learning—A New Paradigm for Undergraduate Education" (1995).

In 1997 the Association of Community College Trustees released a special issue of its *Trustee Quarterly*, "The Learning Revolution: A Guide for Community College Trustees" (O'Banion & Wilson, 2011, p. 4). In 1996 Palomar College hosted the first of five annual national conferences on the learning paradigm. Also in 1996, Walter Bumphus, then chair of the board of the AACC, published an interview with O'Banion and Boggs that focused on student learning and institutional transformation. In 1997 Boggs served as one of the authors of the National Academy of Science publication *Science Teaching Reconsidered*, which included a chapter titled "Linking Teaching with Learning" (National Research Council, 1997).

Terry O'Banion provided a significant boost to the tenets of the learning paradigm when he began to write and speak about the concepts after discussions with Robert Barr and George Boggs. In 1997 Diana Oblinger, former CEO of EDUCAUSE, and Sean Rush edited a book titled *The Learning Revolution: The Challenge of Information Technology in the Academy*, which included O'Banion's chapter "Transforming the Community College from a Teaching to a Learning Institution." That same year, the League for Innovation in the Community College published his *Leadership Abstracts* article "The Purpose, Process, and Prospect of the Learning Revolution in the Community College" (1997c). His book *A Learning College for the 21st Century* (O'Banion, 1997a) and monograph *Creating More Learning-Centered Community Colleges* became guidebooks for colleges to become more learning-focused (O'Banion, 1997b).

In 1997 and 1998 the League for Innovation in the Community College and Public Broadcasting Service (PBS) sponsored three national teleconferences on the learning revolution and the learning college (O'Banion & Wilson, 2011, p. 4). A 1998 survey by the League for Innovation in the Community College revealed that 73 percent of the nation's community college presidents indicated they had initiatives under way for their institutions to become more learning centered (O'Banion & Wilson, 2011, p. 4). Just seven years after the publication of the Palomar College Vision Statement and just five years after leaders and scholars began writing and speaking about learning paradigm concepts, most of the nation's community college leaders had embraced the vision and were engaged in transformation.

In 2000 the AACC and the Association of Community Colleges Trustees (ACCT) published the report of their New Expeditions Initiative, *The Knowledge Net* (2000). It was the first major report that AACC had been involved in since its 1988 *Building Communities* report. The chapter "Learner Connections" referenced the Palomar College vision and mission statements. In 2001 AACC unveiled a new mission statement, "Building a Nation of Learners by Advancing America's Community Colleges."

Today all seven of the higher education regional accrediting agencies require institutions to document student learning outcomes (SLOs). In 2001 the largest of the regional accreditors officially changed its name from North Central Association of Colleges and Schools to Higher Learning Commission. In 2005 Christine McPhail published *Establishing and Sustaining Learning Centered Community Colleges*. A ProQuest search revealed that fifty-eight doctoral dissertations and master's theses have been written since 1993 on the learning college or the learning paradigm.

THE LEARNING COLLEGE PROJECT

In January 2000 the League for Innovation in the Community College launched the Learning College Project to help community colleges around the world become more learning-centered institutions. Twelve vanguard learning colleges (VLCs) were selected by an international advisory committee to help develop model programs and best practices in learning-centered education, with a specific focus on five key areas: organizational culture, staff recruitment and development, technology, learning outcomes, and underprepared students.

The twelve VLCs were Cascadia Community College (Washington), the Community College of Baltimore County (Maryland), Community College of Denver (Colorado), Humber College (Ontario, Canada), Kirkwood Community College (Iowa), Lane Community College (Oregon), Madison Area Technical College (Wisconsin), Moraine Valley Community College (Illinois), Palomar College (California), Richland College (Texas), Sinclair Community College (Ohio), and Valencia Community College (Florida).

Kay McClenney served as the evaluator for the project. Her observations remain valuable for college leaders interested in becoming more outcome focused. She noted that the transformation to a learning college is long, arduous, and exciting as colleges realign institutional priorities, policies, practices, and personnel to focus on learning as the primary business of the college. College representatives struggled with ways to bring innovations to scale and to sustain them. Colleges faced resistance to change and "reform fatigue" from engagement in too many initiatives.

There was some confusion between the terms *learner-centered* and *learning-centered* (McClenney, 2001). Colleges need to be concerned about learners (students), but the outcome is learning. Terry O'Banion addressed this confusion in "The Learning College: Both Learner and Learning Centered" (O'Banion, 1999).

The project participants quickly identified the need for colleges to become more data informed. The desire to develop a culture of evidence was driven by questions such as "How do I know that students are learning what I think I am teaching?" The colleges began to collect more data, to use the data to make decisions, and to demonstrate more commitment to a philosophy of continuous improvement (McClenney, 2003a). The participants committed to asking the questions posed by Terry O'Banion in *Creating More Learning-Centered Community Colleges* (1997b, p. 9):

- Does this action improve and expand learning?
- How do we know this action improves and expands learning?

McClenney noted several positive outcomes for the Learning College Project. The college teams learned from each other about the importance of strategic planning; aligning organizational structure to support learning, learning strategies, learning assessment, programs, and services to support underprepared students; tracking student progress; and the use of technology to support and enhance learning. Many participants spoke of a new level of honesty and rigor in institutional self-examination. Participants began to ask whether institutional resource allocations matched rhetoric about learning. Another important outcome was the belief that people were taking collective responsibility for student learning. The project's cross-functional teams helped to break down institutional silos (McClenney, 2003a, 2003b).

DEFINING STUDENT SUCCESS

In 2012 the American Association of Community Colleges published the report *Reclaiming the American Dream* (21st Century Commission on the Future of Community Colleges, 2012). It is the third major report from the association, following *Building Communities* in 1988 and *The Knowledge Net* in 2000. The report presented a compelling argument for community colleges to change. Although the report recommends a change from a focus on teaching to a focus on learning, the major emphases of the report are on the needs to improve student completion and to close achievement gaps.

Reflecting an outcome of the Learning College Project, the report calls on colleges to move from a culture of anecdote to a culture of evidence.

The focus on completion is one component of the learning paradigm. In the 1993 NISOD presentation, George Boggs pointed out:

> Our criteria for success will be different. Under the old paradigm, we measured success by looking at enrollment growth, revenue growth, program additions, quantity and quality of resources, and quality of entering students. Under the new paradigm, we will be concerned about quality of learning, learning growth and efficiency, increasing the graduation rate, increasing the transfer rate, and increasing the retention rate. (Boggs, 1993)

In response to increasing national interest in college completion, the AACC convened the six major national community college associations (the AACC, the ACCT, the League for Innovation in the Community College, the National Institute for Staff and Organizational Development, the Center for Community College Student Engagement, and Phi Theta Kappa) in April 2010 to issue a joint call to action to improve student completion rates.

The vanguard colleges in the Learning College Project had earlier focused many of their efforts on completion. In her program evaluation comments, McClenney reported that a new seminar requirement at the Community College of Denver had improved first semester completion rates from 60–70 percent to 90 percent or higher. A new orientation course at Moraine Valley Community College improved retention rates, and its students ended the semester with a significantly higher percent of credits earned and significantly higher GPAs. Similar efforts at the other participating colleges also increased student success (McClenney, 2003b).

The focus on completion is important because of the need for a more educated citizenry and workforce. It is also understandable for educators to concentrate on completion because it is more easily measured and perhaps less controversial than measuring student learning outcomes. However, educators should not lose sight of the overall objectives of the learning paradigm.

In the March 1, 2018, issue of the *Chronicle of Higher Education*, in an article titled "How to Make Sure Students Graduate with More Than a Diploma," George Kuh, the founding director of the National Institute for Learning Outcomes Assessment, is quoted as saying, "Yes, it's important that students finish what they start. But graduating isn't enough: Students should be different when they complete college than they were at the outset" (Kuh, 2018). Educators must be careful that a single-minded goal to improve completion rates does not blind them to the need to improve and expand student learning.

Thirty-five states have or are considering some form of outcomes-based funding (also called performance-based funding) for higher education. Policy makers in these states have come to believe that public colleges and universities need to be incentivized to improve certain performance measures, such as graduation or transfer rates. Advocates claim that funding colleges based on student enrollment doesn't motivate institutions to help students to complete. However, outcomes-based funding is controversial.

A 2016 report of the Century Foundation declared that performance-based funding rarely works to increase outcomes (Hillman, 2016). There is also the danger that institutions may limit access for students who are less likely to complete or are likely to lower academic standards in order to increase completion rates. It is important for educators to be actively involved in developing the outcomes-based funding formulas to be sure that both access and quality are protected.

RESISTANCE TO THE LEARNING PARADIGM

In her March 2001 Learning College Project evaluation report, Kay McClenney mentioned that "on some campuses, there is a notable resistance to the language of the learning college among at least some faculty and staff" (McClenney, 2001). George Boggs, Robert Barr, John Tagg, and Terry O'Banion encountered some of the opposition to the language in their talks. The objections centered on the language that seemed to pit teaching against learning. Faculty often didn't see anything new in the learning college concepts. They thought that student learning was always their goal. Many did not recognize something as significant as a paradigm shift.

In a November 28, 1995, nine-page unpublished memorandum to Irving McPhail, then president of St. Louis Community College at Florissant Valley, Brian Gordon, chair of the History Department, stated: "Robert Barr and John Tagg appear to be either snake-oil hucksters looking for work on the staff development circuit . . . or else they are simply ignorant of contemporary community college instructional practice. . . . There isn't a paradigm's worth of difference between the two opposing models of education they try to describe."

Manual Gonzales, a social science professor at Diablo Valley College (DVC) in California, wrote in an article in a campus newsletter on September 25, 1998: "Adopting the Barr-Tagg model . . . will only result in a further blurring of the distinction between high school and college, the final step in the transformation of DVC from an institution of higher learning into Tinker Toy Tech."

In response to the false dichotomy between teaching and learning, Terry O'Banion, in an unpublished paper prepared in 2011 for the AACC 21st Century Commission on the Future of Community Colleges, declared, "The purpose of teaching is improved and expanded learning. Improved and expanded learning is the outcome of effective teaching."

In a January 1999 article in the *American Association for Higher Education Bulletin* titled "What the Learning Paradigm Means for Faculty," George Boggs addressed the concerns that faculty often raise. The article was republished later that year in *Learning Abstracts* by the League for Innovation in the Community College:

> Some faculty members are concerned about the loss of teacher control advocated by proponents of the learning paradigm. In the traditional "instruction paradigm," teachers are subject-matter experts who dispense and explain information to students, primarily via lectures. In the learning paradigm, students are more in control of their own learning, often learning from peers in small groups. Information is more widely available.
>
> Other faculty members equate a focus on learning with becoming so student centered that academic standards drop. They believe that there is a danger of becoming overly concerned about maintaining student self-esteem to the detriment of preparing students for a "real world" that is complex and not always fair.
>
> Faculty members who question the ideas of the learning paradigm do not understand that its primary focus is at the institutional level rather than at the individual faculty member level. In fact, their attention to effective teaching in an environment that is sometimes hostile to their ideas was one of the major factors that led to the proposition that a paradigm shift was needed. It is not an accident that the ideas of the learning paradigm are getting the most attention at institutions that have teaching and learning as primary missions. (Boggs, 1999a, 1999b)

Under the learning paradigm, the most important people in the institution are the learners. The faculty members are key to student goal achievement; they are the designers, managers, promoters, and facilitators of student learning. However, it is not only the faculty who are responsible for the success of the students; everyone at the college has an important role in creating the student learning environment and supporting the mission of student learning.

STUDENT LEARNING OUTCOME ASSESSMENT

Kay McClenney's evaluation of the Learning College Project revealed that the VLCs had discovered that the essential task of defining, assessing, and documenting student learning outcomes (SLOs) was the most challenging (McClenney, 2001). The National Institute for Learning Outcomes Assessment defines student learning outcomes as statements that clearly state the expected knowledge, skills, attitudes, competencies, and habits of mind that students are expected to acquire at an institution of higher education.

In response to the interest in student learning generated by the learning paradigm, all of the regional accrediting agencies have adopted standards requiring colleges and universities to measure SLOs. The Accrediting Commission for Community and Junior Colleges (ACCJC), which accredits community colleges in California, Hawaii, and the Pacific Islands, mentions SLOs liberally throughout its standards. For example, its standard on student learning and support programs states:

> The institution identifies and regularly assesses learning outcomes for courses, programs, certificates and degrees using established institutional procedures. The institution has officially approved current course outlines that include student-learning outcomes. In every class section students receive a course syllabus that includes learning outcomes from the institution's officially approved course outline. (ACCJC, standard II, A 3)

The SLOs remain controversial, however. In a February 23, 2018, article in the *New York Times*, "The Misguided Drive to Measure 'Learning Outcomes,'" Molly Worthen, an assistant professor at the University of North Carolina at Chapel Hill, describes what she calls a bureaucratic behemoth known as learning outcomes assessment. She claims that the "movement's focus on quantifying classroom experience makes it easy to shift blame for student failure wholly onto universities, ignoring deeper socio-economic reasons that cause many students to struggle with college-level work" (2018).

In a March 1, 2018, rebuttal to the Worthen article, Kate Drezek McConnell, the director for research and assessment at the Association of American Colleges and Universities (AAC&U), wrote an article published by *Inside Higher Ed* titled "What Assessment Is Really About." McConnell refers to the important role that faculty play in assessment, pointing out that AAC&U engaged interdisciplinary teams of faculty members from across the country to author the rubrics for its Valid Assessment of Learning in Undergraduate Education (VALUE). McConnell goes on to say, "Worthen's opposition to assessing student learning reads as but a strawman for a much more harmful argument: protecting the life of the mind by writing off entire segments of our society from the intellectual and, yes, economically transformative power of education" (McConnell, 2018).

As the discussions about learning outcomes continue, educators should be careful not to fall into the trap of making the purpose of SLOs just about a report to satisfy an accrediting commission or a state agency. If it becomes the bureaucratic behemoth that Molly Worthen complained about, it will have no real impact on student learning. On the other hand, if faculty members conduct meaningful discussions about what students should be learning and how to measure it, the effect will be positive.

HOW STUDENTS LEARN

Historically, college educators have relied on lectures, reading assignments, writing assignments, problem sets, laboratory work, and fieldwork to promote student learning. Today educators have come to realize that students must be more actively engaged in their learning. For example, evidence from a number of disciplines suggests that oral presentations to large groups of passive students contribute very little to learning (National Research Council, 1997). Learners do not just absorb new information as if their brains were blank slates.

According to the National Academy of Sciences, learning organizes and reorganizes the brain. Learners use their current knowledge to construct new knowledge, and what they know at the moment affects how they interpret new information. Sometimes learners' current knowledge supports new learning; sometimes it hampers learning (National Research Council, 1999, p. xvi). Teachers who build on what students already know and who challenge misconceptions can promote learning.

Students also learn in different ways, sometimes called learning styles or preferences. Some students are auditory learners and can learn from hearing a description; others are visual learners and must read a description or see a demonstration; still others need to physically do something related to what they are trying to learn. Research has confirmed that one single approach to teaching does not work for every student or even for most students (Silver, Strong, & Perini, 1997).

Students must be actively involved in their own learning. Eric Mazur, a professor of physics at Harvard University, has found that he has been able to improve student test scores by engaging his students in discussions of problems. He asks his students to consider a conceptual question individually for a minute and then asks them to turn to their neighbors and convince them of their logic. He says that chaos erupts in his lecture hall as students engage in lively and usually uninhibited discussions of the question. After one or two minutes, he calls time and asks the students to record an answer and a confidence level. Mazur claims that the students have taught him how best to teach them. Nothing clarifies students' ideas as much as explaining them to others (National Research Council, 1997, p. 22).

There are many forms of collaborative or group learning. Collaborative learning, compared with competitive and individualistic efforts, has numerous benefits and typically results in higher achievement and greater productivity; more caring, supportive, and committed relationships; and greater psychological health, social competence, and self-esteem (Laal & Ghodsi, 2012). Learning communities, in which students and faculty are assigned to a common set of classes, have been shown to improve learning outcomes when faculty members teaching the common courses structure assignments that require students to apply what they are studying in one course to other courses and assignments (Zhao & Kuh, 2004).

When he was a faculty member at the University of California at Berkeley in 1978, Uri Treisman conducted a groundbreaking study that demonstrated the effectiveness of collaborative learning. Treisman studied the behavior of Chinese American students, who received the highest grades in his calculus classes, and found that they naturally formed study groups and collaborated in helping each other to learn. Treisman suspected that this same type of collaboration might assist other students to become successful learners and was able to demonstrate improvements in learning. He created an intensive workshop course for minority students to encourage their collaboration and found the results to be dramatic. Black and Latino calculus students who were in the workshop class substantially outperformed not only their minority peers, but also their white and Asian classmates (Treisman, 1992).

The lack of educational success for men of color is a growing national concern. In 2014 Phi Theta Kappa and the Center for Community College Student Engagement conducted focus group interviews that included men of color who were members of the honor society. They expected that these successful students might have come from different backgrounds than the men of color who were not successful. The surprising finding was that the backgrounds were identical.

Both successful and unsuccessful men of color came from single-parent households and grew up in poverty and in high crime areas. What made the difference was that the successful students broke ties with negative acquaintances and instead developed strong relationships with people on campus and in the community who motivated them to learn and become successful (Center for Community College Student Engagement, 2014, p. 10). The report documented the importance of personal connections, a sense of belonging, people who believe in them, high expectations, and instructors who showed an interest in them and a commitment to help them learn (Center for Community College Student Engagement, 2014, p. 8).

Educational technology can be used in powerful ways to support and enhance student learning both in and out of the classroom. It can improve access to education; in many ways, it almost forces a greater engagement between faculty and students while also enabling a greater degree of student collaboration. However, classes that are mostly remote can be a challenge for students who would benefit from the structure and motivation experienced in a physical classroom with an instructor and other students. For that reason, instructors need to regularly interact electronically with online students and to find ways to encourage student-to-student interaction (Boggs, 2018, p. 2).

The Achieving the Dream initiative has demonstrated the effectiveness of several strategies that help students be successful. The Knowledge Center on the Achieving the Dream website provides information on many of these efforts to improve student success. Examples of effective practices include referring students to tutoring, enrolling students in college success skill or freshman experience courses, and use of a math lab.

CONCLUSION

In a relatively short time, the learning paradigm and the subsequent learning college principles significantly impacted all of higher education in the United States and beyond. Current initiatives are centered on a narrower objective of shifting from an emphasis on access to education to both access and success, in which student success is defined by completion of a certificate or a degree. Outcome-based funding formulas for public higher education institutions are spreading across the country, but they are generally based on student progress or completion and not on learning. The emphasis on completion is an important component of the learning paradigm, but not the only one.

Accrediting agencies now require student-learning outcomes; however, they remain controversial—and they are not easy to measure. There is some encouraging work being done by organizations such as the AAC&U and the National Institute for Learning Outcomes Assessment. The National Institute for Staff and Organizational Development continues to link effective teaching with student learning, and the Center for Community College Student Engagement continues its work to help colleges improve student engagement, an important strategy for student success. The League for Innovation in the Community College continues to host an annual learning summit and to publish *Learning Abstracts*, giving educators opportunities to demonstrate and share best practices to promote learning.

Perhaps the most visible changes from the learning paradigm to date are that institutions have become more outcome focused and data informed, and they have accepted responsibility for student success. Students, of course, are the most responsible for their learning and success, but there is a great deal that institutions can do to promote and support student learning. In order for that to happen, college leadership must make it a priority, and everyone in the institution must be relentless in developing a culture of evidence and advocating for student learning.

REFERENCES

Barr, R. (1995). From Teaching to Learning: A New Reality for Community Colleges. *Leadership Abstracts* 8, no. 3 (March).

Barr, R. & Tagg, J. (1995). From Teaching to Learning—A New Paradigm for Undergraduate Education. *Change: The Magazine of Higher Learning* 27, no. 6 (November–December).

Boggs, G. R. (1991). *Palomar College 2005: A Shared Vision*. San Marcos, CA: Palomar College.

Boggs, G. R. (1993). Community Colleges and the New Paradigm. In *Celebrations*. Austin, TX: The National Institute for Staff and Organizational Development.

Boggs, G. R. (1993–1994). Reinventing Community Colleges. *Community College Journal* (December/January): 4–5.

Boggs, G. R. (1995a). The Learning Paradigm. *Community College Journal* (December/January): 24–27.

Boggs, G. R. (1995b). Focus on Student Learning. *Crosstalk: A Quarterly Publication of the California Higher Education Policy Center* 3, no. 2: 18–19.

Boggs, G. R. (1995c). The New Paradigm for Community Colleges—Who's Leading the Way? *The Catalyst: The Journal of the National Council on Community Services and Continuing Education* 25, no. 1: 27–28.

Boggs, G. R. (1999a). What the Learning Paradigm Means for Faculty. *AAHE Bulletin* 51, no. 5 (January): 3–5.

Boggs, G. R. (1999b). What the Learning Paradigm Means for Faculty. *Learning Abstracts* 2, no. 4 (May).

Boggs, G. R. (2018). Rip Van Winkle Goes to College. *Innovation Abstracts* 40, no. 6 (February).

Brint, S., & Karabel, J. (1989). *The Diverted Dream: Community Colleges and the Promise of Educational Opportunity in America*. Oxford: Oxford University Press.

Bumphus, W. (1996). Two Views Toward Learning. *Community College Journal* 67, no. 2 (October/November): 4–6.

Center for Community College Student Engagement. (2014). *Aspirations to Achievement: Men of Color and Community Colleges*. Austin, TX: Center for Community College Student Engagement.

Commission on Research for the California Association of Community Colleges. (1988). *Indicators and Measures of Successful Community Colleges*. California Association of Community Colleges.

Commission on Research for the California Association of Community Colleges. (1989). *Criteria and Measures of Institutional Effectiveness*. California Association of Community Colleges.

Commission on the Future of Community Colleges. (1988). *Building Communities: A Vision for a New Century*. Washington, DC: American Association of Community Colleges.

Hillman, N. (2016). *Why Performance-Based College Funding Doesn't Work*. New York: The Century Foundation.

Kuh, G. (2018). How to Make Sure Students Graduate with More Than a Diploma. *The Chronicle of Higher Education*, March 1.

Laal, M., & Ghodsi, S. M. (2012). Benefits of Collaborative Learning. *SciVerse Science Direct: Procedia-Social & Behavioral Sciences* 31: 486–490.

McClenney, K. (2001). Learning from the Learning Colleges: Observations Along the Journey. *Learning Abstracts* 4, no. 2.

McClenney, K. (2003a). Becoming a Learning College: Milestones on the Journey. *Learning Abstracts* 6, no. 3.

McClenney, K. (2003b). Benchmarking Best Practices in the Learning College. *Learning Abstracts* 6, no. 4.

McConnell, K. D. (2018). What Assessment Is Really About. *Inside Higher Ed*, March 1.

McPhail, C. J. (2005) *Establishing and Sustaining Learning Centered Community Colleges*. Washington, DC: Community College Press.

National Research Council. (1997). *Science Teaching Reconsidered: A Handbook*. Washington, DC: National Academy Press.

National Research Council. (1999). *How People Learn: Brain, Mind, Experience, and School*. Washington, DC: National Academy Press.

New Expeditions Initiative. (2000). *The Knowledge Net*. Washington, DC: Community College Press for the American Association of Community Colleges and the Association of Community College Trustees.

O'Banion, T. (1997a). *A Learning College for the 21st Century.* Phoenix, AZ: The Oryx Press.

O'Banion, T. (1997b). *Creating More Learning-Centered Community Colleges.* Chandler, AZ: League for Innovation in the Community College.

O'Banion, T. (1997c). The Purpose, Process, and Product of the Learning Revolution in the Community College. *Leadership Abstracts* 10, no. 7 (June).

O'Banion, T. (1999). The Learning College: Both Learner and Learning Centered. *Learning Abstracts* 2, no. 2 (March).

O'Banion, T., & Wilson, C. (2011). *Focus on Learning: A Learning College Reader.* Chandler, AZ: League for Innovation in the Community College.

Oblinger, D., & Rush, S. C. (1997). *The Learning Revolution: The Challenge of Information Technology in the Academy.* Alta Loma, CA: Anker Press.

Silver, H., Strong, R., & Perini, M. (1997). Integrating Learning Styles and Multiple Intelligences. *Educational Leadership* 55, no. 1 (September): 22–27.

Treisman, U. (1992). Studying Students Studying Calculus: A Look at the Lives of Minority Mathematics Students in College. *The College Mathematics Journal* 23, no. 5: 362–372.

21st Century Commission on the Future of Community Colleges. (2012). *Reclaiming the American Dream: Community Colleges and the Nation's Future.* Washington, DC: American Association of Community Colleges.

The Wingspread Group on Higher Education. (1993). *An American Imperative: Higher Expectations for Higher Education.* Racine, WI: Johnson Foundation.

Worthen, M. (2018). The Misguided Drive to Measure "Learning Outcomes". *New York Times*, February 23.

Zhao, C.-M., & Kuh, G. (2004). Adding Value: Learning Communities and Student Engagement. *Research in Higher Education* 45, no. 2: 115–138.

Chapter Two

Community Colleges and the Ladder of Student Success

Suzanne Walsh and Mark Milliron

As an invention of the Truman Commission; a child of junior colleges and technical institutes; and a tool for economic development leaders, progressive educators, and social justice crusaders alike, the community college stands alone. Indeed, today's comprehensive community college is a shining example of American innovation in higher education. It has become a mainstay in education ecosystems regionally and nationally, serving millions of students each year. Distinct from its K–12 and university siblings, the community college's place in the family of higher education institutions is unique—primarily because of its focus on helping underserved, and often forgotten, students rise above.

Indeed, from the early days of this "movement"—as many of its most seasoned supporters call it—until today, community colleges and their leaders have been building out and guiding students toward an all-important student success ladder. Along the way they have had to focus on strengthening and solidifying different steps of this ladder, even as they have offered the trip up the ladder to an increasing number of students. The four steps focused on in this chapter are access, learning, completion, and postgraduation outcomes.

The access step remains essential to allow for any kind of advancement for students, of course. Yes, it is a century-old work in progress, but it is still in need of expansion and even repair. The learning step has always mattered but has received significantly more attention over the last twenty-five years. Focused and sometimes frenzied construction on the completion step has been the work of the last decade, however, and is still galvanizing the higher education practice and policy world in compelling ways.

The coming together over the last five years of work on the access, learning, and completion steps is showing the powerful potential of the concept of the student success ladder. Given that the larger higher education field is diving deep into more of these multistep, comprehensive student success efforts, examples of this work are a major focus here. However, the need to begin more intense work on the last step, postgraduation outcomes, is also explored. On to step one.

ACCESS

An educational, economic, and social advancement ladder is of no use to a striving student if he or she cannot even reach the first step. Put simply, access is essential. Of course the "access to what" argument that follows matters as well. But it is difficult to make the case that offering a deep learning opportunity without effective access is an enlightened approach to student success. Not surprisingly, then, access as the student success ladder's first step had to take the lion's share of the early energy.

Indeed, the work of the last century is the story of leaders, builders, educators, and millions of students working on, advocating for, and celebrating the expansion of access. The 1944 GI Bill and the 1947 President's Commission on Higher Education, called for by President Harry S. Truman, made a massive expansion of access a national imperative and helped redefine who had the option to continue on to postsecondary education. The GI Bill and the Truman Commission were a major boost to the community college movement in the United States, culminating in an explosion of access innovation from the 1960s through today's "free community college" efforts. As access expanded, adult basic education, GED, technical training, transfer, associate degrees, workforce certifications, and more were part of the array of options available to millions of new students if they would just take their first steps through the "open door" of community and technical colleges.

The open-door metaphor is core to the ethic of the early builders of the access step on this ladder. The idea was to give new and diverse students new and diverse options. Early leaders and advocates of community college expansion said that these students had the "right to fail." Getting them in mattered most.

Not surprisingly, innovations around flexible scheduling, distance learning, remote learning centers, contract training, and eventually online and blended learning flourished. Moreover, federal, state, and institutional policies, especially the funding models, reflected this focus on access. Funding models, in fact, were always performance based. The key performance metric, however, was enrollment. A "healthy" or "effective" community college was synonymous with a growing college. If a college was successfully expanding access (i.e., had growing enrollment), it was considered a good community college.

LEARNING

Access and Excellence: The Open Door College (Roueche & Baker, 1987) is but one of many publications that tried to shine a brighter light on the need to focus more on strengthening the learning step on the ladder. Not surprisingly, educators from the heady days of the 1960s, 1970s, and 1980s now bristle at the suggestion that learning was not at the core of their work. Indeed, they offered access to an array of learning innovations. But access was the dominant conversation. The policy and practice work of that time is clear evidence of the access focus being the primary one.

In the 1990s Barr and Tagg (1995) made the case that the community college field needed to stop focusing so much of its energy on teaching (being "teaching centered," as they referred to it) and begin focusing first on improving student learning. Soon thereafter, George Boggs (1996) argued that community college leaders needed to make learning, rather than teaching, the overall focus of their efforts; he recommended a new learning paradigm for community colleges. (See chapter 1 in this volume.) Then Terry O'Banion's *A Learning College for the 21st Century* (1997) sounded the clarion call. It made the argument that community college leaders needed to ask the burning questions related to all policies, practices, and people: Are they improving and expanding learning? How do you know?

The learning college movement was born. But essential to the conversation here, this movement brought foundation funding, policy change, and practice innovation to a boil for over fifteen years. The League for Innovation in the Community College launched the grant-funded vanguard learning college project, with leading colleges across North America; began publishing *Learning Abstracts*; and welcomed educators internationally to an annual learning summit focused on improving and expanding learning outcomes. The American Association of Community Colleges (AACC) held learning-centered education convenings, hundreds of colleges did the work of becoming more learning centered in their programs and services, think tanks explored what it meant to take learning seriously, and state and local policy makers tried to shape policies that catalyzed and helped support learning-centered practice.

The second step on the student success ladder was solidifying, to be sure. Then in 2004 a national initiative funded by Lumina Foundation for Education, Achieving the Dream, came together. Building on the promise of the first and second steps—that students should have affordable access to high-quality learning—but adding a nonnegotiable focus on a "culture of evidence" around learning outcomes and an aspiration to close attainment gaps between diverse students, the movement to take the next step on the ladder was put in motion.

COMPLETION

In the early 2000s a series of foundations began to focus on community colleges (Lumina Foundation, Ford Foundation, The Heinz Endowments, College Success Foundation, Kresge Foundation); by 2008, they and other new entrants such as the Bill & Melinda Gates Foundation had started to turn the national conversation to completion. These foundation leaders began to ask a simple but difficult-to-answer question: Are students attending community colleges finishing credentials that help them advance their careers and live more fulfilling lives?

The context was ripe for engagement. Colleges that had been part of Achieving the Dream since the early 2000s had embraced the new culture of evidence and were ready for the next challenge. States, the federal government, and foundations were pushing community colleges to graduate more students for the good of the local and national economies.

To that end, the years 2008 to 2010 were seminal in the completion movement. Focusing on completion of certificates and degrees was becoming more than a passing fad that was "put upon" colleges by policy makers or foundations and was beginning to signal a significant shift for community colleges. Colleges began to look for ideas about how to move beyond the idea of setting ambitious grad-rate and grad-number goals. As the French Renaissance philosopher, Michel de Montaigne (2006), said,

> We take other men's knowledge and opinions upon trust; which is an idle and superficial learning. We must make it our own. We are in this very like him, who having need of fire, went to a neighbour's house to fetch it, and finding a very good one there, sat down to warm himself without remembering to carry any with him home. . . . What good does it do us to have the stomach full of meat, if it do not digest, if it be not incorporated with us, if it does not nourish and support us?

In their effort to own the energy of the completion agenda, community college leaders began to pull together and incorporate the work of the foundations, the American Association for Community Colleges, League for Innovation in the Community College, Community College Research Center, Achieving the Dream, and others to shape a more cohesive vision of student success. Their version would include at least three of the steps on the ladder: access, learning, and completion.

It is important to note that without this combined vision, colleges could improve completion by giving away worthless credentials or closing their doors to the hardest to serve students. Neither was an option given the history and culture of the movement. Moreover, by continuing to build out and improve all three steps on the student success ladder, the work truly comes together into a transformative journey for students.

Economic, Political, and Foundation Catalysts

The collective student success movement—bringing access, learning, and completion together—began to gain real momentum when it was seen to be part of an economic imperative. Indeed, from 2008 to 2012, student success became a rallying cry for economic competitiveness. Dr. Jennifer Engle, then director of higher education data and research at EdTrust and now deputy director for measurement, learning and evaluation at the Bill & Melinda Gates Foundation, recalls:

> We had to start every proposal, report, or article from at least 2008 to 2012 with a statement about how the US had fallen from first in the world in college attainment and thus we were losing the competitiveness game. On the one hand, this was a welcome narrative for those who had been working to increase awareness about the need to improve college access AND success for low-income students and students of color in this country. On the other hand, the narrative was decidedly focused on an economic rather than an equity imperative because there was a sense that a workforce agenda would better resonate politically with decision makers. Many made the argument at the time that our economic goals could not be met without closing equity gaps, but it did shift the priorities of the conversation in a way that persists today. (personal interview 2018)

The economic and equity goals persisted and served as the basis for foundations, states, and the nation to set ambitious goals around completion beginning in 2008. That was the year that Lumina announced its Big Goal to increase the proportion of Americans with high-quality degrees and credentials to 60 percent by the year 2025.

And 2008 was also an election year. It was an opportunity to discuss with candidates higher education as a priority and a core component of the nation's competitiveness. The newly elected president of the United States, Barrack Obama, as well as the second lady of the United States, Jill Biden, led the charge. Community colleges were receiving unprecedented attention.

In 2009 the Bill & Melinda Gates Foundation made its first investments in postsecondary education, and the stated goal at that time was to *double the number of young people* who earn a postsecondary degree or certificate with labor-market value by the time they reach age twenty-six. The strategy focused exclusively on community colleges at its inception and continues to invest in community college initiatives even after it expanded support to all segments of higher education. Today, the postsecondary strategy at the Gates Foundation is focused on closing equity gaps to improve social/economic mobility for low-income and first-generation students and students of color, which contributes to broader economic goals.

The White House Summit on Community Colleges

By 2010, community colleges were solidly part of the national focus on economic competitiveness and were welcomed to the White House for its Summit on Community Colleges, chaired by Jill Biden. The mission statement of the White House summit focused on action:

1. To emphasize the role of community colleges in achieving the president's goal of making America the most educated country in the world by 2020.
2. To demonstrate that community colleges are crucial partners in our efforts to prepare our graduates to lead the twenty-first-century workforce.
3. To highlight the Skills for America's Future initiative, a new Gates Foundation program called Completion by Design, and the Aspen Prize for Community College Excellence.

The 2011 White House summit laid out in very clear terms the important role that community colleges play in the nation's competitiveness. Community colleges were being called upon to respond quickly to a shortage of community college graduates:

> [C]ommunity colleges aren't just the key to the future of their students. They're also one of the keys to the future of our country. We are in a global competition to lead in the growth industries of the 21st century. And that leadership depends on a well-educated, highly skilled workforce. We know, for example, that in the coming years, jobs requiring at least an associate degree are going to grow twice as fast as jobs that don't require college. We will not fill those jobs—or keep those jobs on our shores—without community colleges . . . [and] countries that out educate us today are going to out-compete us tomorrow. (President Barack Obama, in White House Summit on Community Colleges, 2011)

A number of breakout sessions were part of the summit. Of particular note are the recommendations listed here from "Breakout Session 2: Community College Completion," which was moderated by Secretary of Education Arne Duncan and Undersecretary of Education James Kvaal. The ideas sourced from the community college leaders in attendance were pivotal, and many have been achieved in a relatively short time:

1. Better communicate the value of a credential to help the public understand its purpose, quality, and results.
2. Establish common metrics that measure progress and outcomes.
3. Establish block scheduling and directed choice to accelerate time to degree.
4. Consider how developmental education meets the needs of diverse learners.
5. Offer industry-run professional development for faculty.
6. Base state funding on completion, rather than enrollments.
7. Foster an institution-level culture of evidence-based decision making.
8. Be more aggressive about counseling.
9. Strengthen student support services.
10. Create stronger partnerships with industry to ensure work opportunities and job placement; increase teaching opportunities for business representatives.
11. Align graduation and entrance requirements between K–12 and community colleges.
12. Create high school dual-credit opportunities.
13. Use technology to increase capacity.
14. Increase the use of cohort-based education.
15. Grant associate degrees to students who have completed enough credits, even if they are seeking bachelor's degrees (e.g., Project—Win–Win).
16. Award credit for prior learning experiences.
17. Create transparent articulation agreements.
18. Link with President Obama's volunteer service corps to provide tutoring and High Touch for community college students; leverage the knowledge and resource of retirees.

Community colleges began implementing many of the ideas on this list of recommendations, developed further by the AACC 21st Century Commission on the Future of Community Colleges. As de Montaigne suggested, colleges continued to gather ideas from the increasing number of trusted sources and make them their own. Those ideas that made the most significant impact all started with deep data analysis that led to data-informed programmatic and policy changes.

STUDENT SUCCESS LADDER EXAMPLES

As part of Completion by Design, a student success initiative funded by the Bill & Melinda Gates Foundation, nine community colleges in three states worked to do just as the name suggests: design their institutions to help most students complete. This was a big idea in 2010, as community colleges were beginning to more strategically integrate their work on the access, learning, and completion steps on the ladder. To assist the colleges in assessing how they were doing in helping more students to rise up the rungs, the foundation shared "Understanding the Student Experience: Loss and Momentum Framework" (see figure 2.1).

The framework identifies four key points that are part of all students' journeys and the most likely places where students will gain or lose momentum: connection, entry, progress, and completion. It allows an institution to investigate the student experience and "the numerous systems, protocols, departments, and personnel that each and every student encounters on the way to completion outcomes—these are the building blocks of completion"

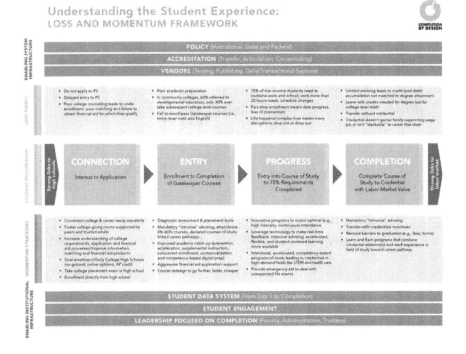

Figure 2.1.   Understanding the Student Experience: Loss and Momentum Framework

(Rassen, Chaplot, Jenkins, & Johnstone, 2016). Most institutions tend to focus resources, staff, and time on the first two phases of connection and entry and thus see the greatest momentum in those phases. Understanding this helps institutions redesign the student experience to adjust resources, staff, and time on progress and completion.

In 2012 the North Carolina Community College System organized all of its grants on student success and mapped them against the framework, finding that just as individual colleges have focused most on the connection and entry stages, most of the grants applied for and received by the system were also focused on connection and entry. Completion by Design colleges each applied the framework and used it to redesign their processes, structures, and resources, resulting on average in colleges meeting three out of five of their 2019 target goals three years ahead of schedule. The framework lives on, and Achieving the Dream has recently updated it to include transition and transfer, to begin pushing toward postgraduation, the next step on the student success ladder.

A related example, the AACC Guided Pathways Project, draws on past community college work, Completion by Design, Achieving the Dream, and the 21st Century Commission. As part of the project, thirty institutions from seventeen states participated in Pathways Institutes to build capacity to design and implement structured academic and career pathways at scale, for all of their students. For further information on this work, see chapter 4 in this volume or review the seminal book *Redesigning America's Community Colleges: A Clearer Path to Student Success* (Bailey, Jaggars, & Jenkins, 2015).

The more prevalent these student success projects by practitioners and discussions by policy makers became, the more important it was for community colleges to be able to define student success metrics that best reflected their unique missions—especially metrics that measured success on the first three steps of the student success ladder. Moreover, there had been a need for a national common accountability framework among community colleges ever since the accountability movement had begun in earnest in 2006 with the issuing of the final report by Secretary of Education Margaret Spellings' Commission on the Future of Higher Education. Community college leaders took the report and began to define metrics and accountability for themselves. This combination of forces and commitment led AACC, Association of Community College Trustees, and the College Board to come together to create the Voluntary Framework of Accountability (VFA).

The public collection and use of data were not new to community colleges. "Since 2002, nearly 800 community colleges had voluntarily agreed to have the results from the Community College Survey of Student Engagement (CCSSE) posted on a public Web site with interactive data search and benchmarking capabilities" (Principles and Plans, n.d.). The challenge for the VFA, however, was to determine how best to measure community college effectiveness in ways that are appropriate and sensitive to the missions of these institutions, while also being relevant and rigorous in addressing the legitimate concern of law-makers and the public interested in the performance of its higher education institutions. The VFA initiative [was] also [intended to] provide a template for college leaders to use to assess and improve institutional outcomes.

NEXT STEPS ON THE STUDENT SUCCESS LADDER

The community college movement continues to build out and hold up the student success ladder as a tool to help more, and more diverse, students rise. Work is still being done at each step to ensure more students ascend the ladder.

In the access world, the affordability crisis is real and rising. The launch of the Hope Center for College, Community, and Justice and the embrace of Sara Goldrick-Rab's *Paying the Price: College Costs, Financial Aid, and the Betrayal of the American Dream* (2016) have helped bring the stunning extra-academic needs of students to light. These sources show how far community colleges are from completing the work on access.

In short, many community college students are too hungry to study (almost 40 percent), too worried about where they will sleep at night to join a student club (upward of 10 percent), or too occupied with child care to make it to class on time. Moreover, the work of the Institute for the Study of Knowledge Management in Education (ISKME) and its Open Education Resource Commons (www.oercommons.org) are helping more community college students access lower-cost curricular resources. More colleges are learning about the importance of food pantries, emergency aid, and transportation vouchers—and especially about braiding social services into student services. Finally, the total cost of college has led to a deep embrace of the "free community college movement" (see chapter 3 in this volume). The work on the access step is far from complete.

On the learning side, the challenge of championing and working toward better programs that help students achieve key learning outcomes has not gone away. Indeed, Terry O'Banion's *Bread and Roses: Helping Students Make a Good Living and Live a Good Life* (2016) continues to catalyze conversations with faculty senates and leadership preparation programs. Conversations about how to anchor programs in measurable twenty-first-century skills are dominating accreditation conversations. Documenting learning outcomes is required by accrediting agencies and increasingly by employers.

In the work of completion, colleges are in the early days. With standing completion rates at most community colleges in the mid- to high 20s, transfer still a challenge in most regions, and equity gaps evident in a range of college outcomes, community college leaders know they are just beginning to champion innovations and institutional transformations on a scale that will change the game for most striving students.

From AACC's Guided Pathways to the Bill & Melinda Gates Foundation's Frontier Set institutions (2018), the models are emerging, and the student success metrics are rising. The energy is there. It will just take sustained and committed work to continue to improve and strengthen each step on the community college student success ladder—particularly work to significantly improve the ability of colleges to provide data for leaders and learners eager to better understand what is working and what is not in the build out and on the journey (Milliron, 2016).

But achieving completion will not be enough. What good is access if students do not learn? What good is learning if they do not have a credential that can help them access the next level of learning or get a good job? And what good is that credential if it does not help them succeed in that job, advance their careers, continue their learning, and empower their personal choices? It is this last question that is starting to come into focus.

Indeed, at the Civitas Learning annual partner summit, best-selling author and editor at large for the *Chronicle of Higher Education* Jeff Selingo made the case that this last question is at the core of what he calls Completion 3.0 (Milliron, 2018). Completion 3.0 is when (1) the employers who require and (2) the stakeholders that fund the institutions that bestow credentials—whether they are badges or certificates, diplomas, or degrees—demand to see the outcomes of students' career and personal pathways after they have crossed the graduation stage.

Completion 3.0 was almost thrust upon the field with gainful employment legislation that would have created a federal requirement for community colleges to embrace this kind of system in place to justify tuition and funding for a wide array of programs. While this one piece of legislation may have been stalled, make no mistake, these postgraduation outcomes will soon become a more important part of how community colleges judge their successes, build programs, and do the daily work of teaching and reaching students.

In the years to come, community college faculty, staff, leaders, and supporters will continue building, strengthening, advertising, celebrating, critiquing, and perfecting this student success ladder. However, the goal will remain the same: help more, and more diverse, students successfully make their way up the ladder to reach their unique goals. Moreover, as the associated institutional transformation work continues, it is vital that community college leaders remember that *each step matters*. The steps form a hopeful whole. And as significantly more striving students successfully stride up this ladder, step by step, communities, states, nations, and the world will also rise.

REFERENCES

Bailey, T. R., Jaggars, S. S., & Jenkins, D. (2015). *Redesigning America's community colleges: A clearer path to student success* (1st ed.). Cambridge, MA: Harvard University Press.

Barr, R. B., & Tagg, J. (1995, November/December). A new paradigm for undergraduate education. *Change*, 13–25. Retrieved from https://www.colorado.edu/ftep/sites/default/files/attached-files/barrandtaggfromteachingtolearning.pdf

Boggs, G. R. (1996). The learning paradigm. *Community College Journal, 66*(3), 24–27.

Goldrick-Rab, S. (2016). *Paying the price: College costs, financial aid, and the betrayal of the American dream.*

Milliron, M. (2016). *Making the most of a healthy change in education: The emerging student success platform.*

Milliron, M. (2018, June 20). *Jeff Selingo podcast: Leaning in and leading in to higher education* [Video blog interview]. Retrieved from https://www.civitaslearningspace.com/CatalyticConversations/jeff-selingo-podcast-leaning-in-and-leading-in-to-higher-education/

Montaigne, M. (2006, September). Essays of Michel de Montaigne. Retrieved from http://www.gutenberg.org/files/3600/3600-h/3600-h.htm

O'Banion, T. (1997). *A learning college for the 21st century* (1st ed.). Lanham, MD: Rowman & Littlefield.

O'Banion, T. (2016). *Bread and roses: Helping students make a good living and live a good life.* Chandler, AZ: League for Innovation.

Principles and plans: A Voluntary Framework of Accountability (VFA) for community colleges. (n.d.). Retrieved from https://vfa.aacc.nche.edu/Documents/PrinciplesandPlans-AVoluntaryFrameworkofAccountability.pdf

Rassen, E., Chaplot, P., Jenkins, D., & Johnstone, R. (2016). Understanding the student experience through the loss/momentum framework: Clearing the path to completion. Retrieved from https://ccrc.tc.columbia.edu/media/k2/attachments/understanding-student-experience-cbd.pdf

Roueche, J. E., & Baker, G. A. (1987). *Access & excellence: The open-door college* (1st ed.). Washington, DC: Community College Press.

White House Summit on Community Colleges. (2011). *Summit report.* Retrieved from https://obamawhitehouse.archives.gov/sites/default/files/uploads/community_college_summit_report.pdf

Chapter Three

The College Promise

Transforming the Lives of Community College Students

Martha Kanter and Andra Armstrong

Throughout the United States, a bold vision for the twenty-first century is shaping a new mind-set for local communities and states. It is called the College Promise. Its origin is centuries old, but to many students, families, communities, and states, it is a new, transformational idea that is sweeping the nation. The College Promise is based on the proposition that a community college or technical education should be as universal, free, and accessible as high school has been since 1929, when Alaska enacted high school for all.

A growing number of four-year colleges and universities are also launching the College Promise, many in partnership with community colleges and others on their own or as required by state legislation. But community colleges are dominant in this dramatic expansion of College Promise programs. In December 2018, the College Promise Campaign in Washington, DC reported quadrupled growth, from fifty-three College Promise programs identified in 2015 to more than 300 underway in forty-four states, with twenty-three established at the statewide level.

From coast to coast, community college trustees and presidents are joining with locally elected officials to build strategic partnerships with leaders from business, education, philanthropy, labor, and nonprofit organizations to keep higher education and the pursuit of the American Dream within reach of their residents. They are enacting College Promise programs, which cover tuition and fees for hardworking students to start and complete a degree or certificate at a community or technical college, freeing students from unmanageable college debt. Many Promise programs also provide support services (e.g., counseling, mentoring, and other services) to enable students to accelerate their progress through high school and college. To receive a College Promise, students must meet eligibility and persistence requirements that illustrate their commitment to complete their educational goals.

These local, state, and national leaders are working together to design and fund sustainable programs for students who live in their cities and towns because they know that a high school education is no longer enough to secure a good job and a decent quality of life. Bubbling up from substantial local engagement that built on the early results of local Promise programs (e.g., in Long Beach, CA; Kalamazoo, MI; Buffalo, NY; El Dorado, AR; and Pittsburgh, PA) and inspired by President Barack Obama's America's College Promise proposal and the Tennessee Promise, many of the nation's governors over the past five years have taken steps to enact legislation or executive orders to initiate and support College Promise programs.

There is no single way to build a Promise. Just as each community college tailors its offerings to meet its local needs, communities and states determine what Promise features and funding works best to drive their economic, social, and civic prosperity. These visionary, committed leaders are leveraging the College Promise because they understand that having an educated, workforce-ready citizenry is essential for the economic, civic, and social health of their regions. They realize that education is a path to a happier, healthier future for individuals, families, local economies, and the greater society.

While College Promise initiatives are a contemporary approach for a new century, the idea behind them is as old as the American Dream, as timeless as the Founding Fathers' notion that education is the catalyst for a prosperous, sustainable democracy. College Promise programs are founded on the supposition embedded in the heart of the American Dream that all people, regardless of their social, economic, or cultural backgrounds, should have the opportunity to make use of their full potential, that everyone should have the opportunity to climb the ladder of economic and social mobility, to enjoy a fruitful livelihood, and to ensure that the next generation is ready and able to build on that success.

A BRIEF HISTORY OF THE COLLEGE PROMISE MOVEMENT

Though the majority of College Promise programs are barely a decade old, the idea behind them is not new. Throughout American history, local, state, and federal leaders have repeatedly risen to the challenge of great economic shifts and changing workforce needs by investing in education. Again and again, lawmakers and other community leaders have set their sights on preparing their residents for the jobs of their time by supporting a free and appropriate public education. Through these investments, the nation has repeatedly brought opportunity to people who thought education was beyond their means. These leaders have understood that an educated citizenry is an essential ingredient in building economic and social prosperity and sustaining a vibrant democracy. The College Promise is this generation's iteration of that age-old idea.

Since the mid-nineteenth century, the United States has invested in public higher education as a way to boost a rapidly changing national economy. Through the Morrill Land Grant Acts of 1862 and 1890, steps were taken to broaden the country's economic development beyond its agrarian roots by offering more Americans the opportunity to earn a college degree, so they could train for industrial occupations, the careers of a brave new era. These laws acted as a watershed, stimulating the careers of Americans entering the twentieth century. They also embedded access to educational opportunities in centralized locations within the states as an essential strategy for "democratizing" postsecondary education and disseminating knowledge, both scientific and pragmatic.

These acts of Congress introduced the notion that colleges and universities could expand their course offerings beyond the liberal arts by adding practical training in evolving occupations, so workers could acquire the knowledge and skills needed by industries to grow their local economies and strengthen their communities.

However, by the dawn of the twentieth century, the notions of community and economic opportunity began to shift once again. In their comprehensive analysis of human and social capital, Goldin and Katz (1998) noted that between 1910 and 1940 towns and cities throughout the country realized they needed to provide residents with skills beyond what was required on the farm or in factories. They knew the jobs of the day required local residents to increase their education by acquiring the necessary language, administrative, and mathematical skills to adapt to the modern workforce. In just three decades, the free high school movement grew, and public high schools expanded dramatically in cities and towns throughout the country. Today these schools, which serve the majority of the nation's youth, are taken for granted.

According to Goldin (1998), in 1910, 19 percent of fifteen- to eighteen-year-olds in America were enrolled in a high school, but only 9 percent earned a diploma. By 1940, nearly three-quarters of American youth were enrolled in K–12 schools. Fifty-one percent of students graduated from high school in 1940. Within just three decades, the free public high school movement had spurred the United States to become the undisputed world leader in educational attainment. And that engendered the most substantial economic expansion ever seen in world history.

In 1944, during the waning days of World War II, Congress passed the Servicemen's Readjustment Act, known as the GI Bill, which propelled education levels beyond high school. Through this massive public investment,

the federal government provided 1.7 million servicemen and women returning home with the opportunity to earn a college education that was free.
Congress passed this bill because it feared that the fragile economy (still
recovering from the Great Depression) might again be plunged into ruin if
these returning service members could not find jobs. The idea was to equip
them with education and expertise for the ever-evolving workforce.

In 1947 President Truman received recommendations from the President's Commission on Higher Education that he relied on to affirm his postwar vision that K–14 education should be "both universal and free." Among
the principal outcomes of the Truman Commission, as it came to be known,
was the recognition that the community college was a national asset; the
commission also popularized the term *community college*.

The GI Bill and Truman Commission's recommendations promoted the
national values of college affordability, equity, and opportunity made possible by the government's support of and investment in higher education. The
shared vision and actions by the Executive Office and Congress—working in
tandem—to educate Americans with a world-class, universally available,
higher education system cemented America's place as the best-educated and
best-prepared country of the postwar era.

The formation and dramatic expansion of America's community colleges
brought the promise of universality and access to millions of Americans who
likely never would have been able to pursue a postsecondary education.
Women and minorities were increasingly represented in the nation's public
two- and four-year colleges and universities, enabled by these actions of the
federal government working with states. As a result, millions more
Americans took advantage of higher education, especially those from the
lower-income rungs whose financial circumstances would have precluded
advancing beyond high school before the postwar boom.

Two decades later, reeling from the civil rights protests following *Brown
v. Board of Education* (1954) and the death of President John F. Kennedy in
1963, the necessity of pursuing an education beyond high school became a
priority for the nation. Building on the opportunity and equity promise of an
affordable higher education for all, Congress passed, and President Lyndon
Johnson signed, the Higher Education Act of 1965. The landmark bill was
designed to make college available for all Americans by providing very low-
interest loans and removing significant financial barriers faced by economically disadvantaged students through generous federal aid grants, paving the
way for the Pell grant legislation to help low-income students take advantage
of community colleges and universities. Chronicled by The Pell Institute for
the Study of Opportunity in Higher Education (2018) for many decades,
these actions enabled millions more Americans to enter college, complete
their degrees and certificates, and advance in their careers and communities.

However, as noted by Mortenson (2012), by the mid-1970s public invest-ment in postsecondary education as a percentage of per capita income began to decline. In the waning decades of the twentieth century, the nation slowly began to pull away from its promise to ensure that America would have the best-educated and most highly skilled population in the world. Even as the American economy grew in the 1990s and early 2000s, the nation's public investments in education declined. Crucial ground was lost in the global economy as other countries outpaced the United States in the percentage of gross domestic product (GDP) committed to education at all levels. These nations began to move ahead of the United States as they prepared their citizens with the knowledge and training needed for twenty-first-century jobs—without requiring them to go into debt.

In just a few generations, the United States went from being first in the world in the proportion of twenty-five- to thirty-four-year-old adults with college degrees. By 2009 the United States had fallen to sixteenth place, according to the Organisation for Economic Cooperation and Development (OECD) (2012). That set the stage for the College Promise expansion.

The momentum to build College Promise programs was inspired by the vision of the Truman Commission, the GI Bill, and two free college pro-grams that emerged in the late twentieth century: the California Community Colleges Board of Governors Fee Waiver, which since 1984 has in essence made college free for low-income community students in the Golden State, and the Indiana 21st Century Scholars Program, which has helped more than seventy thousand low-income students in the Hoosier State afford college since it was established in 1990. The pioneering state program in Indiana went beyond paying college tuition and fees and set clear expectations to incentivize students to stay on track to earn their degrees and certificates on time. Other communities took notice.

Public and private sector leaders launched the Kalamazoo Promise (Mill-er-Adams, 2009) in Kalamazoo, Michigan, in 2005 when a group of anony-mous donors turned to free college as a way to curb residential flight and a lagging economy. The idea was to help the city transform itself by offering all residents the opportunity to go to college without paying tuition, any-where in the state of Michigan, for one to four years. These innovative philanthropists reasoned that the city could reverse the tide of ebbing popula-tion and local industry if their residents had affordable access to the educa-tion and skills needed for the rapidly changing economy. They knew that more businesses would invest or stay in the city if residents prepared for careers in the changing workforce. They understood that fewer people would move away if they could train for those jobs close to home.

The Kalamazoo Promise broke new ground in how it awarded scholar-ships: residency and graduation from one of the city's high schools were the only requirements to receive an award; neither merit nor financial need was considered. Since its creation, this unprecedented experiment in urban development through education has guaranteed potentially every graduate of Kalamazoo High School a full scholarship to attend any approved public or private postsecondary school in Michigan, including the state's community and technical colleges. The amount of tuition funding students receive depends on how long they have been enrolled in the Kalamazoo system. Those who have been in the city's public schools since kindergarten receive a full tuition waiver.

The results are compelling. According to the W. E. Upjohn Institute, the Promise reversed the school district's decades-long decline in enrollment and built a strong college-going culture in the city (Miller-Adams, 2015). Between 2005 and 2014, enrollment in the Kalamazoo Public Schools grew by 24 percent, bringing new financial support and leading to the construction of two new schools, the first to be opened in Kalamazoo in almost forty years. Research by the institute also showed a dramatic increase in the number of students (including minority and economically disadvantaged students) who took advanced placement courses.

Inspired by Kalamazoo's success, three other communities—Denver, CO; Pittsburgh, PA; and El Dorado, AR—launched Promise initiatives between 2006 and 2007. Each program had a unique model and funding scope. While they varied in design, they shared a common goal: to educate and prepare residents for economic and social sufficiency by broadening access to postsecondary education. A grassroots movement to make a community college education as universal and affordable as public high school was born once again.

In the ensuing decade, approximately fifty new College Promise programs emerged as struggling local economies grappled with the challenge of sending more students to college even as the Great Recession unfolded and college costs were spiraling upward as federal and state investments began to wither. These were the early days of College Promise.

On February 24, 2009, President Obama embedded the idea of "free community college" into the nation's consciousness during his first address to a joint session of Congress. In that address, he conveyed the urgent need to prepare Americans for the jobs of the rapidly changing economy through investments in higher education. "In a global economy where the most valuable skill you can sell is your knowledge, a good education is no longer just a pathway to opportunity—it is a prerequisite. . . . That is why it will be the goal of this administration to ensure that every child has access to a complete and competitive education—from the day they are born to the day they begin a career" (Obama, 2009, para. 6).

President Obama urged every American to commit to at least one year of postsecondary education or training beyond high school. To achieve that vision, his administration committed to making college more accessible, affordable, and attainable for all American families so that, as he said to that joint session, "by 2020, America would once again have the highest proportion of college graduates in the world" (Obama, 2009, para. 46).

Six years later, in his January 20, 2015, State of the Union address to Congress, President Obama sought legislation by proposing the creation of federal-state partnership grants that would fund community college tuition and fees for qualified students (Obama, 2015a). Under the proposal, students enrolled at least half-time while maintaining a 2.5 grade point average would be eligible for funds as they worked toward earning their degrees or certificates.

The idea was to provide students with college-level undergraduate general education and career-technical courses in high-demand careers to prepare them for the jobs of the future and increase their economic, social, and civic mobility. Under the plan, community colleges would create evidence-based institutional reforms to improve college persistence, completion, and graduation rates on their campus. And participating states would have had to guarantee the alignment of transferable credits between community colleges and four-year colleges and universities. That legislation came to a halt in the 114th Congress due to the declining bipartisan political environment, but it did inspire the grassroots College Promise movement at the local and state levels, building on the results of the more than fifty local Promise initiatives.

On September 9, 2015, President Obama traveled to Macomb Community College in Warren, Michigan, to announce the creation of the nonpartisan College Promise National Advisory Board, a diverse collection of leaders from education, business, philanthropy, government, student groups, labor, and nonprofit organizations (Obama, 2015b). These assembled leaders agreed to serve as advisers to the nascent College Promise Campaign, a nonpartisan effort to build support for communities and states to make a community or technical college education as universal, accessible, and free as high school has been for a nearly a century. This bipartisan group was charged with providing leadership, advice, and support for the campaign, whose mission was to build support for the creation of College Promise programs at the local and state levels.

At that event, the president introduced Dr. Jill Biden, second lady of the U.S. and community college professor, and Governor Jim Geringer, the former governor of Wyoming who was honored for creating the Hathaway Scholarship in his state, as the board's honorary chair and vice chair. The board was charged to provide leadership, advice, and support for the nascent College Promise Campaign. It is important to note that in 1974 Governor Stanley Hathaway had established the Wyoming Permanent Mineral Trust Fund to run state government, which included higher education. In 2005, during Governor Geringer's administration, legislation to enact the Hathaway Scholarship fund was made possible through a $400 million permanent endowment, funding qualified Wyoming high school graduates to enroll in the University of Wyoming or any of the state's seven community colleges (State of Wyoming, Wyoming Department of Education, 2018).

The idea behind College Promise was not new, but this was the first time there had been a coordinated national drive to build support for educational investments at the grassroots level. As President Obama said at the launch of the College Promise National Advisory Board:

> I have been focused on community colleges. They're at the heart of the American Dream. Community Colleges are everywhere. They're accessible. They're a gateway for folks, who, maybe their parents didn't go to a college, maybe they can't afford a four-year college, maybe the career path they want to follow isn't a traditional one. Everyone willing to work hard deserves a shot at an education. It's (their ticket) to the middle class. (Obama, 2015b, para. 22)

The campaign's mission is to encourage local institutions, communities, and states to fund tuition and fees for residents who make a serious commitment to complete postsecondary education, starting in America's community colleges, attended by more than 40 percent of all undergraduates in the country. The goal is for communities and states to educate and train their residents without burdening them with unmanageable college debt.

THE COLLEGE PROMISE MOVEMENT TODAY

Since its creation in 2015, the College Promise Campaign has built broad public support for communities and states to cover tuition and fees for the first two years of community or technical college and to provide support to help students succeed. While the campaign serves as the nation's most prominent public voice for local and state College Promise programs, it does not promote any single approach. Instead, it convenes leaders from business, education, government, philanthropy, nonprofits, labor, and the students themselves to support the College Promise in their communities and states in ways that fit their specific civic, economic, and social needs. Since 2015 the growth of College Promise programs in communities and states has relied on bipartisan support in numerous communities and at the state level. The Promise programs have been equally enacted and led by Democrat and Republican legislatures and their governors.

To promote the launch and expansion of quality College Promise programs, the campaign widely shares the latest research, high-impact practices, and policy designs for communities and states to build effective and financially sustainable programs that engender student success. It also leverages the results of evidence-based research to engage public and private leaders from diverse sectors in investing in the College Promise in their communities and/or states. Along the way, it underscores the value of free community colleges, showing that an investment in the College Promise is a down payment on the prosperity and vitality of the regions served by the nation's nearly twelve hundred community colleges. And the campaign is also encouraging partnerships between community colleges and four-year colleges and universities to support the goals of College Promise.

From 2015 through 2018 the campaign witnessed rapid expansion in the number of College Promise programs, quadrupling to more than three hundred local initiatives under way in forty-four states and twenty-three in full operation at the statewide level, as previously noted. Across the nation, from Hawaii to Rhode Island, from Seattle to Jacksonville, and from Lansing to Houston, communities are removing barriers and giving students the financial, social, and academic support they need to succeed through College Promise. It's happening in large metropolitan areas such as San Francisco, CA; Detroit, MI; Milwaukee, WI; and Dallas, TX; as well as in smaller cities, towns, and counties like Stockton, CA; Baltimore, MD; Akron, OH; and Laramie, WY.

The driving force behind the swift adoption of the College Promise idea is the growing understanding that communities, states, and ultimately the nation, cannot thrive unless they produce more graduates with college degrees, technical certificates, or apprenticeships, necessary credentials for the shifting demands of the workforce to meet the larger demands of the twenty-first-century economy and the greater society.

Coalitions putting together College Promise programs understand their residents must be prepared for the workforce with the knowledge and skills employers seek to fill job openings. By 2017 there were more than 6.5 million jobs left unfilled because employers could not find workers with the required education or training. That is not good for students, families, or local economies, which is why so many elected officials are working with business, educational, and philanthropical organizations to fill those gaps through free college programs that prepare students for in-demand careers.

Elected officials are forming strategic partnerships to build Promise programs because they know that by 2020 more than six of every ten jobs will require an education beyond high school at a time when only 46 percent of Americans have a college degree or technical certificate, as noted by Carnevale, Smith, and Strohl (2013). These officials, joined by public and private sector leaders and concerned citizens, feel an urgency to address the rising costs of college that are making higher education—even at the community colleges—seem out of reach for the those who need it most: first-generation and low-income students, working parents, disconnected residents, and older adults seeking knowledge and skills or retraining for a new economy.

While tuition and fees at community colleges are considerably less than those at four-year colleges and universities, they represent a small portion of the total cost of attendance. Additional college-crucial costs—textbooks, housing, child care, and transportation—present financial barriers that are difficult for low-income students to overcome. By covering tuition and fees through the College Promise, communities and states seek to alleviate some of that financial burden.

A study published by the Wisconsin Hope Lab and the Association of Community College Trustees (Goldrick-Rab, Richardson & Hernandez, 2017) reported that one in three community college students experience hunger, and that 51 percent lack secure housing, while 14 percent are homeless. These kinds of data spur the development of free college programs as community colleges grapple with how they can help students to and through college, so they can escape the cycle of poverty. And they propel College Promise programs to cover costs beyond tuition and fees.

Communities also understand that a "Promise" isn't indeed a promise unless students complete their courses of study. That is why so many College Promise programs include mentoring, advising, and other academic support to guide students along the path toward completion of their course of study. Each College Promise program launched serves as an inspiration to other communities as they identify ways to remove financial barriers and provide support, so students can earn the credentials they need to thrive in the twenty-first century.

Some noteworthy local and state initiatives that continue to inspire the College Promise movement are discussed in the following subsections.

Tennessee Promise: Inspiring the College Promise Movement

Since its creation in 2014, the Tennessee Promise has been a guiding model for states and communities as they seek to build free college programs that increase the opportunity for students to not only start but complete a community college degree, a certificate, or university transfer requirements. By using a combination of state lottery surplus funds and contributions from both businesses and foundations, the Tennessee Promise also demonstrates how a Promise program can be designed for financial sustainability. As a "last dollar scholarship," students receive Promise funds once they have depleted all other sources of available state or federal student aid, such as the Hope Scholarship or the Pell Grant. Students may use the scholarship at any of the state's thirteen community colleges, twenty-seven colleges of applied technology, or other eligible institutions offering associate degrees.

Governor Bill Haslam introduced the performance-based scholarship, mentoring, and community service program as part of his "Drive to 55" goal to equip 55 percent of Tennesseans with a college degree or certificate by 2025. By offering "free community college" to all qualified recent high school graduates in Tennessee, the Promise has put the first two years of higher education within reach for eligible residents, especially youth and families who believe college is beyond their means. And it enables students to earn a college degree or technical certificate without taking on burdensome college debt.

In addition to covering tuition and fees, the Tennessee Promise adds another crucial element: mandating that Promise students take part in advising and mentoring sessions to boost the chances that they will complete their course of study. It also requires students to give something back: to fulfill community service hours as they work toward earning their certificates and degrees. They must also maintain satisfactory progress, at least a 2.0 grade point average (GPA), to continue receiving funds.

Data from tnAchieves, the administrative arm of the Tennessee Promise, make a compelling case that the Tennessee Promise has led to significant increases in enrollment, persistence, and completion for students taking part in the program. Its research shows that the one-year increase in the college-going rate between 2015 and 2016 was greater than for the seven years 2007–2014. And since the creation of the Promise, the Volunteer State notes that Promise students persist from term to term, and from year one to year two, at higher rates than their non-Promise peers.

For Promise students, the term-to-term persistence rate is approximately 82 percent, while the year one to two persistence rate is approximately 63 percent, or five percentage points higher than for non-Promise students. Data also demonstrate that first-time enrollment at community colleges in Tennessee has increased by 25 percent and Pell-eligible students by 20 percent.

Seeds of the Promise were first planted almost a decade earlier when Governor Haslam served as mayor of Knoxville, TN. In 2008 Haslam and Knox County mayor Mike Ragsdale worked with local philanthropists to create Knox Achieves, a program enabling graduating high school seniors in Knox County, Tennessee, to attend local community and technical colleges without paying tuition and fees.

The idea took off; between 2009 and 2014, Knox Achieves expanded to twenty-seven counties in Tennessee and was renamed tnAchieves (Tennessee Achieves). Early results indicate that the program was reaching its core audience, first-generation and low-income students. In that time tnAchieves students were the first in their family to attend college, and 70 percent came from families with annual incomes of less than $50,000. TnAchieves raised more than $15.5 million in private funds for the last-dollar scholarships and supported more than ten thousand students to attend a community or technical college. Knox Achieves also retained students at a rate 50 percent higher than the state average and reported that 94 percent of tnAchieves students completed their degrees and certificates without taking on debt.

In spring 2017 Tennessee became the first statewide free college program in the country to extend College Promise to adults. The new program, Ten-

nessee Reconnect, builds on the success of the Tennessee Promise model by
providing free college and mentoring scholarships to state residents of any
age who have not earned a college degree. When he signed the Tennessee
Reconnect program into law, Governor Haslam said:

> "This is about jobs, it's about math, and it's about the Tennessee we can be.
> We know that by 2025, at least half the jobs in this state will require a college
> degree or certificate. Mathematically, there's no way to reach that goal just by
> equipping high school graduates with degrees. Just as we want Tennessee
> Reconnect to send a clear message to adults: wherever you fall on life's path,
> education beyond high school is critical to the Tennessee we can be." (*Haslam
> Signs Tennessee Reconnect Act*, 2017, para. 3)

In spring 2018 the College Promise Campaign joined forces with Complete
College America and Achieving the Dream to produce *Promise with a Purpose*, a guide to help states, communities, and individual community colleges
build an intentional framework for student success into their College Promise
programs.

Dallas County Promise

The success of the Tennessee Promise inspired other communities, counties,
and states to build affordable college programs that incorporate mentoring,
advising, and other support services to boost the chances that students not
only start, but finish, their course of study. The Dallas County Promise
launched in fall 2017, just one year after the Dallas County leaders ventured
on a fact-finding mission to visit officials administering the Tennessee Promise. From their weeklong visit to the Volunteer State, this innovative group of
leaders brought back to Texas the best practices for building a financially
sustainable Promise program geared toward ensuring student success.

Dallas County officials launched the Promise to address the growing
skills gap in North Texas, where 65 percent of living-wage jobs require an
education beyond high school but only 37 percent of adults hold a two- or
four-year degree, concerns jointly raised by a county judge, Dallas County
Community College trustees and its chancellor, and presidents of the University of North Texas at Dallas and Southern Methodist University. Their goal
was to provide an affordable path for county residents to complete their
education and to prepare for jobs requiring an associate and/or a bachelor's
degree.

These local leaders understood that financing a college education is most
frequently noted as the biggest challenge for students seeking education beyond high school, especially those from low-income families. And they knew
that more students and families would enter college if they believed they
could afford it. Chancellor May confirmed the challenge these partners took

on when he said: "We know that the greatest barrier to college completion is cost. The Promise is a game-changer for students, businesses, and the communities we serve" (Dallas County Community College District, 2018).

To build the Promise, Chancellor Joe May and leaders from the Dallas County Community College District and its foundation worked with the United Way of Metropolitan Dallas and the Commit Partnership organization to form a coalition representing school districts, local colleges and universities, businesses, nonprofit organizations, and the philanthropic community. Through this collaboration, the Dallas County Promise offers free tuition to entering students regardless of income or GPA who complete the FAFSA or TAFSA and earn eighteen credits a year at any of the seven Dallas County community colleges. Students must enroll in the program during their senior year of high school, where they are assigned a mentor to guide them through to completing their college program of study. County students who successfully complete their associate degrees are then eligible to receive two years of free tuition at Southern Methodist University or University of North Texas at Dallas if they meet GPA requirements upon transfer.

Detroit Promise Path

In Detroit, Michigan, students are receiving the benefit of the Detroit Promise Path, a package of support services designed to boost the success of students enrolled in the city's free community college program. Since 2013 the Detroit Promise has offered to cover up to three years of tuition for recent high school graduates to attend any of the city's five community colleges, once they have exhausted all other sources of federal and state aid. But the program provides more than just financial support.

To receive Promise funds, students must enroll in the Detroit Promise Path, a program that adds a range of support services to the Promise of financial support. The Detroit Chamber of Commerce leads this effort, and MDRC, a nationally known social and education policy and research program, is working with the chamber to support the design and evaluate the program to boost the persistence rates of Promise students.

The innovative program requires students to meet regularly with a dedicated campus coach and to participate in summer enrichment. It also provides Promise students with incentive funding to offset other college costs not covered by financial aid. The Path, which is administered by the chamber, uses a management information system to communicate with students and to monitor their progress.

In July 2017 MDRC published *Enhancing Promise Programs to Improve College Access and Success*, a report that demonstrates the positive impact the Detroit Promise is having on student success. The data show an increase in persistence from semester to semester, including a sizable effect on enrollment in the second semester and on full-time enrollment in the first and second semesters.

Independent research reports like this are beneficial to policy researchers, community leaders, and anyone else investigating how to build financially sustainable and effective College Promise programs. And they also help build the evidence-based literature to link research findings to policies and practices in local communities and states.

Indiana Workforce "Adult Promise" Grant

In 2017 Indiana created the Indiana Workforce Grant, a financial aid opportunity that covers tuition and fees for working-age adults to acquire the skills they need for jobs in high-demand industries (State of Indiana, Indiana Commission for Higher Education, 2017). Indiana governor Eric Holcomb and lawmakers in the Hoosier State launched the program to address the massive skills gap in Indiana, where over two million adults lacked the education and training they needed to compete in the twenty-first-century workforce. They saw the grant as the way to advance the state's economic development and competitiveness.

The grant covers tuition and mandatory fees for students to enroll in high-value certificate programs at Ivy Tech Community College, Vincennes University, or other approved training providers. Students can use the grant for up to two years but may only use the funds for courses that apply directly to their certificate program.

The qualifying programs were selected based on their alignment with Indiana's highest demand sectors. A wide range of factors, including employer demand, wages, job placement, and program completion rates, were the criteria used for identifying these programs. The programs included advanced manufacturing, building and construction, health sciences, information technology and business services, transportation, and logistics.

Home Run Promise, West Sacramento, CA

In May 2016, during his State of the City address, West Sacramento mayor Christopher Cabaldon, a member of the College Promise National Advisory Board, announced his vision to make tuition and fees free for graduating high school students who planned to attend local community colleges in the city. Just six months later, after the city received seed funds from several philanthropic donors and fostered partnerships with its nonprofit and business communities, residents approved a College Promise program. The free college measure was included in a referendum to create the West Sacramento Home Run, a broad-based college-to-career initiative that combines universal preschool, college savings accounts, and paid internships. With a 65 percent margin, the referendum passed with strong support from the city's fifty thousand residents.

The West Sacramento Home Run Promise launched in 2017 through a partnership involving the City of West Sacramento, Washington Unified School District, and Sacramento City College. As a last-dollar program, the initiative requires students to apply for federal and state aid before receiving Promise dollars. It also includes several elements that are intended to boost student success: to receive funds, prospective Promise students must enroll as full-time students and are required to complete and pursue an education plan.

Sharing information about Home Run with more than three hundred public and private sector leaders and residents at his annual State of the City address on May 3, 2018, a year after the Promise launch, the mayor said: "The City of West Sacramento Home Run initiative isn't just making West Sacramento the best place to raise a family and grow up as a child, but it also makes our city the best place to find high-quality talent ready for skilled entry and mid-level jobs" (*Sacramento Oracle* 2018; Hosley, 2018, p. 1). A month later, on June 9, 2018, Mayor Cabaldon joined other mayors in the region at a College Promise reception hosted by the law firm Holland and Knight.

The Boston Bridge Pilot Program

In March 2017 Boston mayor Marty J. Walsh and Massachusetts governor Charlie Baker formed a city-state partnership to support low-income eligible students in Boston to complete a two- and four-year degree in the Bay State that covers tuition and mandatory fees. To qualify for the Boston Bridge, students must enroll full time in the Tuition-Free Community College Plan at one of the city's three community colleges. If they complete their associate degree within two and a half years, they are eligible for the Commonwealth Commitment, whereby the majority of tuition and fees are covered by the state for the remaining two years at designated public colleges and universities in Massachusetts for those who attend full time and maintain a 3.0 GPA.

Through this innovative partnership, the Democrat mayor and the Republican governor provide yet another Promise model for states and communities as they build college and career pathways for their residents. And they demonstrate how government leaders from both sides of the legislative aisle can work together to build College Promise pathways to increase student access and success.

The Boston Bridge is an expansion of the state's Commonwealth Commitment, which provides reduced tuition and fees for the state's community college graduates to attend public colleges and universities in Massachusetts.

It also builds upon Boston's Free Community College initiative, which provides free community college tuition for eligible low-income students.

These are just a few examples of the many local and state College Promise programs that are growing across the nation. It is exciting to see the emergence of a Promise research and evaluation base to help Promise leaders design and implement what works to increase student achievement, better align early learning between K–12 and postsecondary education, and meet the ever-changing workforce and societal demands of the twenty-first century. Say Yes to Education/Weiss Institute, Strive Together, National College Access Network, and other agencies are collaborating with researchers and policy makers to ensure that Promise programs make a significant difference in the lives of America's students.

THE ROAD AHEAD

The College Promise Campaign has witnessed a rapid growth of College Promise programs since its launch in 2015. In just three years, more than three hundred Promise programs are up and running in forty-four states. Twenty-three governors and their legislatures have enacted statewide Promise initiatives for their residents.

Each program that emerges sets an example for other leaders as they seek ways to expand access to and completion of a quality higher education by removing financial and social barriers to higher education and providing needed student support for eligible students. But Promise programs vary. Some are more generous than others. Some have sustainable funding streams while others are seeking funds annually. Some are more merit based while others are more need based, with varying GPA, performance, and other eligibility and persistence requirements. And some have numerous restrictions, severely limiting the number of students who can participate

The College Promise Campaign is working to identify and showcase the Promise programs that have the greatest impact on student access and success, while providing caveats to communities and states about unintended or negative consequences based on evidence-based results from independent scholars and reputable research and policy organizations across the nation.

As the movement evolves, communities and states are reminded that the promise of delivering a College Promise is hollow if students enrolling in a community college, technical college, and/or four-year institution fail to complete their degrees or certificates.

Innovative leaders in community colleges, universities, cities, regions, and states are committed to designing and implementing College Promise programs that marry the promise of college access with the promise of completing a college degree or a technical certificate. They understand that the creation of a College Promise program comes with the essential need to design programs that focus on student success as the end goal, so students can acquire the knowledge and skills they need to obtain a more secure and stable future for themselves and their families.

Now that the idea of College Promise has taken off, the campaign is not only promoting the concept and value proposition of the College Promise, but most important, leveraging the College Promise knowledge base to identify best practices to help local communities and states design the highest impact and financially sustainable programs that meet the specific needs of their targeted student populations. Entering the second phase of its mission, the College Promise Campaign will use its national platform to share the latest research, policies, and program results that demonstrate the impact that high-quality College Promise programs have on the students, families, and communities they serve.

The College Promise Campaign will continue to encourage leaders from business, education, government, nonprofits, labor, students, and philanthropy to form and sustain cross-sector partnerships within their communities and states as they seek ways to increase student success along with workforce and societal goals through Promise initiatives. The idea is to cultivate leadership at the community and state levels to meet the specific educational, economic, and social needs of their regions and the nation as a whole.

CONCLUSION

As noted previously, the idea behind College Promise is not new. At its core, College Promise, also known as "free college," has always placed a priority on engaging and preparing people for gainful employment and to become productive members of the greater society.

In recent years the idea has emerged as a national priority because too many Americans lack sufficient financial resources, social support, and clear pathways to and through postsecondary education that would enable them to upgrade their skills, enter, or advance in the workforce. For far too many people today, the cost of higher education is beyond their reach, even with available federal and state financial aid or other scholarships. College aspirations dampen, work and family responsibilities consume the future space, and making ends meet on a daily basis takes priority. As a result, the American Dream becomes more distant and for too many people, dissipates altogether.

Well-designed and implemented College Promise programs help eliminate financial barriers, ensure access to higher education, and provide students with mentoring, advising, and other support services they need to succeed. Today, throughout the nation, as College Promise programs are

launched and sustained to cover tuition, fees, and in many cases the additional costs of attending college (e.g., textbooks, supplies, food, transportation,
child care, housing) as well as offering student supports (e.g., mentoring,
advising, coaching), they are making the difference between success and
failure for thousands of Americans who want to participate in the American
Dream.

As the College Promise movement evolves in the years ahead, community and state leaders are looking for innovative ways to incorporate sorely
needed program elements to accelerate degree and certificate completion and
boost student success. Seamless, aligned guided pathways in high-demand
fields of study, academic and social guidance, emergency grants, paid internships, redesigned class schedules, and child-care support for student parents,
who comprise 25 percent of all undergraduates, are among the College Promise features that are being leveraged to increase graduation rates.

Since the launch of the College Promise Campaign in 2015, the number
of Promise programs has more than quadrupled as communities and states
have implemented a growing variety of program models. This vast expansion
of the College Promise idea is transforming thousands of lives and serves as
a bellwether for the nation that a free and universal K–14 education can
become a reality for the nation's students and families in the 21st century.

Today's Promise programs are as varied as the student populations they
serve and reflect the unique character of their local institutions, communities,
and states. It is still early in the movement to cite robust data on the long-
term impact of the College Promise, but early research is promising from
communities and states that have updated and sustained their College Promise initiatives for more than a decade, with many evidence-based studies
tracking student achievement, graduation rates, workforce preparedness, and
community and state economic and social development. Each month, more
evidence is collected by leading scholars from across the country to determine the effects of College Promise on boosting educational attainment and
restoring America's leadership position in the world relative to the proportion of adults with high-quality certificates and degrees.

The College Promise Campaign and the Educational Testing Service are
conducting the second phase of research on how communities and states are
building financially sustainable College Promise programs in their regions.
To build the College Promise evidence base on what works, the campaign's
ongoing collaborations are taking place with the University of Pennsylvania's Alliance for Higher Education and Democracy, the Community College
Research Center at Columbia University Teachers College, the University of
Tennessee, Temple University, the University of Alabama's Education Policy Center, MDRC, WestEd, the Upjohn Institute for Employment Development, and Georgetown University's Center on Education and the Workforce,

to name a few of the many institutions investigating the impact of College Promise programs.

It is clear that the College Promise has flourished. The idea of Promise has been established as a potent and galvanizing movement in American postsecondary education. Promise has fast become a linchpin strategy for the efforts of community and technical colleges to increase college access and student success for higher educational attainment with their partners. College Promise is growing new roots among the great movements in American education, fundamentally steeped in the ideals of the Founding Fathers to cultivate an educated citizenry that will sustain American democracy and prosperity for the twenty-first century and beyond.

REFERENCES

American Association of Community Colleges. (2017, October 25). College Promise programs continue to grow. *Community College Daily*. Retrieved from http://www.ccdaily.com/2017/10/college-promise-programs-continue-grow/

American Association of Community Colleges. (2018). *Supporting the college promise*. Retrieved from https://www.acct.org/files/Advocacy/ACCT_AACC_College Promise Toolkit.pdf

Bartik, T. J., & Lachowska, M. (2012). *The short-term effects of the Kalamazoo promise scholarship on student outcomes*. Upjohn Institute Working Paper 12-186. Kalamazoo, MI: W. E. Upjohn Institute for Employment Research. Retrieved from https://doi.org/10.17848/wp12-186

Boston Bridge. (2018). *The Boston bridge*. Retrieved from https://www.bostonpublicschools.org/bostonbridge

Carnevale, A. P., Smith, N., & Strohl, J. (2013, June 26). *Recovery: Job growth and education requirements through 2020*. Retrieved from https://cew.georgetown.edu/cew-reports/recovery-job-growth-and-education-requirements-through-2020/

College Promise Campaign. (2018a, June 9). *City and county playbook—How to build a promise*. Retrieved from http://collegepromise.org/policy-tools/playbook/

College Promise Campaign. (2018b, June 9). *College promise campaign releases promise playbook for local elected officials*. Retrieved from www.collegepromise.org

Complete College, College Promise Campaign, and Achieving the Dream. (2018, April 28). *Promise with a purpose: College promise programs "built for completion."* Retrieved from https://completecollege.org/promise/

Dallas County Community College District. (2018). *Dallas County Promise: Welcome*. Retrieved from https://www.dcccd.edu/pc/scholother/scholarships/dallaspromise/pages/default.aspx

Dallas County Promise. (2018). Scholarship overview. Retrieved from http://dallascountypromise.org/

Goldin, C. (1998). America's graduation from high school: The evolution and spread of secondary schooling in the twentieth century. *Journal of Economic History, 58*(2), 345–374. Retrieved from https://dash.harvard.edu/bitstream/handle/1/2664307/goldin_americagraduation.pdf?sequence=4

Goldin, C., & Katz, L. F. (1998, March). *Human capital and social capital: The rise of secondary schooling in America, 1910 to 1940*. Retrieved from http://www.nber.org/papers/w6439

Goldrick-Rab, S., Richardson, J., & Hernandez, A. (2017, March). *Hungry and homeless in college: Results from a national study of basic needs insecurity in higher education*. Wisconsin Hope Lab and the Association of Community College Trustees. Retrieved from http://www.acct.org/files/Publications/2017/Homeless_and_Hungry_2017.pdf

Haslam, Governor William. (2014, February 3). *Tennessee governor Bill Haslam's 2014 State of the State speech.* Retrieved from http://www.governing.com/topics/politics/gov-tennessee-bill-haslam-annual-speech.html

Haslam signs Tennessee Reconnect Act: State to offer all citizens chance to earn a degree tuition-free. (2017, May 24). Retrieved from https://www.tn.gov/governor/news/2017/5/24/haslam-signs-tennessee-reconnect-act.html

Higher Education Act of 1965. Retrieved from http://legcounsel.house.gov/Comps/HEA65_CMD.pdf

The Library of Congress. (2017, October 26). *Primary documents in American history: Morrill Act.* Retrieved from https://www.loc.gov/rr/program/bib/ourdocs/morrill.html

MDRC. (2017, July). *Enhancing Promise programs to improve college access and success.* Retrieved from https://www.mdrc.org/publication/enhancing-promise-programs-improve-college-access-and-success

Miller-Adams, M. (2009). *The power of a Promise: Education and economic renewal in Kalamazoo.* Kalamazoo, MI: W. E. Upjohn Institute for Employment Research. Retrieved from https://doi.org/10.17848/9781441612656

Miller-Adams, M. (2015). *Promise nation: Transforming communities through place-based scholarships.* Kalamazoo, MI: W. E. Upjohn Institute for Employment Research. Retrieved from https://doi.org/10.17848/9780880995061

Mortenson, T. G. (2012, Winter). *State funding: A race to the bottom.* American Council on Education. Retrieved from http://www.acenet.edu/the-presidency/columns-and-features/Pages/state-funding-a-race-to-the-bottom.aspx

Obama, B. (2009, February 24). *Address before a joint session of the Congress.* Retrieved from https://www.presidency.ucsb.edu/documents/address-before-joint-session-the-congress-1

Obama, B. (2015a, January 20). *Remarks by the president in State of the Union address.* Obama White House Archive. Retrieved from https://obamawhitehouse.archives.gov/the-press-office/2015/01/20/remarks-president-state-union-address-january-20-2015

Obama. B. (2015b, September 9) *Remarks at Macomb Community College in Warren, Michigan.* Retrieved from https://www.presidency.ucsb.edu/documents/remarks-macomb-community-college-warren-michigan-1

Organization for Economic Cooperation and Development. (2012). *Education at a glance 2012: Highlights.* OECD Publishing. Retrieved from http://dx.doi.org/10.1787/eag_highlights-2012-en

Pell Institute for the Study of Opportunity in Higher Education. (2018). *Overview.* Retrieved from http://www.pellinstitute.org/pell_grants.shtml

Sacramento Oracle. (2018, May 3). New West Sacramento city manager named: West Sacramento Home Run initiative milestone announced, new mobility options coming to West Sacramento. Retrieved from http://www.sacramentooracle.com/articles/2018/0504-West-Sacramento-City-Manager-Named-Home-Run-Initiative-Milestones-Mobility-Options/index.php?ID=4766

Servicemen's Readjustment Act (1944). Retrieved from https://www.ourdocuments.gov/doc.php?flash=false&doc=76

State of Indiana, Indiana Commission for Higher Education. (2015, November 18). *21st century scholars: 25 years of supporting student success.* Retrieved from https://www.in.gov/che/files/25th_Anniversary_Brochure_11-18-15_Final_pages.pdf

State of Indiana, Indiana Commission for Higher Education. (2017). Indiana Workforce Grant. Retrieved from https://www.in.gov/che/4773.htm

State of Tennessee, Higher Education Commission. (2018). [Enrollment, persistence, and completion P-20 data from the Higher Education Student Information System (THEC SIS), the Tennessee Longitudinal Data System (TLDS), and the National Student Clearinghouse]. Retrieved from http://thec.ppr.tn.gov/THECSIS/ and http://slds.rhaskell.org/state-profiles/tennessee

State of Tennessee, Higher Education Commission & Student Assistance Corporation. (n.d.). *Drive to 55.* Retrieved from https://www.tn.gov/thec/learn-about/drive-to-55.html and http://driveto55.org/

State of Tennessee, Office of the Governor. (2017, May 24). *Haslam signs Tennessee Reconnect Act.* Retrieved from https://www.tn.gov/governor/news/2017/5/24/haslam-signs-tennessee-reconnect-act.html

State of Wyoming, Wyoming Department of Education. (2018). *Hathaway Scholarship reporting.* Retrieved from https://edu.wyoming.gov/?s=hathaway+scholars; and *About the scholarship.* Retrieved from https://hathawayscholarship.org/hathaway-scholarship/about-the-scholarship

Truman, H. (1947, December 15). *Statement by the president making public a report of the Commission on Higher Education.* Retrieved from https://www.presidency.ucsb.edu/documents/statement-the-president-making-public-report-the-commission-higher-education

University of North Texas at Dallas. (2018). *Dallas County Promise.* Retrieved from https://www.untdallas.edu/county_promise

Upjohn Institute for Employment Research. (2018). *About the Kalamazoo Promise.* Retrieved from https://upjohn.org/about-kalamazoo-promise

US Department of Education. (2018). *College affordability and completion: Ensuring a pathway to opportunity.* Retrieved from https://www.ed.gov/college

US Department of Education, National Center for Education Statistics. (1993, January). *120 years of American education: A statistical portrait.* T. D. Snyder (Ed.). Retrieved from https://nces.ed.gov/pubs93/93442.pdf

US Department of Education, National Center for Education Statistics. (2004). *Digest of education statistics.*

White House, Office of the Press Secretary. (2015, January 9). *Fact sheet—White House unveils America's College Promise proposal: Tuition-free community college for responsible students.* Retrieved from https://obamawhitehouse.archives.gov/the-press-office/2015/01/09/fact-sheet-white-house-unveils-america-s-college-promise-proposal-tuition

Chapter Four

Guided Pathways to College Completion and Equity

Kay M. McClenney

Over the past two decades there have been major changes in the community college field. From the late 1990s through the early 2000s, new and powerful emphasis was placed on student learning and college completion. While those issues were raised within the sector, attention to them was heightened throughout the 2000s by concerns about student outcomes pointedly expressed by policy makers and philanthropies.

A historic shift during this period from an almost exclusive focus on postsecondary access to an equal focus on college completion reflects recognition of the strong relationship between educational attainment and social and economic upward mobility, a central concern for community colleges. The increasing willingness and capacity among colleges to use data about student progress and achievement, along with accumulating evidence about effective educational practice, have added impetus for change.

A number of significant initiatives, several of them briefly described in this chapter, have focused sharply on improving practice and policy in the interest of dramatically increasing college completion and equity.

Even as these accomplishments were acknowledged, concerns escalated about threats to the American Dream and the needed contributions of community colleges to reclaiming it. Leaders and scholars recognized that despite substantial effort, the magnitude of institutional change had been too small to address the scope of the challenges involved in heightening community college student success.

In *Reclaiming the American Dream: Community Colleges and the Nation's Future,* AACC's 21st Century Commission on the Future of Community Colleges laid out the challenge:

> Despite these historic successes, and amidst serious contemporary challenges, community colleges need to be redesigned for new times. What we find today are student success rates that are unacceptably low, employment preparation that is inadequately connected to job market needs, and disconnects in transitions between high schools, community colleges, and baccalaureate institutions (AACC, 2012, p. viii).

The commission acknowledged daunting financial challenges, including persistent underfunding of community colleges, but also pointed to evidence undergirding criticisms of community college performance, while at the same time affirming the institutions' crucial roles. It concluded: "The American Dream is at risk. Community colleges can help reclaim it. But stepping up to the challenge will require dramatic redesign of these institutions, their missions, and most critically, students' educational experiences" (AACC, 2012, p. 1).

One key response to this challenge, and the focus of an explicit commission recommendation, is the work of guided pathways reform. Building on prior work, accumulating evidence, and the lessons of experience, the guided pathways concept has spread rapidly in recent years throughout the community college sector and a handful of pioneering four-year institutions. By mid-2018, more than 250 community colleges across the country were implementing guided pathways. Leading and supporting the work is a network of national organizations, scholars, state officials, state-based student success centers, and institutional leaders at all levels who have the vision and courage to undertake transformational change in the interest of students.

The guided pathways model, described more fully later in this chapter, is centrally based on clear and educationally coherent programs of study that are aligned with requirements for success after university transfer and in the labor market. Default course sequences and learning outcomes are made clear so that each student can work with an assigned adviser to develop a full-program educational plan tailored to that student's needs and interests— and then to monitor progress against that plan.

As necessary, colleges then redesign and realign advising, career exploration, academic and student supports, and instructional approaches to help students *clarify their goals, choose and enter pathways that will lead to goal achievement, stay on their pathways,* and *master the knowledge and skills requisite to their success in employment and further education.* Administrative functions, including support for student onboarding, continuing registration, advising, and financial aid, as well as finance, human resources, and information technology, are aligned to support student progress through their pathways.

EQUITY BY DESIGN

At the heart of guided pathways reform is a passionate commitment to achieving equity in college access and outcomes for students. As colleges fundamentally redesign students' educational experiences, they assume the professional and moral obligation to ensure that institutional policies and practices are specifically designed to promote equity—and conversely, to eliminate unintentional barriers, unconscious bias, and institutional racism. Ideally, every design decision is made with equity in mind.

The change required to implement guided pathways—at scale, for *all* students—is transformational. Guided pathways reform is not just another discrete initiative; rather, it provides a framework for integrating and scaling the best of the prior student success work colleges have undertaken. Beyond that, it necessarily involves changes in institutional culture, policy, processes, and the roles of virtually everyone in the college. It requires a series of substantial shifts in organizational and institutional mind-set; it challenges traditional organizational boundaries; and it needs the active engagement of faculty, staff, and administrators across the institution.

Guided pathways reforms are still relatively new, and major efforts are underway to monitor results and to learn more about large-scale institutional change. The good news is that early results are promising. The other good news is that the field is rising to the challenge.

FOUNDATIONS FOR THE GUIDED PATHWAYS MOVEMENT

Guided pathways reform stands on the shoulders of nearly two decades of work in the community college field—work aimed at strengthening and documenting student learning, heightening student engagement, identifying evidence-based high-impact education practices, improving developmental education, increasing college completion, and attaining equity in college access and outcomes. [1]

In the late 1990s O'Banion (1997) described the changes in higher education architecture and institutional practice necessary to place learning first, creating a "learning college for the 21st century." The ensuing Learning College Project, led by O'Banion and the League for Innovation, involved a select group of community colleges in work aimed at implementing those substantial changes.

Soon thereafter, the Community College Survey of Student Engagement (2002), established by Kay McClenney within the Community College Leadership Program at The University of Texas at Austin, initiated research focused systematically on the community college student experience and the student voice, at the same time pioneering online public reporting of survey results, encouraging disaggregation of those data, and providing for institutional performance benchmarking. The work continues under the leadership of Evelyn Waiwaiole, and through 2017 the Center for Community College Student Engagement had surveyed more than 2.9 million students (representing a population of 6.4 million) at 951 colleges in fifty states.

Notably, the center identified for the field a set of high-impact practices in community college education (CCCSE, 2013) and then went on to argue that those practices are likely to be most powerful when combined and integrated inescapably into students' educational experiences, in contrast to discrete, stand-alone college services offered as options for students (CCCSE, 2014).

The launch of Achieving the Dream (ATD) with twenty-seven colleges in 2004, with support from the Lumina Foundation, promoted a sea change in the willingness and capacity of participating community colleges to collect, analyze, and use data—particularly longitudinal student cohort data—to understand student progress and attainment and then to target strategies for improvement. Over time, ATD's approach has evolved to focus on a framework encompassing institutional capacities in (1) leadership and vision, (2) data and technology, (3) equity, (4) teaching and learning, (5) engagement and communication, (6) strategy and planning, and (7) policies and practices (Achieving the Dream, 2018).

Achieving the Dream's early years yielded important lessons for the community college field. As noted in an early evaluation conducted jointly by MDRC and the Community College Research Center (CCRC) (Rutschow et al., 2011), the field learned that many of the interventions undertaken by colleges were directed only to limited aspects of the student experience (e.g., developmental education or the college intake process); the interventions typically involved relatively few students; and while some strategies certainly resulted in positive outcomes for the students who participated, the interventions overall were not large enough or sustained enough to produce the magnitude of improvement in student persistence and completion that colleges sought to achieve. Over time, these insights have led to increased emphasis on scaled practice and whole-institution change.

In some ways, these lessons were reinforced through the Developmental Education Initiative (DEI), which ATD launched in 2009 with funding from the Bill & Melinda Gates Foundation (BMGF). While working diligently to address a crucial community college issue, the fifteen participating ATD colleges struggled during the project's three-year life to achieve scaled implementation of their promising developmental education reforms. Thus, the project illuminated some of the challenges—cultural, political, financial, and logistical—of moving from pilot efforts to scale (Quint, Jaggars, Byndloss, & Magazinnik, 2013).

As the 21st century progressed into its second decade, CCRC and others conducted a growing body of research that helped substantially to guide policy and practice. These advances occurred in three broad areas, as described in *The Movement Toward Pathways* (CCRC & AACC, 2015a, p. 2):

> First, the field began to draw insights from behavioral economics to argue that the community college environment was too complex and confusing for students, suggesting that college-level programs needed to be simplified and made more coherent. The implications of behavioral economics research for community college practice were formally articulated in a BMGF-funded CCRC paper, *The Shapeless River* (Scott-Clayton, 2011).
>
> Second, CCRC and others produced research showing that students who gained early momentum (by passing the gateway courses in a program of study in their first year of college) were much more likely to graduate than those who took time to "find themselves" (Attewell, Heil, & Reisel, 2011; Jenkins & Cho, 2012).
>
> Third, research by CCRC and others on developmental education concluded that developmental assessments did not accurately identify students' needs, and traditional developmental coursework did not help underprepared students succeed at higher rates, while accelerated and contextualized coursework held more promise (e. g., Bailey, 2009; Edgecombe, 2011; Jenkins et al., 2010; Perin, 2011; Scott-Clayton, 2012; Zeidenberg, Cho, & Jenkins, 2010).

With the beginning in 2011 of the Completion by Design (CBD) initiative, funded by the BMGF, community colleges built on lessons from ATD's early work and on the accumulating research from the CCRC and others. Aimed at redesigning student experiences to increase success and college completion, CBD was based on the following principles for redesign, all of which have become recognized components of guided pathways reforms:

- Accelerate entry into coherent programs of study.
- Minimize the time required to get college-ready.
- Ensure that students know the requirements to succeed.
- Customize and contextualize instruction.
- Integrate student supports with instruction.
- Continually monitor student progress and proactively provide feedback.
- Reward behaviors that contribute to completion.
- Leverage technology to improve learning and program delivery.

(Chaplot, Rassen, Jenkins, & Johnstone, 2013, p. 5)

While there was substantial variety in the approaches undertaken by CBD colleges (ultimately, nine institutions in Florida, North Carolina, and Ohio), CBD reports that the colleges on average "had met three out of five of their 2019 target goals three years ahead of schedule" (CBD, 2018). These targets were expressed through metrics indicating early student momentum in their educational journeys. As noted in *The Movement Toward Pathways* (CCRC & AACC, 2015a, p. 2):

> CBD's variety in implementation did provide CCRC with the opportunity to observe the implications of different combinations of these elements. [CCRC'S] *resulting report to BMGF . . . suggested that the most successful colleges used the college-level program of study as a central organizing point for college reforms.* At the same time, the experience with CBD and associated insights led to the solidification and elaboration of the guided pathways model articulated in CCRC's book, *Redesigning America's Community Colleges* (Bailey, Jaggars, & Jenkins, 2015).

Several CBD colleges, including Davidson County Community College (NC), Lorain County Community College (OH), Miami-Dade College (FL), and Sinclair College (OH), as they continue to demonstrate promising results, have become leaders in the guided pathways movement.

REDESIGNING AMERICA'S COMMUNITY COLLEGES

An extended "defining moment" for community colleges came with the 2015 publication of Bailey, Jaggars, and Jenkins's important book, *Redesigning America's Community Colleges: A Clearer Path to Student Success.* Marshaling the available evidence, the authors described community colleges as typically operating under a "cafeteria" model that offers students too many choices, too little educational coherence, insufficient purpose and structure, unclear pathways, and spotty feedback on their progress.

While the cafeteria model worked well for colleges as they sought primarily to ensure *access* to postsecondary education, it creates substantial challenges when it becomes clear that access without *success* is an empty promise. In addition to the access mission, colleges now are called to increase completion rates by helping students to enter and complete programs that lead efficiently to seamless transfer and to credentials with value in the labor market.

The book urges colleges to *redesign* programs of study and support services comprehensively and at scale, in order to promote student progress, completion, and learning. The authors conclude: "We have argued that instead of expecting students to find their own way through college, colleges need to create clear, educationally coherent program pathways that are aligned with students' end goals, help students explore and select a pathway of interest, and track and support students' progress along their chosen pathway" (Bailey, Jaggars, & Jenkins, 2015, p. 199).

THE AACC PATHWAYS PROJECT: BUILDING CAPACITY FOR REFORM AT SCALE IN THE COMMUNITY COLLEGE FIELD

By 2015, with momentum added by *Redesigning America's Community Colleges* (Bailey, Jaggars, & Jenkins, 2015), there was a striking convergence of research and lessons of experience, as leaders and their organizations—at the national, state, and institutional levels—confronted the reality that large-scale results require large-scale institutional change. Typically, the changes made thus far, in the interest of student success, had not been comprehensive enough, integrated enough, or scaled enough to achieve the desired improvements in college completion and in transfer and employment outcomes, particularly among low-income students and students of color.

Recognizing those realities, the American Association of Community Colleges (AACC), with funding from the BMGF, launched in 2015 the national AACC Pathways Project, focused on building capacity for community colleges to design and implement structured academic and career pathways *at scale*, for *all* of their students.

Notably, the project goals reflected AACC's commitment to follow through strategically on recommendations set forth in the report of the 21st Century Commission on the Future of Community Colleges, *Reclaiming the American Dream* (AACC, 2012). In particular, the commission's report emphasized the imperative for community colleges to fundamentally redesign students' educational experiences, and it identified a specific implementation strategy: "Construct coherent, structured pathways to certificate and degree completion. This strategy should aim to incorporate high-impact, evidence-based practices; integrate student support with instruction; promote implementation at scale; rigorously evaluate the effectiveness of programs and services for students; and courageously end ineffective practices" (AACC, 2012, p. 16).

National Partners

For collaborative work on the Pathways Project, AACC gathered a group of seven national partner organizations, all committed to the goals of achieving major gains in college completion and equity and each bringing special expertise. The partners are ATD, the Aspen Institute College Excellence Program, the Center for Community College Student Engagement, the CCRC, Jobs for the Future, the National Center for Inquiry and Improvement, and Sova. Leading the AACC Pathways work is Gretchen Schmidt, a nationally recognized expert on guided pathways reform.

The Pathways Institute Series

The project developed a model series of six institutes, each two and a half days in length and each engaging five-person teams of varying composition from a competitively selected group of thirty colleges. The institutes supported committed community colleges in work to design and implement clear, structured student pathways to high-quality credentials that are aligned both to university transfer and to jobs with value in the labor market.

College teams attended the six institutes in 2016–2018. Each event focused on a crucial aspect of institutional change and pathway design/implementation; each required advance work by the colleges; and each resulted in products developed by the participating college teams, including action plans and assessment of continuing needs for campus engagement, professional development, and technical assistance. The institute format featured a mix of expert presentations, interactive topic-focused sessions, and planning sessions for the college teams, facilitated by pathways coaches.

College Participation

The thirty diverse community colleges selected for the Pathways Project demonstrated serious commitment to transformational work at scale, aimed at improving both college completion and equity in student outcomes (see table 4.1). The project required consistent participation of college CEOs as institute team members and recommended that governing board members be part of the college teams for the first and final institutes. Over time, most colleges chose to rotate new participants into their institute teams, seeing that the learning events built expertise about the *what* and *why* of guided pathways while broadening engagement of leaders at all levels of the college. Institutions received no direct project funding, but onsite institute costs were covered by the project.

Knowledge Development

An important project component is focused on building knowledge that will strengthen the work, multiply its future impact, and inform the field. Project colleges agreed to collect, monitor, and report data on defined metrics depicting early student momentum in their college experience. CCRC leads (through 2022) the data analysis and reporting, as well as extensive on-campus interviews aimed at learning about implementation challenges and management of large-scale institutional change.

In addition, the Center for Community College Student Engagement conducted student focus groups at Pathways colleges, providing authentic voices and video documentation that enrich understanding of Pathways reform and its effects on students. Finally, an online resource center (www.

Table 4.1.   AACC Pathways Colleges (Cadre 1.0)

AACC Pathways Colleges (Cadre 1.0)

Alamo Colleges (TX)	Bakersfield College (CA)
Broward College (FL)	Cleveland State Community College (TN)
Columbus State Community College (OH)	Community College of Philadelphia (PA)
Cuyahoga Community College (OH)	El Paso Community College (TX)
✓Front Range Community College (CO)	Indian River State College (FL)
Irvine Valley College (CA)	Jackson College (MI)
Lansing Community College (MI)	Linn-Benton Community College (OR)
Monroe Community College (NY)	Mt. San Antonio College (CA)
Northeast Wisconsin Technical College (WI)	Paris Junior College (TX)
Pierce College District (WA)	○Prince George's Community College (MD)
St. Petersburg College (FL)	San Jacinto College (TX)
Skagit Valley College (WA)	Stanley Community College (NC)
South Seattle Community College (WA)	Tallahassee Community College (FL)
Tulsa Community College (OK)	Wallace State College (AL)
Western Wyoming Community College (WY)	Zane State College (OH)

pathwaysresources.org), developed for broad use by community colleges and others, is a key outcome to which all partner organizations have contributed.

Achieving Scale

A central objective of the AACC project was to design and test an approach that can be replicated with additional groups of institutions. Even as the institute series was implemented with the thirty original colleges, the institute models and related tools and resources were made available for replication with groups of colleges in Texas, California, and the Maricopa Colleges

(AZ), and to the state-based student success center network coordinated by Jobs for the Future. In 2017 AACC launched Pathways 2.0, a second cadre of Pathways colleges, and 2018 marked the beginning of a series of regional pathways workshops for colleges seeking an introduction to the work. Institute materials and a pathways coaching guide are among the numerous tools included in the online Guided Pathways Resource Center, as AACC continues to support pathways design and implementation at increasing scale across the community college field.

THE GUIDED PATHWAYS MODEL: AN OVERVIEW

The guided pathways model[2] is an *integrated, institution-wide* approach to student success. Central to the model are clear, educationally coherent program maps that include specified course sequences, progress milestones, and program learning outcomes. Faculty and advisers ensure that these pathways are aligned to transfer options in the field of study and to expectations for related jobs and careers in the local or regional labor market.

Beginning with their earliest connections with the college, students are assisted in exploring academic and career options, choosing first a general meta-major or area of interest and then a specific program of study, and then developing—ideally by the end of their first term—a full-program educational plan. These plans simplify subsequent student decision making, and they enable colleges to provide predictable class schedules, frequent feedback, and targeted support as needed to help students stay on track and complete their programs more efficiently. They also facilitate faculty work to ensure that students are building the knowledge and skills they will need to succeed in employment and further education.

The four essential practice areas of the guided pathways model are briefly described below, along with conditions essential to the institutional change required. The model is also depicted in figure 4.1, a graphic representation developed collaboratively by ten national partner organizations involved in leading and supporting pathways reforms.

Guided Pathways Essential Practices

Clarify Paths to Student End Goals

- Simplify students' choices with default *program maps* developed by faculty and advisers that show students a clear pathway to completion, further education, and employment in fields of importance to the region.

Guided Pathways: Planning, Implementation, Evaluation

Creating guided pathways requires managing and sustaining large-scale transformational change. The work begins with thorough planning, continues through consistent implementation, and depends on ongoing evaluation. **The goals are to improve rates of college completion, transfer, and attainment of jobs with value in the labor market; and to achieve equity in those outcomes.**

PLANNING	IMPLEMENTATION

ESSENTIAL CONDITIONS
Make sure the following conditions are in place - prepared, mobilized, and adequately resourced - to support the college's large-scale transformational change:
- Strong change leadership throughout the institution
- Faculty and staff engagement
- Commitment to using data
- Capacity to use data
- Technology infrastructure
- Professional development
- Favorable policy (state, system, and institutional levels) and board support
- Commitment to student success and equity

PREPARATION/AWARENESS
Understand where you are, prepare for change, and build awareness by:
- Engaging stakeholders and making the case for change
- Establishing a baseline for key performance indicators
- Building partnerships with K-12, universities, and employers
- Developing flowcharts of how students choose, enter, and complete programs
- Developing an implementation plan with roles and deadlines

SUSTAINABILITY
Commit to pathways for the long term and make sure they are implemented for all students by:
- Determining pathways to sustainability (state, system, and institutional levels)
- Redefining the roles of faculty, staff, and administrators as needed
- Identifying needs for professional development and technical assistance
- Revamping technology to support the redesigned student experience
- Reallocating resources as needed
- Continuing to engage key stakeholders, especially students
- Integrating pathways into hiring and evaluation practices

CLARIFY THE PATHS
Map all programs to transfer and career and include these features:
- Detailed information on target career and transfer outcomes
- Course sequences, critical courses, embedded credentials, and progress milestones
- Math and other core coursework aligned to each program of study

HELP STUDENTS GET ON A PATH
Require these supports to make sure students get the best start:
- Use of multiple measures to assess students' needs
- First-year experiences to help students explore the field and choose a major
- Full program plans based on required career/transfer exploration
- Contextualized, integrated academic support to help students pass program gateway courses
- K-12 partnerships focused on career/college program exploration

HELP STUDENTS STAY ON THEIR PATH
Keep students on track with these supports:
- Ongoing, intrusive advising
- Systems for students to easily track their progress
- Systems/procedures to identify students at risk and provide needed supports
- A structure to redirect students who are not progressing in a program to a more viable path

ENSURE STUDENTS ARE LEARNING
Use these practices to assess and enrich student learning:
- Program-specific learning outcomes
- Project-based, collaborative learning
- Applied learning experiences
- Inescapable student engagement
- Faculty-led improvement of teaching practices
- Systems/procedures for the college and students to track mastery of learning outcomes that lead to credentials, transfer, and/or employment

EARLY OUTCOMES
Measure key performance indicators, including:
- Number of college credits earned in first term
- Number of college credits earned in first year
- Completion of gateway math and English courses in the student's first year
- Number of college credits earned in the program of study in first year
- Persistence from term 1 to term 2
- Rates of college-level course completion in students' first academic year
- Equity in outcomes

Revisit conditions, sustainability, and implementation. Continuously improve pathways by building on elements that work and adjusting or discarding elements that are not serving all students well.

EVALUATION

Contributors to this model for Guided Pathways are: American Association of Community Colleges (AACC), Achieving the Dream (ATD), The Aspen Institute, Center for Community College Student Engagement (CCCSE), Community College Research Center (CCRC), Complete College America, The Charles A. Dana Center, Jobs for the Future (JFF), National Center for Inquiry and Improvement (NCII), and Public Agenda.

Figure 4.1. Guided Pathways Model

- Establish *transfer pathways* through alignment of pathway courses and expected learning outcomes with transfer institutions, to optimize applicability of community college credits to university majors.

Help Students Choose and Enter a Pathway

- Bridge *K–12 to higher education*, assuring early remediation in the final years of high school through strong K–12/postsecondary partnerships.
- Redesign traditional remediation as an *"on-ramp" to a program of study*, which helps students explore academic and career options from the beginning of their college experience; aligns math and other foundation skills coursework with a student's program of study; and integrates and contextualizes instruction to build academic and nonacademic foundation skills throughout the college-level curriculum, particularly in program gateway courses.
- Provide *accelerated remediation* to help very poorly prepared students succeed in college-level courses as soon as possible.

Help Students Stay on Path

- Support students through a strong *advising* process, embedded and ongoing in the pathways experience and supported by appropriate technology, to help students make informed choices, strengthen clarity about transfer and career opportunities at the end of their chosen college path, ensure they develop an academic plan with predictable schedules, monitor their progress, and intervene when they go off track.
- Embed *academic and nonacademic supports* throughout students' programs to promote student learning and persistence.

Ensure That Students Are Learning

- Establish program-level *learning outcomes* aligned with the requirements for success in employment and further education in a given field and apply the results of learning outcomes assessment to improve the effectiveness of instruction across programs.
- Integrate *group projects, internships, and other applied learning experiences* to enhance instruction and student success in courses across programs of study.
- Ensure incorporation of *effective teaching practice* throughout the pathways.

Essential Conditions for Guided Pathways Reforms

Research and experience in the field indicate that the following conditions and institutional capacities are essential for motivating and supporting higher education institutions and systems as they undertake the large-scale institutional changes necessary for implementing guided pathways effectively and at scale:

- *Leadership* demonstrating skills for managing and sustaining large-scale transformational change.
- Broad and authentic *engagement* of college faculty and staff—particularly advisers—in the design, implementation, evaluation, and ongoing improvement of pathways for students.
- *Institutional will and capacity to use data and evidence* to design academic and career pathways, monitor student progress, and implement needed improvements over time.
- *Technological tools and infrastructure* appropriate to support student progress through guided pathways.
- Commitment to the level of *strategically targeted professional development* that will be required to design and implement pathways at scale.

- *Policy conditions* established at the state, governing board, system, and institutional levels that provide incentives, structures, and supports for pathway design and implementation at scale, while removing barriers.
- A *continuing action research agenda* that examines the efficacy of guided pathways and develops practical knowledge and tools to support effective implementation at scale.

LARGE-SCALE INSTITUTIONAL TRANSFORMATION: CHALLENGES AND EARLY RESULTS

The work of designing and implementing guided pathways at scale is not small, and it is not for the faint of heart. It entails large-scale institutional change that ultimately affects the roles of virtually everyone working in a college. When initially introduced to the pathways idea, college personnel often assume that pathways design begins and ends with establishing a course sequence for a program of study. By contrast, a description of likely design steps for each program pathway illustrates the greater magnitude of change involved and the work required of faculty and advisers:

- Create the default program course sequence, aligning course-level learning outcomes that accrue to desired program-level outcomes and identifying crucial milestone courses. Ensure that program completion requirements typically do not exceed sixty credits.
- Determine "the right math" for the pathway—that is, the mathematics that students actually need to learn for success in the major field and in the workforce.
- Discuss and recommend which general education core courses and elective courses may best serve to augment and enrich students' experiences in the pathway, with an eye toward educational coherence and relevance.
- Identify discipline-appropriate experiential/applied learning experiences that can be integrated into coursework along the pathway.
- Integrate discipline-appropriate, inescapable academic supports into course syllabi and students' experiences.
- Align discipline-appropriate cocurricular learning experiences with coursework for students in the pathway.

Increasingly, as pathways colleges identify meta-majors—clusters of related programs (labeled at various colleges as career and academic communities, fields of interest, institutes, schools, areas of study, etc.)—they are building valuable choice architecture for students. They also are creating opportunities for faculty and student support professionals to apply their ingenuity in transforming the meta-majors from lists in brochures or on websites into vibrant, large-scale learning communities. Colleges are using color coding, logos, name tags, lanyards, T-shirts, ball caps, designated spaces, Facebook Workplace pages, college orientations, contextualized success courses or first-year experiences, and other strategies to build students' identification with their meta-majors and thus both their level of engagement with faculty, advisers, and fellow students and their sense of belonging in the college.

In addition to the substantial work just described, most colleges also will need to fully redesign their student onboarding processes and their advising systems. Then there are major adjustments in business processes and technology infrastructure to support students' entry into and progress through their pathways. Everything changes.

Davis Jenkins and his colleagues at the CCRC have articulated a series of significant "mind-set" shifts that colleges need to make if they are to design and implement effective guided pathways for their students (Jenkins, Lahr, Fink, & Ganga, 2018). Explicitly noted is the necessary work to rethink program mapping, student onboarding, student advising, and teaching and learning—all efforts aligned with the four guided pathways practice areas previously described. For example, the mind-set shifts described with regard to "rethinking student onboarding" are the following:

- *From* job and transfer support for students approaching completion *to* career and college exploration and planning for all students from the start of college
- *From* current semester schedules *to* full-program educational plans
- *From* academic assessments of students' readiness for college-level work *to* holistic assessments of students' plans, goals, and challenges
- *From* prerequisite remediation *to* corequisite academic support
- *From* algebra and English composition courses as college gatekeepers *to* courses (not just math and English) crucial for program success
- *From* a la carte dual credit courses in high school *to* exploration of career/ academic pathways beginning in high school

(Jenkins et al., 2018, p. 4)

As might be expected, the work of transformational change is intellectually challenging, time-intensive, and at times politically risky. Rob Johnstone, founder and president of the National Center for Inquiry & Improvement (NCII), has provided a service to the field in describing questions and concerns that naturally arise among faculty, student support professionals, and others as pathways reforms are introduced.

The first installment, *Guided Pathways Demystified* (Johnstone, 2015), addresses philosophical and conceptual concerns, exploring questions about higher education values; considerations about control, enrollment, and workload; and apprehensions about potential impacts on students' learning and development, which are all issues, Johnstone asserts, that must be openly addressed if colleges are to successfully pursue a guided pathways effort. In the follow-up publication (Johnstone & Karandjeff, 2017), the necessary dialogue progresses to questions focused more on pathways planning and implementation. Issues range from culture change to practical concerns and operational changes.

Challenges notwithstanding, guided pathways reforms have progressed to the status of a serious movement within the community college sector. As Jenkins et al. (2018, p. 2) note:

> Major national initiatives such as the American Association of Community Colleges' (AACC) Pathways Project are helping colleges throughout the country to implement the reforms and refine the model. Higher education agencies and statewide organizations such as the Student Success Centers are also facilitating guided pathways reforms in numerous states, including Arkansas, California, Connecticut, Michigan, New Hampshire, New Jersey, New York, North Carolina, Ohio, Oregon, Tennessee, Texas, Virginia, and Washington.

The elements of the guided pathways model, as previously discussed, are research based; even so, the model is relatively new and will require continuing testing and evaluation. Results from guided pathways implementations are being analyzed by national research organizations, notably the CCRC, by state systems, and by the institutions themselves.

To ascertain early results, many colleges are using a set of early-momentum key performance indicators (KPIs) developed by CCRC (Jenkins & Bailey, 2017), including metrics for credit accumulation in the first year; completion of college-level English, math, or both in the first year; program credits earned in the first year; and fall-to-spring persistence. These metrics are associated with longer-term student outcomes, including college completion, and so are useful to institutions in monitoring progress in their pathways work. Selected examples of early results in community colleges are briefly described here.

Data from Cleveland State Community College (TN) (Jenkins et al., 2018) show trends from 2010 through 2016 for the percentage of fall first-time-ever-in-college (FTEIC) students who completed 6+, 12+, 24+, and 30+ credit hours during their first academic year. Percentages increased significantly at all levels of credit accumulation; at the highest levels, the percentage of students completing 24+ credit hours in the first year almost tripled, and the percentage completing 30+ credit hours (though still a small number of students) more than quadrupled.

At the five Alamo Colleges (TX),[3] the percentage of FTEIC students who completed both college-level math and college-level English in their first year (an early-momentum KPI) increased from 11 percent in 2010 to 29 percent in 2016. Further, illustrating the relationship between this early-momentum indicator and longer-term outcomes, results of a CCRC analysis indicate that for fall 2014 FTEIC students who entered the Alamo Colleges and completed any college credential (at any institution), the three-year completion rate was 32 percent for students who had completed college-level math and English in their first year, compared to 8 percent for those who did not meet that KPI.

For Indian River State College (FL), the two-year graduation rate for full-time students from 2011 to 2015 was analyzed by race/ethnicity (Jenkins et al., 2018). The rates for all groups increased significantly—from 26.1 to 36.4 percent for white students, from 20.7 to 33.7 percent for Hispanic students, and from 12.5 to 23.4 percent for black students. The equity gaps were reduced, particularly for Hispanic students, but were not eliminated.

Between 2010–2011 and 2014–2015 at Lorain County Community College (OH), the percentage of entering students who completed nine credit hours in their program of study in their first academic year (an early-momentum KPI) increased from 19 to 30 percent. Turning to a look at college completion in the same institution, results show that Lorain County increased its three-year graduation rate for first-time, full-time students from 8 percent for the 2008 cohort to 23 percent for the 2014 cohort (Jenkins et al., 2018).

The challenges of achieving institutional transformation through guided pathways reform are substantial. Results are very promising, but still preliminary. The road to full scale across the community college sector is still long. The need for courageous and tenacious leadership is evident. For community colleges, even taking all of these challenges into account, guided pathways provide the opportunity to achieve their aspirations for student success and equity—and thus to keep America's promise.

NOTES

1. This section draws substantially from a paper first developed by the Community College Research Center (CCRC), with subsequent contributions by the AACC Pathways Project and the author. See CCRC and AACC (2015a).

2. This overview is drawn, and slightly adapted/updated, from a document developed by the CCRC and the author, on behalf of the AACC Pathways Project. See CCRC and AACC (2015b).

3. Early momentum and completion rates calculated by the Alamo Colleges, following metrics developed by the CCRC for the colleges in the AACC Pathways Project.

REFERENCES

Achieving the Dream, Inc. (2018, July 9). *Our approach*. Retrieved from http://www.achievingthedream.org/our-network/our-approach

American Association of Community Colleges (AACC). (2012). *Reclaiming the American dream: Community colleges and the nation's future.* Washington, DC: Author.

Attewell, P., Heil, S., & Reisel, L. (2012). What is academic momentum? And does it matter? *Educational Evaluation and Policy Analysis, 34*(1), 27–44.

Bailey, T. (2009). Challenge and opportunity: Rethinking the role and function of developmental education in community college. *New Directions for Community Colleges, 145,* 11–30.

Bailey, T., Jaggars, S., & Jenkins, D. (2015). *Redesigning America's community colleges: A clearer path to student success.* Cambridge, MA: Harvard University Press.

Center for Community College Student Engagement (CCCSE). (2013). *A matter of degrees: Engaging practices, engaging students* (High-impact practices for community college student engagement). Austin: The University of Texas at Austin, Community College Leadership Program.

Center for Community College Student Engagement. (2014). *A matter of degrees: Practices to pathways* (High-impact practices for community college student success). Austin: The University of Texas at Austin, Program in Higher Education Leadership.

Chaplot, P., Rassen, E., Jenkins, D., & Johnstone, R. (2013). *Principles of redesign: Promising approaches to transforming student outcomes.* Seattle, WA: Completion by Design.

Community College Research Center (CCRC) & American Association of Community Colleges (AACC) (2015a). *The movement toward pathways.* Retrieved from https://www.pathwaysresources.org/wp-content/uploads/2018/04/TheMovementTowardPathways_Final.pdf

Community College Research Center (CCRC) & American Association of Community Colleges (2015b). *What is the pathways model?* Retrieved from https://www.pathwaysresources.org/wp-content/uploads/2018/04/PathwaysModelDescription_Final.pdf

Community College Survey of Student Engagement (CCSSE). (2002). *Engaging community colleges: A first look.* Austin: The University of Texas at Austin, Community College Leadership Program.

Completion by Design (CBD). (2018, July 11). Retrieved from https://www.completionbydesign.org/s/

Edgecombe, N. (2011). *Accelerating the academic achievement of students referred to developmental education* (CCRC Working Paper No. 30). New York: Columbia University, Teachers College, Community College Research Center.

Jenkins, D., & Bailey, T. (2017). *Early momentum metrics: Why they matter for college improvement* (CCRC Research Brief No. 65). New York: Columbia University, Teachers College, Community College Research Center.

Jenkins, D., & Cho, S.W. (2012). *Get with the program: Accelerating community college students' entry into and completion of programs of study* (CCRC Working Paper No. 32). New York: Columbia University, Teachers College, Community College Research Center.

Jenkins, D., Lahr, H., & Fink, J. (2017). *Implementing guided pathways: Early insights from the AACC Pathways colleges.* New York: Columbia University, Teachers College, Community College Research Center.

Jenkins, D., Lahr, H., Fink, J., & Ganga, E. (2018). *What we are learning about guided pathways, part 1: A reform moves from theory to practice.* New York: Columbia University, Teachers College, Community College Research Center.

Jenkins, D., Speroni, C., Belfield, C., Jaggars, S. S., & Edgecombe, N. (2010). *A model for accelerating academic success of community college remedial English students: Is the Accelerated Learning Program (ALP) effective and affordable?* (CCRC Working Paper No. 21). New York: Columbia University, Teachers College, Community College Research Center.

Johnstone, R. (2015). *Guided pathways demystified: Exploring ten commonly asked questions about implementing pathways.* Retrieved from http://ncii-improve.com/wp-content/uploads/2017/06/PWs-Demystified-Johnstone-111615.pdf

Johnstone, R., & Karandjeff, K. (2017). *Guided pathways demystified II: Addressing 10 new questions as the movement gains momentum.* Retrieved from http://ncii-improve.com/wp-content/uploads/2017/09/GP-Demystified-II-091517.pdf

O'Banion, T. (1997). *A learning college for the 21st century.* Phoenix, AZ: The Oryx Press.

Perin, D. (2011). *Facilitating student learning through contextualization* (CCRC Working Paper No. 29). New York: Columbia University, Teachers College, Community College Research Center.

Quint, J. C., Jaggars, S. S., Byndloss, D. C., & Magazinnik, A. (2013). *Bringing developmental education to scale: Lessons from the Developmental Education Initiative*. New York: MDRC.

Rutschow, E. Z., Richburg-Hayes, L., Brock, T., Orr, G., Cerna, O., Kerrigan, M. R., . . . Martin, K. (2011). *Turning the tide: Five years of Achieving the Dream in community colleges*. New York: MDRC.

Scott-Clayton, J. (2011). *The shapeless river: Does a lack of structure inhibit students' progress at community colleges?* (CCRC Working Paper No. 25). New York: Columbia University, Teachers College, Community College Research Center.

Scott-Clayton, J. (2012). *Do high-stakes placement exams predict college success?* (CCRC Working Paper No. 41). New York: Columbia University, Teachers College, Community College Research Center.

Zeidenberg, M., Cho, S.-W., & Jenkins, D. (2010). *Washington State's Integrated Basic Education and Skills Training Program (I-BEST): New evidence of effectiveness* (CCRC Working Paper No. 20). New York: Columbia University, Teachers College, Community College Research Center.

Chapter Five

The Community College Baccalaureate Movement

Evolutionary and Revolutionary

Deborah L. Floyd and Michael L. Skolnik

The American community college embodies the fusion of many great ideas that are congruent with egalitarian values and philosophies. A more educated citizenry adds value to communities, and local community colleges play an important role in providing relevant localized education to all citizens, regardless of their ability to pay.

Community colleges' missions and programs have evolved over time, mainly in response to local needs and wants for education and training. Early junior colleges were bridges between secondary schools and universities. Then community-based colleges provided the first two years of a baccalaureate degree for transfer, developmental support for those not yet ready for college-level studies, and career and vocational training designed to fill local workforce needs. Until recently, however, community colleges were limited to offering certificates, diplomas, and associate degrees, with baccalaureate degrees and beyond reserved for universities and four-year colleges.

Over time, great strides have been made to ensure that general education associate degrees (AA and AS) articulated well with university baccalaureates. But unfortunately not all community college graduates were ensured access to university baccalaureate degree programs due to geography, flexibility, and costs.

Access to baccalaureate degrees has been very limited for community college applied, workforce, and technical associate (AAS and some AS) graduates because of the access reasons previously cited and because many universities do not offer technical baccalaureates such as bachelor of technology, bachelor of applied technology, and bachelor of applied science. Without access to affordable and accessible baccalaureate degrees, the community college associate degree has been effectively "terminal" for many students, limiting graduates' opportunities for higher incomes and greater contributions to society.

The idea of the community college baccalaureate (CCB) degree emerged to provide greater opportunity for individuals to advance their education and to meet national and local needs for a more highly educated workforce. The early CCBs were designed to meet local and specific applied workforce needs, an earmark of the vast majority of those offered now. Beginning slowly, but gaining momentum over the past two decades, the CCB movement has found its footing.

Generally, states have been very specific about what can be offered, perhaps a response to the concerns of four-year institutions and governing bodies that do not want unnecessary degree duplication, competition, or costs. In some states, however, community colleges are offering baccalaureates in education and nursing, a departure from the applied technical degrees, in response to community and workforce demands.

AN IDEA WHOSE TIME HAS COME: THE COMMUNITY COLLEGE BACCALAUREATE

As Koch and Garner (2013) suggest, the CCB is an idea whose time has come. As more citizens hunger for credentials and degrees that will enhance their earning potential and improve their lives, the CCB movement is gaining momentum. The CCB is revolutionary in that it involves community colleges adding to their repertoire a new academic credential they had not previously awarded, but it is also evolutionary in building upon their history of continuously adapting their programs to meet emerging needs of the populations and locales they serve.

The original CCB idea was to add a new function to the mission of the community college: offering four-year bachelor's degree programs in applied fields of study for which there was a demand from industry. According to its proponents, the CCB was intended as an *addition* to other community college functions, not a replacement for them. In particular, there was no intention that the CCB would be a substitute for traditional transfer; some colleges have expanded their transfer activity with four-year institutions simultaneously while adding new CCB programs. However, while the introduction of the CCB into a community college is usually accompanied by a statement to the effect that this does not reflect an intention for the institution to become a four-year college, that has sometimes happened.

Frequently the CCB curriculum has been constructed largely by adding third and fourth years to the curriculum of existing associate degrees. A benefit of this approach is that it provides an efficient pathway for graduates of associate degree programs to continue on to the bachelor's degree. However, in other cases CCB programs have been created from scratch, and sometimes associate degree programs have been terminated in conjunction with the development of a related bachelor's degree program.

The CCB was intended to serve two principal goals. It serves the goal of increased accessibility to the baccalaureate by helping to overcome the barriers of distance, cost, lack of program affinity, and limited credit transfer. It also helps by providing a different kind of baccalaureate experience that may be more attractive and effective for learners who perform best in a more hands-on setting that is more connected to the world of work. In these ways, it attempts to make the baccalaureate more accessible to groups that have been underserved by four-year institutions, such as low-income families, minorities, single parents, and persons living in rural areas (Skolnik et al., 2018). The other goal is to provide a new type of graduate who is thought to be in demand by industry and is more job ready than the traditional four-year college graduate.

Students in two-year programs of career and technical education in community colleges constitute an important potential pool of baccalaureate students. More than a third of students who enter postsecondary education start in community college (Shapiro et al., 2017), and about half of associate degree students in community colleges are in applied programs. In view of national concern about the decline in the bachelor's degree attainment rate in the United States relative to other countries (College Board, 2008; Lumina Foundation, 2015; Pell Institute for the Study of Economic Opportunity, 2011), career program students in the community colleges are too large a pool of talent to neglect.

TERMINOLOGY AND MODELS

As CCB programs continue to evolve, many innovative models have emerged, but the terminology to describe the models, programs, and even colleges lags and is often confusing and inconsistent. The term *community college baccalaureate* has been used to describe partnership degrees wherein the four-year college or university offers the upper division courses and awards the degree. It has also been used to describe models in which the baccalaureate degree is fully delivered and awarded by community colleges. Most community colleges provide some type of partnership programming toward baccalaureate attainment, but these programs are not considered CCB degrees by most definitions.

Many questions arise regarding naming terminology. For instance, when a community college offers and awards even one baccalaureate degree, is that college then considered a *four-year college* or a community college? And, if a community college drops the term *community* from the name or changes to a *state college,* or adds *university* to its name, is the college still considered a community college? Answering these questions is fraught with challenges, as these institutions and programs continue to evolve and agencies, researchers, and even the colleges themselves are not consistent with the application of terms. For purposes of this chapter, the CCB is defined as a degree conferred by a baccalaureate/associate institution, which captures colleges formerly named as community colleges and others.

Historically, community colleges have guided students through many diverse pathways for baccalaureate attainment through implementation of several models that require partnerships, planning, and collaboration between a community college and a four-year college or university (Floyd & D. A. Walker, 2003; Floyd & K. P. Walker, 2005, 2009; Floyd, 2005, 2006). The tried and true articulation baccalaureate degree model (often referred to as a 2 + 2 model) ensures acceptance of lower division credits or an associate degree by a four-year institution and is the most common model, but it often requires that students complete upper division courses on a four-year college or university campus.

University center and concurrent use baccalaureate models require partnerships but focus on providing local access to courses and programs, often through shared facilities or centers on community college campuses. Albert Lorenzo (2005) described university centers and further classified them into six submodels: co-location model, enterprise model, virtual model, integrated model, sponsorship model, and hybrid model. *University extension baccalaureate models* result in baccalaureate degree programs that are offered by centers or campuses that are university branches or are affiliated with universities, such as Oklahoma State University Institute of Technology and four campuses of the State University of New York (SUNY). In all of these partnership models the four-year college or university confers the baccalaureate degree.

Inverted baccalaureates (3 + 1 or "upside down" degrees) are degrees that articulate with technical courses, wherein students complete three years of technical studies and the final year of general education (Ignash, 2012; Floyd & Walker, 2009). *Workforce baccalaureates* is a term often used to describe the rationale for the baccalaureate degree as one that addresses local workforce needs in areas such as nursing, teaching, and business or technology. This term has also been used synonymously with *applied baccalaureates*. Inverted, applied, and workforce baccalaureates may be conferred by community colleges and universities alike, especially through university branches and centers.

HISTORY OF THE COMMUNITY COLLEGE
BACCALAUREATE IDEA

While throughout the twentieth century some junior colleges evolved into four-year colleges, the movement among community colleges to offer their own baccalaureate degrees began in earnest in the late 1980s with Parkersburg Community College's requests and eventual approvals to offer business, applied technology, and elementary education degrees to meet local workforce demands in rural West Virginia. Parkersburg later affiliated with the University of West Virginia and became known as the University of West Virginia at Parkersburg.

In 1993 Vermont Technical College was approved to offer baccalaureates to address local workforce needs in business, information technology, architecture, aeromechanical engineering technology, and general education. In the 1990s Utah approved Utah Technical College and Dixie College to offer baccalaureate degrees in business, community health, elementary education, and nursing.

Georgia's Dalton Junior College and Macon Junior College began offering market-driven degrees in education, health, business, and nursing baccalaureates in the mid- to late 1990s and later converted to four-year colleges named Dalton State College and Macon State College. About the same time, Westark Community College obtained approval to offer baccalaureate degrees in workforce areas, including manufacturing technology. Subsequently, Westark's name and governance changed to the University of Arkansas–Fort Smith.

During the early years of this movement, community college and university leaders worked to strengthen partnerships through articulation, extension, and university center models, which resulted in the "net effect" of more baccalaureate degree offerings in local communities (Floyd, Skolnik, & Walker, 2005; Floyd & Walker, 2009; Lorenzo, 2005). But partnership models did not always adequately address the need for specialized workforce baccalaureates in geographically and fiscally accessible ways. Thus, community college leaders, in response to local workforce needs, designed new types of workforce and applied baccalaureates in specific fields that were often conferred as bachelor of applied science (BAS), bachelor of applied technology (BAT), and bachelor of science (BS) degrees. Very few offered bachelor of arts (BA) degrees.

The CCB movement gained enormous traction and momentum in 2001 when Florida's legislature enacted Senate Bill (SB) 1162, which granted Florida's oldest community college, St. Petersburg Junior College, authorization to offer select baccalaureates to meet local needs and workforce demands (Floyd & Falconetti, 2013; Floyd & Walker, 2009; Furlong, 2005). At the same time, a handful of colleges in Florida were authorized as "pilots," which included two rural community colleges (Chipola Community College and Okaloosa-Walton Community College) and a large urban college (Miami Dade Community College).

In 2008 landmark legislation was enacted in Florida that changed the state system of community colleges to the Florida College System, authorized local boards to name local colleges, and allowed expansion of the baccalaureate degree offerings with the application processes overseen by the Florida College System. Currently, baccalaureate degrees are offered by all but one of Florida's twenty-eight colleges, and the total number of baccalaureate programs is 189. The areas in which the programs are offered include teacher education, organizational management, applied health sciences, nursing, supervision and management, dental hygiene, information technology, cyber-security, business and management, paralegal studies, orthotics and prosthetics, health services administration, energy technology management, emergency management, electrical and computer technology, radiologic and imaging sciences, cardiopulmonary sciences, and international business and trade.

Soon thereafter, in 2003, Texas followed with legislation authorizing Midland College, Brazosport College, and South Texas College to offer technology management baccalaureates to meet local workforce needs. With subsequent approvals at two other institutions, five community colleges have now gained authorization to award ten bachelor of science and bachelor of technology degrees.

Nevada followed during 2004–2007 with Great Basin College and the College of Southern Nevada approved to offer programs such as teacher education, dental hygiene, social work, and management. Today three of Nevada's four community colleges are authorized to deliver eighteen baccalaureate degree programs.

The CCB movement continued to gain momentum in 2005 when Washington State approved four community colleges to offer workforce and applied baccalaureate degrees as "pilots"; it added three more in 2008. The 2005 enabling legislation was amended in 2010 to allow all of Washington's community colleges to award bachelor's degrees, with State Board for Community and Technical College oversight and assurances that the degrees are of high quality, are not offered by a nearby four-year college, and are offered in response to workforce demands.

Today, Washington offers eighty-five baccalaureates at twenty-five community and technical colleges in areas such as applied management, cybersecurity, nursing, information technology, various allied health fields, forest resource management, respiratory care, computing and software development, digital gaming and interactive media, and teacher education.

In 2010 Colorado's legislature authorized Colorado Mountain College to offer up to five baccalaureate degree programs to meet local workforce demands. In 2014 lawmakers also granted authority to the Colorado Community College System to approve applications to offer bachelor of applied science degrees that addressed local workforce needs. The Colorado Commission on Higher Education considers and approves baccalaureate degree proposals, and today four colleges offer a total of nine baccalaureate programs.

In 2012 Michigan followed by enacting legislation that authorized its twenty-eight community colleges to offer baccalaureate degrees in specific areas of concrete technology, maritime technology, energy production, and culinary arts. By early 2018 six colleges offered (or were approved to offer) six bachelor of science degrees in these fields.

The CCB movement gained even more momentum in 2014 when California established a statewide bachelor's degree pilot program at fifteen community colleges; each college was limited to one bachelor's degree program and must receive program approval from the California Community College Board of Governors. The fifteen California community colleges currently offer fifteen bachelor of science degrees in workforce areas such as mortuary science, dental hygiene, respiratory care, occupational studies, biomanufacturing, health information management, and automotive technology.

KEY PLAYERS IN THE CCB MOVEMENT

Changing the mission of a two-year community college by adding four-year baccalaureate degrees was, and continues to be, controversial. Early critics argued that offering baccalaureate degrees at community colleges was "mission creep" and that offering these programs would detract from the core missions of technical and occupational education, academic transfer education, developmental education, and community programming. Advocates argued that offering these new baccalaureate degrees was a natural evolution of the community college mission to provide relevant education and training opportunities locally.

Community college leaders worked tirelessly, often with a missionary zeal, to gain approval to offer their own baccalaureate degrees in direct response to identified community needs and wants. They worked to offer a compelling vision, a persuasive rationale, and inspirational leadership. Quite often, multiple attempts and approaches were employed to eventually obtain governance approval at the local and state levels. Even today, with many states granting at least one community college authorization to offer baccalaureate degrees, critics abound, and challenges continue.

The number of people in community colleges, state agencies, universities, government, and national associations who have made significant contributions to advancement of the CCB idea is so large that it is not possible to mention all of them. Some have served on the Board of the Community College Baccalaureate Association (CCBA), such as longtime board members Linda Thor, retired chancellor, Foothill–De Anza Community College District; Ali Esmaelli, dean of baccalaureate programs, South Texas College; and current board chair Michael Hansen, president of the Michigan Community College Association.

Many other practitioners contributed to the dialogue early in this movement, such as Albert L. Lorenzo, retired president of Michigan's Macomb Community College, who helped shape discussions about baccalaureate models (Lorenzo, 2005). Critics, including James Wattenbarger (2000), added value to this movement by reminding community colleges not to abandon their core missions and purposes.

In addition, following is a list of many other practitioners who helped create, support, document, implement, and bring the idea of the community college baccalaureate degree to fruition:

- The late Eldon Miller, president of Parkersburg Community College and later the University of West Virginia at Parkersburg, quietly and successfully championed bringing baccalaureate degrees to his college's Appalachian service area in 1989 as an early CCB agent of change.
- Kenneth P. Walker, retired president of Edison Community College (FL) (renamed Edison State College), was the preeminent spokesperson for the CCB, especially for about fifteen years beginning in the late 1990s. Ken was the founding president of the CCBA and remains a tireless advocate for initiatives to bring improved opportunities for the baccalaureate to the community college campus. His publications include coediting *The Community College Baccalaureate: Emerging Trends and Policy Issues*, along with several articles and book chapters (Walker, 2001, 2005; Walker & Floyd, 2005).
- Beth Hagan, retired executive director of the CCBA under Ken Walker's leadership and after his retirement, has provided dynamic leadership for the CCBA in its role as a clearinghouse for knowledge and a national forum for discussion. In addition, CCBA works with institutions, higher education agencies, and governments to foster knowledge and awareness of models for improving opportunities for the baccalaureate.
- Carl Kuttler, retired president of St. Petersburg College (SPC), was the flag bearer for Florida's 2001 legislative authorization that allowed SPC to begin the process to offer baccalaureate degrees in high-need areas such as information technology, nursing, teacher education, and health careers. Today, SPC offers over two dozen baccalaureate degrees in areas such as veterinary technology, international business, paralegal studies, dental hygiene, sustainability management, business administration, public policy and administration, nursing, and various areas of teacher education.

- Thomas E. Furlong Jr., retired senior vice president for baccalaureate programs and university partnerships at SPC, spearheaded the early implementation of authorization, accreditation, and curriculum development at SPC. He also authored a number of articles and book chapters documenting the development of the baccalaureate programs at SPC and changes the college made to support the delivery of baccalaureate degree programs (Furlong, 2005). In retirement, he is assisting various colleges with transitions necessary to offer baccalaureate degrees.
- Ron Remington, retired president of the Community College of Southern Nevada (CCSN) and past president of rural Nevada's Great Basin College (GBC), spearheaded the 1999 approval for GBC to offer the first CCB in Nevada. Later, as president of CCSN, Ron worked tirelessly to advocate CCB approval. Nancy and Ron Remington documented the evolutionary change processes of GBC in the Floyd, Skolnik, and Walker (2005) book and later were responsible for the edited book *Alternative Pathways to the Baccalaureate* (Remington & Remington, 2013). Ron was a founding CCBA board member.

In addition to the many practitioners who have been responsible for the development, improvement, accreditation, and success of CCB programs, several higher education scholars have contributed to the CCB idea through research that has documented, explained, and interpreted the community college baccalaureate:

- The late Barbara Townsend's contributions included drawing attention to the need for and limitations of pathways to the baccalaureate for students in applied associate degree programs, offering cautious views for consideration (Townsend, 2005).
- John Levin examined the CCB's origins early in the movement and offered scholarly insights about the likely impact in the context of globalization and neoliberalism (Levin, 2004).
- Debra D. Bragg's research on the CCB included contributions to the development of an important line of research on the applied baccalaureate as it has developed in both four-year and two-year institutions (Bragg & Ruud, 2012; Bragg & Soler, 2017; Townsend, Bragg, & Ruud, 2009).
- Deborah L. Floyd and Michael L. Skolnik have been studying and writing about phenomena related to the CCB for more than two decades. They met at an annual conference of the CCBA, and shortly thereafter, with Kenneth Walker, edited the first book on the CCB, *The Community College Baccalaureate: Emerging Trends and Policy Issues* (Floyd, Skolnik, & Walker, 2005). Both have written on many different aspects of the CCB. For Deborah these have included community college programs in teacher education (Floyd & Walker, 2003), applied and workforce baccalaureates

(Floyd, Falconetti, & Felsher, 2012; Floyd & Walker, 2005, 2009), graduate education issues (Floyd, Felsher, & Catullo, 2012), and the CCB
movement in Florida (Floyd & Falconetti, 2013; Floyd, Falconetti, &
Hrabak, 2009). Michael has examined theoretical explanations of the origin of CCB (Skolnik, 2009), competition between community colleges
and universities in baccalaureate level education (Skolnik, 2011), and
international comparisons of CCBs (Skolnik, 2016a, 2016b).

THE COMMUNITY COLLEGE BACCALAUREATE
IN AN INTERNATIONAL CONTEXT

Although the United States is the focus of this chapter, it is important to note
that a number of other countries have started to offer baccalaureate degree
programs and programs of shorter duration than a bachelor's degree. The
CCBA is an international organization which from the beginning has had
strong participation from Canadians and has almost always had at least one
Canadian on its board, including one of the coauthors of this chapter. Other
Canadian board members include Paul Byrne, former president of Grant
MacEwan College, longtime board member; David Ross, president of South-
ern Alberta Institute of Technology; and more recent board member Henry
Decock, associate vice president of academic partnerships at Seneca College.

Leesa Wheelahan and Gavin Moodie's research addresses ways in which
community colleges and their counterpart institutions in other countries enable students who start postsecondary education in these institutions to complete a bachelor's degree. Their international research has focused particularly on Australia, Canada, the United Kingdom, and the United States (e.g.,
Wheelahan, Moodie, Billet, & Kelly, 2009; Wheelahan et al., 2017).

STATE IMPLEMENTATION:
POLICIES AND LEGISLATIVE ACTIVITY

States policies and legislative activity are consistently shifting as the landscape of higher education evolves, in an effort to align degree authorization
and approvals with local and state needs. Expanding community colleges'
authorization to offer baccalaureate degrees is not without controversy (Fulton, 2015). Most efforts to change authorization are not successful, especially
during the early request and expansion stages. For instance, in 2015 Michigan's legislature failed to pass a bill to expand its 2012 authorization of
twenty-eight community colleges beyond baccalaureates in energy production, concrete technology, maritime technology, and culinary arts.

California also proposed legislation to expand approval beyond the original fifteen community colleges, which failed. Similarly, in 2015 Texas legis-

lators introduced several bills to expand community college authorization to award baccalaureate degrees, and they all failed to pass. In 2018 even the most established CCB state, Florida, was threatened by a failed senate bill that would have changed the name of the Florida College System back to the Florida Community College System and limited current baccalaureate degree offerings. The Florida bill gained significant momentum as critics' arguments about "mission creep" and failed articulation with universities fueled the debates.

The Education Commission of the States (Fulton, 2018) reported that twenty-four states allow community colleges to award baccalaureate degrees and that several more have recently proposed legislation to do so. The commission clarifies that CCB degrees are intended to address local workforce needs, especially in high-demand fields. Among the many core elements of state policies, Fulton (2015) describes state policies that address the location of program offerings, number of institutions and degrees, programmatic demand by students and employers, approval processes, resources and cost effectiveness, and reporting requirements.

Fulton (2018) reported that between January 1, 2017, and April 30, 2017, thirteen states introduced fifty-four bills related to CCBs, and four states enacted legislation. She noted legislative activity in California, Colorado, Florida, Idaho, Maryland, Missouri, Nevada, New Jersey, Ohio, Oregon, Pennsylvania, South Carolina, and Texas. Ohio's 2018–2019 budget bill requires the establishment of a process by which community and technical colleges may offer applied baccalaureate degrees in specific areas and with unique approaches. Texas approved legislation in 2017 that allows the higher education coordinating board to authorize additional programs in applied fields to meet workforce needs, but an approved community college may not offer more than three baccalaureate degree programs at the same time. Colorado legislation in 2018 authorized the expansion of nursing applied degrees, and Idaho legislation in 2017 approved amendments that clarified that community college upper division programs and services are subject to specific approval requirements.

IDENTIFICATION OF CCB STATES, INSTITUTIONS, AND PROGRAMS

The Carnegie Classification of Institutions of Higher Education 2015 update of the Undergraduate Instructional Program classification was used as the base for developing an inventory of CCB states, institutions, and programs reported in this chapter. Specifically, those higher education institutions categorized under the classification "Baccalaureate/Associate Colleges" were selected for further examination.

Baccalaureate/associate colleges are defined thus: "These institutions awarded both associate's and bachelor's degrees, but the majority of degrees awarded were at the associate's level" (The Carnegie Classification of Institutions of Higher Education, n.d.-a, para. 14). It is important to note that the 2015 updates are based on degree conferrals (not offerings) for 2013–2014 as reported to the National Center for Education Statistics (NCES) through the IPEDS Completions collection (The Carnegie Classification of Institutions of Higher Education, n.d.-b). The number of public baccalaureate/associate colleges in the 2015 update was 101, of which 98 were in the fifty states and three were in territories (American Samoa, Northern Marianas, and Puerto Rico).

An online search was conducted on each of these institution's websites to determine the number of baccalaureate programs, variety of programs, and types of degrees offered by each college in 2018. The data for California, Colorado, Florida, Georgia, Michigan, Ohio, Texas, and Washington were further updated through information from the states' community college associations and systems. The online search resulted in the elimination of one institution from the Carnegie list as a result of a consolidation of two institutions in Georgia, and another in Wisconsin was found not to be offering any baccalaureate degree programs. The online search also revealed the presence of forty baccalaureate-awarding institutions that were not in the 2015 list of baccalaureate/associate colleges. The biggest change was for the state of Washington, which went from fourteen institutions with sixty-nine baccalaureate programs to twenty-five institutions with eighty-five programs.

The resulting inventory, shown in table 5.1, indicates that as of July 2018, 957 baccalaureate programs were being offered by 136 CCB institutions in twenty states. The difference between the number of states shown in table 5.1 and the Education Commission of the States estimate of twenty-four is likely due to differences in definitions and methodologies for identifying CCB programs.

Table 5.1 shows that the states with the largest numbers of institutions awarding baccalaureate degrees are Florida (27), Washington (25), Ohio (20), and California (15). Of the 21 Ohio institutions, 17 are campuses of Ohio universities. The 2 CCB institutions in Oklahoma, as well as some of the CCB institutions in other states, are also campuses of universities. In total, 34 of the 136 CCB institutions (25 percent) identified in table 5.1 are campuses of universities as opposed to being independent community colleges. These institutions account for nearly half of all CCB programs—462 of 957 programs. Some of these institutions became affiliated with universities only after they began to offer baccalaureate programs as independent community colleges, while others began as two-year campuses of a multi-campus university and subsequently added bachelor's degrees.

State	Number of Host Institutions Awarding a Baccalaureate Degree	Number of Baccalaureate Programs	Types of Baccalaureate Degrees Offered
Arkansas	1	28	BA, BAS, BBA, BGS, BS, BSN, BSW
California	15	15	BS
Colorado	4	9	BA, BAS, BASS, BSBA, BSN
Florida	27	188	BAS, BS
Georgia	8	77	BA, BAS, BBA, BS, BSBM, BSM, BSN, BSW
Hawaii	1	3	BAS
Indiana	1	4	BS
Michigan	6	6	BS
Nevada	3	18	BA, BAS, BS, BSW
New Mexico	1	13	BA, BAIS, BBA, BEng, BS, BSN
New York	6	147	BBA, BFA, BS, BT, BTech, BArch
North Dakota	1	1	BAS
Ohio	20	168	BA, BAH, BAS, BBA, BCJ, BIS, BRIT, BS, BSAM, BSBA, BSC, BSE, BSEd, BSH, BSN, BSHP, BSS, BSSW, BSW, BTAS, BSSpS
Oklahoma	2	4	BT
Pennsylvania	5	63	BA, BS, BSB, BSN
Texas	5	10	BAS, BAT
Utah	2	75	BA, BFA, BIS, BM, BS, BSN
Vermont	1	18	BS, BSN
Washington	25	85	BAA, BAS, BS, BSN
West Virginia	2	25	BA, BAS, BASBA, BAT, BSBA, BSN, RBA
TOTALS	136	957	

Table 5.1

Other factors that may influence the identification of CCB institutions are whether an institution may be deemed to have "evolved" from a community college into some other type of postsecondary institution or if the terminology used to classify colleges and CCB institutions is inconsistently applied. For example, some may question whether the Florida colleges are still community colleges since most have changed their names to "state college" and the statewide community college system is now known as the Florida College System.

Ten years ago Floyd and Walker (2009) described some of the challenges of classifications due to various baccalaureate degree models and inconsistent use of terminology to describe these degrees. They defined terminology such as inverted baccalaureates, university centers, and articulation baccalaureates, whereby the baccalaureates are conferred by a university partner but provide the "net effort" of new bachelor's degrees for community college clientele. While these partnership models are valuable, table 5.1 only reflects institutions that are approved to confer baccalaureates, not partner with others to confer them.

To put the number of CCB institutions shown in table 5.1 in perspective, according to the National Center for Education Statistics, the number of two-year institutions in the United States in 2016–2017 was 885 (National Center for Education Statistics, 2018). The public postsecondary institutions whose degree granting consists exclusively or predominantly of associate degrees include these 885 two-year institutions plus the 136 baccalaureate/associate institutions indicated in table 5.1, giving a total of 1,021 institutions. Taking that figure of 1,021 as an estimate of the number of community colleges, the 136 CCB institutions could be said to comprise 13.3 percent of American community colleges.

The degree titles, such as bachelor of applied science and bachelor of technology, shown in the last column of table 5.1, reflect the preponderance of applied programs. The bachelor of science programs are primarily in applied fields of study, and traditional types of bachelor of arts degrees are infrequent or nonexistent in community colleges in most states. Programs in nursing or teacher education are frequent, but the majority of programs are in areas that are not normally found in four-year institutions, such as diesel technology, digital marketing, sustainable building technology, construction management, industrial logistics, supply chain management, maritime technology, energy production and distribution management, technology management, equine and ranch management, airframe manufacturing technology, and industrial automation.

The word *applied* is a fitting descriptor for CCBs not only because their goal is to prepare graduates for specific occupations, but also because of their pedagogy and curriculum (Skolnik, 2013). Extending the same practices that characterize the associate of applied science programs that typically provide their foundation, CCB programs make extensive use of hands-on learning, learning by doing, and work-integrated learning. As the fields of the degrees are defined by the world of practice rather than by the organization of academic disciplines, learning often tends to begin "as an outgrowth of practical problems and situations and progresses, depending on the intensity of focus, toward more general knowledge" (Walker & Floyd, 2005, p. 97).

The conclusions of Moodie et al. (forthcoming) regarding the nature of applied baccalaureate programs in Ontario colleges of applied arts and technology also fit baccalaureate programs of American community colleges. According to Moodie et al., applied knowledge in these programs derives from two sources: "disciplinary knowledge, recontextualized for a field of practice," and the field's "established rules and practices which have been restructured as systematic procedural knowledge" (Moodie et al., in press). Moodie et al. note that college baccalaureate programs play a particularly important role in systematizing rules and procedures of practice for emerging occupations that do not yet have existing institutions to systematize such knowledge.

IMPACT OF THE COMMUNITY COLLEGE BACCALAUREATE

There has been relatively little empirical research on the impact of the CCB. Graduate dissertations constitute a particularly important source of information on this impact, and quite helpful surveys of dissertation research—which were a valuable resource for the preparation of this chapter—have been provided by Hrabak (2009) and Liu, Simpson, and Adam (2017).

After a little more than two decades, the CCB movement is still at a relatively early stage of development. Although there is at least one community college involved in CCB activity in twenty states, in the majority of these states the numbers of institutions and programs are very small. In only two states—Florida and Washington—can it be said that baccalaureate programs have a major presence in systems of independent community colleges.

While the overall impact of the CCB at the national level is limited by its modest scale, specific impacts can still be significant. Although there has to date been only a small amount of research on the impact of the CCB, where it has been implemented the CCB appears to have

- increased the output of new teachers and nurses, especially in Florida (Daun-Barnett, 2011; Manias, 2007; Neuhard, 2013);
- made the baccalaureate more accessible to students who would not otherwise have been able to attain it (Manias, 2007), especially those with high financial need (Neuhard, 2013);

- enabled people to advance their education without having to leave their communities and enabled communities to retain educated workers (Bragg & Soler, 2017; State of California, 2017; Grothe, 2009); and
- helped employers find workers who possess both the technical and non-technical skills employers need (Grothe, 2009).

While there has been very little research on employment outcomes of CCB graduates, there is some evidence that CCB programs have enabled community college students to significantly increase their earning power compared to what it would have been with an associate degree (Kaikkonen & Quarles, 2018). One study reported that in the short term, employment outcomes for CCB graduates are comparable to those of graduates of traditional baccalaureate programs (Cominole, 2017).

Much of the research on the impact of the CCB has focused on the changes that occurred when an institution that had not previously offered bachelor's degree programs began to offer them. Many of these changes were found in institutions that offered only a small number of bachelor's degree programs:

- Many institutions dropped the word *community* from their names, changing the names to "state college" or just "college" (Floyd & Falconetti, 2013).
- While often the new bachelor's degree programs have been built on existing associate degree programs, in some cases the bachelor's degree programs have replaced associate degree programs (State of California, 2017).
- In several cases the entire institution's general education curriculum has been revamped to give it the depth and complexity appropriate to support bachelor's degree programs (Hofland, 2011).
- Generally, institutions have enhanced library resources, academic support services, and financial assistance (Ames, 2015; Hofland, 2011; Martinez, 2018).
- The impact on faculty has been mixed, with many welcoming the challenge of upper division teaching and others concerned about possible loss of status because they do not possess a doctorate (Davis, 2012; Essink, 2013).
- Introduction of baccalaureate programs has helped to strengthen the entire workforce development function of the community college (Hernandez, 2014).

FUTURE OF THE COMMUNITY COLLEGE BACCALAUREATE

Starting with just a few institutions before 2000, the number of CCB institutions (including institutions with the word *university* in their names) has grown to 136 by July 2018. The growth of the CCB might have been even greater if not for two factors: the tight control exercised by state legislatures and regulatory agencies, and uncertainty among prospective students about how employers may perceive the community college bachelor's degree.

In most states where there has been some adoption of the CCB, approval was given initially to only a limited number of community colleges and for only a limited number of programs. For example, in Texas three community colleges were given authorization in 2003 to offer up to five bachelor's degree programs each, but subsequently the Texas Higher Education Coordinating Board recommended that CCB programs should be allowed only as a last resort, and by 2013 only four CCB programs had been approved at the three institutions (Russell, 2013).

Not until 2017 was a bill enacted that would allow an expansion of the CCB in applied sciences, applied technology, and nursing, but that bill limits an individual college to no more than three baccalaureate programs. Where state restrictions on numbers have been eased, for example in the state of Washington, the expansion has been considerable, suggesting the potential for substantial growth.

While students have expressed gratitude to community colleges for making bachelor's degree programs more accessible, they also worry about the marketability of the degrees (Bragg & Soler, 2017). Students seem to be attracted to the idea of an applied bachelor's degree offered in the friendly confines of the community college environment, but they are unsure about whether employers and other educational institutions will view the CCB as a "normal" bachelor's degree. Consequently, some CCB programs that have received state approval have not been able to start due to insufficient numbers of students.

Moodie (2009) has suggested that in regard to questions of this type, there is often a tipping point after which new forms and practices that were regarded as novel and unproven become accepted. It is difficult to say exactly where this tipping point occurs. For example, one might ask whether now that community colleges in Florida account for about 10 percent of bachelor's degrees awarded by public institutions, their degrees are considered "normal" bachelor's degrees.

The two barriers noted here may to some extent be interdependent. That is, states may be more inclined to allow expansion of the CCB the more they see students voting with their feet for these degrees. On the other hand, the steady increase in the number of institutions awarding bachelor's degrees and in the numbers of programs they offer may help prospective students overcome any ambivalence they may have about enrolling in a new type of bachelor's degree program. In addition, data on positive employment outcomes of graduates may help students and regulatory agencies overcome whatever misgivings they have about community college bachelor's degrees.

It is not possible to construct a time series showing the growth of CCB programs because the historical data that are available are based on different definitions and reflect different data sources and coverage. Even if it could be constructed, such a time series of data points might be of limited value because the growth of the CCB has depended upon key policy decisions in different states, decisions that often were the result of unpredictable and idiosyncratic factors.

A single decision that could have major implications for the growth of the CCB is the policy stance that California will take with respect to community college bachelor's degrees at the conclusion of the pilot project that was initiated in 2014. Similarly, the growth of the CCB over the next decade could be influenced significantly by whether states such as Texas and Michigan ease restrictions on numbers of programs and whether other states such as Illinois and Arizona decide to allow their community colleges to award baccalaureate degrees.

The factors that appear to have driven the growth of the CCB over the past two decades are likely to continue and perhaps even strengthen in the coming decade, suggesting the likelihood of continued and possibly substantial growth in the CCB activity. These factors are

- concern about the costs of bachelor's degrees in universities;
- concern about America's need for a more highly educated workforce, both as a function of increased demands on workers in a knowledge society and to remain competitive with other countries that have been increasing their levels of educational attainment; and
- concern about disparities in baccalaureate degree attainment between members of more privileged groups and groups that historically have been underserved by universities.

There are many other issues for the future of the CCB besides its scale. This chapter concludes by noting five important challenges for policy, practice, and research:

- *Equity considerations*: Little is yet known about how successful the CCB has been in enabling members of groups that historically have been underserved by four-year institutions to earn a baccalaureate and enjoy the career success that has been associated with baccalaureate attainment. Progress along this dimension needs to be monitored, and policies and practices may have to be devised that will realize the potential of the CCB to improve opportunities for underserved groups.

• *Reshaping community college missions*: Although the CCB was originally intended as a "simple" addition to a community college's mission, its adoption appears to be having an unanticipated impact on institutions. There is a dearth of knowledge about how the activity profiles and priorities of institutions have evolved after offering CCBs. For example, what has the increased emphasis on advanced career and technical education meant for the vitality of the academic transfer function? How many of the community colleges that are offering baccalaureate programs may for all practical purposes leave the community college sector over the next decade to become four-year colleges or some new type of hybrid postsecondary institution?

• *The research function in community colleges*: In other types of higher education institutions that offer bachelor's degree programs, research is a normal part of a professor's job. As the baccalaureate becomes a more prominent feature of community colleges, will there be pressure for faculty to be more involved in research, both to enhance their knowledge and skills and to provide opportunities for students to gain research experience?

• *Postgraduate study*: The CCB is not intended to be a terminal educational credential, but little is known about the admissibility of CCB graduates to university postgraduate programs and professional programs that require an undergraduate degree for admission. What policies might be necessary to ensure that CCB graduates have access to additional opportunities to advance their education? Is it conceivable that community colleges that have a successful track record in offering applied bachelor's degree programs may be allowed also to offer applied master's programs, as their counterpart institutions in some other countries do?

• *Internationalization*: To date the CCB has developed as a pragmatic American solution to an American problem, in isolation from other countries that have experienced similar developments. In contemplating future development of the CCB, might it be helpful to interact more with comparable institutions in other countries—for example, through the World Congress of Colleges and Polytechnics—and consider such initiatives as international exchanges for faculty and students and collaborative programs with institutions in other countries?

CONCLUSION

The CCB is a highly innovative idea that was developed by passionate leaders who advocated for increased access to bachelor's degrees locally, especially in applied and workforce fields. That has been the hallmark of the CCB: meeting community needs and providing access. It is also the hallmark of the community college's egalitarian mission.

While this idea has already had a noticeable impact, there is a long way to go to realize its potential. Enabling community colleges to award baccalaureate degrees has done much to expand access in the states where a substantial number of community colleges have been authorized to award baccalaureate degrees and many CCB programs are being offered. However, the majority of states still do not allow the CCB, and in many of the states that do allow it there are stringent limits on the number and types of baccalaureate degrees that may be offered.

It appears that the CCB has been particularly effective in opening doors to the baccalaureate for place-bound students who might not otherwise have access to a bachelor's degree program, and there is some indication that it has been of benefit to students for whom ability to pay is a barrier to baccalaureate study. The CCB has also greatly increased access to applied and workforce baccalaureate degrees, since that is the focus of most of the degrees.

A novel discovery of the research undertaken for this chapter is that a quarter of baccalaureate/associate institutions identified here as CCB providers are campuses of universities (or colleges with the word *university* in their names), and these campuses account for nearly half of all CCB programs. A valuable project for future research would be to compare the baccalaureate programming of independent community colleges with that of university-affiliated colleges with respect to such matters as access, graduation rates, the student experience, or labor market outcomes for CCB graduates.

Early critics of the movement called it "mission creep," but increasingly the CCB has been seen as a natural evolution, building on the community colleges' mission to serve the needs of the geographic areas of which they are part and to afford access to programs for students who might not otherwise be able to seek an advanced degree. The CCB may be viewed as a revolutionary concept, for it has major implications for most aspects of the community college and for its relationship with other types of postsecondary institutions.

To be sure, there are many unanswered questions surrounding the CCB, some of which are noted previously. Some of the most important questions are: How will these degrees be viewed by university graduate schools, and are CCB graduates viewed as academically prepared for graduate admission? What is the impact of the CCB on meeting local workforce needs, and how are these graduates viewed by employers? What impact have these new CCB degrees had on the mission of the community college and on its other programs and functions, including funding? What are the lessons learned from states and colleges that have offered the CCB, and how can these lessons be utilized to improve policy and assist those considering the CCB?

Evolutionary and revolutionary: the CCB is no longer just an idea whose time has come; it is a very present reality. And while it may be a natural evolution of the community college mission, it requires a new way of looking at how programs are delivered and who delivers them. Change is always replete with challenges. Going forward, the CCB movement will require proactive and visionary leadership to tackle such change and such challenges. By 2030, will most American two-year community colleges have been authorized to offer baccalaureate degrees? Time will tell.

REFERENCES

Ames, S. I. (2015). *Developmental stages of community colleges and their employees that emerge as a result of offering an applied baccalaureate degree* (Unpublished doctoral dissertation). Fielding Graduate University, Santa Barbara, CA.

Bragg, D., & Ruud, C. (2012). Why applied baccalaureates appeal to working adults: From national results to promising practices. In D. L. Floyd, R. A. Felsher, & A. M. Falconetti (Eds.), Applied and workforce baccalaureates [Special issue]. *New Directions for Community Colleges, 158,* 73–86.

Bragg, D. D., & Soler, M. C. (2017). Policy narratives on applied baccalaureate degrees: Implications for student access to and progression through college in the United States. *Journal of Vocational Education & Training, 69*(1), 123–146.

The Carnegie Classification of Institutions of Higher Education. (n.d.-a). *Undergraduate Instructional Program classification.* Retrieved from http://carnegieclassifications.iu.edu/classification_descriptions/ugrad_program.php

The Carnegie Classification of Institutions of Higher Education. (n.d.-b). *Undergraduate Instructional Program methodology.* Retrieved from http://carnegieclassifications.iu.edu/methodology/ugrad_program.php

College Board. (2008). *Coming to our senses: Education and the American future.* New York: Author.

Cominole, M. B. (2017). *Employment outcomes for graduates of Washington state's applied baccalaureate degree programs* (Unpublished doctoral dissertation). North Carolina State University, Raleigh.

Daun-Barnett, N. (2011). Community college baccalaureate: A fixed effects, multi-year study of the influence of state policy on nursing degree production. *Higher Education Policy, 24*(3), 377–398.

Davis, K. A. (2012). *Faculty perception of educational innovation as it pertains to the community college baccalaureate degree* (Unpublished doctoral dissertation). Capella University, Minneapolis, MN.

Essink, S. E. (2013). *The community college baccalaureate: A mixed methods study of implementation and best practices* (Unpublished doctoral dissertation). University of Nebraska, Lincoln.

Floyd, D. L. (2005). Community college baccalaureate in the US: Models, programs and issues. In D. L. Floyd, M. L. Skolnik, & K. P. Walker (Eds.), *The community college baccalaureate: Emerging trends and policy issues* (pp. 25–47). Sterling, VA: Stylus Publishing.

Floyd, D. L. (2006). Achieving the baccalaureate through the community college. In D. D. Bragg & E. A. Barnett (Eds.), *Academic pathways to and from the community college: New directions for community colleges.* San Francisco, CA: Jossey-Bass.

Floyd, D. L., & Falconetti, A. M. G. (2013). The baccalaureate movement in Florida: A decade of change. In N. Remington & R. Remington (Eds.), *Alternative pathways to the baccalaureate* (pp. 85–107). Sterling, VA: Stylus Publishing.

Floyd, D. L., Falconetti, A. M. G., & Felsher, R. A. (2012). Applied and workforce baccalaureate models. *New Directions for Community Colleges, 158,* 5–12.

Floyd, D. L., Falconetti, A. M. G., & Hrabak, M. R. (2009). Baccalaureate community colleges: The new Florida system. *Community College Journal of Research & Practice, 33*(2), 195–202.

Floyd, D. L., Felsher, R. A., & Catullo. L. (2012). Graduate education issues and challenges: Community college applied and workforce baccalaureates. In D. L. Floyd, R. A. Felsher, & A. M. Falconetti (Eds.), *Applied and workforce baccalaureates: New directions for community colleges.* San Francisco, CA: Jossey-Bass.

Floyd, D. L., Skolnik, M. L., & Walker, K. P. (Eds.). (2005). *The community college baccalaureate: Emerging trends and policy issues.* Sterling, VA: Stylus Publishing.

Floyd, D. L., & Walker, D. A. (2003). Community college teacher education: A typology, challenging issues, and state views. *Community College Journal of Research and Practice, 27*(8), 643–663.

Floyd, D. L., & Walker, K. P. (2005). Applied and workforce baccalaureates. In D. L. Floyd, M. L. Skolnik, & K. P. Walker (Eds.), *The community college baccalaureate: Emerging trends and policy issues* (pp. 95–102). Sterling, VA: Stylus Publishing.

Floyd, D. L., & Walker, K. P. (2009). The community college baccalaureate: Putting the pieces together. *Community College Journal of Research and Practice, 33*(2), 90–124.

Fulton, M. (2015, April). *Community colleges expanding role into awarding bachelor's degrees.* ECS Education Policy Analysis. Retrieved from https://www.ecs.org/wp-content/uploads/State-Information-Request_Community-College-Bachelors-Degrees.pdf

Fulton, M. (2018, May 1). Response to information request, Education Commission of the States. Retrieved from https://www.ecs.org/wp-content/uploads/State-Information-Request_Community-College-Bachelors-Degrees.pdf

Furlong, T. E. (2005). St. Petersburg College. In D. L. Floyd, M. L. Skolnik, & K. P. Walker (Eds.), *The community college baccalaureate: Emerging trends and policy issues* (pp. 103–128). Sterling, VA: Stylus Publishing.

Grothe, M. (2009). *The community college applied baccalaureate degree: Employers' and graduates' perspectives* (Unpublished doctoral dissertation). Oregon State University, Corvallis.

Hernandez, K. (2014). *Community college mission statements in an era of the new community college baccalaureate* (Unpublished doctoral dissertation). University of Miami, Miami, FL.

Hofland, B .S. (2011). *A case study of the community college baccalaureate: What happened in ten years?* (Unpublished doctoral dissertation). University of Nebraska, Lincoln.

Hrabak, M. R. (2009). The community college baccalaureate movement: Cutting-edge dissertation research. *Community College Journal of Research and Practice, 33*(2), 203–212.

Ignash, J. M. (2012). Articulation to and from the applied associate degree: Challenges and opportunities. In D. L. Floyd, R. A. Felsher, & A. M. Falconetti (Eds.), *Applied and workforce baccalaureate. New directions for community colleges.* San Francisco, CA: Jossey-Bass.

Kaikkonen, D. A., & Quarles, C. L. (2018). The effect on earnings of an applied baccalaureate degree. *Community College Review.* Retrieved from https://www.sbctc.edu/resources/documents/colleges-staff/research/bachelor-applied-science-research/effect-on-earnings-ab-degree-kaikkonen-and-quarles-v2.pdf

Koch, A. K., & Gardner, J. N. (2012). The comprehensive community college baccalaureates: An idea whose time has come. In N. Remington & R. Remington (Eds.), *Alternative pathways to the baccalaureate* (pp. 178–189). Sterling, VA: Stylus Publishing.

Levin, J. (2004). The community college as a baccalaureate-granting institution. *The Review of Higher Education, 26*(1), 1–22.

Liu, Q., Simpson, D., & Adam, E. (2017). Appendix 2: A review of theses on college baccalaureates. In L. Wheelahan, G. Moodie, M. L. Skolnik, Q. Liu, E. Adam, & D. Simpson, *CAAT baccalaureates: What has been their impact on students and colleges? Appendices* (pp. 18–25). Toronto: Centre for the Study of Canadian and International Higher Education, OISE-University of Toronto.

Lorenzo, A. L. (2005). The university center: A collaborative approach to baccalaureate degrees. In D. L. Floyd, M. L. Skolnik, & K. P. Walker (Eds.), *The community college baccalaureate: Emerging trends and policy issues* (pp. 73–93). Sterling, VA: Stylus Publishing.

Lumina Foundation. (2015). *Lumina's goal.* Retrieved from http://www.luminafoundation.org/goal_2025

Manias, N. (2007). *The baccalaureate colleges in Florida: A policy evaluation* (Unpublished doctoral dissertation). University of South Florida, Tampa.

Martinez, E. (2018). Changes, challenges, and opportunities for student services at one baccalaureate degree-granting community college. *Community College Review, 46*(1), 82–103. doi:10.1177/0091552117744049

Moodie, G. (2009). Australia: The emergence of dual sector universities. In N. Garrod & B. Macfarlane (Eds.), *Challenging boundaries: Managing the integration of post-secondary education* (pp. 59–76). London: Routledge.

Moodie, G., Skolnik, M. L., Wheelahan, L., Liu, Q., Simpson, D., & Adam, E. G. (2018). How are "applied degrees" applied in Ontario colleges of applied arts and technology? In M. Gallacher & F. Reeve (Eds.), *New frontiers for college education: International perspectives* (pp. 137–147). London: Routledge.

National Center for Education Statistics. (2018). Characteristics of degree-granting postsecondary institutions. Retrieved from https://nces.ed.gov/programs/coe/indicator_csa.asp

Neuhard, I. P. (2013). *Examining Florida's policy of expanding access through community college baccalaureate degrees: An analysis of enrollment trends, demographic characteristics, and systematic impacts* (Unpublished doctoral dissertation). University of Florida, Gainesville.

Pell Institute for the Study of Economic Opportunity. (2011). *Developing 20/20 vision on the 2020 degree attainment goal.* Retrieved from http://www.pellinstitute.org/downloads/publications-Developing_2020_Vision_May_2011.pdf

Remington, N., & Remington, R. (2013). *Alternative pathways to the baccalaureate: Do community colleges offer a viable solution to the nation's knowledge deficit?* Sterling, VA: Stylus Publishing.

Russell, A. B. (2013). Update on the community college baccalaureate. In N. Remington & R. Remington (Eds.), *Alternative pathways to the baccalaureate* (pp. 67–84). Sterling, VA: Stylus Publishing.

Shapiro, D., Dundar, A., Huie, F., Wakhungu, P. K., Yuan, X., Nathan, A., & Bhimdiwali, A. 2017. *Completing college: A national view of student attainment rates—fall 2011 cohort* (Signature Report No. 14). Herndon, VA: National Student Clearinghouse Research Center.

Skolnik, M. L. (2009). Theorizing about the emergence of the community college baccalaureate. *Community College Journal of Research and Practice, 33*(2), 125–150. doi:10.1080/10668920802564873

Skolnik, M. L. (2011). Re-conceptualizing the relationship between community colleges and universities, using a conceptual framework drawn from the study of jurisdictional conflict between professions. *Community College Review, 39*(4), 352–375. doi:10.1177/0091552111424205

Skolnik, M. L. (2013). Reflections on the nature and status of the applied baccalaureate degree. In N. Remington & R. Remington (Eds.), *Alternative pathways to the baccalaureate* (pp. 128–147). Sterling, VA: Stylus Publishing.

Skolnik, M. L. (2016a). How do quality assurance systems accommodate the differences between academic and applied higher education? *Higher Education, 71*(3), 371–378. doi:10.1007/s10734-015-9908-4

Skolnik, M. L. (2016b). Situating Ontario's colleges between the American and European models for providing opportunity for the attainment of baccalaureate degrees in applied fields of study. *Canadian Journal of Higher Education, 46*(1), 38–56.

Skolnik, M. L., Wheelahan, L., Moodie, G., Liu, Q., Adam, E., & Simpson, D. (2018). Exploring the potential contribution of college bachelor's degree programs in Ontario to reducing social inequality. *Policy Reviews in Higher Education,* 1–22. doi:10.1080/23322969.2018.1455532

State of California. (2017). *California community colleges: Interim evaluation of baccalaureate degree pilot program.* Sacramento, CA: Legislative Analyst's Office.

Townsend, B. K. (2002, April). *Terminal students do transfer*. Paper presented at the annual meeting of the American Association of Community Colleges, Seattle, Washington.

Townsend, B. K. (2005). A cautionary view. In D. L. Floyd, M. L. Skolnik, & K. P. Walker (Eds.), *The community college baccalaureate: Emerging trends and policy issues* (pp. 179–190). Sterling, VA: Stylus Publishing.

Townsend, B. K., Bragg, D. D., & Ruud, C. M. (2009). Development of the applied baccalaureate. *Community College Journal of Research and Practice, 33*(9), 586–705.

Walker, K. P. (2001). Opening the door to the baccalaureate degree. *Community College Review, 29*(2), 18–27.

Walker, K. P. (2005). History, rationale and community college baccalaureate association. In D. L. Floyd, M. L. Skolnik, & K. P. Walker (Eds.), *The community college baccalaureate: Emerging trends and policy issues* (pp. 9–23). Sterling, VA: Stylus Publishing.

Walker, K. P. & Floyd, D. L. (2005). Applied and workforce baccalaureates. In D. L. Floyd, M. L. Skolnik, & K. P. Walker (Eds.), *The community college baccalaureate: Emerging trends and policy issues* (pp. 95–102). Sterling, VA: Stylus Publishing.

Wattenbarger, J. (2000, April 17). Colleges should stick to what they do best. *The Community College Week*, pp. 4–5.

Wheelahan, L., Moodie, G., Billet, S., & Kelly, A. (2009). *Higher education in TAFE*. Adelaide, SA: National Centre for Vocational Education.

Wheelahan, L., Moodie, G., Skolnik, M. L., Liu, Q., Adam, E. G., & Simpson, D. (2017). *CAAT baccalaureates: What has been their impact on students and colleges?* Toronto: Centre for the Study of Canadian and International Higher Education, OISE-University of Toronto.

Part II

Ideas as Internal Functions

While the ideas in the previous section can be viewed as external national initiatives, the ideas in this section may be viewed as internal functions, since they are all key components of the basic structure of the comprehensive community college. Workforce education and developmental education have been core functions for decades. The first community college was located in a high school, and community colleges have created alliances and programs with high schools ever since.

As community colleges matured, they became more accountable to federal and state agencies, accrediting associations, and their own communities. Responding to these external pressures, community colleges created their own practices and programs of institutional effectiveness. And while demographics could be viewed as an external force, community colleges usually respond idiosyncratically, tailoring their own programs to the needs and characteristics of their own students.

The five ideas discussed in this section are similar to the five ideas in part I in that books, articles, toolkits, and guides have been written about how to implement them. Some of these ideas are also supported by national organizations, grants, and strong advocates. But they differ in that community colleges may choose to participate in the national initiatives identified in part I.

Community colleges have no choice about participation in the five areas discussed in this section; they must respond to demographics, build alliances with high schools, and create programs in workforce education, developmental education, and institutional effectiveness. These are long-term and bedrock ideas that provide a foundation for the contemporary community college, and recent developments in these areas continue to transform the community college world.

Chapter Six

Institutional Effectiveness

From Intuition to Evidence

Barbara Gellman-Danley and Eric V. Martin

Many will recall the phrase "community college movement," demonstrating the force behind the birth of two-year colleges and the passion that continues to fuel the sector to include its laser focus on student success. The mantra "community is our middle name" further speaks to the centrality of community colleges, emphasizing the importance of partnerships and regional engagement in sustaining their unique mission. With its focus on students and community, a sector once seen as the only alternative to those who might not get into a traditional college has become one of choice. The evolving purpose and growing importance of community colleges thus necessitates, now more than ever, measurable outcomes of success for the learners *and* for the institution itself.

In light of this central importance, public and government officials alike are increasingly asking for institutions to demonstrate their effectiveness and that such institutional effectiveness (IE) be rooted in evidence and not mere intuition. Community colleges are working together to meet this demand, as they always have, despite the rising challenges to American higher education. From the "learner-centered college" to Achieving the Dream (ATD), Guided Pathways, the completion agenda, and the Voluntary Framework of Accountability (VFA), the nation's community colleges are taking the journey toward IE seriously and transforming themselves in the process. The complexities of this journey bear further analysis.

This chapter undertakes such analysis with several ambitious aims. Specifically, it describes the rise of IE for regional accrediting agencies and community colleges alike, conveys IE success stories and real-world challenges identified in a survey of the Higher Learning Commission's (HLC's) community colleges, and offers recommendations to inform next steps on the road to IE.

FROM QUALITY IMPROVEMENT
TO INSTITUTIONAL EFFECTIVENESS

While it may not have been labeled at that time, the goal of continuous improvement inspired early community college leaders and their successors. In recent years a shift from quality improvement to IE on community college campuses has become evident as astute institutional leaders and their trustees—often leaders from industry and health care themselves—are versed in theories of continuous quality improvement (CQI). These leaders seek to move beyond CQI (an often-amorphous activity) to specific measures of effectiveness such that quality is demonstrably improved and open to external validation. This same movement, from the broader concept of quality improvement to the specific activities of IE, has been under way among the regional accreditors, stemming from the historical underpinning of regional accreditation, and evident in the accreditors' current criteria and standards.

Historical Progression and Current Standards

The assurance of quality has been the focus of regional accreditation for more than a century. According to Ewell (2008), during the originating years of regional accreditation, the focus among elite institutions was to "recognize and distinguish colleges of quality" through a process of *peer affirmation*, as opposed to modern-day *peer review* (p. 21). This early approach defined regional accreditation for many years until it began to be replaced in 1913 by strict quantitative measures of quality in the form of the institution's enrollment, the number of departments at the institution, the qualifications of its faculty, and the number of volumes in the library (Ewell, 2008).

In 1934, following a series of what they called "experiments," the North Central Association (NCA, now known as the Higher Learning Commission) adopted an entirely new approach to accreditation in response to the rise and increasing diversification of institutions of higher learning (Ewell, 2008). According to Davis in 1945, through its new approach toward accreditation the NCA recognized that "an institution should be judged in terms of the purposes it seeks to serve" (cited in Ewell, 2008, p. 31).

This emergence, as Ewell (2008) explains, created the first mission-based approach to accreditation, in which the holistic judgment of institutional functions across varying institutional contexts replaced strict adherence to the previous quantitative measures of quality applied uniformly to all institutions. He summarizes: "From 1934 onward, in what would eventually become the dominant posture for the regionals, the process of accreditation was intended primarily to help colleges and universities improve" (Ewell, 2008, p. 31).

Today the clearest indications of regional accreditors' commitment to institutional quality and their visible progression toward IE reside in their respective criteria and standards. A complete listing of these indicators is beyond the scope of this chapter, but the following illustrate this point:

- From the Higher Learning Commission (HLC), subcomponent 5.D.2.: "The institution learns from its operational experience and applies that learning to improve its institutional effectiveness, capabilities, and sustainability, overall and in its component parts" (Higher Learning Commission, 2014, para. 32).
- From the Middle States Commission on Higher Education (MSCHE), standard VI: "An accredited institution possesses and demonstrates the following attributes or activities . . . periodic assessment of the effectiveness of planning, resource allocation, institutional renewal processes, and availability of resources" (Middle States Commission on Higher Education, 2015, p. 12).
- From the New England Association of Schools and Colleges (NEASC), standard 2.2: "The institution systematically collects and uses data necessary to support its planning efforts and to enhance institutional effectiveness" (New England Association of Schools and Colleges, 2016, para. 18).
- From the Northwest Commission on Colleges and Universities (NWCCU), standard 4.A.1.: "The institution engages in ongoing systematic collection and analysis of meaningful, assessable, and verifiable data . . . as the basis for evaluating the accomplishment of its core theme objectives" (Northwest Commission on Colleges and Universities, 2017, p. 35).
- From the Southern Association of Colleges and Schools Commission on Colleges (SACSCOC), section 7.1: "The institution engages in ongoing, comprehensive, and integrated research-based planning and evaluation processes that (a) focus on institutional quality and effectiveness and (b) incorporate a systematic review of institutional goals and outcomes consistent with its mission" (Southern Association of Colleges and Schools Commission on Colleges, 2017, p. 19).
- From the Western Association of Schools and Colleges (WASC): "The institution considers the changing environment of higher education in envisioning its future. These activities inform both institutional planning and systematic evaluations of educational effectiveness" (Western Association of Schools and Colleges, 2013).

The requirements of the Accrediting Commission for Community and Junior Colleges (ACCJC) are particularly instructive, as it is the only accreditor working exclusively with community and junior colleges. Its requirements related to quality improvement and IE are conveyed in standard I.B.9.: "The institution engages in continuous, broad based, systematic evaluation and planning. [It] integrates program review, planning, and resource allocation into a comprehensive process that leads to accomplishment of its mission and improvement of institutional effectiveness and academic quality" (Accrediting Commission for Community and Junior Colleges, 2014, p. 3).

Later, in standard IV.B.1., ACCJC underscores the role of the CEO regarding IE: "The CEO provides effective leadership in planning, organizing, budgeting, selecting and developing personnel, and assessing institutional effectiveness" (2014, p. 15).

HIGHER LEARNING COMMISSION SURVEY OF COMMUNITY COLLEGES ON INSTITUTIONAL EFFECTIVENESS

The similarity of the regional accreditors' standards related to IE signal the very form of unity that they are often said to lack. That unity is mirrored in the community college sector, where institutions share a commitment and approach to improving and demonstrating their effectiveness; as among the accreditors, however, there is not necessarily one way to measure effectiveness.

The question that remains today is how, if at all, institutional effectiveness can be measured in ways that support the mission of community colleges *and* the concomitant increasing demands of the communities they serve. In order to explore this issue, the HLC formulated a member survey in the summer of 2018. The commission emailed 858 representatives at two-year institutions within its nineteen-state region and received 115 completed surveys (a response rate of 13.4 percent), which included presidents, provosts, academic deans, and those responsible for IE.

Findings

Survey respondents were first asked, "Has institutional effectiveness been appropriately defined in the higher education community?" The revelation that only 20 percent agreed that there was such an understanding does not come as a surprise. A resounding 41.7 percent said "no," and the institutional representatives provided several reasons, discussed later in this chapter. Another 28.7 percent responded "maybe," and the other 9.57 percent stated that they simply did not know. As with accreditors, community college personnel know quality assurance when they see it, and they are quick to point out when it is failing. The same applies to IE. One explanation about the lack of clarity on a shared definition is given by Seymour and Bourgeois (2018) in the *Institutional Effectiveness Fieldbook*: "The challenge of defining institutional effectiveness is largely due to its not being a smaller, more circumscribed idea. Instead, IE is a boundary-buster that infringes on organizational turf and defies the pigeonholing that makes organization life easier for many individuals. But that more robust, cross-functional aspect is also what makes it a powerful force for creating coherence and driving positive change" (p. 11). External perceptions and political challenges add further complications. For example, the nation's community colleges are frequently challenged on completion rates as a means of demonstrating IE. Yet it is difficult *not* to be defensive when sitting in front of a congressional committee whose members quote the low completion rate of 10 percent for community college students, despite the fact that context and limited data might present a very different story.

Bailey, Jaggars, and Jenkins (2015) depict the challenges well, stating that "while these colleges have helped educate millions, it is also true that many, probably a majority, of students who enter higher education through a community college do not achieve their long-term educational objectives" (p. vi). They point out that despite this they found

> no deficiencies in the enthusiasm, dedication, or skill of the faculty and staff of community colleges, but rather observe problems in the structure of the colleges and of the overall system of higher education – a structure that may have served this country well in the 1960s and 1970s when community colleges were a core part of the nation's effort to dramatically expand access to higher education, but which is not well suited to the needs and challenges they now confront. (2015, p. vii)

Accepting these challenges, HLC's survey asked respondents for their own definition of IE, ways to measure it, and best practices. Examples of these definitions and responses follow:

- The extent to which an institution has vision, processes, procedures, and outcomes to ensure student success and continuous improvement (Arapahoe Community College, CO).
- Using data and nondata methods to explore an institution's strengths and weaknesses and then develop strategies to improve. Consistent evaluation and use of results for improvement define institutional effectiveness (Clovis Community College, NM).
- Institutional effectiveness supports a culture of inquiry, evidence, accountability, and continuous improvement related to all college functions and activities (Gateway Technical College, WI).
- Institutional effectiveness is the degree to which the organization is achieving its mission-based objectives (Jackson College, MI).
- An organization's effectiveness is a product of its collective self-awareness, its propensity for self-evaluation and self-reflection, and its obses-

sion with achieving excellent results. For an institution to be truly effective, every single employee needs to be committed to actively improving performance (Kankakee Community College, IL).

- A systemic approach and organizational structure that provide meaningful information to the right stakeholders at the right time, guiding strategic direction and resource allocation to achieve high-quality institutional outcomes (Maricopa Community Colleges–Rio Salado Community College, AZ).
- IE escapes definition until the institution type is clearly defined. Generally, IE is defined as meeting the tenets for why the entity was created in the first place. IE measures the success of aligning the institution's mission and goals in respect to the founding tenets (Northeast Community College, NE).
- Institutional effectiveness is the result of the college reaching or exceeding its measurable goals and objectives as defined and informed by the college's mission and vision and external legal and accreditation expectations (Northwest Arkansas Community College, AR).
- With decreased state funding of community colleges, as is seen in Illinois, an effective institution would be one that just stays open (Sauk Valley Community College, IL).
- We believe that institutional effectiveness is a journey, a very exciting, and very rewarding journey (Southeast Technical Institute, SD).

One respondent to HLC's survey perhaps best conveyed the need for a clear definition and commonly understood framework for IE: "I run an IR/IE department, and I can't explain it in a way that the intelligent layman would understand." Yet even against this stark backdrop, widespread belief in the central importance of IE and commitment to its success, particularly among institutional leaders, will likely ensure its long-term success. Other research has revealed the necessary groundwork taking shape.

The commitment of institutional leaders to the success of IE has been documented by Bartolini, Knight, Carrigan, Fujidea, LaFleur, and Lyddon (2016, p. 4) in a study in which they interviewed twelve leaders, including current presidents, presidents emeritus, a chancellor, and a provost, all of whom represented a variety of institutional types. Although the interviewees varied in terms of the adoption of IE on their respective campuses, all agreed on its importance. Among their results, Bartolini et al. (2016, p. 4) stated:

Participants identified advantages of the IE model as improved effectiveness and efficiency of decision making; improved institutional accountability and ability to establish priorities; the ability to carry out benchmarking and identify best practices; greater timeliness, accuracy and richness of evidence; durability of decision support processes; better connection of people and systems; heightened ability to focus on student success; and the potential to influence policy.

The only disadvantage cited was the difficulty in identifying candidates for the chief institutional effectiveness officer position who possess the necessary skill set.

As seen in the earlier listing, respondents to HLC's survey voiced similar support for IE. At the same time, they provided additional insights into the confusion about IE, its location at a college, and required skill sets:

- I meet a lot of people with IE in their titles, and we all do a wide variety of different tasks, which leads me to believe that IE is more of a catchall function than a clearly defined specialty (Gateway Technical College, WI).
- I think this term means many things to many different groups. There is no cohesive meaning across all higher education sectors/institutions (Hutchinson Community College, KS).
- It's a great term, but it seems to have different meanings for different people. Some measure effectiveness by processes, and the extent to which those processes are mapped. Some measure effectiveness by student achievement in a particular course or program (Iowa Lakes Community College, IA).
- It seems that each institution has come up with its own definition (Pikes Peak Community College, CO).
- There are many measures to evaluate the effectiveness of a college or university. While scholars have pondered the question, a unified definition seems to continue to escape us (University of Cincinnati, Clermont College, OH).

Even with such core considerations unresolved, the community colleges that responded to the survey suggested a variety of current practices and ideas firmly rooted in IE. The ideas fell into five categories: (1) the crucial role of leadership in advancing IE and the organizational culture; (2) integrating IE into strategic planning priorities and mission; (3) the impact of accreditation and the resultant alignment of quality assurance with IE, and focusing on that agenda after being "inspired" by accreditation requirements; (4) organizational structure, reengineering the community college to create a centralized office of IE, and assuring participation across the college; and (5) externally initiated programs that support and influence institutional effectiveness programs and measures.

1. Leadership and Organizational Culture

Several survey responses focused on the essential role of leadership in moving toward and sustaining IE and improvement activities on a campus:

- We have started the concept of a working strategic plan that included specific targets and key performance indicators that are measurable. The plan is discussed annually with the leadership team, and data are presented for each item. This allows for a structured, data-driven approach to institutional planning. It helps to focus the leaders of the institution on the strategic goals and allows for progress toward these goals to be examined annually (Connors State College, OK).
- The new president brought CQI principles and created KPIs (key performance indicators) and dashboards. Things expanded from there, with metrics in strategic planning, development of a Strategic Enrollment Management (SEM) plan, and program review processes. Many of these were being done for reporting purposes, but the institution did not have the focus (McHenry County College, IL).
- One element of our institutional effectiveness involves student completion. To that end, we have established 90/80/70 goals—i.e., 90 percent student fall-winter persistence; 80 percent student fall-fall persistence, and 70 percent student achievement of a credential of market value, transfer, or employment. The idea was a collective one emanating from the president, board, and leadership council that resulted in our "Total Commitment to Student Success" (TCS^2), which governs all of our work (Jackson College, MI).
- As a newly appointed president, I was concerned about the college's graduation and retention rates. So we began a college-wide goal to improve both categories. An institutional effectiveness team was formed that is comprised of faculty, administrators, professional support, classified staff, and the director of institutional research. The board of trustees is updated monthly on the progress. We benchmarked the data and began to identify issues and barriers that currently existed. Our graduation rate in 2012–2013 was 22 percent and in 2015–2016 increased to 51 percent (Spoon River College, IL).

2. Strategic Planning and Mission

Many survey responses linked planning and mission to IE:

- When reviewing our last strategic planning cycle in the spring of 2014, we determined that based on our assessment cycle we needed to establish and measure and ultimately improve our institutional KPIs that flowed down to the department, program, class, and individual levels (Carl Sandburg College, IL).
- In 2011, as part of the strategic planning process, the institution recognized an opportunity to improve academic advising services. The college

turned the opportunity into a strategic priority (Pikes Peak Community College, CO).

- The effectiveness of an institution is based upon its ability to execute its mission. The implementation and monitoring has taken place in the measurement of the key outcomes defined by the mission (Dunwoody College of Technology, MN).
- Faculty training, focus groups, and team meetings were part of the implementation process to ensure understanding, feedback, and buy-in. The power of the Strategic Improvement Process (SIP) indicators was the linkage to key measures on the strategic plan, making the connection between performance at the classroom level [and] the college level very clear and important to the entire college community and ultimately to individual performance. The SIP plans are key elements of the Fox Valley's Strategic Alignment Model (Fox Valley Technical College, WI).

3. *The Impact of Accreditation and Quality Assurance*

Institutional responses highlighted linkages between IE efforts and accreditation activities, including HLC's elective programs (the Assessment Academy and the Persistence and Completion Academy, now known as the Student Success Academy), as well as the Academic Quality Improvement Program (AQIP)—an accreditation pathway that will soon sunset after nearly two decades of fostering institutional success. In all cases, a "culture of evidence" validates effectiveness:

- Based on HLC visiting team recommendations, we are changing from an institutional research model to an institutional effectiveness model. We modified our operational plans to include ways of measuring our success from simply reporting the results to rating each element's effectiveness. These ratings culminate in scores that can be compared to find areas of weakness upon which to improve (Labette Community College, KS).
- HLC's Assessment Academy brought us together with other schools facing the same challenges—this is the real support—making connections with other schools and developing relationships in which we support one another (Lac Courte Oreilles Ojibwa Community College, WI).
- The work evolved out of accreditation requirements, the IR [institutional research] function, and the need for integrated planning and alignment between the executive leadership at the college and the functional areas of the college. Our institutional definition encompasses IR, assessment, compliance, accreditation, grants, analytics, and development. We worked with all deans and leadership faculty. The president has supported the direction and funded these roles consistently (Maricopa Community Colleges–Rio Salado Community College, AZ).

- To address issues of retention and completion, our school established a Center for Student Success in 2014. All outreach and services to students experiencing difficulties are coordinated. Each student is assigned a Student Success Coach. Data are used to ascertain the effectiveness of individual strategies. Implementation was driven by our involvement in the HLC Persistence & Completion Academy. Our retention increased by 7 percentage points in one year to an all-time high of 82 percent (Mitchell Technical Institute, SD).
- In 2009 one of Moraine Valley's AQIP Action Project teams developed and implemented the college's Continuous Improvement Objective Results (CIOR) process, designed to connect planning, budgeting, measuring effectiveness, and reporting on how results were used to continuously improve processes. In 2016 a second AQIP Action Project team developed and implemented a new planning process entitled Plan, Evaluate, and Improve (PIE) to replace the CIOR process. This is the team that developed the college's definition of institutional effectiveness. In January 2017 the college also formed a team charged with defining Strategic Priority Indicators (SPIs). These institutional-level SPIs serve as a means of tracking the college's goal of becoming a more data-informed decision-making entity. The PIE process has now been institutionalized and is again being used for FY19 planning, and departments were encouraged to use SPI data, as appropriate, when developing their FY19 PIEs (Moraine Valley Community College, IL).

4. Organizational Reengineering

In this category, respondents commented on the organizational and structural changes stemming from the infusion of IE processes and activities. Many noted the importance of reengineering to assure success:

- Gateway created an integrated program effectiveness (PE) function within our institutional effectiveness division in 2013–2014. In response to faculty confusion over the requirements to measure student learning, maintain up-to-date curriculum, and participate in program review, we organized a team of staff who worked on those functions and designed a single process with integrated deadlines and common forms to clarify faculty's responsibilities. Each program also has a faculty PE chair with assigned hours to gather data and communicate with our office. Since we've started the process, we've maintained 100 percent participation in assessment of student learning (Gateway Technical College, WI).
- An Institutional Effectiveness Office has been designated to include institutional research, accreditation, and assessment for student learning. More recently assessment in nonacademic programs is being implemented. This

office is now part of the VP for student affairs administrative unit and reports directly to the president. This approach has worked effectively for creating an awareness of institutional effectiveness and a focus on improvement (North Dakota State College of Science, ND).

- About four years ago, our institution decided that we needed to create an official office for institutional effectiveness so that increased attention could be directed to the ever-increasing data needs including federal and state reporting. The Associate Vice President for Institutional Effectiveness is now also the AVP for Academic Affairs and has a full-time staff member to assist with data analysis. Locating the office under Academic Affairs allows for more visibility and collaboration (Rose State College, OK).

- The integrated and functional approach of IE professionals is a powerful agency for change at any college. Starting with an organizational structure to advance strategic outcomes has been a great learning experience for our college (Maricopa Community Colleges–Rio Salado Community College, AZ).

5. *Externally Initiated Programs*

A range of responses touched upon other externally initiated programs such as ATD, Guided Pathways, the completion agenda, Complete College America (CCA), or simply placing IE functions on a campus under the umbrella of performance-based funding in states. Achieving the Dream is discussed first, followed by survey responses.

In 2004 the Lumina Foundation launched Achieving the Dream: Community Colleges Count. This initiative was explicitly designed to improve outcomes, including helping academically underprepared students succeed at college-level work, increasing semester-to-semester persistence, and improving rates of degree completion (Bailey et al., 2015, p. 7). Bailey and colleagues explain:

> The experience of the ATD initiative during its first five to seven years provides a good picture of the state of community college reform in the first decade of the twenty-first century, just as the completion agenda took hold. The initiative was explicitly designed to increase the academic success of community college students by building a "culture of evidence" in which administrators, faculty, and others would use data to identify barriers to student success and develop reform strategies to overcome those identified barriers. The initiative assigned experienced administrators—usually retired community college presidents—as coaches for the participating colleges (2015, p. 8).

Accreditors require a culture of evidence versus the old "I know quality when I see it" intuitive approach. Guided Pathways is another way student success rates can improve. The guided pathways approach to redesign starts with students' end goals in mind, then rethinks and redesigns programs and support services to enable students to achieve those goals (Bailey et al., 2015, p. 16). HLC survey respondents noted these approaches and other external support ideas available to them:

- We carefully evaluate all student success programs. This began out of Achieving the Dream work and has continued in our Pathways and other student success programs. Success programs have an evaluation plan developed by the program leaders in collaboration with the Office of Institutional Effectiveness (OIE), and OIE provides templates to develop the plan and metrics to support the evaluation. We had a great deal of initial support in developing this from our ATD data coach (Columbus State Community College, OH).
- We took a great deal of time to collaboratively develop a Strategic Enrollment Management (SEM) plan in our continuous quality improvement process. We have followed Complete College America strategies and have developed a SEM plan with assistance from excellent consultants (Central Wyoming College, WY).
- The Completion Agenda has changed the measure for IE. Ohio's 100 percent performance-based funding provides IE metrics (Clark State Community College, OH).
- Our student success data (retention, graduation, transfer) [were] not getting better, so the president formed a student success task force. That ultimately led to participation in the AACC Pathways program and implementation of several Pathways initiatives (Front Range Community College, CO).
- We used our student outcomes assessment system as a guide, making our purpose statements into outcomes to be assessed. We then unified all the data gathering methods (internal, external, direct measures, indirect measures) into purpose statements—putting it all together in a dashboard. Folks are using the same data as we are—IPEDs, Noel-Levitz, community college benchmarking project, the Kansas study, etc. (Neosho County Community College, KS).
- We adopted the Degree Qualifications Profile (DQP) in 2011 and have been working to incorporate its outcomes into all of our courses and programs. We have been collecting assessment data on these efforts and can point to attainment of the DQP's outcomes as a measure of effectiveness (North Central Michigan College, MI).
- Our effort to improve academic advising was successful, as the 2015 CCSSE survey results indicated a statistically significant increase in usage

of and satisfaction with academic advising (Pikes Peak Community College, CO).

These examples reflect multistate collaboration among community colleges, often provided with external financial support. Many of the programs encourage a cohort approach, establishing important networking and shared goals, a great asset to the participating community colleges and those watching the results.

The final question of the survey asked participants if they were members of yet another nationwide initiative, the VFA, designed by the American Association of Community Colleges (AACC). Nearly one-third of respondents were members. Some benefits of participation include the development of pathways, revising advising systems, and benchmarking against other institutions. Completion and transfer data lead to more comprehensive and reliable figures than can be found in some federal databases.

Institutions participating in the VFA quickly learn that it tells the full story of their organization, including offering substantive insight into its successes and challenges. Regarding the latter, institutions are then able to identify the core areas on which quality improvement initiatives must focus.

In spite of its success, the number of institutions participating in the VFA remains low. Ideally, IE efforts across community college campuses will boost participation in the VFA, which in turn will maximize available data and deepen the growing portfolio of information to benefit other institutions. As is discussed in the next section, regional accrediting agencies are trying to assist in the overarching effort to amass useful data through collaborative research of their own that is focused on graduation rates and student success.

A SURVEY OF INSTITUTIONS
BY REGIONAL ACCREDITING AGENCIES

Whereas HLC's survey of member institutions provides examples of the changing winds of higher education and the obstacles that stand in the way of measuring institutional effectiveness, it did not address specific challenges related to student success and graduation rates. Suffice it to say, both are of central importance to regional accreditors and the institutions they recognize.

For this reason, the Council of Regional Accrediting Commissions (C-RAC) mobilized in 2018 to study the graduation rates of a cross-section of institutions and, especially important, the efforts of the institutions to increase their graduation rates even if in some cases those rates were already high. C-RAC's report, "A One-Year Review of the C-RAC's Graduation Rate Information Project," bears mention in this chapter because it can both align with and further inform the work being completed in elective programs such as those previously discussed. Moreover, C-RAC's study will be of interest to IE leaders on individual campuses who are taking on the challenge of low graduation rates.

Although discussing the detailed findings of the C-RAC study is beyond the scope of this chapter, the following bears mention here. The C-RAC study (2018, p. 26) found that all institutions are seeking to improve graduation rates by creating policies and procedures to address key issues, such as time to degree and stackable credentials; building programs, structures, and personnel to support student success through mandatory advising, summer bridge programs, and one-stop student support offices; and using software/technology to establish early warning systems for at-risk students. Most will agree that the success of these efforts at any institution will bear a strong correlation to the success of the institution's overall IE activity.

OBSERVATIONS AND RECOMMENDATIONS

As seen throughout this chapter, many strong initiatives are under way that are intended to help institutions improve their own effectiveness, with the common goal of improving student success. Both the HLC Survey and the C-RAC graduation rate study are modest means toward this same end. A telling insight expressed in the HLC survey was that, "Each year we spend more time and money on measures and I'm not certain measuring what we currently measure changes much. In the meantime, many students do great in spite of us, but other students leave worse than when they came" (Lamar Community College, CO).

While many respondents agree that there is a lack of clarity about the meaning of *student success* and how institutions must innovate to improve their effectiveness in this area, the commitment to success at community colleges remains unquestionable. Based on the wide range of inputs amassed for this narrative, here are six recommendations to help community colleges become more effective in meeting their goals:

1. Definition: Work collaboratively across the institution to agree upon a definition of institutional effectiveness and how it will be measured. Be certain all levels of the college and its stakeholders are aware of this definition and that all departments have an IE plan with measurable metrics. The plan should be created by staff from academic, student support, administrative, and all other units of the college. Submit reports on outcomes established each year, including plans for continuous improvement.
2. Leadership and organizational culture: Be certain that institutional effectiveness is a priority for the CEO and governing board. Make IE

part of the presidential review as well as the board's annual self-assessment. Demonstrate administrative and board support and intentional leadership in advancing the IE agenda.

3. Strategic planning and mission: Integrate IE into all strategic plans, including those of the institution, each department, and for individual employees. Tie the goals to metrics, including the budget. Assure that all goals align with the college's mission.

4. The impact of accreditation: Educate everyone at the institution about accreditation standards, criteria, and expectations, both regional and specialized, when appropriate. Shift thinking about accreditation as a mandatory requirement to its being a source for quality assurance and thought leadership. Work with accreditors to align IE initiatives. Participate in opportunities for learning from accreditors, including annual conferences, training opportunities, and participation as peer reviewers. Participation in peer review enables a win-win for the college, in that participants are giving back to the higher education community and learning a great deal for their own institutions.

5. Organizational reengineering: Identify organizational structures to elevate IE as a priority. Hire individuals with training, experience, and skills in IE. Carefully consider the reporting structure to position IE as an institutional priority.

6. Externally initiated programs: Participate in national initiatives and research available to strengthen IE for community colleges. Create a team of IE ambassadors to share knowledge from those programs as they are integrated across the college. Share success stories that might be leveraged into new initiatives across the country.

Community colleges are facing many challenges, including the complex issue of IE and moving from relying on intuition about success to a culture of evidence. While there are great variances across colleges, much can be learned by working collaboratively. Taking ownership of the IE agenda and outcomes is crucial. If colleges do not do this well, external stakeholders will impose their own standards. Embrace the excellent examples and success stories available across the sector, recognizing that the community college system in America is a unique and crucially important part of higher education. It is, indeed, a journey.

REFERENCES

Accrediting Commission for Community and Junior Colleges. (2014). *Eligibility requirements, accreditation standards, and commission policies.* Retrieved from https://accjc.org/eligibility-requirements-standards-policies/

Bailey, T. R., Jaggars, S. S., & Jenkins, D. (2015). *Redesigning America's community college: A clear path to student success.* Cambridge, MA: Harvard University Press.

Bartolini, B., Knight, W., Carrigan, S., Fujieda, E., LaFleur, M., & Lyddon, J. (2016). *Presidential perspectives on advancing the institutional effectiveness model.* Retrieved from https://www.ahee.org/files//2016/04/Presidential-Perspectives-on-Advancing-the-IEModel_AHEE_April_2016.pdf

Council of Regional Accrediting Commissions. (2018). *A one-year review of the C-RAC's graduation rate information project.* Retrieved from https://docs.wixstatic.com/ugd/68d6c2_5bc3e173acf242e585c4c07fc8660dd9.pdf

Ewell, P. (2008). *U.S. accreditation and the future of quality assurance.* Washington, DC: The Council for Higher Education Accreditation.

Higher Learning Commission. (2014). *Criteria for accreditation.* Retrieved from https://www.hlcommission.org/Policies/criteria-and-core-components.html

Middle States Commission on Higher Education. (2015). *Standards for accreditation and requirements of affiliation.* Retrieved from https://www.msche.org/standards/

New England Association of Schools and Colleges. (2016). *Standards for accreditation.* Retrieved from https://cihe.neasc.org/standards-policies/standards-accreditation/

Northwest Commission on Colleges and Universities. (2017). *Accreditation handbook.* Retrieved from http://www.nwccu.org/wp-content/uploads/2016/02/Accreditation-Handbook-2017-edition.pdf

Seymour, D., & Bourgeois, M. (2018). *Institutional effectiveness fieldbook: Creating coherence in colleges and universities.* Santa Barbara, CA: Olive Press Publishing.

Southern Association of Colleges and Schools Commission on Colleges. (2017). *The principles of accreditation: Foundations for quality enhancement.* Retrieved from http://www.sacscoc.org/pdf/2018PrinciplesOfAcreditation.pdf

Western Association of Schools and Colleges. (2013). *Handbook of accreditation 2013 revised.* Retrieved from https://www.wscuc.org/book/export/html/924

Chapter Seven

Recognition, Reform, and Convergence in Developmental Education

Bruce Vandal

Complete College America's report, "Remedial Education: Higher Education's Bridge to Nowhere," published in 2012, made a provocative and powerful case that remedial education—long viewed as a means of increasing access to higher education—did just the opposite, denying hundreds of thousands of students access to college-level math and English courses and ultimately decreasing the likelihood that they would ever earn a postsecondary credential.[1] Using data collected from CCA's Alliance of States, the report found that over 50 percent of new students entering community college enrolled in developmental education courses, and that low-income students and students of color were far more likely to be placed in developmental education than the general student population.

Over 67 percent of new entering black students, 58 percent of Hispanic students, and almost 65 percent of Pell-eligible students started their postsecondary experience in a sequence of one, two, three, or more courses they had to pay for and complete before having access to college-level math and English courses. Further, the report found that only 22 percent of students who enrolled in developmental education completed gateway courses within two years.

Most significantly, the report found that while students of color and low-income students were more likely to be placed in developmental education, they were less likely to complete gateway math and English courses than the overall population who enrolled in developmental education. The conclusion arrived at was that developmental education did not increase student success in college-level math and English courses but created an achievement gap—particularly for black and low-income students.[2]

For those studying the effectiveness of developmental education, the findings of the report were not earth shattering; they merely reflected what already had been revealed in previous studies. A series of papers released by the Community College Research Center transformed a national conversation on the role of assessment, placement, and developmental education in higher education. The papers have moved the study and practice of developmental education in an entirely new direction that recognizes the root causes of failure of developmental education.

Recommendations from the CCA report included a set of evidence-based reforms that are restructuring how students who require assistance to complete gateway math and English are supported. There is now a growing convergence on systemic reforms in which the vast majority of new entering community college students are placed in college-level courses and, when necessary, provided academic support while enrolled in college-level support as a corequisite.

Tom Bailey's synthesis of the research, "Challenge and Opportunity: Rethinking the Roles and Function of Developmental Education in Community College,"[3] revealed the inherent structural flaws in the design of developmental education and suggested that the benefits of prerequisite developmental education did not outweigh the considerable negative impact of the existing structure of a multi-billion-dollar intervention.[4] Many had questioned the role of developmental education as a tool for ensuring access to a postsecondary credential, but Bailey's study put the debate in a new light.

Bailey challenged the practice of using standardized assessments that resulted in the placement of the majority of new entering community college students into multiple-semester developmental education sequences. He suggested that instead of achieving its objective of fully preparing students for success in higher education, the system was placing an artificial barrier between students, particularly low-income students and students of color, and a postsecondary credential.

Likewise, two papers, one by Judith Scott-Clayton[5] and a second by Clive Belfield and Peter Crosta,[6] found that a large percentage of students who are capable of completing gateway math and English courses are wrongly placed in developmental education. Both studies found that deemphasizing the high-stakes standardized placement exams as the primary tool for placement and incorporating the use of high school GPA to assess student readiness for college-level math and English courses resulted in many more students starting their postsecondary paths in college-level math and English courses.

These studies, along with a range of innovations in the field, have resulted in a fundamental restructuring of developmental education that is achieving dramatic improvements in gateway math and English success. Policy makers, who have long been skeptical of developmental education, are taking note of these reforms by passing legislation that is pushing entire state postsecondary systems to scale these reforms. In the end, it is likely that the reform of developmental education will be the cornerstone of a movement that ushers in a set of other reforms that ensure millions more students, particularly low-income students and students of color, are able to earn a postsecondary credential.

It is an inescapable fact that increasing graduation and transfer rates at community colleges requires that students who are placed in developmental education successfully complete gateway math and English courses in a timely manner. With estimates from research suggesting that as many as 60 percent of all new entering students enroll in developmental education courses,[7] it was inevitable that the question of its effectiveness would be examined to determine whether it contributed to degree completion—particularly for the high percentage of students of color and low-income students placed into developmental education.

Questions about the effectiveness of an intervention that most new entering students at community colleges must navigate before progressing into gateway math and English courses leading into a program of study were a primary driver for a set of national initiatives to build the capacity of community colleges to increase college graduation and transfer rates for their students. Large-scale initiatives like Achieving the Dream, Developmental Education Initiative, and the state-based Developmental Studies Redesign Initiative generated new innovations that informed institutional practice across the field.

Along with generating innovations and new thinking on community college student success, these initiatives resulted in powerful new data sets for the study of community college outcomes, particularly in developmental education. The result was a deeper examination of the effectiveness of developmental education and a clearer understanding of how the structural design of developmental education impacts student outcomes.

RECOGNITION AND REFORM: DEVELOPMENTAL EDUCATION REDESIGN

Bailey's overview of the research on developmental education, published in 2008, found that the impact of developmental education on student outcomes was highly suspect. The synthesis of the research examining the structure of developmental education found that when students were placed into a sequence of one, two, or three developmental courses in either math or English, they rarely completed their full remedial education sequence. Of those who enrolled in a remedial reading sequence, only about 44 percent completed their developmental sequence, and only 31 percent enrolled in developmental math completed their sequence within three years.[8]

Bailey further contended that low completion rates in developmental education sequences had little do with the effectiveness of teaching in the courses or the capacity of students to complete them. In fact, many students were successful in the courses in which they were enrolled.[9]

Instead he described a problem in which students enrolled in developmental education sequences failed to enroll in and complete the full sequence. Consequently, few students placed in developmental education ever enrolled in and completed gateway math and English courses. CCA's data found that among its Alliance of States, only 22 percent ever enrolled in and completed gateway courses.[10] In the end, only a few placed in developmental education earned a postsecondary credential. Only about one in four students enrolled in developmental education ever earned a postsecondary credential in eight years.[11]

The recognition that student attrition from long remedial sequences was at the root of student failure coincided with a set of reforms focused on accelerating students through developmental education sequences. Two separate initiatives—the Developmental Education Initiative, created by MDC with Achieving the Dream, and the Developmental Studies Redesign Initiative at the Tennessee Board of Regents—set in motion a set of reforms that attempted to collapse the length of developmental education sequences. In both initiatives, the primary reform focused on breaking down developmental education courses into a sequence of competencies or modules that enabled colleges to place students in developmental education only for the competencies they were lacking, thus enabling students to complete their developmental education requirements in shorter and less time-intensive segments.

The modularization of developmental education into competencies enabled a more precise placement of students and the ability to move them through each module at a pace that coincided with student learning styles. In some cases, students could rapidly complete multiple competencies in a single semester that in a traditional course structure might have required two semesters to complete. Conversely, students who needed more time and were not able to complete a "course's worth" of content in a single semester could pick up where they left off the previous semester without the penalty of repeating material they had already mastered.

The modularization of developmental education aligned well with a growing movement in higher education to use technology to address basic skill needs of students. Products like Pearson's My Math Lab and My Writing Lab, ALEKS, and other competency-based learning platforms quickly took root on college campuses through the Emporium Model, in which faculty would provide customized instruction to students as they worked through content at a computer terminal. Students worked at their own pace, and faculty could provide individualized instruction to students as they moved through each module.

Early results were promising, with students completing their developmental education courses at higher rates.[12] However, modularization did not appear to resolve the fundamental structural challenge of student attrition.[13] Data from Virginia and North Carolina found no real increase in college-level course completion in the first year. In fact, the breaking of courses into multiple modules exacerbated the attrition problem by creating even more exit points from the sequence. Many students paused between the modules, which delayed rather than accelerated their progression through the sequence.[14]

Another set of reforms took the student attrition problem to heart by advocating for the collapsing of developmental education sequences, limiting developmental education to no more than a single semester, with students immediately enrolling in the college-level course the following semester. The Carnegie Foundation for the Advancement of Teaching and Learning's Quantway/Statway model, the Charles A. Dana Center's New Math Pathways Initiative, and the California Acceleration Project (CAP) all developed accelerated models that had similar attributes.

In addition to limiting developmental education to a single semester, all three approaches made significant efforts to back map the content from the college-level course in order to identify the content to be addressed in the developmental education course. The focus in developmental education courses moved away from teaching a set of prerequisite skills that students should have mastered in high school to teaching the essential content necessary to complete the college-level course. In many cases, particularly in math, many concepts were left on the cutting room floor, allowing for the accelerated approach of only requiring the single semester developmental education course.

While all three strategies had the objective of increasing gateway course completion by significantly reducing the length of the developmental education sequence, an underlying principle of the reforms focused on the fact that many students were unnecessarily required to prepare for and enroll in college algebra as their default college-level math course. Instead, the three projects emphasized that students should only be required to prepare for and then enroll in math courses that were most relevant to their program of study. Math faculty leaders argued that college algebra, as a general rule, was designed to prepare students to enroll in calculus,[15] and that students who were not pursuing a program of study requiring calculus should enroll in a rigorous alternative course like quantitative reasoning.[16]

The Carnegie Math Pathways, New Math Pathways, and CAP models advocated for colleges to develop and offer multiple gateway math courses with content that was appropriate for a student's major. All three initiatives were constructed with the intention of first placing students who were not pursuing a calculus-based program of study in alternative college-level math courses such as statistics or quantitative reasoning. If students required additional support in those courses, it should be focused on the content necessary to succeed in the college-level course.

Results from the single-semester approach were promising. Eliminating all but a semester of developmental education did reduce the number of attrition points for students who previously had been placed in multiple semesters of developmental education. As a result, a higher number and percentage of students both enrolled in and completed gateway math courses.

Initial results from the Carnegie Math Pathways initiative resulted in approximately 50 percent of students at community colleges and four-year institutions completing gateway statistics courses, significantly more than traditional developmental education at the participating institutions, where success rates ranged between 5 and 16 percent. Community colleges that implemented Quantway experienced a 60 percent success rate in gateway quantitative reasoning, and four-year institutions saw 74 percent of students completing college-level quantitative reasoning. Traditional developmental education students had college-level quantitative reasoning success rates between 21 and 25 percent.[17]

The New Math Pathways Initiative, now called Dana Center Math Pathways, saw success rates in college-level math courses improve by eleven percentage points after enrolling students in college-level math courses aligned to students' programs of study and limiting developmental education instruction to one semester.[18]

CAP also found positive results from single-semester models, with success rates in transfer-level math courses at 38 percent, compared to the 12 percent achieved through traditional prerequisite remedial education sequences. The English version of the CAP model found success rates of 38 percent, compared to 20 percent for traditional prerequisite remedial education sequences.[19]

CCA's "Bridge to Nowhere" report showcased another developmental education reform that was well aligned with the student attrition problem of traditional prerequisite developmental education. "Corequisite remediation," as it was described in the report, advocated for placing students directly into college-level courses in math and/or English and providing academic support while students were enrolled in college-level courses as a corequisite. The argument was that by placing students directly into college-level courses, the problem of student attrition would be solved, enabling students who would have been filtered from postsecondary education through long remedial sequences to enroll in and complete college-level math and English courses and to do so in significantly less time.

CCA's interest in corequisite remediation peaked after seeing results achieved through two corequisite models implemented at the Community College of Baltimore County and Austin Peay State University. Both models, while substantially different in their designs, were achieving success rates in college-level courses that were two to three times better than the success rates from traditional prerequisite developmental education.

The Accelerated Learning Program (ALP) was devised by Peter Adams and his colleagues at the Community College of Baltimore County (CCBC). After an extensive examination of CCBC's data on the success of developmental students that revealed the student attrition problem on his campus, he convinced faculty to pilot the ALP model of co-enrolling students into college-level courses and a developmental English course.

In the ALP model, students assessed as needing additional support enroll as a cohort into the college-level English course along with other students who have placed directly into the college-level course. ALP students attend the college-level course, with the college-level-placed students, for three hours a week and also attend class with their fellow ALP students and the same instructor as the college-level course for an additional three hours. The ALP students benefit from additional time on task, a smaller class size in the developmental section, and more time with the instructor. Crucial to the model is that the content in the developmental section is closely aligned with the college-level course, and the singular objective is to ensure students complete the college-level course.

Developmental instruction in ALP is not focused on a set of prerequisite skills that may or may not be relevant to the college-level course, but instead provides just-in-time support on challenges students are facing in the college-level course.[20] The results of the pilot revealed significant improvements in the number and percent of students completing college-level English. A study conducted by the Community College Research Center found that ALP students were completing college-level English at nearly twice the rate of students placed in traditional remedial education. Some 75 percent of ALP students completed college-level English, compared to 38.5 percent for students in traditional remedial education. Further, the study found that ALP students were more likely to complete the second college-level English course, earn more credits, and persist.[21]

At Austin Peay State University, traditional prerequisite developmental education had been largely replaced by the Structured Learning Assistance (SLA) model. As in the ALP model, Austin Peay students who were assessed below college level in math or English were placed in a college-level math or English course and then required to concurrently enroll in a separate SLA lab that met for an additional two hours a week. Students in SLA received additional support in the lab on content related to the college-level course.[22] Unlike ALP, SLA did not rely on the college-level course instructor to teach in the corequisite lab. In addition, the lab did not require students to pay tuition to enroll. Instead, students paid a less-expensive lab fee.

Despite the differences between the two models, the results were remarkably similar. Students enrolled in SLA passed college-level quantitative reasoning at a 78 percent rate, compared to 11 percent for students in traditional prerequisite remedial education. Students in SLA statistics completed college-level statistics at a 65 percent rate, compared to 8 percent for students in prerequisite remediation, and SLA English students passed college-level English at a 70 percent rate, compared with 49 percent for students in traditional remedial education.[23] In addition, SLA students earned more credits and were more likely to persist than under other models implemented through Tennessee's Developmental Studies Redesign Initiative, further building the evidence for corequisite support over modularized models.[24]

CCA's confidence in the corequisite model deepened after states receiving grants from CCA and the Bill & Melinda Gates Foundation, as part of the Completion Innovation Challenge Initiative, implemented a range of developmental education reforms to include modularization and other accelerated models. Studies found that corequisite support was clearly the most effective model, consistently achieving results similar to those found among other institutions implementing corequisite models.

Several of the states that participated in the Completion Innovation Challenge Initiative committed to scaling corequisite remediation to serve between 50 and 100 percent of students who would otherwise be placed in traditional developmental education. West Virginia, Indiana, Georgia, and Tennessee scaled corequisites in both math and English, and Colorado scaled in English. The results from the scaling of corequisites were remarkably similar to those achieved through the pilot efforts in each of the states, once again producing success rates in college-level courses that were two to three times the success rate for students in traditional developmental education.[25]

The potential of corequisite remedial education to dramatically improve college math and English pass rates did not go unnoticed in the field. Researchers and college leaders began to recognize that single-semester models of developmental education still struggled with attrition rates, with many students not enrolling or completing college-level courses after completing their single semester of developmental education. At that point, the Carnegie Math Pathways, Dana Center Math Pathways, and California Acceleration Project all incorporated corequisite models into their strategies.

In addition, corequisite remediation continues to spread among the states. Complete College America is working with twelve states through a grant from the Michael and Susan Dell Foundation to scale corequisites. California and Texas have both recently passed legislation and/or system-level policy to scale corequisite support for the vast majority of students who require additional academic support. Ohio, Georgia, City University of New York, and the State University of New York have pledged to scale corequisite support as part of the Strong Start to Finish Initiative managed by Education Commission of the States and funded by the Bill & Melinda Gates Foundation, Kresge Foundation, and Great Lakes Higher Education Corporation.

Despite results at scale that are reporting some of the greatest improvements in college-level success rates to date, questions remain about whether corequisite remediation is a viable and scalable model for meeting the needs of all students. Key questions remain about the depth of research conducted on the reform and whether the reform would work for all students.[26] Recent studies with more sophisticated methodologies, however, are continuing to show the positive results of corequisite remediation.

A randomized controlled experiment of a corequisite model implemented at the City University of New York showed positive effects of the corequisite model when compared to traditional and enhanced developmental education courses. The study examined three different student populations: students who remained in the traditional developmental education elementary algebra course, students in the corequisite statistics course, and students who received additional academic support while enrolled in the developmental education elementary algebra course. The findings from the study revealed that students enrolled in the corequisite course completed the college-level course at a rate sixteen percentage points higher than those assigned to developmental algebra. Corequisite students also earned more credits than students assigned to traditional developmental education.[27]

A study commissioned by the Bill & Melinda Gates Foundation and conducted by the Boston Consulting Group examined the impact of a range of developmental education reforms, from modularization to corequisite support, at various community colleges. Researchers reported that a fully scaled corequisite model was the most effective approach, reducing the ratio of students who enroll in developmental education to those who complete college-level math from fifty-four-to-one to four-to-one.[28]

An interesting dimension of the study was that the corequisite model featured in the report defaulted all new entering students into corequisite courses, allowing students to either test out of the model or choose a more traditional remedial option after the semester began if they were struggling in the corequisite. The Community College of Denver (CCD) approach recognized that completing gateway math was such a significant barrier to college completion for their students, they thought it was important to give all students the opportunity to benefit from the corequisite model. In effect, the CCD model used corequisite support as the default gateway course design for all students.

On the question of whether students who are assessed at the lowest levels can benefit from corequisite support, the Tennessee Board of Regents reported that students assessed at the lowest levels with ACT scores below 13 on math or English performed significantly better in corequisites than in traditional prerequisite developmental education. According to the report, community college students with an ACT of 13 or below in math were ten times more likely to pass a college-level math course in a corequisite model than students with the same ACT scores who were placed in a traditional developmental education sequence. Students who fell below an ACT of 13 in English were twice as likely to complete a college-level English course through a corequisite English course as students in traditional developmental English.[29]

California researchers reported a similar result when examining data from their Multiple Measures Assessment Project. The analysis by the RP Group found no clear-cut point in their multiple measure assessment model at which students would pass transfer-level quantitative reasoning, statistics, or English courses at a higher rate after placement in a traditional prerequisite remedial sequence than if they were placed directly in the transfer-level course and received corequisite support. In other words, the RP Group analysis found no evidence that prerequisite remedial education is ever more effective than placement in corequisite remediation.[30]

While there is ample evidence that students assessed at even the lowest levels are more likely to complete gateway math and English in corequisite models than in traditional models, there is still a population of students who are not successful in corequisite models. In the past, the prevailing standard for determining the "lowest level" student was a score on a standardized exam. There is a growing recognition that the causes of student failure are far more complicated and cannot be measured by a single assessment. A new body of research and practice is focusing on the overall academic mind-set of new entering students to understand why many students fail to complete gateway math and English courses.

When the Tennessee Board of Regents recognized that academic assessments were not predictive of student success in a corequisite model, they began to explore the data in greater depth. One significant finding from their research was that students who succeeded in corequisite models, regardless of their entering ACT scores, were more likely to complete nearly all credits for courses in which they were enrolled. Conversely, students who did not succeed in corequisites, regardless of ACT score, completed very few college credits. In fact, the most likely outcome for students who did not succeed in a corequisite model was that they would not earn any college credits in the term they were enrolled in a corequisite. The study concluded that student success was not a function of academic readiness, but of overall college readiness.[31]

To better understand that finding, the Tennessee Board of Regents designed an academic mind-set survey for students. The survey found that students who scored low on academic mind-set were less likely to succeed in corequisite courses, regardless of ACT score. Given these results, Tennessee and Georgia are broadening their efforts to successfully onboard students into their institutions. They are designing interventions focused on assessing and addressing the academic mind-set of new entering students and ensuring new students pursue a first-year experience that not only focuses on gateway course completion but ensures they have made a purposeful choice of a program of study by the end of their first academic year.

The City University of New York's CUNY Start Program takes a more holistic approach to student support that considers a full range of college readiness skills beyond instruction in math and English. The CUNY Start model works with those students deemed at greatest risk of failure once enrolled and provides intensive academic and other college readiness support for a semester to ensure they can fully matriculate, enroll in college-level math and English in the first semester, and begin their program of study in earnest. Students are not charged tuition but pay a $75 fee to participate in the program the semester before enrolling at a CUNY institution.

Early findings show that students who participate in CUNY Start are far more likely to be ready for college-level math and English courses after a semester of traditional prerequisite developmental education. The study found that 57 percent of CUNY Start students were ready for college-level math, compared to only 25 percent of students in the control group. For students needing academic support in math, English, and reading, 38 percent of CUNY Start students were ready for college-level work in all three subjects, compared to only 13 percent of the control group. [32]

CUNY Start, while showing positive effects for students, is not a panacea. CUNY's long-term strategy is to combine CUNY Start with its plan to scale corequisite support, providing a comprehensive approach to serving all students as the focus of the Strong Start to Finish project design. Time will tell whether the combination of prematriculation strategy and corequisite support will dramatically increase the success of students assessed as needing support in multiple academic areas. [33]

RECOGNITION AND REFORM: PLACEMENT

Reforms to developmental education are showing tremendous improvements in student success in gateway math and English courses for thousands of students across the nation. The success of accelerated strategies, particularly corequisite support, has fundamentally challenged the mental model of college readiness, calling into question how colleges assess students and place them in developmental education.

Two separate studies released by the Community College Research Center in 2012 confirmed that beyond the structural flaws of developmental education sequences, most colleges are placing far too many students in developmental education who could be successful in college-level courses. The studies illustrate the ineffectiveness of using only placement exams to predict student success in college-level courses, the effectiveness of high school grade point average and high school course taking for predicting student success, and the value of using multiple measures to determine college readiness.

Judith Scott-Clayton's "Do High-Stakes Placement Exams Predict College Success?" examined data from a prominent community college system and discovered that a significant percentage of students who were placed in developmental math and English courses using a college placement exam could have passed a college-level math or English course if given the opportunity. [34] The study found that over 30 percent of students placed in developmental courses could have passed a college-level math course with a "B" or better, and over 50 percent of students could have passed a college-level math course with a "C" or better.

Not only did the research reveal the ineffectiveness of placement exams, it also found that high school GPA was a better predictor of success in college-level math and English courses than placement exams, and the combination of both exams and high school GPA was an even more effective measure of student success. [35] Likewise, in a separate study Belfield and Crosta found that high school GPA was a far more effective predictor of student success in college-level math and English courses, students' college GPA, and the number of credits students earn in college. [36]

The research on the ineffectiveness of placement exams started a larger conversation on the use of multiple measures to determine readiness for college-level math and English courses. The North Carolina and Virginia community college systems were among the first to recognize the value of high school performance when determining college readiness. Both states developed systems that gave students multiple bites at the college placement apple. By first using high school GPA to determine readiness for college-level math and English courses, then college entrance exams for students who didn't reach the GPA standard, and finally diagnostic exams to more precisely determine student academic deficiencies, the system gave students multiple opportunities to prove their readiness for college-level courses.

In California, researchers and practitioners were embarking on their own research on the use of multiple measures. Unlike the rest of the country, California had been using multiple measures for placement for many years. Initial reforms agreed to by the California Community College System Chancellor's Office after a lawsuit filed by the Mexican American Legal Defense and Education Fund required that institutions not rely on a single assessment to determine placement in college-level, or as California colleges term them, transfer-level courses. [37]

As in the rest of the nation, policies and practices for assessment and placement were inconsistently implemented and misaligned among institutions.[38] For example, high school transcript data, GPA, and course taking were often incorporated into placement systems at many colleges, but still were only marginally used, while traditional placement assessments continued to be the primary tool in most placement systems.[39]

Despite these challenges, innovative efforts to more effectively use multiple measures began to emerge. Most noteworthy were reforms at Long Beach City College, where institutional researchers Andrew Fuenmayor, John Hetts, and Karen Rothstein linked high school transcript data from their local school district with course record information and found a significant association between high school and college performance in math and English.[40] The strength of the research resulted in a pilot project called the Promise Pathways Initiative, in which students were placed in transfer-level math and English courses based on their high school performance. The new system resulted in dramatic increases in placement and enrollment in transfer-level math and English courses, without any measurable reduction in the success rate of students in those courses.[41]

The Long Beach City College research resulted in the Student Transcript-Enhanced Placement Study (STEPS 2.0) at eleven California colleges, which adapted the Long Beach City College analysis of the relationship between high school and postsecondary performance in transfer-level math and English.[42] The STEPS 2.0 study revealed two noteworthy findings. First, high school performance (GPA, course level in subject, course grades in subject) was not as strong a predictor of performance on placement exams as K–12 standardized exams. Second, high school performance was far more predictive of success in transfer-level courses. In other words, standardized test performance predicted future standardized test performance, and high school coursework was a more effective predictor of success in transfer-level college coursework.[43]

The findings from the STEPS 2.0 research consequently resulted in further experimentation with multiple measure processes that relied on a combination of high school GPA, high school course levels in each subject area, performance in high school courses by subject, and placement exams. Several California community colleges that have implemented the recommended placement standards using multiple measures are consistently finding a higher number of placements in transfer-level math and English courses without any measurable drop in student success in transfer-level courses.[44]

The research in California has tremendous implications for creating more equitable outcomes across income, race, and ethnicity. As in the rest of the nation, students of color and low-income students were more likely to be placed in developmental education in California. Consequently, the existing ineffective placement system had an even greater negative impact on under-served populations.

A study conducted by Gregory Stoup at the RP Group found that the most significant factor in creating attainment gaps in higher education was placement in developmental education. Stoup found that gaps in student progress that begin with the placement of students in developmental education persist throughout students' progress through a program of study.[45] Consequently, system leaders and policy makers alike began to recognize that reliance on assessments to place students in developmental education was causing inequities in California community colleges.[46]

It is clear that research and practice are creating an entirely new mental model for understanding the readiness of new entering students for college-level math and English. In effect, the research reveals that high school faculty, by and large, are very effective at assessing the readiness of their students for college-level courses. It can no longer be assumed that college faculty and the assessments they use to measure the readiness of students should be the default method for determining student access to college level courses The immediate impact of this new mental model will likely be significant reforms to assessment and placement policies and practices by requiring the use of multiple measures, with a particular emphasis on building systems that use high school performance as a foundation for student assessments.

CONVERGENCE

The field is beginning to appreciate the inherent structural flaw of prerequisite remedial education and to witness the evidence of student success in college-level math and English courses by implementing multiple measures placement and corequisite remediation. National postsecondary education leaders, policy makers, institutional leaders, and practitioners are converging around the transformation of developmental education into an enterprise that recognizes that access and quality are no longer mutually exclusive.

New evidence is proving that access can be achieved and quality learning can be maintained through a fundamental recognition that the problems of student success were never about the lack of academic readiness of students or the inability of faculty to maintain high academic standards in diverse classrooms. By merely recognizing the learning students demonstrated in high school and focusing instruction on students passing gateway courses, colleges can see dramatic improvements in gateway course success and ultimately greater college completion rates.

The transformation is well under way, and there is reason to believe that it will only accelerate as state legislatures, systems, and institutional boards of trustees absorb the large-scale impact the reforms have had at the institutional, system, and state levels.

National higher education policy and practice organizations have realized that the evidence of student success from these reforms is compelling enough to support the transformation of developmental education at scale. The "Core Principles for Transforming Remediation within a Comprehensive Student Success Strategy: A Joint Statement,"[47] published by Achieving the Dream, American Association of Community Colleges, the Charles A. Dana Center, Complete College America, Education Commission of the States, and Jobs for the Future, outlines six principles to ensure that systemic reform of developmental education is the foundation of comprehensive student success strategies that campuses should pursue to dramatically increase college completion rates. The principles advocate for strategies to ensure the following:

- Every student's postsecondary education begins with an intake process to choose an academic direction and identify the support needed to pass relevant credit-bearing gateway courses in the first year.
- Enrollment in college-level math and English courses or course sequences aligned with the student's program of study is the default placement for the vast majority of students.
- Academic and nonacademic support is provided in conjunction with gateway courses in the student's academic or career area of interest through corequisite or other models with evidence of success in which supports are embedded in curricula and instructional strategies.
- Students for whom the default college-level course placement is not appropriate, even with additional mandatory support, are enrolled in rigorous, streamlined remediation options that align with the knowledge and skills required for success in gateway courses in their academic or career area of interest.
- Every student is engaged with content of required gateway courses that is aligned with his or her academic program of study—especially in math.
- Every student is supported to stay on track to a college credential, from intake forward, through the institution's use of effective mechanisms to generate, share, and act on academic performance and progression data.

These principles are the common DNA among a wide range of national initiatives to fundamentally redesign community colleges to build clear pathways into and through postsecondary programs of study. Among them are Complete College America's Momentum Pathways Framework; the Strong Start to Finish Initiative, funded by a consortium of national funders and managed by Education Commission of the States; the Student Success Center Network, directed by Jobs for the Future; and the Guided Pathways initiative of the AACC.

Policy makers and state- and system-level leaders alike are moving aggressively to fully scale developmental education reforms. System or state higher education executive offices in Tennessee, Georgia, West Virginia, Indiana, and Idaho have either passed system-level policy or otherwise declared a commitment to fully scale corequisite support for nearly all students entering their institutions. Other states, including Colorado, Montana, Missouri, Oklahoma, Massachusetts, Hawaii, Ohio, Nevada, Kentucky, New York, and New Hampshire, are methodically working toward state or system goals to scale corequisite support.

Florida, Connecticut, and most recently Texas and California have passed state legislation to default most students into college-level courses by either exempting them from being placed in developmental education (Florida), limiting the length of the developmental sequence (Connecticut), requiring that most students needing developmental education receive it as a corequisite (Texas), or requiring the use of multiple measures for placement and setting a very high evidence bar for colleges that want to place students in prerequisite developmental education (California).

States that have passed legislation have found bipartisan agreement that these reforms make sense for most students. For legislators, the emerging evidence relieves their discomfort with investing in developmental education structures that are an ineffective redundancy in the education system, while recognizing the importance of ensuring access to higher education for academically underprepared students. As a result, legislation that incorporates the elements of the redesigned system is finding broad consensus and rapid adoption.

Community colleges might find the prospect of developmental education reform legislation sweeping the nation unsettling. But there is an emerging understanding of how to go about building high quality with all key stakeholders at the table that can ensure legislation that has the greatest opportunity to achieve its goals.

California's passage of Assembly Bill 705 represents a watershed moment in the developmental education reform movement. Years of public investment in developmental education reform and K–12 alignment work resulted in a substantial higher education infrastructure for innovation and research. Those investments ultimately led to the groundbreaking research conducted by the RP Group for the California Community Colleges and faculty-led reform efforts like the California Acceleration Project.

Innovations in the field, beginning with new models of developmental instruction at institutions like Los Medanos and Chabot Colleges, resulted in a cadre of faculty leaders who not only moved reform at their institutions, but created a network for the dissemination of successful reforms, ultimately leading to a grassroots base of faculty reformers. As the evidence on the effectiveness of multiple measure placement and corequisite support began to mount, early adopters grew impatient with slow and incremental reforms. The result was a growing coalition of faculty reformers, the research community, system-level leaders, and an advocacy organization called the Campaign for College Opportunity engaging state legislators on the prospects of passing legislation to trigger large-scale reform. The legislation, rooted in a commitment to greater higher education access and the elimination of attainment gaps, gained broad support from legislators and was passed.

Equally important to the passage of the legislation was the activation of the broad coalition to provide opportunities for faculty and institutional leaders to receive the support and professional development they needed to effectively implement reforms consistent with proven practice. While full-scale implementation of Assembly Bill 705 will not occur until fall 2019, there has been independent recognition from institutional and public policy researchers alike that the bill will result in radical improvements in student outcomes. [48]

At a time when higher education has fully recognized that its future is intimately tied to ensuring both access and success for the growing new majority of students on its campuses who have been traditionally underserved by its institutions, the fundamental redesign of developmental education represents the first crucial reform of the college completion movement. Large-scale reforms to developmental education are setting in motion new systemic structures that can result in dramatic improvements in college enrollments, retention, and completion, driven by the closing of systemic attainment gaps that have been higher education's greatest and most pressing challenge to student success.

NOTES

1. Complete College America. (2012). *Remedial Education: Higher Education's Bridge to Nowhere.*   https://www.insidehighered.com/sites/default/server_files/files/CCA%20Remediation%20ES%20FINAL.pdf.

2. Ibid.

3. Bailey, Tom. (2008). *Challenge and Opportunity: Rethinking the Role and Function of Developmental Education in Community College.* Working Paper No. 14. Community College Research Center, Teacher's College, Columbia University.

4. Complete College America. (2012). *Remedial Education: Higher Education's Bridge to Nowhere.*   https://www.insidehighered.com/sites/default/server_files/files/CCA%20Remediation%20ES%20FINAL.pdf.

5. Scott-Clayton, Judith. (2012). *Do High Stakes Placement Exams Predict College Success?* Working Paper No. 41. Community College Research Center, Teachers College, Columbia University.

6. Belfield, Clive, and Crosta, Peter. (2012). *Predicting Success in College: The Importance of Placement Tests and High School Transcripts.* Working Paper No. 42. Community College Research Center, Teachers College, Columbia University.

7. Core Principles for Transforming Remediation within a Comprehensive Student Success Strategy. (2015). *Achieving the Dream.* American Association of Community Colleges, Charles A. Dana Center, Education Commission of the States, Jobs for the Future.

8. Bailey, Tom. (2008). *Challenge and Opportunity: Rethinking the Role and Function of Developmental Education in Community College.* Working Paper No. 14. Community College Research Center, Teacher's College, Columbia University.

9. Ibid.

10. Complete College America. (2012). *Remedial Education: Higher Education's Bridge to Nowhere.* https://www.insidehighered.com/sites/default/server_files/files/CCA%20Remediation%20ES%20FINAL.pdf.

11. Bailey, Tom. (2008). *Challenge and Opportunity: Rethinking the Role and Function of Developmental Education in Community College.* Working Paper No. 14. Community College Research Center, Teacher's College, Columbia University.

12. Twigg, Carol A. (n.d.). *Tennessee Board of Regents: Developmental Studies Redesign Initiative.* National Center for Academic Transformation.

13. Bickerstaff, Susan, Fay, Maggie P., and Joy Trimble, Madeline. (2016). *Modularization in Developmental Mathematics in Two States: Implementation and Early Outcomes.* CCRC Working Paper No. 87. Community College Research Center, Teachers College, Columbia University.

14. Kalamkarian, Hoori S., Raufman, Julia, and Edgecombe, Nikki. (2015). *Statewide Developmental Education Reform: Early Implementation in Virginia and North Carolina.* Community College Research Center, Teachers College, Columbia University.

15. Saxe, Karen, and Braddy, Linda. (2015). *A Common Vision for Undergraduate Mathematical Sciences in 2025.* Mathematical Association of America.

16. Dana Center Math Pathways. (2016). *DCMP Call to Action: The Case for Mathematics Pathways.* Charles A. Dana Center, University of Texas-Austin.

17. Hoang, Hai, Huang, Melrose, Sulcer, Brian, and Yesilyurt, Suleyman. (2017). *Carnegie Math Pathways 2015–2016 Impact Report: A Five Year Review.*

18. Zachary Rustow, Elizabeth. (2018). *Making It Through: Interim Findings on Developmental Students' Progress to College Math with the Dana Center Mathematics Pathways.* Center for the Analysis of Postsecondary Readiness.

19. Hayward, Craig, and Willett, Terrence. (2014). *Curricular Redesign and Gatekeeper Completion: A Multi-College Evaluation of the California Acceleration Project.* The Research and Planning Group for the California Community Colleges.

20. Accelerated Learning Program. http://alp-deved.org/what-is-alp-exactly/

21. Cho, Sung-Woo, Kopko, Elizabeth, Jenkins, Davis, and Smith Jaggars, Shanna. (2012). *New Evidence of Success for Community College Remedial English Students: Tracking the Outcomes of Students in the Accelerated Learning Program (ALP).* Working Paper No. 53. Community College Research Center, Teachers College, Columbia University.

22. Structured Learning Assistance Program, Austin Peay State University.

23. Griffy, Loretta. (n.d.). Course Redesign Co-Requisite Models. Center for Teaching and Learning. Austin Peay State University.

24. Boatman, Angela. (2012). *Evaluating Institutional Efforts to Streamline Postsecondary Remediation: The Causal Effects of the Tennessee Developmental Course Redesign Initiative on Early Student Academic Success.* National Center for Postsecondary Research, Community College Research Center and MDRC.

25. Complete College America. (2016). *Corequisite Remediation: Spanning the Completion Divide.*

26. Logue, Alexandra. (2018). The Extensive Evidence of Co-Requisite Remediation's Effectiveness. *Inside Higher Education.*

27. Logue, Alexandra, Watanabe-Rose, and Douglas, Daniel. (2016). Should Students Assessed as Needing Remedial Mathematics Take College-Level Quantitative Reasoning Courses Instead? A Randomized Controlled Trial. *Educational Evaluation and Policy Analysis 38*(3).

28. Laverdiere, Renee, and Mullin, Chris. (2018). *Compressing the Sequence: Corequisite Remediation Increases Completion and Improves Efficiency.* Boston Consulting Group and Strong Start to Finish.

29. Denley, Tristan. (n.d.). *Co-Requisite Remediation: Full Implementation 2015–16.* Office of the Vice Chancellor for Academic Affairs, Tennessee Board of Regents.

30. Multiple Measures Assessment Project (MMAP). (2018). *Summary of Methodology for English and Math Phase II Rule Sets and AB 705 Adjustments*. RP Group and Educational Results Partnership.

31. Ibid.

32. Scrivener, Susan, Gupta, Himani, Weiss, Michael J., Cohen, Benjamin, Scott Cormier, Maria, and Brathwaite, Jessica. (2018). *Becoming College-Ready: Early Findings from a CUNY Start Evaluation*. MDRC and Community College Research Center, Teachers College, Columbia University.

33. *CUNY Awarded $2.1 Million Grant to Scale Equity-Focused Student Success Strategies*. (2018).

34. Scott, Clayton. (2012). *Do High Stakes Placement Exams Predict College Success?* Working Paper No. 41. Community College Research Center, Teachers College, Columbia University.

35. Ibid.

36. Belfield, Clive, and Crosta, Peter. (2012). *Predicting Success in College: The Importance of Placement Tests and High School Transcripts*. Working Paper No. 42. Community College Research Center, Teachers College, Columbia University.

37. Willett, Terrence. (2013). *Student Enhancement Placement Study (STEPS) Technical Report. The Research & Planning Group for California Community Colleges.*

38. Ibid.

39. Ibid.

40. Fuenmayor, Andrew, Hetts, John, and Rothstein, Karen. (2011). *Assessing Assessment: Evaluation Models of Assessment and Placement*. Long Beach, CA: Long Beach City College.

41. Hetts, J., and Willett, T. (2012). *Assessing Transcript-Based Placement*. Long Beach, CA: Association of Institutional Research Annual Forum.

42. Willett, Terrence. (2013). Student Enhancement Placement Study (STEPS) Technical Report. The Research & Planning Group for California Community Colleges.

43. Ibid.

44. Multiple Measures Assessment Project. (March, 2017). California Acceleration Project Conference, Sacramento, CA.

45. Stoup, Gregory. (2016). *Using Data to Identify Emergent Inequities and the Effective Practices to Address Them*. RP Group.

46. Iriwn, Jacqui, and Ortiz Oakley, Eloy. (2018). Trust Students, Not Tests, to Open Pathway to Community College Success. *EdSource*.

47. *Core Principles for Transforming Remediation within a Comprehensive Student Success Strategy: A Joint Statement*. (2015). Achieving the Dream, American Association of Community Colleges, Charles A. Dana Center, Education Commission of the States, and Jobs for the Future.

48. Rodriquez, Olga, Cuellar Mejia, Marisol, and Johnson, Hans. (2018). *Remedial Education Reforms at California's Community Colleges: Early Evidence on Placement and Curricular Reforms*. Public Policy Institute of California.

BIBLIOGRAPHY

Bailey, Tom. (2008). *Challenge and Opportunity: Rethinking the Role and Function of Developmental Education in Community College*. Working Paper No. 14. Community College Research Center, Teacher's College, Columbia University.

Belfield, Clive, and Crosta, Peter. (2012). *Predicting Success in College: The Importance of Placement Tests and High School Transcripts*. Working Paper No. 42. Community College Research Center, Teachers College, Columbia University.

Bickerstaff, Susan, Fay, Maggie P., and Joy Trimble, Madeline. (2016). *Modularization in Developmental Mathematics in Two States: Implementation and Early Outcomes*. CCRC Working Paper No. 87. Community College Research Center, Teachers College, Columbia University.

Boatman, Angela. (2012). *Evaluating Institutional Efforts to Streamline Postsecondary Remediation: The Causal Effects of the Tennessee Developmental Course Redesign Initiative on Early Student Academic Success.* National Center for Postsecondary Research, Community College Research Center and MDRC.

Cho, Sung-Woo, Kopko, Elizabeth, Jenkins, Davis, and Smith Jaggars, Shanna. (2012). *New Evidence of Success for Community College Remedial English Students: Tracking the Outcomes of Students in the Accelerated Learning Program (ALP).* Working Paper No. 53. Community College Research Center, Teachers College, Columbia University.

Complete College America. (2012). *Remedial Education: Higher Education's Bridge to Nowhere.*

Complete College America. (2016). *Corequisite Remediation: Spanning the Completion Divide: Breakthrough Results Fulfilling the Promise of College Access for Underprepared Students.* http://completecollege.org/spanningthedivide/

Core Principles for Transforming Remediation within a Comprehensive Student Success Strategy. (2015). Achieving the Dream. American Association of Community Colleges, Charles A. Dana Center, Education Commission of the States, and Jobs for the Future.

CUNY Awarded $2.1 Million Grant to Scale Equity-Focused Student Success Strategies. (2018). http://www1.cuny.edu/mu/forum/2018/02/06/cuny-awarded-2-1-million-grant-to-scale-equity-focused-student-success-strategies/

Dana Center Math Pathways. (2016). *DCMP Call to Action: The Case for Mathematics Pathways.* Charles A. Dana Center, University of Texas-Austin.

Denley, Tristan. (n.d.). *Co-Requisite Remediation: Full Implementation 2015–16.* Office of the Vice Chancellor for Academic Affairs, Tennessee Board of Regents.

Fuenmayor, Andrew, Hetts, John, and Rothstein, Karen. (2011). *Assessing Assessment: Evaluation Models of Assessment and Placement.* Long Beach, CA: Long Beach City College.

Griffy, Loretta. (n.d.). *Course Redesign: Co-Requisite Models. Center for Teaching and Learning.* Austin Peay State University. https://slideplayer.com/slide/4770705/

Hayward, Craig, and Willett, Terrence. (2014). *Curricular Redesign and Gatekeeper Completion: A Multi-College Evaluation of the California Acceleration Project.* The Research and Planning Group for the California Community Colleges.

Hetts, J., and Willett, T. (2012). *Assessing Transcript-Based Placement.* Long Beach, CA: Association of Institutional Research Annual Forum. http://forum.airweb.org/2013/Documents/Presentations/1708_94318854-0d27-410b9e32-41fc835de98a.pdf

Hoang, Hai, Huang, Melrose, Sulcer, Brian, and Yesilyurt, Suleyman. (2017). *Carnegie Math Pathways 2015–2016 Impact Report: A Five-Year Review.*

Irwin, Jacqui, and Ortiz Oakley, Eloy. (2018). Trust Students, Not Tests, to Open Pathway to Community College Success. *EdSource.* https://edsource.org/2018/trust-students-not-tests-to-open-pathway-to-community-college-success/596996

Kalamkarian, Hoori S., Raufman, Julia, and Edgecombe, Nikki. (2015). *Statewide Developmental Education Reform: Early Implementation in Virginia and North Carolina.* Community College Research Center, Teachers College, Columbia University.

Laverdiere, Renee, and Mullin, Chris. (2018). *Compressing the Sequence: Corequisite Remediation Increases Completion and Improves Efficiency.* Boston Consulting Group and Strong Start to Finish. https://www.linkedin.com/pulse/compressing-sequence-co-requisite-remediation-strong-start-to-finish/

Logue, Alexandra. (2018). The Extensive Evidence of Co-Requisite Remediation's Effectiveness. *Inside Higher Education.* https://www.insidehighered.com/views/2018/07/17/data-already-tell-us-how-effective-co-requisite-education-opinion

Logue, Alexandra, Watanabe-Rose, and Douglas, Daniel. (2016). Should Students Assessed as Needing Remedial Mathematics Take College-Level Quantitative Reasoning Courses Instead? A Randomized Controlled Trial. *Educational Evaluation and Policy Analysis 38*(3).

Multiple Measures Assessment Project. (March 2017). California Acceleration Project Conference, Sacramento, CA.

Multiple Measures Assessment Project (MMAP). (2018). *Summary of Methodology for English and Math Phase II Rule Sets and AB 705 Adjustments. RP Group and Educational Results Partnership.*

Rodriquez, Olga, Cuellar Mejia, Marisol, and Johnson, Hans. (2018). *Remedial Education Reforms at California's Community Colleges: Early Evidence on Placement and Curricular Reforms*. Public Policy Institute of California.

Saxe, Karen, and Braddy, Linda. (2015). *A Common Vision for Undergraduate Mathematical Sciences in 2025*. Mathematical Association of America.

Scott-Clayton, Judith. (2012). *Do High Stakes Placement Exams Predict College Success?* Working Paper No. 41. Community College Research Center, Teachers College, Columbia University.

Scrivener, Susan, Gupta, Himani, Weiss, Michael J., Cohen, Benjamin, Scott Cormier, Maria, and Brathwaite, Jessica. (2018). *Becoming College-Ready: Early Findings from a CUNY Start Evaluation*. MDRC and Community College Research Center, Teachers College, Columbia University.

Stoup, Gregory. (2016). *Using Data to Identify Emergent Inequities and the Effective Practices to Address Them*. RP Group. https://accelerationproject.org/Portals/0/Documents/pathways-stoup.pdf?ver=2016-08-16-185647-180

Structured Learning Assistance Program, Austin Peay State University. https://www.apsu.edu/asc/sla/index.php

Twigg, Carol A. (n.d.). *Tennessee Board of Regents: Developmental Studies Redesign Initiative*. National Center for Academic Transformation. http://www.thencat.org/States/TN/TN%20Outcomes%20Summary.htm

Willett, Terrence. (2013). *Student Enhancement Placement Study (STEPS) Technical Report*. The Research & Planning Group for California Community Colleges.

Zachary Rustow, Elizabeth. (2018). *Making It Through: Interim Findings on Developmental Students' Progress to College Math with the Dana Center Mathematics Pathways*. Center for the Analysis of Postsecondary Readiness.

Chapter Eight

The Evolving Mission of Workforce Development in the Community College

James Jacobs and Jennifer Worth

Postsecondary workforce development is one of the major innovations of the modern community college. These approximately eleven hundred institutions, considered as a group, are the best existing institutional candidates for a national workforce system in the United States. They provide workforce education for a diverse group of Americans, from younger students transitioning out of high school, to anyone of any age who wants to acquire skills to enter the labor market, to adults already working who wish to improve their existing skills. No other nation has developed such an extensive educational network of local institutions able to respond to its talent needs.

Most significant, this unique innovation, developed over the past century, was neither a conscious product of federal policy nor the simple implementation of an educational blueprint from one educational theorist or the university system. Rather, it originates from local community activists who stimulated the fundamental DNA of the community college to respond to students and workers in the community who had to obtain skills to meet the needs of local industry. By focusing on local needs, they built a network of institutions that can respond to a national workforce agenda.

Unlike in many other advanced nations that have established a work-based learning system to increase employment skills, here in the United States it is the community college approach that has emerged as an important source of workplace learning. Its explicit goal is to provide open-door, relevant occupational education and training to a diversified workforce, thereby reflecting the combination of responsiveness to employers' skill needs and students' concern for employment.

The essential features of this workforce approach are (a) curricula driven by the needs of local industry; (b) delivery systems sufficiently flexible to meet the diverse needs of students and industry; and (c) a mixture of work-based and classroom learning, often with the actual equipment used at the workplace, and significant counseling and other wraparound services. These features combine to help students succeed at postsecondary education and gain important training with less than a four-year degree.

Many nations both in the advanced and developing world are rapidly copying this form of education for their workforce systems. Thus, the evolution of this workforce development model is one of the major innovations that community colleges have brought to worldwide postsecondary education efforts. This chapter discusses the ways this innovation continues to evolve to meet the needs of students, employers, and local communities.

THE EARLY HISTORY OF THE
COMMUNITY COLLEGE CONCEPT

The workforce mission was embedded within the origins of the modern community college. The earliest "junior colleges" were established with both a traditional liberal arts curriculum modeled after four-year university systems and programs that responded to the local needs of employers. Many of these junior colleges were established to relieve the research universities of the effort to educate large numbers of freshmen and sophomores so they could instead focus on their research mission. At the same time, alongside these programs for first- and second-year students, the colleges also developed occupational courses to serve local business and industry. As William Rainey Harper noted in 1900, "many students who might not have the courage to enter upon a course of four years' study would be willing to do the two years of work before entering business or the professional school" (cited in Cohen & Brawer, 1996, p. 214).

Community college workforce programs were often deemed "terminal degrees" because, unlike the liberal arts programs that prepared students to transfer to a four-year institution, the curriculum in the occupational areas focused on skills to meet the specific needs of local employers (O'Banion, 2016, p. 21). In their early years of development many community colleges viewed preparation for new jobs that required more than a high school diploma as their major goal. The American Association of Junior Colleges took a leadership role in the movement for terminal education and created its Commission on Junior College Terminal Occupations in 1939 to advocate the employment mission of these institutions on a national level (Cohen & Brawer, 1996, p. 215).

In the post–World War II period, the occupational mission of the community colleges was solidified on the national level through efforts such as the GI Bill, which funded college for veterans. Specifically, the President's Commission on Higher Education, popularly named the Truman Commission, called for the formation of more community colleges:

> To meet the needs of the economy our schools must train many more young people for employment as medical secretaries, recreational leaders, hotel and restaurant managers, aviators, salesmen in fields like life insurance and real estate, photographers, automotive and electrical technical and . . . medical technicians, dental hygienists, nurses' aides, and laboratory technicians. (Grubb & Lazerson, 2004, p. 87)

Soon to be added to this list was nursing; indeed, within the Nursing Department at Teachers College, Columbia University, Mildred L. Montag, citing the Truman Commission, created the first associate degree of nursing program in 1951. Until then most nurses were trained in "diploma programs," a quasi-apprenticeship training system managed by hospitals. Montag's program combined the technical requirements for nursing with liberal arts courses, justifying this new combination with a rationale that remains relevant today: "Skill in the art of communication, knowledge of the economic system, understanding of people and social institutions, and an appreciation of the privileges and obligations of citizenship are all necessary if the student is to be able to function effectively as a person as well as a technician" (Quigley & Bailey, 2003, p. 22).

The rationale used to establish the associate degree of nursing program became a vital underpinning in the development of a national consensus that community colleges were the public institutions that could produce the skills needed for what were called the "semiprofessional" occupations. These occupations required more than a high school diploma, but less than a four-year degree. The growth of these occupations across many sectors of the American economy aided in the incorporation of community colleges within the framework of federal policy.

Federal workforce policy, originally initiated to support high school vocational education in 1917 with the Smith-Hughes Act, has been updated in more recent iterations to include funding for community colleges. In addition, the Truman Commission, which promoted postsecondary education for returning GIs in 1946, supported job skills programs at community colleges (Grubb & Lazerson, 2004, pp. 87–89).

Access to these funding sources, combined with a local desire for greater postsecondary education for the broad middle class, stimulated the vast and rapid expansion of community colleges in the period from 1950 to 1975. During this quarter century, the number of public community colleges grew by 150 percent (Cohen, 1998, p. 187). Most were developed through initiatives of local citizens, who in part were responding to the need of their communities for some form of postsecondary education beyond a high school diploma. They offered accessible, low-cost, relevant postsecondary education that would provide a gateway to economic opportunity for the expanding middle class. The American community college workforce programs evolved to meet the needs of their local communities.

THE IMPACT OF MODERN TECHNOLOGIES AND BUSINESS ORGANIZATION ON WORKFORCE DEVELOPMENT

By 1975 there were over one thousand community colleges enrolling over five million students, equal to all postsecondary enrollment twelve years earlier (Cohen, 1998). Their credit programs were typically found in two relatively separate parts of the institution: the traditional liberal arts classes, designed to enable transfer to a four-year institution, and the occupational classes, created for students who wanted to enter the workforce. In addition, often separate from these programs, many of the colleges developed work-based learning programs such as apprenticeships. Some also began offering occupational "enrichment" programs in their noncredit continuing education divisions for adults who wanted to start their own businesses by obtaining an appropriate skill in such areas as small engine repair, interior design, or real estate.

These program distinctions were reflected in the demarcation of degrees offered by the institutions. Colleges offered transfer programs with an associate of arts or sciences degree; the associate of applied science degree was considered terminal; and a number of occupational programs awarded students a one-year, short-term certificate. Programs in continuing education offered no degrees, but sometimes the noncredit programs helped students secure a license or certificate that had value.

However, this neatly siloed organizational structure was disrupted by changes in the workplace and by public policy advocates who began to use the community colleges to support their economic development activities. New international competition encouraged companies to rapidly adopt computer-based technologies to increase their productivity. Companies' focus on technologies meant not only hiring individuals with greater skill sets but also increasing the skills of their current workforce. Thus, the implementation of these technologies altered the long-term distinctions between education and training—a far greater change than just the introduction of individual computer devices or programmable logic computers. The impact of these contemporary trends on the workforce development mission of community colleges increased the scope and value of workforce education.

The conventional wisdom among workforce educators bifurcated technical learning into (a) teaching generalizable skills that were found in any
technology, such as design, machining, or information technology and (b)
training in the mastery of specific skills associated with the specific internal
process of a company. Most vocational educators traditionally believed that
workforce education should be the responsibility of the educational institutions, but training was the responsibility of the employer. The new computer-
based technologies challenged this distinction because, to master them, both
generalizable skills and specific training on vendor software had to be taught
simultaneously (Jacobs, 1987, pp. 6–10).

Further, business practices changed as the result of both modern technologies and international competition. Not only were businesses becoming lean-
er, with layers of supervision eliminated and replaced by teams, but they
developed a new emphasis on quality with the rediscovery of statistical process control, an American-invented methodology for measuring and control-
ling quality in manufacturing, which was used very successfully by Japanese
manufacturers. The new business practices needed to be introduced to incumbent workers, and American manufacturers turned to community colleges as training institutions (Jacobs, 1989).

Promoting an even more extensive partnership, some companies—especially those with multisite locations dispersed throughout the United States—
began to consider community colleges as a potential delivery system to meet
their talent needs. In the early 1980s General Motors initiated a national
training program for mechanics for its dealers, starting at Delta Community
College in Michigan (Dougherty & Bakia, 1999, pp. 17–21). Following on
that positive experience, General Motors then created the Automotive Service Education Program (ASEP), in which students took automotive classes
focused solely on GM vehicles. When the students completed the program,
they were absorbed into a GM dealership.

Ford, Toyota, and Chrysler soon followed with their own programs,
thereby forcing many community colleges to create separate facilities and
courses for these specific dealership programs. The design software firm
Autodesk initiated an alliance of colleges to serve as a training platform for
companies that adopted its computer-aided design (CAD) packages, giving
colleges access to its software and training for college faculty to serve clients
of Autodesk. These new industry-college partnerships created formal ties
between the colleges and companies to perform company-specific training
functions.

While many courses were integrated within the credit career and technical
programs, others were developed outside the regular programs, resulting in
the establishment of some new centers for technical training. These partnerships were noted by community college leaders, and in 1988 the American
Association of Community Colleges (AACC) also acknowledged their sig-

nificance in its major publication, *Building Communities*: "Partnerships with employers for training and retraining must be recognized as a vital component of the continuing education program in community colleges" (American Association of Community Colleges, 1988, p. 39).

These new company demands for training and education were also integrated into the economic development strategies of states (Rosenfeld, 1992). Until the late 1970s most successful state economic development policies consisted of a combination of investment in appropriate physical assets (railroad sidings, large parcels of land) and tax incentives to attract new investment. However, as the companies began to focus on their human capital, technology, and internal organizational needs, states initiated innovative programs to attract firms through training grants and the development of new public organizations dedicated to their "modernization."

This new emphasis on these economic development factors led to the establishment of state units such as the Michigan Modernization Service and the Ben Franklin Centers in Pennsylvania, which provided technical assistance to aid many small and medium-sized manufacturing companies in implementing modern technologies. Community colleges played roles in these new organizations and were often called upon to train workers from the firms served. By the early 1990s these state innovations had sparked the development of a program inside the US Department of Commerce, the Manufacturing Extension Partnership (MEP), which was a federal/state effort to promote modernization among small and medium-sized manufacturing firms (Modernization Forum Skills Commissions, 1993).

As policy makers considered their options for designing training for these firms, the community colleges became logical implementers. They had four major characteristics that were very attractive to both the firms and policy makers concerned about economic development: they were located near most major clusters of firms, were low cost, and could provide flexible schedules for the firms. Perhaps most important, colleges employed leaders and staff committed to the success of the firms as part of their educational mission. Thus, new state training programs in community colleges blossomed in many states (Jacobs, 1992).

THE ACCELERATION OF COMMUNITY COLLEGE AND BUSINESS PARTNERSHIPS

The national recession of 1982 accelerated efforts to link community colleges and the private sector. It was not the first downturn in the economy in the postwar period, but it was the first major recession to occur when a substantial number of community colleges existed. As a result, for the reasons previously suggested, companies and policy makers turned to the community colleges to aid in economic recovery.

Thus, added to the colleges' growing student market were displaced workers: individuals who needed new skills to reenter the workforce. The AACC responded to these changes with the creation of a new task force, Keeping America Working. For the first time job training initiatives such as the federal Comprehensive Employment and Training Act (CETA) program, which morphed into the Job Training Partnership Act, began to actively depend on community colleges as sources of training for dislocated workers (Day, 1985).

The growth of workforce development activities within community colleges produced new organizations to aid their new workforce development missions. One of the first was the Center for Occupational Research and Development (CORD), established in 1980 by Dan Hull in Waco, Texas. CORD assumed that one of the major needs of community colleges was the development of technical training programs more advanced than their previous vocational efforts, and it thus promoted the new institutional responses at community colleges to implement more sophisticated technical education and training (Hull & Grevelle, 1998).

These stand-alone entities, which could deal with the new technical workforce needs of the local industries, were often called advanced technology centers (ATCs). Most ATCs were not created within the traditional career and technical programs of the community college but were parallel to them and often administered by a new organization that emerged out of continuing education. Most of the relationships between ATCs and local companies were governed by contracts that were developed between the community college and the company and that defined customized training to be offered by the college (Grubb, Badway, Bell, Bragg, & Russman, 1997).

These new ventures served to orient community colleges around the needs of industry far more than the traditional vocational education programs. While the mission was to develop programs that would prepare students for entry-level work, for the most part in the early 1980s, traditional career and technical education was organized around the federal funding streams initiated more than half a century earlier, in 1917, by the Smith Hughes Act. The federal initiative of the 1980s, the Perkins Act, was organized around grants to states for curriculum development, equipment purchases, and leadership development. However, large corporations—especially the manufacturing sector—had facilities all over the nation. Community colleges, originally created to serve a local geographical area, had to figure out how to deal with the needs of companies in many parts of the country.

The Development of Community College Consortia to Serve Businesses Training Needs

In 1984, therefore, a group of ten community colleges, called the Mid-American Training Group, was established across state lines. The group placed an advertisement in the *Wall Street Journal* announcing its existence and desire to serve the needs of companies with facilities near the colleges. A similar organization, the Consortium of Manufacturing Competitiveness (CMC), comprised of community colleges located in various southern states, was created through the work of Stuart Rosenfeld of Regional Technology Strategies (Rosenfeld, 1992, pp. 18–19). These early consortia reflected the initial efforts of colleges to network with each other and the dominant industries in their regions to better meet the needs of students, industries, and communities.

The Advent of the Shadow College within the Community College

The impact of these national alliances created a new sense of awareness of the potential power of community colleges among policy makers far beyond their traditional supporters in the Department of Education and Department of Labor. The traditional sources of federal financial support through the Perkins Act or the Job Training Partnership Act did not apply to many of the company-specific training and state-sponsored economic development activities. A new group of specialists emerged in the community colleges to create new programs and expand funding sources. Most of these specialists did not have traditional vocational education backgrounds in specific technologies, nor were they part of the traditional academic structure of the institution. More likely to come from continuing education backgrounds, they used their marketing and sales skills to solicit business and industry contracts. Community college leaders saw the value of these new programs and allowed them to bypass the traditional vocational education programs.

By the late 1990s these new units within the community colleges were identified as the "shadow college." Many of these were stand-alone operations outside the traditional credit-based organizational structure of the community college that reported directly to the Office of the President. They were the college's local representatives to business and industry, as well as to state and often national economic and workforce policy makers. Their separation from the traditional college programs was encouraged by some community college presidents, who believed their shadow colleges would provide significant new revenue streams. As a result, they were given internal resources and attention not normally afforded many of the regular occupational programs (Jacobs & Teahen, 1997, p. 14).

Many shadow college units were established as auxiliary enterprises with the specific intention of becoming self-sufficient, although most of their operations were housed within the institution, meaning that expenses for buildings, utilities, and even salaries were subsidized by their institutions.

However, in part because of the shadow college's emphasis on financial accountability, the individuals who were attracted to work there were the most entrepreneurial and risk taking of community college personnel. They valued their independence from the institution and often conflicted with traditional parts of the college. Many came from local industry or were involved in marketing, grant writing, or public relations work. But as the shadow colleges grew, many began renting their own facilities and often had their own equipment and separate advanced technology facilities. Their style of work mirrored high-performance organizations in the private sector (Jacobs & Teahen, 1997, p. 15–16).

Often there was considerable internal conflict within community colleges between the shadow colleges and traditional vocational education programs. The traditional programs were concerned that the shadow colleges' activities competed with them. In many instances, however, faculty hired by the shadow colleges were paid less and were excluded from faculty bargaining units. The shadow college administrators often complained that their students lacked access to counseling and other wraparound services provided to traditional students. In addition, since many of the programs operated as "noncredit," the conventional federal student aid programs such as Pell Grants were not available to their students (Grubb et al., 1997, pp. 40–42). Sometimes the conflict extended outside the institution, as both the traditional vocational programs and the new contract education programs competed to market their programs to the same firms.

The Evolution of Definitions of Community College Student Success

There were also conflicts over definitions of a successful college program. Whereas traditional community college programs focused on student employment and earnings, many of the shadow college programs were considered successful if they contributed to enhancing the competitive position of the firms requesting the training. Moreover, while there was an academic calendar and structure to the credit classes in the traditional programs, the customized units operated year-round without credit, delivering instruction anywhere and anytime, producing a very different operating culture that stressed agility and responsiveness more than organizational consistency (Van Noy, Jacobs, Korey, Bailey, & Hughes, 2008, pp. 26–28).

In many instances, record keeping and discussions of how to evaluate the noncredit activities were central to issues of institutional effectiveness

(Grubb et al., 1997, p. 42). During this period, many of the colleges with large noncredit organizations developed an important perspective that became fundamental to this divide: all learning is learning. This meant that regardless of whether a course was for credit or not, it was the responsibility of the institution to ensure that learning took place and that the goals of the institution were reflected. This perspective became very important for the community colleges twenty years later, when states began to develop significant measures of accountability that stressed measurable outcomes regardless of credit or noncredit status.

Moreover, the growth of noncredit education allowed community colleges to respond to two major developments in private-sector skill development practices. The first was that skill standards and other forms of nondegree certification were established as norms in some of the emerging information technology sectors. While some standards and certifications were maintained inside the supply chain programs of major companies, a good many emerged from the needs firms had in their hiring practices, especially in the information technology sector. They served as signals to indicate that those who earned these certificates had specific knowledge of a software product or operating system.

These certifications, such as Microsoft Mouse or Cisco systems academies, were organized around the products of the vendors, and they raised a significant pedagogical issue for educators: Was this training or education or both? (Jacobs & Grubb, 2006, pp. 134–137). In addition, if the goals were related to performance, not seat time or course completion, wouldn't education for these certifications be best taught in the shadow college rather than in the traditional course sectors?

Even in the traditional occupational courses, the new computer technologies were having an impact. It was hard to teach anything in information technology programs that was not vendor specific—for example, teaching CAD required the adoption of a specific system—and whether it was in the credit or noncredit program meant making a choice. So the development of education for these new certifications posed significant issues that would reemerge in the present period of workforce development at community colleges (Carnevale & Desrochers, 2001).

The Role of New Technologies in Community College Education

Another issue within the private sector was the growing significance of continuous training and adjustment as the new technology-infused workplace required more than technical skills. As more work was performed in teams and continually assessed, with rapid adjustments through performance measurement, worker mastery of "soft skills" such as communications and project management became vital for firms (Jacobs, 2001).

Demands for both soft and technical skills resulted in a significant repurposing of adult education programs in the 1990s. Whereas in the past adult education had been considered primarily a public K–12 school function to ensure that all adults could obtain a high school diploma through passage of the GED, a new policy consensus emerged that called for career preparation as one of the fundamental aspects of adult education. It reflected the increasing skills needed in the workplace and the reality that a high school diploma was not sufficient for much of entry-level work. Thus, states began to shift some of the responsibility for adult education to community colleges.

Research on programs in states such as Washington indicated that income and employment potential rose significantly for adults who were prepared not only for obtaining their high school diploma, but also for success in a community college technical program. The development of programs to bring adults into community colleges was often initiated on the noncredit side but soon became part of the credit programs as well—and served to underscore an additional mission of the community college: the preparation of low-skilled adults for college success (Liebowitz & Taylor, 2004).

During this period, however, not all the changes to community college workforce programs were outside the traditional for-credit sectors of the institutions. The new computer-based technologies required substantially upskilling technical workers. To wit, one very significant new federal policy initiative in workforce education emerged with Congress's passage of the Scientific and Advanced-Technology Act in 1992. The act sought "to encourage, guide, and support our nation's community and technical colleges in preparing science and engineer technicians to support U.S. employers in advanced and emerging technical fields" (Teles, 2012, p. 15). It established the Advanced Technological Education (ATE) program, designed to provide funding for community college faculty to develop curricula that would produce technicians in the emerging fields of telecommunications, nanotechnologies, and cybersecurity. These degree programs were in technical areas that could lead to a four-year degree.

While the initial funding of the program was only $40 million—significantly less than federal funding for community college programs from the US Departments of Labor and Education—it was expanded and funded by Congress over the next fifteen years. By 2010 over $720 million in accumulated funds had been invested by the National Science Foundation (NSF) in new technical programs. This NSF-ATE funding became an important source of revenue for many innovative occupational programs within the traditional credit parts of the institution.

These programs also brought together technical instructors with science and mathematics instructors to form new coalitions within the community college that supported goals to increase the numbers of high school students prepared in science and technology. And as the skills required by many occupations continued to increase, the ATE was very important in orienting community colleges toward an understanding of the future trends in industry (Teles, 2012, pp. 19–21).

The Link between High Schools and Community Colleges to Promote Early Attention to Careers

A major federal initiative in the 1990s linked community colleges and high schools to develop new alliances so that students acquired both occupational skills and knowledge of career opportunities in the areas of science and technology (see chapter 9 in this volume). This program, named Tech Prep and administered through the US Department of Education, provided specific funding for collaborations among high schools, community colleges, and employers focused on preparation for work. In Tech Prep, community colleges and secondary vocational educators were working together, and these early experiments provided a significant foundation for many of the dual enrollment and early college programs that emerged after 2000. In many ways the significant roles now played by community colleges in offering postsecondary education to high school students were based on the original efforts of Tech Prep (National Assessment of Vocational Education, 2004, pp. 171–193).

Community College Entrance into the Four-Year Degree Arena

Community colleges were also advancing their own response to workplace demands for skills beyond an associate degree. In addition to developing better ties between their programs and four-year degree programs, some community colleges believed they should advance their own four-year degree programs to accommodate the growing need to train technicians. The concept of the applied baccalaureate began to be widely discussed in community colleges in the late 1990s.

Applied baccalaureates were bachelor's degrees in specific technical areas that filled the specific needs of dominant industries in the community not being addressed by area four-year colleges and universities. They were awarded in areas such as criminal justice, CAD, and niche training areas such as nuclear power technologies (Floyd, Skolnik, & Walker, 2005). (See chapter 5 in this volume.) In some states such as Florida, community college leaders convinced the legislature to develop four-year degree programs on their campus; other states such as Washington and California are still exploring these programs.

These attempts by community colleges to develop their own four-year programs were often met with furious political opposition from four-year institutions (Makela, Bragg, & Harwell, 2015). The battle lines were drawn especially in one very crucial area, nursing, where the four-year colleges fought hard against community college development of their own bachelor of science in nursing (BSN) programs. Motivating this dispute were changes in the health-care industry, which began to value BSN over nursing associate degrees (Karp, Jacobs, & Hughes, 2003). This conflict continues today and reveals an important challenge for future workforce programs at community colleges, as the skills needed by employers will require more four-year degrees even for entry-level work.

WORKFORCE DEVELOPMENT AS
A PRIORITY OF COMMUNITY COLLEGES

As the new millennium got under way it became increasingly clear to community college leaders, policy makers, business and industry, and federal and state legislators that workforce development was not only a central mission of the community college; some saw it as a priority of the community college. As Jamie Merisotis, president of the Lumina Foundation, said, "[T]o deny that job skills development is one of the key purposes of higher education is increasingly untenable" (quoted in Altschuler, 2014, para. 5). When the majority of community college students are enrolled in workforce programs compared to liberal arts programs, and when workforce programs are funded extensively by state and federal agencies and by foundations over other community college programs, then it becomes even clearer where the priority is.

If workforce education is to continue to evolve and remain a priority for community colleges and for the nation, a number of key issues and developments need to be addressed. Some of the more pressing ones are reviewed in the following section.

Relationship of Credit and Noncredit Education

Noncredit workforce education continues as an area of growth at most community colleges. Noncredit programs are more flexible than credit programs and are more easily tailored to the needs of business and industry. In addition, individuals, particularly adults, are attracted to the noncredit programs because they offer short-term programs linked to specific jobs.

There is growing awareness, however, that credit and noncredit programs should not be separate but rather aligned with each other to provide students opportunities for immediate and long-range skill development. Many colleges are developing "bridges" within their institutions whereby noncredit courses are linked to credit programs so adults who come for an immediate job training program can then more easily access credit programs if their career plans change. To better assist students in exploring such transitions, counseling and other wraparound services are now being made available to students enrolled in noncredit courses and programs.

The Role of the Philanthropic Community in Workforce Preparation

In the past decade there has been considerable interest from philanthropic organizations in the workforce development activities of community colleges. Many foundations took note of community colleges as potential vehicles to promote their goal of enabling all Americans to achieve self-sufficiency through sustainable-wage jobs. They supported programs targeted to low-income workers, funded projects previously supported only by the US Department of Labor, and promoted state initiatives to eliminate poverty and increase literacy. Many foundations place priority on equity and the elimination of poverty, and they are beginning to understand that workforce education programs in community colleges that focus on educating low-income students to secure sustainable-wage jobs align perfectly with their goals.

Many foundations champion changes in policy to ensure a better return on their investments and often support statewide projects as a laboratory for more significant change. The Bridges to Opportunity Program funded by the Ford Foundation is an example of a large-scale effort in six states, in which community colleges focused on the needs of low-income citizens. When community colleges collaborated with state policy makers, substantial changes occurred in the existing state workforce programs and in the programs and practices of the participating community colleges.

When community colleges and foundations collaborate and align their goals and resources, some very creative and substantive programs emerge. The Mott Foundation developed a program with a group of colleges to integrate occupational training and basic skills for adults who lacked a high school diploma. The Walmart Foundation established a project with the League for Innovation in the Community College that focused on training entry-level workers for the retail sector. The Kresge Foundation supported efforts to develop new methods to award college credits to adults with previous work experience.

There are a number of important outcomes of this kind of alliance between foundations and community colleges. Community colleges can test out innovations they could not otherwise afford, and many of these innovations lead to institutional change. Colleges in the same state and across states, brought together by the foundations, learn about new programs and new practices they can adapt. College staff working on the projects begin to appreciate that not only are they involved in efforts to improve their own institution, but they are also engaged in substantive work to improve the nation. In a period when state and federal resources for colleges are waning, the philanthropic community will become even more important to future workforce activities at community colleges.

Training Dislocated Workers

In the Great Recession of 2008–2010, the American economy lost over 8.7 million jobs. Unemployed adults streamed into community college workforce programs for retraining in new fields, since many of their old jobs had been eliminated. Because of their flexibility, community colleges were ideal venues for this new challenge, which expanded the scope of workforce programs.

Michigan developed its own program, No Worker Left Behind, which resulted in 140,000 adults receiving two years of free community college training in occupational programs. Thus, community colleges in that state and others became the central institution for preparing dislocated adult workers (State of Michigan, 2009). Not only were the colleges the "go to" institutions for relevant workforce preparation, they also provided literacy training, counseling, and other forms of wraparound services such as food pantries and assistance with housing and transportation.

The Great Recession also motivated a major federal response solely devoted to expanding the workforce capacity of community colleges. With strong support from the Obama administration in 2009, Congress passed legislation initiating a $2 billion US Department of Labor program to increase the capabilities of community colleges to help unemployed adults learn skills for high-wage, high-demand technical occupations: the Trade Adjustment Assistance Community College and Career Training Program (TAACCCT).

When this program came to an end in September 2018, over 256 grants had been awarded, impacting 60 percent of the nation's community colleges. TAACCCT provided staff development funds and funds to purchase additional technical equipment. In addition, it stimulated colleges to form collaborative networks both within their states and around specific industries. These networks will have a very important impact on how the colleges work together on programs in the future (US Department of Labor, 2018).

Reimagining Apprenticeship

Unlike many other nations, the workforce system in the United States has always been primarily school based. Yet parallel to the educational sector, a collective bargaining trade union apprenticeship system has developed. The formal arrangements for a "registered" apprenticeship were structured through the US Department of Labor, and these apprenticeships are generally found only in unionized workplaces, primarily in the manufacturing and construction sectors. This means a relatively small number of workers have been involved. By 2013 there were about 287,750 apprentices in the workforce, or about 0.2 percent of the workforce (Newman & Winston, 2016, p. 188)

Community colleges play a role in the traditional apprenticeship programs by often supplying the "classroom" components of the system. In addition, many community colleges are active with employers who are either nonunion or choose not to work within the Department of Labor regulations and therefore develop their own independent work-based learning programs, such as internships, cooperative education, and other forms of employee training. Paradoxically, however, as the traditional apprentice sectors of unionized workers diminished significantly over the past twenty years, there was a growing interest on the part of companies and policy advocates in the expansion of apprenticeship as a work-based learning system.

This interest was motivated by the private sector, which expressed a persistent concern that entry-level skills were not being adequately addressed in current workforce programs. In addition, policy makers were focused on the need for a better work-preparation system for high school students who were not choosing to attend college. As the costs of college attendance rose, there was a call for expansion of the apprenticeship system as an alternative to taking more technical classes.

Both the Trump and Obama administrations have argued for the expansion of the apprenticeship system. First, they would like to see a rigorous apprenticeship program that is outside the traditional collective bargaining model and that is not tied to union/management relations. Second, they would like to see apprenticeship programs expanded to include new occupations such as insurance and information technology. With the leadership of the AACC, community colleges are beginning to explore expanding their workforce programs to include apprenticeship training. One goal is to update the apprenticeship system to capitalize on the value of work-based learning coupled with the awarding of an educational degree such as an associate degree.

Entrepreneurial and Innovative Activities

The recovery from the Great Recession made it clear there were not enough jobs to meet the need in many communities. Community college workforce development activities needed to include programs that would create economic opportunities through entrepreneurial activities. In many parts of the country, the dominant industries shed thousands of jobs, and because of technical changes and new overseas investments, the jobs were not coming back. Many community colleges therefore began creating programs to support entrepreneurs through business assistance centers, which provided technical assistance for companies that wished to obtain federal procurement contracts. These assistance centers often served to promote student-run enterprises. Other colleges collaborated with private-sector programs such as Goldman Sachs's 10,000 Small Businesses to train current entrepreneurs on how to expand their businesses.

Colleges such as LaGuardia Community College in New York and Lorain County Community College in Ohio developed business incubators to help start-up local enterprises. These were not just buildings to house new businesses but places with technical equipment to aid in product design and development. Such centers, called "maker spaces," were yet another way that the colleges extended their workforce development activities into the creation of new economic activity in communities hard hit by the economic downturn (Oakley & Bynum, 2017).

With these activities, the colleges were responding to the overall economic development needs of communities and the nation more than to the demand by the local private sector to meet its education and training needs. The colleges were responding to the need of the community for greater economic activity to create growth and prosperity, not to the specific demands of one company. However, the two were often closely related.

For instance, Macomb Community College's Innovation Fund, which was funded by both the college and JPMorgan Chase, provided funds for companies that offered employment opportunities for students in highly skilled work. As JPMorgan Chase director of workforce initiatives Chancy Lennon put it: "Detroit-area entrepreneurs are vital to southeast Michigan's continued economic recovery, and the Innovation Fund is a catalyst for creating sustained growth and employment throughout the region" (Macomb Community College, 2014, p. 1).

While some might question whether these applied economic development activities move community colleges away from their main mission of student success, these activities play a key role in their communities. First, they respond to the needs of local small businesses by providing employment for students. Second, aiding business formation at the local level validates the significance of the college to the community and is instrumental in obtaining local support for local college funding requests. Finally, promoting student involvement in local entrepreneurial activities encourages vital skills and the individuals who possess them to stay in the community.

Community College Workforce Development Networks

As colleges respond to their communities with more specialized workforce development programs and activities, collaboration with other community colleges working with similar industries or facing similar community economic development priorities is extremely important. While most community colleges are organized within their states, these networks establish close ties with colleges in many different states and permit the colleges to play a national role while still operating locally.

For example, in 2008 many communities in the Midwest faced massive layoffs of workers in manufacturing, and community colleges responded by organizing a peer learning group called the Community College Workforce Consortium (CCWC). These colleges developed joint programs to deal with the changes within their communities, learning to share resources, programs, and services across a variety of training programs.

Another example, developed through the efforts of Gateway College in Kenosha, Wisconsin, is the National Coalition of Certification Centers (NC3). This organization now includes over seventy-five colleges working in partnership with employers such as Snap-on Tools, Trane, and Fiat Chrysler Automobiles to develop comprehensive curriculum and skills certifications in important career fields. The goal is to develop transferable certifications that will enhance opportunities for students to be employed (National Coalition of Certification Centers, 2018).

The Increasing Significance of STEM

As the skills needed by employers continue to increase, there is a need for a substantial number of individuals who possess technical knowledge based on mathematics and science. While health-care occupational programs traditionally mandated significant numbers of science courses, many community college programs in the business and manufacturing sectors have not required much of a STEM (science, technology, engineering, and mathematics) emphasis. The mathematics most often taught has been "shop math," focused on very rudimentary mathematical calculations involving fractions and percentages. However, as firms have expanded the roles of technicians who maintain, assemble, and often repair the equipment, software, and processes in the workplace, there is an increasing requirement for more science and mathematics courses in occupational programs.

STEM programs are designed to increase the capabilities of community college students to perform advanced work in fields such as mechatronics, cybersecurity, and laboratory technician. Most of these programs assume students will continue in a four-year institution to complete a degree. While these programs seem to have a great deal of promise, the idea of STEM is still only in the initial stages of development. Based on National Student Clearinghouse data, the Community College Research Center (CCRC) has estimated that only about 6 percent of all community college students who transferred to a four-year school and received a bachelor's degree in six years or less were in STEM-related fields (Jenkins, 2018).

The Emergence of Guided Pathways for Workforce Program Students

One of the most important and widespread new developments in workforce programs has been another major community college innovation, guided pathways. This effort was initiated in part as a response to the growing significance of certificates and degrees in certain fields in the United States. If jobs in the future require more workers to hold postsecondary credentials, then one important new criterion for the success of workforce development programs is program completion. While the United States had more individuals participating in postsecondary education among advanced countries, the completion rates among young adults (ages twenty-five to thirty-four) placed America twelfth behind many other advanced countries (Bailey, Jaggers, & Jenkins, 2015, pp. 5–6).

As evidence mounted that college students, especially in the community college, were not achieving their goals, the Obama administration set a goal for millions more individuals to earn college degrees by 2020. The Bill & Melinda Gates Foundation, in its project Completion by Design, set a goal that 50 percent of community college students would earn a certificate or an associate degree, or transfer, by 2020. The Lumina Foundation adopted a "big goal": 60 percent of Americans will earn a quality degree or certificate by 2025. Over two-thirds of the states initiated accountability funding measures that were generally tied to degrees or certificates. A new national community college organization was formed, Achieving the Dream, which promoted reforms within community colleges to ensure that student success—typically measured by earning a degree or certificate or transferring—was the primary goal of the institution (Bailey et al., 2015, p. 7).

To reach these various goals, community colleges began to adopt the concept of the guided pathway. "The guided pathway approach to redesign starts with students' end goals in mind and then rethinks and redesigns programs and support services to enable students to achieve these goals" (Bailey et al., 2015). Researchers and leaders strongly agreed that students needed a clearly defined pathway to achieve their goals, and it was the responsibility of the institution to provide these pathways. By 2015 over one-quarter of all community colleges in the nation were involved in these efforts. (See chapter 4 in this volume.)

The credit workforce programs were now faced with the need to adjust their activities to institutional changes suggested by the guided pathways approach. While workforce development programs always had strong accountability measures, such measures were primarily external to the institution and based on whether or not students got a job and how much they earned. Program initiation, design, and completion tended to be more ad hoc, developed to fit the needs of local employers. Workforce programs had been creating career pathways for many years, but the guided pathways concept required workforce educators to integrate pathways with liberal arts programs and to measure success by degrees and certificates earned. In addition, guided pathways required students to participate in wraparound services such as advising and counseling to help them better navigate the system.

Many of these strategies, however, are of dubious value to incumbent workers who are coming to the institution as "skill builders": individuals seeking to increase their employment skills to provide for themselves and their families. Somewhat paradoxically, despite the continued efforts to bring credit and noncredit education together, the emphasis on guided pathways has led adults to pass up credit courses to selectively complete a series of courses on the noncredit side (Jacobs, 2017) more pertinent to their immediate needs.

CONCLUSION

The Great Recession of 2008–2010 stimulated enrollments in community college workforce programs to new heights. Adults facing employment disruption sought out community college programs to gain skills for new jobs. Furthermore, the Obama administration considered community colleges an "undervalued asset in our country" (Obama, 2009), and many programs were developed to position community colleges as the major workforce training providers in the nation.

In the coming years the community colleges' workforce development mission will need to adapt to three major trends. First, changes in the economy are producing a dual challenge for the colleges. As more jobs require higher skills, the education levels demanded by employers will continue to rise. This means that more community college workforce programs must assume that students should be prepared to complete a degree at a four-year institution or complete a community college baccalaureate.

Except for allied health areas, most career and technical programs lack consistent integration between the skills programs and their "foundation" or basic liberal arts and sciences areas. Most occupational programs do not require these courses for certificates, and even if students want to complete a degree, occupational faculty consider them add-ons to be undertaken after they complete their technical program sequence. This is a mistake because not only do survey data clearly indicate that most career and technical students wish to obtain a four-year degree, but the evolution of many of these occupations means they will soon *require* a four-year degree.

Even in work-based learning programs such as apprenticeships, particularly the younger students view them as a first step toward a four-year degree. The work of Anthony Carnevale at the Georgetown Center on Education and the Workforce has been very important in emphasizing that degrees in specific college majors lead to income gains, and his data support the belief that both specific degree skills and general skills matter in the long run for anyone attending a community college workforce program (Carnevale, Jayasundera, & Gulish, 2015).

Second, the heterogeneity of students continues to intensify, challenging the ability of community colleges to offer a variety of workforce programs. Workforce programs must meet the needs of high school students looking for a career, existing workers needing skills to increase their mobility, and dislocated workers looking for a career change. The ability to provide not simply the instruction, but also the support services needed, to make these students successful thus becomes an important goal of the programs. They will require a coherent and well-developed progression of classes that have knowledge validity; that is, students need to learn relevant subject matter so they can fulfill their goals.

For some liberal arts courses, this bar is met through well-prepared faculty who are familiar with their subject matter, keep up to date, and can continue to hone and develop their skills. However, career and technical courses have an additional burden to consider: How well do their programs meet the current, and most important, future needs of employers within their communities? Unlike other areas of the community college curriculum, career and technical education must be relevant to the employment and earnings of the students.

Given a decade or more of funding cuts to community colleges in most states, it is likely that many community college career and technical programs have not managed to keep up with some of the technical changes in the occupational areas they educate and train students. This is a special concern in health, manufacturing, and business sectors that have integrated information technology. For example, few colleges have the capability to deal with the impact of big data issues at the workplace.

In many colleges the information technology (IT) programs are maintained as discrete career and technical programs, while most companies integrate IT skills within their various business units, resulting in significant IT demands in jobs related to medical record technologies or mechatronic technology. Truck driving programs remain traditionally focused, neglecting the potential impact of autonomous vehicles. Police academies rarely focus on cybersecurity training. Artificial intelligence raises another dimension for many of the programs, particularly in the areas of accounting, marketing, and graphic and commercial design. The shift in many industries away from metals to composites, aluminum, and even additive manufacturing is not often reflected in construction and manufacturing curricula.

Finally, the recent evolution in workforce education is producing a wide variety of activities and initiatives well beyond courses or programs. The workforce mission is not a separate stand-alone mission, but rather integrated into all the rest of the college. This includes everything from serving as a place where entrepreneurial skills are taught, to providing technical expertise to local firms, to developing programs to serve the needs of high school students transitioning into career pathways, to promoting advanced technical training that results in a four-year degree. These activities do not fall under one administrative dean or a division of vocational education. They emerge out of many parts of the institution. The challenge in the future will be for college leaders to develop an organizational rationale that creates opportunities for all parts of the institution to participate.

Perhaps the best opportunity is for colleges to concentrate on STEM initiatives, which will provide the basis for workforce programs to be linked to four-year college programs. Increasingly, job growth is not in areas that call only for some secondary education, but in sectors that require a four-year degree. Clearly credit students understand this, as most national data indicate that students entering community colleges have four-year degrees as their goal. In many occupational areas where community colleges are strong—such as nursing programs—the employer desire for a four-year degree is already very apparent in most metropolitan labor markets. Moreover, the anticipated adoption of artificial intelligence by many sectors of the economy suggests that there will be even less employment for those without a four-year degree.

Thus, community colleges must continue to remain responsive to the unfolding needs of their communities for more employees who have four-year degrees and/or possess the appropriate basic skills to obtain these degrees. Clearly there will be many students, primarily adults, who need to acquire skills quickly so they can obtain meaningful work. Community colleges need to continue to provide that opportunity, but they also need to indicate to students that they will need credentials of value if they are to be competitive in the labor market. This challenge will continue to inform the future of workforce development in the American community college.

Surveying the current status of workforce development in community colleges, there are significant grounds for optimism. Polls of the American population consistently rate community colleges positively as institutions that provide value. Moreover, a recent Gallup poll indicated confidence in community colleges was highest among Americans who did not possess a four-year degree (Busteed & Newport, 2018). Indeed, the public is aware of these institutions, considers their workforce mission an important innovation, and supports the college and its workforce mission with enthusiasm. With that support, the future is very bright.

REFERENCES

Altschuler, G. (2014). A defense of liberal learning. *Inside Higher Ed.* Retrieved from https://www.insidehighered.com/views/2014/05/15/essay-new-book-beyond-university

American Association of Community Colleges (AACC). (1988). *Building communities: A vision for a new century.* Washington, DC: Author.

Bailey, T. R., Jaggers, S. S., & Jenkins, D. (2015). *Redesigning America's community college: A clearer path to student success.* Cambridge, MA: Harvard University Press.

Busteed, B., & Newport, F. (2018). *Words used to describe "higher ed" make a difference.* Washington, DC: Gallup.

Carnevale, A. P., & Desrochers, D. M. (2001). *Help wanted . . . credentials required: Community colleges in the knowledge economy.* Princeton, NJ: ETS Press.

Carnevale, A. P., Jayasundera, T., & Gulish, A. (2015). *Good jobs are back: College graduates are first in line.* Washington, DC: Center on Education and the Workforce.

Cohen, A. M. (1998). *The shaping of American higher education: Emergence and growth of the contemporary system.* San Francisco, CA: Jossey-Bass.

Cohen, A. M., & Brawer, F. B. (1996). *The American community college* (3rd ed.). San Francisco, CA: Jossey-Bass.

Day, P. R. (1985). *In search of community college partnerships.* Washington, DC: American Association of Community Colleges.

Dougherty, K. J., & Bakia, M. F. (1999). *The new economic development role of the community college.* New York: Columbia University, Teachers College, Community College Research Center.

Floyd, D. L., Skolnik, M. L., & Walker, K. P. (2005). *The community college baccalaureate: Emerging trends and policy issues.* Sterling, VA: Stylus Publishing.

Grubb, W. N., Badway, N., Bell, D., Bragg, D., & Russman, M. (1997). *Workforce, economic, and community development: The changing landscape of the "entrepreneurial" community college.* Berkeley: University of California, National Center for Research in Vocational Education.

Grubb, W. N., & Lazerson, M. (2004). *The education gospel: The economic power of schooling.* Boston: Harvard University Press.

Hull, D., & Grevelle, J. H. (1998). *Tech prep the next generation.* Waco, TX: Cord Communications.

Jacobs, J. (1987). *Training and public policy.* Ann Arbor, MI: Industrial Technology Institute.

Jacobs, J. (1989). Training the workforce of the future. *Technology Review, 92,* 66–72.

Jacobs, J. (1992). *Customized training: A priority for Michigan community colleges.* Watertown, NY: State University of New York Jefferson, Center for Community Studies.

Jacobs, J. (2001). What is the future for post-secondary occupational education? *Journal of Vocation Education, 26*(2), 172–205.

Jacobs, J. (2017, October). Adults and community college degrees. *Inside Higher Education.* Retrieved from https://www.insidehighered.com/views/2017/10/09/community-colleges-should-focus-more-educating-adults-essay.

Jacobs, J., & Grubb, W. N. (2006). The limits of "training for now": Lessons from information technology certification. In T. Bailey & V. S. Morest (Eds.), *Defending the community college equity agenda* (pp. 132–54). Baltimore, MD: Johns Hopkins University Press.

Jacobs, J., & Teahen, R. (1997). Shadow colleges and NCA accreditation: A conceptual framework. In *A collection of papers on self-study and institutional improvement* (pp. 13–19). Chicago: North Central Association of Colleges and Schools.

Jenkins, D. (2018). [National Student Clearinghouse data on fall 2010 FTEIC, degree-seeking community college cohort]. Unpublished CCRC analysis.

Karp, M. M., Jacobs, J., & Hughes, K. L. (2003). *Credentials, curriculum, and access: The debate over nursing preparation.* Washington, DC: Community College Press.

Liebowitz, M., & Taylor, J. C. (2004). *Breaking through: Helping low-skilled adults enter and succeed in colleges and careers.* Boston: Jobs for the Future.

Macomb Community College. (2014). *Year one report: Innovation fund.* Warren, MI: Macomb Community College.

Makela, J. P., Bragg, D. D., & Harwell, E. (2015). *Applied baccalaureate degrees in STEM and technician education: Program implementation in five regions of the United States.* Champaign: University of Illinois at Urbana-Champaign, Office of Community College Research and Leadership.

Modernization Forum Skills Commission. (1993). *Skills for industrial modernization.* Dearborn, MI: Author.

National Assessment of Vocational Education. (2004). *Final report to Congress.* Washington, DC: U.S. Department of Education.

National Coalition of Certification Centers. (2018). *History of NC3.* Retrieved from https://www.nc3.net/about/history-of-nc3/

Newman, K. S., & Winston, H. (2016). *Reskilling America: Learning to labor in the twenty-first century.* New York: Metropolitan Books.

Oakley, E. O., & Bynum, L. A. (2017). An engine of economic growth and a front door to entrepreneurship. *Community College Journal, 87*(3), 5–6.

Obama, B. (2009). *President Obama's remarks on the American graduation initiative, Macomb Community College, Warren, MI, July 14.* Retrieved from https://www.scribd.com/document/17363960/President-Obama-s-Remarks-on-the-American-Graduation-Initiative-Macomb-Community-College-Warren-MI-July-14-2009-Transcript-Video-Link

O'Banion, T. (2016). *Bread and roses: Helping students make a good living and live a good life.* Phoenix, AZ: League for Innovation.

Quigley, M. S., & Bailey, T. (2003). *Community college movement in perspective: Teachers College responds to the Truman Commission.* Lanham, MD: Scarecrow Press.

Rosenfeld, S. A. (1992). *Competitive manufacturing: New strategies for regional development.* New Brunswick, NJ: State University Press.

State of Michigan. (2009). *No worker left behind—outcomes for the first 18 months.* Lansing, MI: Department of Energy, Labor, and Economic Growth.

Teles, E. (2012). Curriculum and teaching strategies for STEM technicians. In D. Hull, *Career pathways for STEM technicians.* Waco, TX: CORD Publications.

US Department of Labor. (2018). *TAACCCT program summary.* Washington, DC: Author.

Van Noy, M., Jacobs, J., Korey, S., Bailey, T., & Hughes, K. L. (2008). *The landscape of noncredit workforce education: State policies and community college practices.* New York: Columbia University, Teachers College, Community College Research Center.

Chapter Nine

Eliminating the Gap between High School and College

What the Next Generation of
Transition Programs Must Do

Joel Vargas, Sarah Hooker, Michael Collins, and Ana Bertha Gutierrez

The key to a career that makes a good living is no longer a high school diploma, but a postsecondary credential or degree (Carnevale and Cheah 2018). While community colleges provide accessible paths to both, too many students exit high school and fail to take the next step into college—or start and drop out (*Remediation* 2012). Especially for students who are the first in their families to go to college and from low-income backgrounds—for whom this is most likely to happen—improving the transition from high school into the first year of college is an important part of fulfilling the promise of community colleges to improve economies and economic mobility.

Increasing college completion is not merely a matter of high schools better preparing students or colleges implementing interventions for entering students. It also requires high schools and community colleges working *together* to make a smoother handoff of students between the two systems to set them up for success. This idea—of *high-school-to-college transition partnerships*—has gained broad acceptance as a desirable practice at community colleges.

This is a stark contrast from two decades ago, when the general attitude of community colleges toward high schools was "just give us students who are ready," and the primary goal of high schools was to get students to the graduation stage rather than through the college door. Now there is a growing appetite on both sides for collaborating to increase college success and arguably a movement toward intertwined missions: high schools have been pushed to expand their goals to include ensuring that their students are prepared for college and career, and community colleges have been pushed to think more about developing the pipeline of students transitioning into their institutions.

The embrace of high-school-to-college transition partnerships has increased over the past two decades, sparked by a number of societal trends, especially more demand for young people to earn a postsecondary credential in order to find good jobs; increased attention on low postsecondary completion rates, especially for people from low-income backgrounds, who are hurt most by growing loan debt without credentials to show for it; and the realization that too many high school graduates are not ready for the next step into college, ending up stuck in college remediation.

This idea has spawned the spread of models aimed at smoothing the transition and truly preparing high school students for college success, including

- dual enrollment and early college schools that enable students to earn college credit while in high school;
- twelfth-grade college-transition courses that provide a route for underprepared seniors to avert remediation in college; and
- career pathways that deepen and apply academic learning by connecting the high school curriculum to postsecondary programs of study (and work-based learning).

But like many worthy notions, broader acceptance and expansion can lead to a wider range of quality and results, and some evidence suggests that there is both stronger and weaker implementation of high-school-to-college transition partnerships coinciding with their growth. One of the reasons for this variation is that strategies associated with the idea are often relegated to the periphery of other core changes that colleges are undertaking to improve student success.

The early success of these individual strategies has ironically put them at risk of being adopted as stand-alone (even symbolic) solutions rather than as strategies integral to larger systemic change goals, including authentic alignment and partnerships with K–12 systems, credentialing paths that maximize short-term income outcomes and also provide opportunities for further education, and guided pathways that create a more coherent and structured educational experience so that more students reach key educational milestones and careers. This is the next generation of work surrounding collaborative high school to college efforts, if these efforts are to contribute in a meaningful way to the equitable and large-scale success of community college students.

In this chapter the authors recount the evolution of efforts associated with high-school-to-college transition partnerships, describe approaches that epitomize the integrated role they should play in community college improvement writ large, describe their impact so far and why it is not as great as it could be, and envision how this idea might look when it truly transforms community colleges.

TRANSITIONS: A BRIEF HISTORY

High schools and colleges are operated, funded, and governed by different sets of structures and policies. Even though the first community college, Joliet Junior College in Illinois, ironically grew in 1901 out of a high school wanting to make postsecondary education more accessible for its graduates (Joliet Junior College 2018), there is a fundamental difference between secondary and postsecondary education. High school is part of a compulsory system that the state requires students to attend, typically through high school age, and community college is a voluntary system that students choose to attend.

This accounts for many key differences, including why public K–12 students pay nothing to attend, while college students pay tuition or receive aid from state and federal governments to cover the cost of attendance. It is a factor in why K–12 learning standards, assessments, and graduation requirements are so often set by state governments, while states generally exert less control in public college systems, which have a tradition of academic freedom and shared governance with faculty.

Also, as high schools operate in loco parentis ("in the place of a parent"), educators there generally view the support of students as being their responsibility. In contrast, students are in college by their own volition, and the general collegiate ethos is that it is the students' responsibility to manage their own learning—that is, sink or swim—which is one of the reasons the transition from high school to college can be so jarring for them.

A New Era of P–16 Efforts

There was little sense until the early 2000s that K–12 and postsecondary institutions ought to act more as aligned parts of a singular education pipeline than as loosely coupled systems. In the early years of the millennium, a convergence of interests, goals, innovations, and evidence fueled more systematic, state, and national attention to the need for secondary and postsecondary education to work better together. Larger forces began to push for the improvement of K–12, higher education, and the transition between the two.

They included both state and federal governments and philanthropy advocating for more consistently rigorous standards in elementary and secondary education, and higher completion rates in postsecondary education—particularly in community colleges. These separate pressures came together as policy makers and influencers realized that achieving each goal could be partly facilitated by having the K–12 system and higher education system work more as a P–16 system (the "P" is included to signal the importance of prekindergarten education).

K–12 Standards

The pinnacle of standards-based reform in K–12 education arguably spanned 2001 to 2009. It culminated with the formation by forty-eight governors and state education leaders of the Common Core State Standards Initiative to develop a shared set of K–12 standards in math and English that aligned with the expectations of higher education for entering students.

The lead-up to this moment was marked by the landmark 2001 No Child Left Behind (NCLB) reauthorization of the Elementary and Secondary Education Act, itself an important development in K–12 standards-based reform. The law, a bold new assertion of the federal role in education, required that states assess students at specified grade levels based on state standards, make the results transparent to the public through an accounting of annual yearly progress, and define consequences and supports for students and schools not meeting standards. NCLB and years of developments leading up to its passage actually laid bare the fact that states had very different education standards.

Thus, the Common Core effort was marked by both a commitment to common standards across states and the recognition that careers with good wages required postsecondary education. Accordingly, all state standards should be aligned to the knowledge and skills needed to be successful in math and English at the college level. This was a major force pushing K–12 and higher education system leaders to work together to align what was taught and assessed in high school with what colleges expected of entering students in nonremedial courses. It was a product of and punctuated by years of work during this period by national networks of states—including K–12, college, and industry representatives—convened by Achieve, Inc. (itself created by governors and leading businesses in 1996) and other advocates for more rigorous K–12 standards.

Correspondingly, many states also created statewide P–16 councils—composed of leaders from local and state-level K–12 and postsecondary systems with (typically) advisory authority (Education Commission of the States 2018)—and other local and state secondary-postsecondary groups whose goal was to better coordinate and align the systems, sometimes examining and recommending changes to high school graduation requirements and programs that could create a more seamless education pipeline.

Community College Improvement Efforts

At the same time, community colleges were feeling pressure from policy makers to increase student completion rates. Starting in 2004, Lumina Foundation and the Bill & Melinda Gates Foundation elevated attention to the need for community college improvement and lent support to colleges engaged in this endeavor, including Achieving the Dream, Completion by Design, and Jobs for the Future's (JFF) Postsecondary State Policy Network.

These initiatives often included a focus on the importance of secondary-postsecondary efforts to align standards and expectations so that more high school graduates would enter college with momentum toward their goal of earning a degree or credential. For example, a JFF brief by Michael Collins on tenets for improving developmental education practices and policies included "preventative strategies" such as early assessment testing of high school students (Collins 2009). The multistate, multicollege Completion by Design initiative developed and tested strategies within a "loss/momentum framework" for students that included a focus on "connection from interest in college enrollment to application"—including strategies such as early colleges and dual enrollment. In 2013 JFF documented that four states had incorporated dual enrollment into their higher education performance-based funding models—a major reform lever for states trying to improve college success rates—by rewarding colleges that encouraged high school students to complete college courses early (Struhl 2013).

The Influence of Research

A surge of seminal research revealing significant misalignment between the requirements for high school graduation and college readiness further fueled improvement efforts. For example, a national study called the Stanford Bridge Project found that colleges in six states used a wide variety of homemade and standardized instruments to assess entering students for placement into college-level or remedial courses (Venezia, Kirst, and Antonio 2003). This lack of consistency and connection to K–12 standards—in addition to the lack of K–12 guidance counseling—was especially damaging for first-generation college students, who were least likely to be able to navigate this cacophony on their own. Clifford Adelman's research for the US Department of Education, *Answers in the Toolbox*, showed the strong relationship between college success and a rigorous high school curriculum, particularly in math, and how many students did not take or have access to such a curriculum (Adelman 1999).

The Center for Higher Education Management Systems illustrated in stark terms, using milestones of educational pipeline progression, how few students actually completed college, earning a credential or degree. Roughly one in five ninth graders graduated from high school on time, went directly to college, returned for a second year, and graduated within 150 percent of program time by 2006 (NCHEMS Information Center 2018). The pipeline metaphor began popping up at policy conferences focused on college readiness and success and pointed to the need for action at multiple junctures to stem the steady loss of students.

JFF and other organizations also proposed ideas for promising policies and practices to fix these disconnections and create a more seamless P–16 system. In numerous publications, the Community College Research Center noted the rise of and potential for "high school to college" mechanisms, such as career pathways and dual enrollment, to support student success (Community College Research Center 2018).

The JFF conferences of policy makers and influencers in 2003 and 2007 issued calls to "Double the Numbers" of low-income students completing college. The JFF-edited volume *Double the Numbers* and its 2007 companion book, *Minding the Gap*, took stock of some of the most promising state efforts and imagined the kinds of data systems, governance arrangements, incentives, and other infrastructure needed to better bridge the secondary and postsecondary systems. The books and convenings, notable for participation by many leading policy makers and influencers, constituted a rising chorus of voices harmonized around strategies targeting the transition between the final years of high school and the first years of college.

Innovations at Work

Coinciding with pressures for more coordination between secondary and postsecondary systems was emerging evidence about the positive effects of joint efforts aimed at improving college readiness and success. One of the most promising ideas JFF advanced was early college high schools, started by thirteen state and national organizations with a large investment by the Bill & Melinda Gates Foundation. The blending of high school and two years of college in these schools for low-income youth provided an important lens for understanding how secondary and postsecondary policies, systems, and cultures could work better together to create more seamless routes to degrees and credentials. The partnerships spawned by this investment created 280 schools in twenty-five states serving over eighty thousand students annually.

Emerging research about these schools over the years suggested and eventually showed conclusively that the early college investments were paying off in improved high school graduation, college enrollment, and completion rates (Berger et al. 2014; Edmunds et al. 2015). Simultaneously, research suggested that expanding dual enrollment—a key component in early college schools that was scalable—could help more high school students enroll in and complete college, including low-income youth (Karp et al. 2007).

Other research widened the lens on the elements of successful college readiness and success programs and confirmed the importance of secondary-postsecondary alignment and collaboration. The American Youth Policy Forum published a volume in 2009 that examined commonalities among twenty-three education programs, with evidence from rigorous research on preparing students for college success (Hooker and Brand 2009). Among other findings, they noted that what bound the various approaches was a focus on "rigor and academic support," "relationships," and "partnerships and cross-systems collaboration."

Policies and State Systems Promote Growth

The clear need for stronger P–16 alignment, combined with the emergence of promising approaches, also led to increasingly bigger and bolder policies and investments promoting collaborative high school to college transition efforts by state policy makers and systems, solidifying their place among important strategies to improve student success in college.

Early Assessments and Expansion of Dual Enrollment

Several states created policies to promote the expansion of the transition strategies that lead students to college completion by creating some infrastructure to support secondary and postsecondary system collaboration. The California State University's (CSU) Early Assessment Program, started in 2002, created a statewide opportunity for high school students to gauge their level of college readiness in English and math by taking an optional test during their junior year. Students could use the results to determine where they needed to improve during their senior year in order to be prepared for college-level study.

Students demonstrating proficiency in those assessments were able to bypass CSU's mandatory English and math placement tests (The California State University 2018). This effort took a statewide approach to incorporating early assessments for college readiness and also led to CSU's early development of senior year transition courses enabling unprepared students, upon successful completion, to get up to speed and avoid developmental education in the freshman year.

Another area in which states led the policy charge was expanding dual enrollment opportunities. For example, 2005 HB 1 legislation in Texas required all districts to offer students the chance to earn at least twelve credits through dual credit opportunities, including advanced placement or international baccalaureate. In 2015, HB 505 removed restrictions on the grade levels and number of courses that could be taken, thereby establishing the infrastructure within the state education system to offer access to dual enrollment to all students.

Similarly, in Ohio the College Credit Plus Act mandated that all high schools provide pathways for participating students to earn fifteen to thirty college credits toward a college major or career path. This policy intended to transform dual enrollment from an opportunity provided to select students in certain districts into a clearly defined program accessible to all.

Career Pathways

In 2011 a report issued by the Harvard Graduate School of Education, *Pathways to Prosperity*, expanded the boundaries of the idea that high schools and community colleges ought to be working in tandem to promote student success (Symonds, Schwartz, and Ferguson 2011). It argued that many good careers in fast-growing industries were accessible without a bachelor's degree, and instead with postsecondary certificates and credentials in technical career areas, including information technology, health care, and advanced manufacturing. Given this, the report advocated for more models combining the early college approach with a focus on accelerating students toward these credentials and opportunities for further education, creating career pathways in grades 9 through 14.

With the country still in a slow recovery from the 2008 recession, this message resonated with policy makers. The US Department of Labor invested $100 million in the Youth Career Connect program, which emphasized career pathways in high school with an "Integration of Postsecondary Education and Training" (US Department of Labor 2018).

States also made investments in high school career pathways, creating additional pressure and rewards for working early with high school students, especially in coordinating and aligning pathways across high school and college. In the nation's most populous state, the California Career Pathways Trust (California Department of Education 2018) provided a $500 million investment via two rounds of grants to create or expand career pathway programs for grade nine through the first two years of college. This program required that high schools and community colleges work together, coordinating and sharing resources in their pathway work.

Additional policies and programs in California provide further building blocks to support grades 9 through 14 career pathway expansion efforts.

Policy Shifts

Increasing acceptance of the idea that high schools and colleges ought to couple their efforts to create stronger transitions into and through postsecondary education has also been codified and encouraged in federal and state policy. In 2015 the federal Every Student Succeeds Act, the latest iteration of the Elementary and Secondary Education Act, heightened emphasis on post-secondary readiness for the K–12 system. Consequently, many states have opted to include dual enrollment, along with advanced placement and international baccalaureate, as performance indicators in their state accountability systems for high schools.

The dual enrollment Pell Grant experiment provides an estimated ten thousand Pell-eligible high school students with opportunities to use dual enrollment to take community college coursework for free to test whether federal college aid can be used more efficiently (US Department of Education 2018). Considered together, these policies serve to establish crucial infrastructure for the cross-system partnerships needed to align and coordinate transition points between high school and college. They also elevate a cultural shift starting to take root that encourages K–12 and postsecondary systems to use these strategies to build more permanent bridges between them and to use partnerships as a "new normal" for promoting student success.

A GOOD IDEA SPREADS

Again, the notion that colleges and K–12 districts should partner to improve student transitions across systems has rapidly taken root. Policy incentives and mandates, funder-driven initiatives, and community demands are increasingly pushing two-year colleges to expand their sphere of activity and influence down into the high school level, at the same time that high schools are being called on to demonstrate that their graduates are prepared for college and careers. The popularity of transition initiatives is evidenced by their impressive rate of uptake.

Between 1995 and 2015 the number of high school dual enrollees in community colleges more than quadrupled, rising from 163,000 to 745,000. By 2010 high school dual enrollees represented 15 percent of "first time in college" students in community colleges nationally. In a handful of states, they accounted for as much as 25 to 37 percent (Fink, Jenkins, and Yanagiura 2017). The National Center for Education Statistics reported that approximately 1.4 million students nationwide were enrolled in dual enrollment courses during the 2010–2011 school year—the most recent year for which such data were reported—and all signs point to continuing strong growth in the years since then (Thomas et al. 2013).

Particularly rapid rises can be seen in states that adopted policies designed to guarantee access to the opportunity for all high school students to earn a certain amount of college credit for free. In Texas, for instance, dual enrollment numbers swelled by 650 percent from 2000 to 2015 (Texas Higher Education Coordinating Board 2016). Community colleges serve over 90 percent of Texas's dual enrollees.

Within this context, the concept of transition courses, which are intended to address students' remedial needs before high school graduation, has similarly evolved from a set of boutique partnerships between school districts and colleges into a strategy that has been codified and scaled. A recent national study found that seventeen states offered transition curricula through state-led initiatives in 2017—up from eight states in 2012–2013—and locally driven initiatives still abound (Fay, Barnett, and Chavarín 2017).

Policy makers' enthusiasm for high-school-to-college transition strategies does not appear to be waning. Instead, dual enrollment is such a high priority that nine state governors cited it among the policy priorities referenced in their State of the State addresses in 2018 (American Association of State Colleges and Universities 2018). In addition, sixteen governors mentioned career and technical education (CTE) among their top educational priorities, particularly in light of the changing economy and the rise of automation (Whinnery and Pompelia 2018). Many of these CTE proposals involve community and technical colleges playing a key "bridging" role between secondary education and business.

Increased interest from both policy makers and the general public has created mounting pressure on school districts and community colleges to expand their collaborative efforts and reach an ever-greater number of students.

IMPLEMENTATION: PRINCIPLES OF STRONG PRACTICE

While the idea of transition strategies such as dual enrollment, early college high schools, and career pathways has exploded in popularity, their design and implementation vary significantly. In many cases, adaptations of a model represent new innovations that could be more effective in a particular context or that aim to address common barriers to scale or sustainability. Nonetheless, the most successful transition initiatives tend to retain a focus on a similar set of principles: best practices that research has linked to improved outcomes for older adolescents, underrepresented students, and those who are the first in their families to access higher education. These include

1. acceleration with support as the rule;
2. scaffolding transitions and supporting navigation of systems; and
3. supportive relationships, building social capital, and culturally responsive practices.

Each of these principles can be applied to a range of reform efforts in K–12 schools, as well as initiatives on college campuses. However, they are particularly powerful when employed as part of pathways that link the worlds of high school and college, ensuring that their influence is not lost as a student moves through the transition zone between the two.

Acceleration with Support as the Rule

To meet the heterogeneous needs of students coming to education with different levels of knowledge and skill, educational systems have historically varied curricular offerings rather than changed support systems and instruction to ensure that all students have access to equally rigorous curricula (Graham 1984). For example, when students struggle, educators are apt to slow down the pace of learning or put them in less rigorous courses that may not prepare them for college and careers. This approach fails large numbers of students who could have succeeded if challenged and sufficiently supported. Most college students who start out placed in developmental courses never move on to the required college-level courses in the same subjects (*Remediation* 2012).

Strong high-school-to-college transition programs place an emphasis on keeping, deepening, and speeding the pace and rigor of learning joined with proper support and instructional innovation. The goal is not to hold students back until they have met traditional markers of college readiness, but rather to hasten their progress through extra interventions.

This is one of the reasons Tennessee's program Seamless Alignment and Integrated Learning Support (SAILS) is effective. First designed by Chattanooga State Community College and local high school faculty, its success has spawned statewide expansion with investments by the legislature. High school students testing below the college-ready level on the ACT, who would likely take developmental coursework in college, have the opportunity to take SAILS in their senior year of high school instead. SAILS provides early intervention through blended learning lessons (online instruction coupled with high school teacher support) in key math competencies that students need for college success. After completing SAILS, students may take a tuition-free college math class while still in high school for dual credit. Students who pass all five competencies are guaranteed entry into college-level math at any public postsecondary institution in the state.

As the state has continued to expand SAILS, the program was projected to have reached over fifty thousand Tennessee students by the 2016–2017 school year. Two years earlier, the state projected that SAILS had already saved students about $64 million in tuition costs by avoiding developmental education (Higher Ed for Higher Standards 2016).

This principle is not about lowering standards, but about strengthening preparation strategies and support systems so that students have an equal opportunity to meet high standards. Instead of tracking students and focusing on only the highest achievers, exemplary transition programs share the premise that all students can achieve college and career readiness with the right interventions.

Scaffolding Transitions and Supporting Navigation of Systems

Transition programs were created and continue to exist, to a large extent, because it is widely acknowledged that the different levels of the education system operate as separate realms, with their own structures, cultural norms, and systems of reward and punishment. Compared to high schools, higher education institutions—especially large, broad-access colleges—are notoriously challenging places to navigate. Succeeding in this context—or even accessing the resources that are in place to help those who are struggling— often requires considerable insider knowledge, which is especially hard to come by for students who are the first in their families to pursue postsecondary education (Tinto 1993). Strong transition programs take many forms, but they share a common principle of "scaffolding" experiences early in the college trajectory and explicitly building the nonacademic knowledge that contributes to persistence and completion.

As an example of a strategy that spans the gap between secondary and postsecondary education, many community colleges and their K–12 partners have experimented with placing high school dual enrollees in the same college success courses taken by incoming college students. These courses, which are offered for college credit and in many cases are required for degree-seeking students, typically introduce students to the college's library systems, academic support labs, and other resources, and include individualized academic and career planning. By taking these classes as early as ninth grade, students have a scaffolded opportunity to practice college success skills and hone them with increasing independence throughout high school.

Effective programs also provide structures and clear guidance to link the high school curriculum with college degrees and major requirements, as well as actual jobs in high-demand industries. While many students take a seemingly random assortment of dual enrollment courses based on their schedules or interests, some high school and college partnerships place a stronger emphasis on ensuring that dual enrollment is connected to a longer-term degree plan.

As one example, high school students in the Wonderful Agriculture Career Prep program, launched by the agrobusiness Wonderful Company in California's Central Valley, earn forty to sixty college credits in specific career pathways such as plant science and agriculture technology. The program depends on partnerships with three community colleges, two four-year universities, and seven high schools. The partnership agreements between each college and high school spell out the required course sequence for each grade level to ensure that each student in the Ag Prep cohort meets the program's goals, and the curriculum also incorporates work-based learning. Students graduate with all the courses needed for admission to California's four-year universities, but they are also qualified with an associate degree to move directly into a skilled job with Wonderful.

The Ag Prep program exemplifies a career pathway approach that integrates a rigorous academic curriculum and benefits from strong cross-sector partnerships. The intentional program design takes the guesswork out of choosing college courses and uses students' time in high school as efficiently as possible.

Supportive Relationships, Social Capital Development, and Culturally Responsive Practices

Perhaps the most powerful element shared by strong transition programs is a focus on relationships, social capital, and culturally affirming practices. Personalization and strong relationships—between peers as well as between adult mentors and students—have been repeatedly cited as crucial factors promoting a sense of integration in the postsecondary environment, which in turn promotes persistence (Karp 2011; Karp, Hughes, and O'Gara 2010; Bensimon 2007).

Positive relationships also build the social capital of first-generation students by increasing access to crucial information and resources to assist with academic as well as personal and financial challenges. The strong research base on the importance of relationships and social capital has influenced the spread of transition programs, college student success initiatives, and transfer preparation programs that are based on cohort models. These programs can have an even greater impact when they are based in culturally responsive teaching and positive identity development, which aim to address the sense of isolation, and in many cases exclusion and discrimination, that students from underrepresented groups often experience on college campuses (Bensimon 2007; Rendon 1994).

The Puente Program is an intersegmental program that draws on the assets of students' home cultures to support the success of first-generation students in California, many of whom are Latino. With an overall goal of increasing bachelor's degree completion for educationally disadvantaged students and preparing these individuals to return to their communities as professionals and mentors, the program operates at thirty-eight high schools and sixty-five community colleges.

At both the high school and college levels, cohorts of Puente students take a sequence of English courses that draw heavily on Mexican and Latin American literature. College students also participate in a college success class taught by a Puente counselor and mentoring from local professionals; meanwhile, the high school counseling program engages entire families in college-planning workshops. The program has a long history of success at the community college level—measured by transfer rates that are higher than state averages for all students—and has also demonstrated academic gains for high school students (Puente n.d.).

Even though Puente's high school and college programs were designed to operate as separate efforts, it is worth noting that both epitomize the principles of supportive relationships, social capital development, and culturally responsive practices. It is quite likely that local high schools and colleges with their own Puente Programs in the same vicinity would easily find synergies by coupling their efforts, if they are not doing so already.

The Potential Pitfalls of Replication

The examples highlighted in this section reflect research-based principles that promote successful transitions and college persistence. However, none of these models is a silver bullet, and trouble arises when initiatives are replicated without addressing the underlying dysfunction of disconnected systems.

Early college, dual enrollment, and career pathways have become part of the community college and K–12 lexicon. Ironically, that brand recognition runs the risk of losing sight of the principles of design and practice that drive the success or weakness of any approach that attempts to promote stronger high-school-to-postsecondary transitions for students, especially traditionally underserved youth. When a model starts to be championed and perceived as a panacea, implementers may displace the goal. The goal is not to replicate the model (though that may be one step toward the real goal) but to use the principled strategies it coalesces to transform and systematize the ways that high schools and colleges work together to better serve all students.

TROUBLE ON THE HORIZON?

Challenges with Evidence

For all the interest in and proliferation of transition programs, they vary widely, and the research on their effectiveness is mixed. Rigorous research has found positive effects for dual enrollment and early college. But there are few rigorous studies of other transition efforts that find a significant impact of their effectiveness in increasing college completion.

There is descriptive evidence on success courses and transition courses, most of which is mixed. The logic of transition strategies is intuitive, but the empirical evidence that exists to this point is limited in its ability to guide their design, implementation, and establishment in state- and district-level policies across the nation. It is crucial that research continue. One of the issues that might be blunting the impact of transition strategies is that they are typically implemented in isolation from other completion strategies.

Challenges with Variation

A challenge in understanding the impact of transition strategies is the wide variation in their design and implementation. Strategies with the same name—college success courses, for example—often have different curricular components, making it difficult to compare results across them. After a 2012 study on student success courses found positive impacts, there was growth in the number of success courses implemented across the country (Karp et al. 2012). But the wide variation of success courses means that generalizing the effects are problematic and success outcomes vary.

Similarly, there is a great deal of variance in dual enrollment, curricular elements, policy structures, and outcomes. The Community College Research Center has shown that although future college outcomes for dual enrollees nationally on balance are stronger than for non-dual enrollees, outcomes vary widely by state, suggesting that specific policies and practices matter (Fink, Jenkins, and Yanagiura 2017).

Challenges with Quality

Dual enrollment and early college are among the more robust transition strategies, in part because they integrate high school and college. Yet even here, there is some debate around the rigor and quality of college credits that students take in high school. Raymund Paredes, commissioner of higher education in Texas, raised the question of quality in an article in the *Austin American Statesman* when he noted that over forty thousand students taking dual enrollment courses in Texas had not demonstrated college readiness through the state's college-readiness assessment or the SAT or ACT.

And unlike advanced placement, in which students must pass an exam to earn credit, there is no mechanism to validate whether students have mastered learning outcomes associated with college courses. That said, rigorous research has shown that dual enrollees in Texas go on to enroll in and complete associate and bachelor's degrees at significantly higher rates than other high school students with similar demographic backgrounds and academic achievement (Struhl and Vargas 2012).

Nonetheless, as dual enrollment expands, it is important for research to shed more light on the question of the equivalency between dual enrollment courses taken in high school and college courses taken on the college campus. While high school teachers must meet certain standards to be eligible to teach college courses for dual enrollment, faculty at the college have expressed concern over whether the courses taught by the high school are truly college-level courses. These concerns must be addressed or refuted with more evidence.

Challenges of Isolated Interventions

Even as the field will need more research about the elements of good implementation, there is an equally if not larger challenge and opportunity in strengthening high-school-to-college transitions. Such strategies often lack connection to more comprehensive student success strategies at community colleges. Admittedly, the goal of transition strategies varies. For some, such as transition courses, the primary goal is college readiness. For others, the goal is accumulation of college credits. And for yet others, like early college, the goal is completing an associate degree.

High school transition strategies may not be living up to their potential for impact, in part because they are all too often a single-point intervention that is not connected to a broader comprehensive student success strategy. From the evidence on completion in *Redesigning America's Community Colleges* (Bailey, Jaggars, and Jenkins 2015), it is known that isolated interventions that do not consider a student's full pathway are less likely to result in successful completion.

According to researchers at the Community College Research Center: "Simply putting into place a transition course, without deep dialogue and strong collaboration between the two sectors in order to help shape the student's entire senior year, is unlikely to improve student outcomes" (Bailey, Jaggars, and Jenkins 2015, 141). Any uptick in success outcomes that might occur from a single intervention washes out without sustained attention to the subsequent stages of a students' progress toward a credential (Bailey, Jaggars, and Jenkins 2015).

ALTERNATIVE VISIONS/THE FUTURE

Rather than considering transition strategies in and of themselves, there is an opportunity to increase their impact by considering them as part of a coherent credential pathway that is aligned to students' education and work goals. Bailey, Jaggars, and Jenkins note that "transition curricula may be most helpful when students begin the process of academic and career exploration, for example, by exploring meta-majors available at local community colleges and state universities, which could allow students to transition more quickly into a specific programs of study when they enter college" (2015, 141). This will require redesigning transition strategies, because the majority, with the notable exception of early college, only consider the front end of the student experience. Transition courses and summer bridge programs, for example, do not consider the full student experience along a credential pathway.

The premise that students need a more explicit choice architecture leading them to their end goal undergirds the guided pathway reform effort that is taking root in community colleges nationwide. (See chapter 4 in this volume.) The guided pathway approach focuses course taking on highly structured program maps for the students' full educational experience, from the time they enter college through the time they earn a credential.

Guided pathways have four major components: clarify the path, help students choose a path, help students stay on their path, and ensure that students are learning (PathwaysResources.org 2018). Guided pathways are informed by evidence from multiple disciplines, including behavioral economics, organizational effectiveness, learning theory, and lessons learned from implementation of major community college completion reform efforts over the last decade.

These reforms have grown from a novel idea to a national movement in community colleges. A number of states have adopted or considered policies encouraging or requiring higher education institutions to adopt guided pathways. For example, the California Community Colleges Chancellor's Office released the *Vision for Success*, framing the chancellor's vision for transforming the college system to increase student completion of degree/certificate programs, transfer to four-year institutions, and pathways to jobs providing a living wage.

To support this vision, the 2017 legislation SB 539 provides an incentive grant to help establish guided pathways as the vehicle for this transformation across all 114 community colleges in California. Pending legislation for the Community College Student Achievement Act will generate further incentives to create a "coherent, integrated, and system-wide approach that provides students with instruction, advising, support services, and financial aid."

At the national level, the American Association of Community Colleges (AACC) is leading a major Pathways project. Thirty colleges in seventeen states are "building capacity for community colleges to design and implement structured academic and career pathways at scale, for all of their students" (AACC 2018).

Yet guided pathway reforms typically focus on "regular" students who are enrolled in community college and do not strongly feature programming at the secondary level; in most cases, they have developed separately from the high-school-to-college transition programs at the same institutions.

Drawing on the known evidence and the lessons from implementation, there is an opportunity to develop an alternative vision that integrates transition strategies more centrally into the guided pathways model. This integration requires rethinking both strategies and developing an alternative vision in which they become a coherent completion agenda, as opposed to two different strategies, one primarily developed by faculty and administrators working in high school and the other developed by faculty and administrators working in colleges. Integrating transition strategies into guided pathways will require secondary and postsecondary collaboration on the design, delivery, and validation of a new model for which secondary and postsecondary institutions share responsibility (Vargas and Venezia 2015).

In *Redesigning America's Community Colleges*, Bailey, Jaggars, and Jenkins (2015) argue that postsecondary institutions might need to first do the work of structuring and mapping a focused set of credential pathways within the institution. This is the first element of guided pathways: clarify the path. Clear and structured programs give high school students and their counselors better targets to aim at so that the standards and expectations for successfully transitioning from high school to college are more transparent.

But more than the clear signaling about standards, assessments, and performance expectations, closer integration of transition strategies and guided pathways would include joint consideration of both career and transfer outcomes that are aligned with jobs that pay family-supporting wages and transfer to four-year institutions with junior status. Secondary and postsecondary collaboration is also needed at this stage to identify course sequences, including the specific mathematics and English gateway courses associated with different programs of study.

Lorain County Community College in Ohio is an example of an institution that is already leading the way by linking its dual enrollment offerings with its institution-wide guided pathway reforms. The college has created roadmaps of courses spanning from ninth grade dual enrollment all the way to the completion of bachelor's degrees in more than twenty majors. Students in the My University Pathways program can finish their associate degree by high school graduation and a bachelor's degree, offered in conjunction with the college's university partners, only two years later—at 80 percent lower cost than a traditional four-year-degree plan.

Once the college-level programs of study are clearly mapped and student end goals have been thoroughly considered, secondary and postsecondary institutions can collaborate on the second element of guided pathways: help students get on a path. The second element is primarily about providing support to help students clarify their education and work goals. This type of directed educational planning course taking is not a typical feature of transition strategies.

Dual enrollment, for example, is often à la carte. High school students may—and often do—take college-level courses that are not necessarily connected to each other, nor are they necessarily connected to a student's end goals for education and work. But dual enrollment can be jointly redesigned by secondary and postsecondary stakeholders to help students make progress toward their end goals.

Early career exploration or exploration of meta-majors could occur at local colleges so that high school students could develop early momentum in college-level programs of study when they transition to college. North Carolina moved in this direction by passing a state-level policy—Career and College Promise—that requires all college courses for dual credit to be aligned to one of three pathways—the general education core, CTE, or Cooperative Innovation High Schools (early colleges)—so that the courses count toward students' credentials.

The third element of guided pathways—help students stay on their path—is primarily about student progression through the college. This stage features ongoing advising, tracking student progression, and helping students who are not progressing find credential pathways that might be a better fit for their goals. Secondary and postsecondary collaboration on a feedback loop could be helpful at this stage. Sharing information on high school students' performance in college-level programs of study may identify gaps in high school curriculum and identify areas that secondary and postsecondary faculty and administrators might improve.

The fourth element of guided pathways—ensure that students are learning—could benefit from secondary and postsecondary collaboration on developing learning outcomes for student pathways. Increasingly, project- and work-based learning are important elements of credential pathways as high schools and colleges attempt to prepare their students to be successful in collaborating with others and transitioning from school to work. While there are few examples of the secondary-postsecondary integration described above, the Pathways to Prosperity Initiative, co-led by JFF and the Harvard University Graduate School of Education, is a rare effort promoting this kind of integration of transition strategies and guided pathways.

The guided pathway model has direct implications for how colleges are partnering with local high schools, as the pillars that undergird the model call for clarifying the path to college for students. The call to provide clear bridges between high school and college is pushing the systems to build the collaborative and cross-system partnership needed to do so, setting the stage for the pockets of transition programs and approaches to come together in more powerful ways—and on a much larger scale than we have seen in the past.

CONCLUSION

The idea that colleges and high schools should work together to create bridges and better transitions between their educational realms has transformed community colleges, insofar as it is becoming normalized as something colleges need to do—and have a growing appetite for doing—to promote student success at their institutions. But as strategies associated with the idea are implemented and expanded, they will not live up to their potential to achieve transformative outcomes unless they are integral to other core changes that colleges are undertaking to improve student success and continue to be researched for their efficacy and variations in design.

The guided pathway model is an example of how to think through scenarios for systemic integration of these collaborative secondary-postsecondary approaches precisely because it is a comprehensive framework that touches the core of the community college enterprise. But the main point is no less true for community colleges that are undertaking similar reforms by another name and developing partnerships with high schools to promote college readiness and success.

REFERENCES

Adelman, Clifford. 1999. *Answers in the Tool Box: Academic Intensity, Attendance Patterns, and Bachelor's Degree Attainment*. Washington, DC: U.S. Department of Education.

American Association of Community Colleges (AACC). 2018. "AACC Pathways Project." Accessed July 15, 2018. https://www.aacc.nche.edu/programs/aacc-pathways-project/.

American Association of State Colleges and Universities. 2018. "State Policy Update: The 2018 Gubernatorial State of the State Addresses and Higher Education." Accessed July 5, 2018. https://www.magnetmail.net/actions/email_web_version.cfm?ep=QFJgARdkNjq 7GOq_AnzZUUEYmckw8FohSkY0hyppgZtBgLUhN6exLi_2byUo29h5__ iiT8PshccVEDNU-3SbfjT4UR81JsuzY4R_Q_69B9gGUZpHn3IwEmTGiagxLrtn.

Bailey, Thomas R., Shanna Smith Jaggars, and Davis Jenkins. 2015. *Redesigning America's Community Colleges: A Clearer Path to Student Success*. Cambridge, MA. Harvard University Press.

Bensimon, Estela Mara. 2007. "The Underestimated Significance of Practitioner Knowledge in the Scholarship on Student Success." *Review of Higher Education* 30, no. 4: 441–469.

Berger, Andrea, Lori Turk-Bicakci, Michael Garet, Joel Knudson, and Gur Hoshen. 2014. *Early College, Early Success: Early College High School Initiative Impact Study*. Washington, DC: American Institutes for Research.

California Department of Education. 2018. "California Career Pathways Trust (CCPT)." Accessed July 10, 2018. https://www.cde.ca.gov/ci/ct/pt/.

The California State University. 2018. "About the Early Assessment Program." Accessed July 10, 2018. https://www.calstate.edu/eap/about.shtml.

Carnevale, Anthony P., and Ban Cheah. 2018. *Five Rules of the College and Career Game*. Washington, DC: Georgetown University Center on Education and the Workforce.

Collins, Michael Lawrence. 2009. *Setting Up Success in Developmental Education: How State Policy Can Help Community Colleges Improve Student Outcomes*. Boston: JFF.

Community College Research Center. 2018. "High School to College." Accessed July 15, 2018. https://ccrc.tc.columbia.edu/High-School-to-College.html.

Edmunds, Julie, Fatih Unlu, Elizabeth Glennie, Lawrence Bernstein, Lily Fesler, Jane Furey, and Nina Arshavsky. 2015. "Smoothing the Transition to Postsecondary Education: The Impact of the Early College Model." *Journal of Research on Educational Effectiveness* 10, no. 2: 297–325.

Education Commission of the States. 2018. "P-16/P-20 Councils—All State Profiles." https://www.ecs.org/wp-content/uploads/State-Information-Request_-P-20-Accountability-Measures-and-Report-Cards.pdf. Accessed July 4, 2018.

Fay, Maggie P., Elisabeth A. Barnett, and Octaviano Chavarín. 2017. *How States Are Implementing Transition Curricula: Results from a National Scan.* New York: Community College Research Center.

Fink, John, Davis Jenkins, and Takeshi Yanagiura. 2017. *What Happens to Students Who Take Community College "Dual Enrollment" Courses in High School?* New York: Community College Research Center.

Graham, Patricia. 1984. "Schools: Cacophony about Practice, Silence about Purpose." *Daedalus*, 113, no. 4, 29–57.

Higher Ed for Higher Standards. 2016. "Precollege Interventions Help Increase College Readiness, Reduce Remediation." http://higheredforhigherstandards.org/scalingsails/.

Hooker, Sarah, and Betsy Brand. 2009. *Success at Every Step: How 23 Programs Support Youth on the Path to College and Beyond.* Washington, DC: American Youth Policy Forum.

Joliet Junior College. 2018. "First Community College." Accessed July 4, 2018. http://www.jjc.edu/about-jjc/history.

Karp, Melinda Mechur. 2011. *Toward a New Understanding of Non-Academic Student Support: Four Mechanisms Encouraging Positive Student Outcomes in the Community College.* CCRC Working Paper No. 28. New York: Community College Research Center.

Karp, Melinda Mechur, Susan Bickerstaff, Zawadi Rucks-Ahidiana, Rachel Hare Bork, Melissa Barragan, and Nikki Edgecombe. 2012. *College 101 Courses for Applied Learning and Student Success.* CCRC Working Paper No. 49. New York: Community College Research Center.

Karp, Melinda Mechur, Juan Carlos Calcagno, Katherine L. Hughes, Dong Wook Jeong, and Thomas R. Bailey. 2007. *The Postsecondary Achievement of Participants in Dual Enrollment: An Analysis of Student Outcomes in Two States.* New York: Community College Research Center.

Karp, Melinda Mechur, Katherine L. Hughes, and Lauren O'Gara. 2010. "An Exploration of Tinto's Integration Framework for Community College Students." *Journal of College Student Retention* 12, no. 1.

NCHEMS Information Center. 2018. "Welcome to the NCHEMS Information Center." Accessed July 4, 2018. http://www.higheredinfo.org.

PathwaysResources.org. 2018. "Guided Pathways: Planning, Implementation, Evaluation." Accessed July 10, 2018. https://www.pathwaysresources.org/wp-content/uploads/2018/02/PathwaysGraphic462017.pdf.

Puente. N.d. "Puente Success Data." http://puente.berkeley.edu/content/puente-success-data.

Remediation: Higher Education's Bridge to Nowhere. 2012. Washington, DC: Complete College America. https://completecollege.org/wp-content/uploads/2017/11/CCA-Remediation-final.pdf.

Rendon, Laura I. 1994. "Validating Culturally Diverse Students: Toward a New Model of Learning and Student Development." *Innovative Higher Education* 19, no. 1: 33–51.

Struhl, Ben. 2013. *Rewarding Dual Enrollment in Performance-Based Funding Formulas: How States Can Create Incentives for College to High School Partnerships.* Boston: JFF.

Struhl, Ben, and Joel Vargas. 2012. *Taking College Courses in High School: A Strategy Guide for College Readiness.* Boston: JFF.

Symonds, William C., Robert B. Schwartz, and Ronald Ferguson. 2011. *Pathways to Prosperity: Meeting the Challenge of Preparing Young Americans for the 21st Century.* Cambridge, MA: Harvard Graduate School of Education.

Texas Higher Education Coordinating Board. 2016. "Overview: Dual Credit." http://www.thecb.state.tx.us/reports/PDF/9052.PDF?.

Thomas, Nina, Stephanie Marken, Lucinda Gray, and Laurie Lewis. 2013. *Dual Credit and Exam-Based Courses in U.S. Public High Schools: 2010–11.* Washington, DC: National Center for Education Statistics.

Tinto, Vincent. 1993. *Leaving College: Rethinking the Causes and Cures of Student Attrition,* 2nd ed. Chicago: University of Chicago Press.

US Department of Education. 2018. "FACT SHEET: Expanding College Access Through the Dual Enrollment Pell Experiment." Accessed July 10, 2018. https://www.ed.gov/news/ press-releases/fact-sheet-expanding-college-access-through-dual-enrollment-pell-experiment.

US Department of Labor. 2018. "Division of Youth Services: Youth Career Connect." Accessed July 5, 2018. https://doleta.gov/ycc/.

Vargas, Joel, and Andrea Venezia. 2015. *Co-Design, Co-Delivery, and Co-Validation: Creating High School and College Partnerships to Increase Postsecondary Success.* Boston: JFF.

Venezia, Andrea, Michael W. Kirst, and Anthony L. Antonio. 2003. *Betraying the College Dream: How Disconnected K–12 and Postsecondary Education Systems Undermine Student Aspirations.* Stanford, CA: The Stanford Institute for Higher Education Research.

Whinnery, Erin, and Sarah Pompelia. 2018. *Governors' Top Education Priorities in 2018 State of the State Addresses.* Denver: Education Commission of the States. https://www.ecs.org/ wp-content/uploads/Governors_Top_Education_Priorities_in_2018_State_of_the_State_ Addresses.pdf.

Chapter Ten

Demography as Opportunity

Nikki Edgecombe

For far too long institutions and policies have operated as if racial and ethnic differences are problematic—in more recent decades while embracing diversity as a virtuous if somewhat amorphous concept. W. E. B. Du Bois starkly captured this sentiment in *The Souls of Black Folk* at the turn of the twentieth century when he wrote of the black experience, "How does it feel to be a problem?" He went on to articulate an aspirational vision for the future of his community and country:

> The history of the American Negro is the history of this strife,—this longing to attain self-conscious manhood, to merge his double self into a better and truer self. . . . He simply wishes to make it possible for a man to be both a Negro and an American, without being cursed and spit upon by his fellows, without having the doors of Opportunity closed roughly in his face. (1969, pp. 45–46)

Blacks in present-day America may no longer face the legally sanctioned, overt hostility Du Bois references, but they and other racial and ethnic minorities continue to lack the "opportunity" he argues is central to their ability to self-actualize, engage, contribute, and lead as citizens.

Equal access to a high-quality education has been at the center of the opportunity debate, and the importance of community colleges in that debate has grown significantly. The nation's twelve hundred community colleges provide low-cost postsecondary education and a viable pathway to economic security and mobility. Today, they enroll the plurality of postsecondary students and, crucially, serve a majority of students from underrepresented racial and ethnic groups as well as lower income students (Ma & Baum, 2016).

These features of the sector have not brought it the recognition and spoils it deserves. On the contrary, they have left the sector underresourced, unable to compete against politically connected state four-year systems and flagship campuses for limited public funds. Worse yet, they have unfairly stigmatized the sector as institutions and systems struggle to redress the accumulated disadvantage experienced by much of their student body. Societal understandings of disadvantage are laden with value judgments and often perceived as inherent individual and institutional failings rather than a reflection of the nation's history and its economic and social policies.

What is an underresourced and stigmatized higher education sector to do? This chapter presents an idea to reshape words and deeds in ways intended to leverage the benefits of the nation's changing demographics and dispel deficit orientations toward the populations community colleges enroll. *Demography as opportunity* is a simple idea grounded in a commitment to affirm the worth of the students who attend community colleges by being responsive to their life circumstances.

As the demography of the nation changes—the United States is predicted to be majority minority by 2045 (Frey, 2018)—human capital investment in students from racial and ethnic groups, many of whom are first-generation college goers and low income, is crucial to the nation's vitality. This idea is optimistic in that it views diversity as an asset and community college graduates as central actors in equitable economic growth. But it is not Pollyannaish. Discrimination and prejudice continue to be prevalent and generate crippling effects. These realities must be confronted. Demography as opportunity attempts to do so with community colleges at the front lines of inclusivity and justice for generations to come.

THE UNDERPINNINGS

Demography as opportunity marries the racial and ethnic shifts under way in the country and in higher education with equity perspectives on historically disenfranchised populations. It is a constellation of policy and practice—not a plug-and-play model—and abides by implementation principles common to well-executed change efforts. It attends to both people and place and aspires to strengthen communities and the nation by investing in the increasingly diverse population of college goers. Community colleges are the ideal venue for demography as opportunity, not only because of whom they serve but also because of what they do.

An Increasingly Diverse United States

Several factors drive the US shift to a majority minority nation (Frey, 2018; Colby & Ortman, 2014). First, immigration by individuals from Asian and African countries as well as from Mexico and South America significantly outpaces that of individuals from European countries. Roughly one million immigrants arrive in the United States each year (Colby & Ortman, 2014).

In 2016, over 40 percent of the people who obtained permanent resident status immigrated from Asia and about 10 percent came from Africa. Immigrants from Mexico accounted for 16 percent of people obtaining permanent resident status. These figures were considerably higher than those for European countries, which cumulatively accounted for just under 9 percent of people who obtained permanent resident status in 2016 (United States Department of Homeland Security, 2017).

Second, birthrates among the US white population are lower than birthrates among nonwhite populations. The number of births for non-Hispanic white women was slightly down from 2014 to 2015, whereas the number of births for Hispanic women increased by 1 percent; the number of births to non-Hispanic black women was essentially unchanged (Martin, Hamilton, Osterman, Driscoll, & Mathews, 2017). Given low US fertility rates overall, international migration is expected to drive US population growth in the coming decades (Batalova & Alperin, 2018).

Finally, the demographic trend toward a majority minority has more recently been accelerated by an increase in death rates among white adults. A prime driver of this increase is the US opioid crisis. The opioid overdose rates for the white population increased from 7.8 deaths per 100,000 people in 2007 to 17.5 deaths per 100,000 people in 2016 (Kaiser Family Foundation, 2018).

These broader demographic trends, in turn, are driving changes to the racial and ethnic composition of the postsecondary sector. In fall 2015 roughly 44 percent of all undergraduate students were nonwhite: 19 percent were Hispanic, 14 percent were black, and 7 percent were Asian/Pacific Islander (Snyder, de Brey, & Dillow, 2018). Between 2015 and 2026, postsecondary enrollment rates of nonwhite Hispanic, black, and Asian/Pacific Islander students were expected to increase by 26 percent, 20 percent, and 12 percent, respectively, compared to 1 percent for white students (Hussar & Bailey, 2018).

As low-cost institutions in proximity to home and family, community colleges have increasingly emerged as crucial access points for students from racial and ethnic groups historically underrepresented in higher education. Fifty-six percent of all Hispanic undergraduates attend community colleges; the comparable figure for black undergraduates is 44 percent (Ma & Baum, 2016). Nearly four in ten community college students receive Pell grants, and 70 percent applied for some form of financial aid (Ma & Baum, 2016). Many of these Hispanic and black students, in particular, are not traditional-age students coming directly from high school. Moreover, many have enrolled in college previously.

The increasing diversity of postsecondary education broadly and the community college space more specifically provides a unique opportunity for an entire higher education sector to contribute in very tangible ways to a more egalitarian society. To do so, systems and institutions must provide relevant education and robust enough supports to counteract centuries of discrimination and neglect that were often codified in policy and law. In addition, institutional actors must adopt more equity-minded perspectives about these disenfranchised populations to ensure policy and practice do not simply maintain inequality.

The Effects of Discriminatory Policy

The demographic shifts under way are all the more meaningful in light of historical policies that in many cases disadvantaged these very populations (Katznelson, 2005). For black Americans, Jim Crow set up separate and unequal education systems and legalized discrimination in commerce and other dimensions of daily life (Woodward, 1974). Through the New Deal, Federal Housing Authority (FHA) resources were supposed to increase homeownership after the Great Depression. However, aspiring black homeowners were essentially shut out of FHA mortgage guarantees due to restrictive covenants and redlining (Rothstein, 2017).

The effects of these sanctioned forms of discrimination were crippling and functionally undermined the ability of black families to build intergenerational wealth and accrue even modest political power (Baradaran, 2017). Crucially, they blocked investment in human capital by starving whole communities of well-resourced educational institutions across generations, profoundly stunting social mobility.

When the Servicemen's Readjustment Act (commonly known at the GI Bill) was passed in 1944, it was lauded as the most egalitarian piece of bipartisan legislation ever passed. In the midst of Jim Crow–era discrimination, the GI Bill was notable for making no distinctions by race for eligibility for its wide range of benefits. Veterans Administration studies suggested that white and nonwhite program participation rates were comparable. The GI Bill is even credited with helping to integrate select colleges and universities. It also drove significantly higher enrollments at historically black colleges and universities (HBCUs).

Despite the legislation's color-blind language and these positive developments on average, the actual administration of the GI Bill, particularly in the South, was less egalitarian. The legislation was intentionally designed to give states and localities discretion over how benefits were administered to returning servicemen. Absent this provision, the bill would not have gained support from southern legislators. As Katznelson (2005) describes, "To cultivate this support, [Washington officials] made clear that they were disinclined to challenge the region's race relations and enforce equal treatment for all veterans" (p. 123). The result was localities denying certain benefits, creating obstacles to eligibility, and generally discouraging black soldiers from fully utilizing the programs of the GI Bill, including the higher education tuition and stipend benefits.

Underlying the exclusionary features of a lot of public policy is a deficit orientation to racial and ethnic minorities. Deficit orientations ascribe differences in outcomes for nonmajority or disempowered groups to "inadequate socialization, or lack of motivation and initiative" (Bensimon, 2005). They rely on stereotypical characterizations of poverty and disadvantage. Policy and its administration reflect this deficit orientation by explicitly or tacitly excluding racial and ethnic minorities from benefits, creating barriers to eligibility, or instituting compliance and accountability measures that are meant to shame or signal a lack of worthiness.

At its most dangerous, this kind of policy advances supremacist ideology that positions whites as superior to racial and ethnic minorities and views any accommodation to minority groups on the losing end of a zero-sum game. For example, redlining assessed African American neighborhoods as having lower homeownership value than white neighborhoods and attempted to maintain residential segregation. In instances when blacks began to integrate neighborhoods, whites fled—as such change reflected in their view a decline in property value and social order (Kruse, 2005).

Higher education funding is another example of discrimination. Private research universities, which enroll the lowest percentage of students from underrepresented racial and ethnic minority groups, spend five times what community colleges do on per student operating expenses (Kahlenberg, 2015). This dramatic difference in spending illustrates a disturbing value proposition: institutions serving the most advantaged students (who could likely succeed with significantly less) are more worthy of public and private dollars than those serving more disadvantaged students (who need more). The United States has a long history of layering such policies one upon another over generations such that their negative impacts accumulate—deepening disadvantage and helping to further ingrain deficit perspectives.

Demography as opportunity seeks to strengthen the community college sector from the outside by building the political (and thus policy) influence of the emerging minority majority. To do so, it must attend to institutional policies and practices that will make community colleges more responsive to the needs of this demographic block. Equity-minded perspectives may help in that regard.

Moving Toward Equity Perspectives

One of the fundamental challenges regarding demography as opportunity as a clarion call for change is the persistence of higher education attainment gaps by race and ethnicity and by income (Lumina Foundation, 2018). They are persistent and demoralizing. According to a National Student Clearinghouse report, black undergraduates who begin their higher education at two-year public institutions earn baccalaureate degrees at rates more than 15 percentage points lower than their white peers (Shapiro et al., 2017). While college graduation rates have gone up nationally in recent decades, attainment gaps by race and ethnicity have continued and, in some cases, grown (Nichols, Eberle-Sudre, &Welch, 2016). It is easy to be discouraged in the face of these outcomes—to begin to view the disparities as inevitable. A growing body of higher education scholarship provides alternative perspectives, which can be the basis for the kind of constructive action demography as opportunity requires.

Bensimon (2005) uses organizational learning theory as the framework to explain why institutions struggle to achieve equitable outcomes across racial and ethnic groups (Argyris & Schön, 1996). She positions the responsibility for the current disparities squarely with institutional actors—administrators, faculty, and staff—not students:

> I (along with my colleagues at the Center for Urban Education) believe that institutional actors, as a consequence of their beliefs, expectations, values, and practices, create or perpetuate unequal outcomes and that the possibility for reversing inequalities depends on individual learning that holds the potential for bringing about self-change. That is, individuals—the ways in which they teach, think students learn, and connect with students, and the assumptions they make about students based on their race or ethnicity—can create the problem of unequal outcomes. Such individuals, if placed in situations where they learn the ways in which their own thinking creates or accentuates inequities, can also learn new ways of thinking that are more equity minded. (p. 100).

The opportunity for self-awareness of which Bensimon writes relies on the cognitive frame individuals bring to their work. Cognitive frames are the filters through which individuals make sense of their worlds. In higher education institutions seeking reconciliation with their histories of racial discrimination, "cognitive frames represent conceptual maps and determine what questions may be asked, what information is collected, how problems are defined, and what action should be taken" (Bensimon, 2005). They determine what is seen and what goes unseen. As such, in any serious change effort, they represent the place where the work must first begin to ensure inequity is not simply reproduced.

The cognitive frames to which Bensimon (1989) refers are shaped by everyday lived experiences and information resources (including scholarship on higher education and communities of color) that attribute deficits to the students, not institutions. Deficit orientations (or perspectives, as Bensimon calls them) are not benign. They are the basis of discriminatory treatment of underrepresented racial and ethnic groups and have real-world negative implications for the self-efficacy and behaviors of students (Steele & Aronson, 1995).

Harper (2010) provides an alternative—antideficit achievement—framework explicitly designed to learn from positive stories, such as students who successfully complete degrees in science, technology, engineering, and math (STEM). He argues that the right policy and practice solutions will remain elusive if the focus is exclusively on the educational failure of disenfranchised groups. The antideficit achievement framework draws on a range of theories, including crucial race theory, social and cultural capital, and theories of college retention, among others, to examine multiple dimensions of achievement (Harper, 2010).

Missing from the scholarship of Bensimon (2005), Harper (2010), and other like-minded academics are the zero-sum assessments of opportunity and access likely to undermine policy and practice. Moreover, these scholars welcome color-conscious conversations. Attempts to mute discussions of racial exclusion and discrimination, they argue, do nothing to advance equity of educational outcomes.

Demography as opportunity likewise draws on this transparency and candor in service of its goals. Institutional leaders can consider the following principles as inspiration:

1. Know your students.
2. Understand the obstacles to their success.
3. Adopt and adapt responsive policy and practice.
4. Scale and institutionalize continuous improvement.

These principles draw from research and practice on institutional change efforts. They also are infused with insights from the lived experiences of leaders in the fight for racial equity and social justice. The next section discusses each of the principles.

THE PRINCIPLES

Demography as opportunity is meaningful to the extent it is embraced by institutional leaders and infused in an institutional culture. It requires belief in students shadowed in doubt for generations and the rejection of ideologies of supremacy and skewed perceptions of worthiness. Principles alone will not offset entrenched bias. Therefore, community colleges must contextualize the implementation of the principles in the type of wholesale changes to culture and belief systems akin to the equity perspectives just discussed. Simultaneously, the field must aggressively challenge the systemic underinvestment in the sector and the students it serves.

Know Your Students

Community colleges are organized and operate in ways similar to how they did so at their founding. Academic programs are largely segregated from workforce development. Likewise, student services operate independently from academic offerings. But it is not 1970, when two-year institutions served mostly white men who enrolled in college full time (Hussar & Bailey, 2018). As such, an important first step in strengthening community colleges to serve an increasingly diverse group of students is to truly know those students.

Knowing your students entails capturing more and better information about students' backgrounds and college and career goals prior to and upon entry. Some of this information may be drawn from K–12 administrative data sets—to the extent K–12 and higher education data systems can be linked or data easily transferred. Because many community college students do not enroll immediately after high school, it is also important for community colleges to leverage their application systems to collect information beyond compulsory demographic characteristics. For example, a series of simple "yes/no" or multiple-choice questions about students' English-language proficiency may yield information that can be used to strengthen and target English-language learning supports.

Similarly, colleges can use academic advising sessions and orientations to collect the kind of information perhaps less suited for an online application. For instance, in these venues, it makes sense to learn more about students' intended majors and career goals. Are they seeking a terminal associate degree? Would they like to transfer, and do they know where? In addition, in-person interactions provide an opportunity to explore more complicated phenomena, like academic confidence and sense of belonging, and connect students with supportive peer groups.

To know the students also requires colleges to know their communities. It is not always the case that community college faculty and staff live in the same neighborhoods as the students they serve. Often leadership is well-integrated in the business and political communities but has limited ties to the diversity of neighborhoods where their students live. Therefore, demography as opportunity believes administrators, faculty, and staff must proactively forge connections to the everyday lives of students. When sustained and built from positions of mutual respect, connections through K–12 schools, religious institutions, civic organizations, nonprofit organizations, or direct one-on-one outreach will generate a wealth of information about the many strengths of communities of color as well as more nuanced understandings of the challenges students and families may face.

Understand the Obstacles to Their Success

A bounty of research has highlighted a range of policies and practices that have undermined the success of community college students, particularly underrepresented minorities and low-income students. These include inaccurate placement systems (Scott-Clayton, Crosta, & Belfield, 2014), late registration policies (Smith, Street, & Olivarez, 2002), and multicourse and multisemester developmental education sequences (Bailey, Jeong, & Cho, 2010), among others. A majority of community colleges, nonetheless, maintain these policies and practices despite evidence of their negative effects. Why?

Sometimes they have no alternatives, as is often cited as being the case with assessment and placement. In many instances, financial considerations drive decision making, such as in the case of late registration, which generates revenue in the short term. While these reasons are legitimate, maintaining practices that harm students is never justified and frankly would not be tolerated in settings where students (and parents) have more social capital, like highly selective, elite institutions.

Demography as opportunity argues that maintaining harmful policies and practices is an untenable position. Community colleges must chip away at the cumulative disadvantage they create by dismantling the systems, small and large, that sustain that disadvantage and by providing academic and nonacademic supports that are robust enough to offset its profound effects.

Colleges seeking to better understand the obstacles to student success must begin by investing in the examination of students' experiences across measures ranging from academic performance to sense of belonging to labor market outcomes. This will require data collection and analysis and is best initiated as a transparent and collaborative process. It is an even more powerful tactic when done as part of a multi-institution network.

Eventually colleges should get to a place where data collection is built into the student experience, and analysis and review of those data are embedded in professional expectations and institutional strategy. To the extent analysis shows that the measures are low—relatively or in absolute terms—or that substantial disparities exist across different types of students for the same measure, colleges must prepare to intervene.

It is easy to get lost in the data and lose sight of the big picture. So change leaders must inquire beyond any particular metric and seek to understand the underlying causes of negative (or positive) outcomes. This may entail following up with students who have dropped out and inquiring about their college experiences and life circumstances. It may require confronting one's own biases and preconceived notions in service of genuine understanding. Undoubtedly this process requires talking to students and assessing not just their difficulties but also their strengths.

Adopt and Adapt Responsive Policy and Practice

Innovation abounds in the community college sector. Yet as discussed, many policies and practices known to have negative effects on students are maintained. Efforts to change these policies and practices can be hampered by financial considerations, time constraints, complexity, a lack of will and ability, compliance, and many other issues. Moreover, if change agents lack a complete and clear understanding of the underlying obstacles to success, there is a strong likelihood that any new policy or practice will be inadequate. Demography as opportunity views policies as guideposts and practices as tactics designed to publicly elevate the needs of underrepresented and low-income students.

The "best practice" marketplace provides empty assurances of quick fixes. In reality, meaningful institutional change is a strategic endeavor that requires college leaders to adopt and adapt or develop and adapt the kinds of policies and practices that are responsive to students' most crucial needs (Edgecombe, Cormier, Bickerstaff, & Barragan, 2013). For historically underserved student populations, these needs may include deeper social and academic engagement (to offset isolation and build a sense of belonging and academic confidence), which colleges may try to facilitate through mentorship, culturally responsive curriculum and pedagogy, psychosocial supports, and access to programs that lead to high-wage employment. No matter the remedy, adaptation is essential given the unique contours and constraints of different contexts.

In addition, college leaders must be on the lookout for unintended consequences: how new and existing policies and practices may interact in ways that adversely impact students. This inquiry can begin during the planning process, in which various implementation scenarios are tested for interactions. Targeted interventions, such as black male initiatives, typically operate across academic programs and must attend to known and unknown cultural or structural barriers within different majors that may mitigate the effects of the program.

Universal interventions, such as financial incentives designed to encourage full-time enrollment, may encourage more working students to register for fifteen credits but should anticipate that students will need guidance regarding the time management implications. Once rolled out, new policies and practices must be evaluated with an eye toward unintended consequences. These consequences may be identified through disaggregated data as well as qualitative inquiries into students' experiences and perceptions.

Scale and Institutionalize Continuous Improvement

Yesterday's solution is always at risk of becoming today's problem. Developmental education is a case in point. Decades ago, practitioners realized that a lot of academically underprepared students were enrolling in open access institutions, most notably community colleges, and instituted a seemingly rational system to assess and remediate their academic skills in advance of college-level coursework. The problem is that the system evolved into a multisemester, multicourse sequence that the majority of students never complete. And the negative consequences of this system have disproportionately affected underrepresented minority and low-income students.

This cautionary tale suggests that a reframing of traditional notions of scaling and institutionalization may be warranted to protect against good ideas going bad. Demography as opportunity offers a new perspective. It retains predominant elements of scale; that is, the expansion of effective policies and practices to serve all students who can benefit (Edgecombe et al., 2013). Institutionalization, however, is no longer simply about the allocation of institutional resources such that the policies and practices become normative core functions. It now incorporates continuous improvement as a check to ensure the benefits of policies and practices continue to accrue to those who need them most.

Continuous improvement is a long-standing concept of organizational development (Bhuiyan & Baghel, 2005). However, community colleges have struggled to seamlessly integrate it into their business model, given the cultural shift (from individual to systems thinking) and the resource commitment required. Staff must assess new and ongoing initiatives and then convene the appropriate colleagues to review and reflect on the findings and plot corrections in policy and practice. In some instances, external support is required. The subsequent planning and implementation of these corrections, in turn, require significant staff and other resources and must be subject to reassessment. Ideally, strategic planning has provided a systems orientation and positioned continuous improvement efforts within institutional priorities, including those tied to student diversity.

There is nothing revolutionary about the principles of knowing your students, understanding the obstacles to their success, adopting and adapting responsive policy and practice, and scaling and institutionalizing continuous improvement. Yet as an underresourced sector, community colleges struggle to implement them consistently and in service of more equitable outcomes. The next section discusses ways similarly positioned institutions have adhered to these principles and in doing so have turned the tide for the historically disenfranchised students they proudly serve.

THE INSPIRATION

Demography as opportunity has yet to shape community college policy and practice in ways that current trends suggest it should. As a result, gaps in credential attainment and other measures of achievement persist. This stagnation is attributable, at least in part, to the view that the sector's diversity is a weakness, not a strength. Such an orientation shapes attitudes and behaviors in ways that limit the range of solutions put forward and stall action. But there are historical and contemporary examples that portend the potential impact of demography as opportunity.

Cornering the Market on Strengths

Institutions that have served disenfranchised populations have a history of industriousness from which demography as opportunity draws. Industriousness was a necessity given a lack of resources and prohibitions on certain activities and societal rights. Education, both formal and informal, is one such activity.

Enslaved peoples of African descent, for example, surreptitiously pursued literacy and numeracy learning at great risk during the eighteenth and nineteenth centuries (Williams, 2005). During Jim Crow, leaders of all-black schools provided rigorous and affirming educational environments despite being intentionally starved for resources (Walker, 1996).

In recent decades, certain minority-serving institutions have strategically invested in particular areas and earned strong reputations for producing disproportionate numbers of graduates in high-demand and advanced fields (Gasman & Conrad, 2013). While not widespread, the effects of carving out these kinds of niches—or stated another way, cornering the market—have been profound on a handful of institutions and thousands of their graduates.

Vanessa Siddle Walker (1996) chronicled this history for African Americans under legal segregation in the South in *Their Highest Potential*. As she writes,

> to remember segregated schools largely by recalling only their poor resources presents a historically incomplete picture. Although black schools were indeed commonly lacking in facilities and funding, some evidence suggests that the environment of the segregated school had affective traits, institutional policies, and community support that helped black children learn in spite of the neglect their schools received from white school boards. Most notably, in one of the earliest accountings by Thomas Sowell, the schools are remembered as having atmospheres where "support, encouragement, and rigid standards" combined to enhance students' self-worth and increase their aspirations to achieve. (p. 3)

In her historical account of Caswell County Training School (CCTS), Walker vividly describes a school community with active parents, engaged students, and committed teachers. She also describes how the county board of education undermined attempts to provide students with transportation to school and thwarted CCTS expansion initiatives, among other obstructionist tactics. Nonetheless, the CCTS family persevered, preparing hundreds of students over many decades, including Walker, with the skills and dispositions required to contribute to society in productive ways.

Some eighty-five years later, the Meyerhoff Scholars Program at the University of Maryland Baltimore County (UMBC) is the leading producer of African American graduates who earn MDs/PhDs in the nation and draws on the same traditions as CCTS. This program enrolled nineteen African American male freshmen in its first cohort in 1989 and now serves undergraduate students of all backgrounds who intend to pursue doctoral degrees in the sciences and engineering and are committed to the success of underrepresented minorities in those fields. It provides a four-year merit scholarship and a range of academic supports and enrichment opportunities to academically prepared students interested in pursuing postgraduate degrees and research-based careers.

The program culture emphasizes mutual support, high expectations, and accountability within a highly structured oversight model. Entering students participate in a six-week summer bridge program and study groups and engage in undergraduate research opportunities early on, including summer research internships. The program has yielded impressive results: Meyerhoff Scholars were 5.3 times more likely to enroll in or complete a doctoral program in STEM or a combination STEM PhD/MD program than a control group (University of Maryland Baltimore County, n.d.).

Georgia State University (GSU) has garnered considerable attention for eliminating racial and ethnic achievement gaps (Fausset, 2018; Quinton, 2013). In 2003, only about one-third of all GSU students earned a bachelor's degree in six years. The rates for African Americans and Latinos were 29 percent and 22 percent, respectively. By 2017, the overall six-year graduation rate had increased to 54 percent, outpaced by the rates of African Americans (58 percent) and Latinos (55 percent) (Renick, 2017).

College officials attribute both the overall increase in graduation rates and the elimination of attainment gaps across races and economic groups to a set of strategic initiatives, many of which are technology enabled, designed to create more personalized college experiences responsive to students' evolving needs. These initiatives have included the development of a data-analytics-driven advising system; integration of peer tutors in high-failure introductory math courses; targeted deployment of retention grants; and the introduction of meta-major-based, first-year learning communities, among others.

The development process for these initiatives was driven by in-depth assessment of the underlying obstacles to student success. And in some cases they have generated better outcomes at low to no cost. For example, the data-analytics-driven advising cost $200,000 in new technology and about $2,000,000 per year in additional staffing. In its first year, year-to-year retention increased approximately four percentage points, generating over $10,000,000 in annual tuition and fees (Drawdy & Renick, 2018).

Another notable higher education trailblazer has been Paul Quinn College in Dallas, Texas. Founded in 1872 by ministers from the African Methodist Episcopal Church to educate freed slaves and their children, Paul Quinn College is the nation's only federally authorized urban work college. Under the leadership of President Dr. Michael Sorrell, Paul Quinn adopted a student work program model in fall 2015, in which all residential, full-time students engage in on- or off-campus work experiences that underwrite a portion of their educational costs while helping them to develop the skills, habits, and work experience crucial to success in the twenty-first-century labor market. Students work between three hundred and four hundred hours each academic year in order to earn a $5,000 tuition grant and a stipend of between $1,000 and $1,500 (Paul Quinn College, n.d.). Under this work program model, students can graduate from Paul Quinn with their degree and $10,000 or less in student loan debt.

Consistent across these historical and contemporary examples of institutions and programs is an unwillingness to accept the status quo. There is no surrender within the black community of Caswell County, North Carolina, in its pursuit of a high-quality primary and secondary education. Similarly, Freeman Hrabowski, the acclaimed president of UMBC, never questioned the ability of underrepresented minorities to excel in STEM and become the next generation of scholars and teachers in the field so as to seed yet the next generation. He persevered and found philanthropists Robert and Jane Meyerhoff, who seeded hope, opportunity, and a tangible path to prosperity—not just a scholarship.

Georgia State, typical in many ways of the nation's broad-access urban universities, has been willing to upend institutional policy and practice in service of more personalized support to predominantly minority and low-income students at the times when they are most in need. Finally, the leadership of Paul Quinn College threw out the rulebook of low-risk incrementalism that has governed change in higher education. In the work college, it found a business model that made college more affordable for students while providing them the practical employment experience that makes them better students and more successful graduates.

THE CALL TO ACTION

In a country as wealthy and ingenious as the United States, why are so many left behind? Why have community colleges, poised as potentially the most powerful vehicles of economic mobility and social change, been unable to consistently achieve their laudable missions for all students?

On the one hand, the answers to these questions are complex. They require leaders to reconcile the contradictions in the nation's founding, premised on liberty and freedom for all but mired in enslavement and subjugation of African and native peoples as well as women. This reconciliation has never happened, and therefore the insidious effects of this foundational hypocrisy have permeated the country's culture, norms, and institutions in ways that feel unalterable.

On the other hand, the answers to these questions seem quite obvious. Eliminate discriminatory policies and practices and develop the compensatory measures to redress the effects of centuries of prejudice and bias. Fund community colleges at levels adequate to boost overall attainment while closing the achievement gap. Invest strategically and disproportionately in historically underserved communities until the wage and wealth gaps are eliminated. Unfortunately, such commonsense solutions are untenable in the current zero-sum political culture. They would disrupt a social order that powerful interests work mighty hard to maintain.

But the country is changing. Within thirty years, people of nonwhite Hispanic, Asian, and African descent will represent the collective majority of US residents. And community colleges are projected to enroll most of the postsecondary students from these racial and ethnic groups. Demography as opportunity posits that it is neither plausible nor preferable to continue on the current path. Systems and policies must be directed toward expanding opportunity for this new majority, not consolidating power within a shrinking minority.

Institutions and practices must be aggressively and unapologetically equity focused, not stalled by the inertia and incrementalism that discourage leaders from rocking the higher education boat. The virtues and rewards of a robust pluralist society are many: diverse perspectives, collective responsibility, informed debate, health and well-being, civic engagement, economic prosperity, and respect for institutions, among others. Will community college and other institutional leaders help break the current cycle and do what is necessary to reap these rewards?

REFERENCES

Argyris, C., & Schön, D. A. (1996). *Organizational learning II: Theory, method, and practice.* Reading, MA: Addison-Wesley.

Bailey, T., Jeong, D. W., & Cho, S. (2010). Referral, enrollment, and completion in developmental education sequences in community colleges. *Economics of Education Review, 29*(2), 255–270.

Baradaran, M. (2017). *The color of money: Black banks and the racial wealth gap.* Cambridge, MA: Harvard University Press.

Batalova, J., & Alperin, E. (2018, July 10). *Immigrants in the U.S. states with the fastest-growing foreign-born populations.* Washington, DC: Migration Policy Institute. Retrieved from https://www.migrationpolicy.org/article/immigrants-us-states-fastest-growing-foreign-born-populations

Bensimon, E. M. (1989). The meaning of "good presidential leadership": A frame analysis. *Review of Higher Education, 12*(2), 107–123.

Bensimon, E. M. (2005). Closing the achievement gap in higher education: An organizational learning perspective. *New Directions for Higher Education, 131,* 99–111.

Bhuiyan, N., & Baghel, A. (2005). An overview of continuous improvement: From the past to the present. *Management Decision, 43*(5), 761–771.

Colby, S. L., & Ortman, J. M. (2014). *Projections of the size and composition of the U.S. population: 2014 to 2060* (Current Population Reports). Washington, DC: US Census Bureau. Retrieved from https://census.gov/content/dam/Census/library/publications/2015/demo/p25-1143.pdf

Drawdy, R. (Host), & Renick, T. (Guest). (2018, July 17). Improving graduation rates at Georgia State University [Audio podcast]. Retrieved from https://www.helixeducation.com/resources/enrollment-growth-university/improving-graduation-rates-timothy-renick/

Du Bois, W. E. B. (1969). *The souls of black folk.* New York: New American Library.

Edgecombe, N., Cormier, M. S., Bickerstaff, S., & Barragan, M. (2013). *Strengthening developmental education reforms: Evidence on implementation efforts from the Scaling Innovation project* (CCRC Working Paper No. 61). New York: Community College Research Center, Teachers College.

Fausset, R. (2018, May 15). Georgia State, leading U.S. in Black graduates, is engine of social mobility. *The New York Times.* Retrieved from https://www.nytimes.com/2018/05/15/us/georgia-state-african-americans.html

Frey, W. H. (2018, March 14). The US will become "minority white" in 2045, Census projects [The Avenue blog]. Washington, DC: The Brookings Institution. Retrieved from https://www.brookings.edu/blog/the-avenue/2018/03/14/the-us-will-become-minority-white-in-2045-census-projects/

Gasman, M., & Conrad, C. F. (2013). *Minority serving institutions: Educating all students.* Philadelphia: University of Pennsylvania Graduate School of Education, Center for MSIs.

Harper, S. R. (2010). An anti-deficit achievement framework for research on students of color in STEM. *New Directions for Institutional Research, 148,* 63–74.

Hussar, W. J., & Bailey, T. M. (2018). *Projections of education statistics to 2026* (NCES 2018-019). Washington, DC: National Center for Education Statistics, Institute of Education Sciences, US Department of Education.

Kahlenberg, R. D. (2015). *How higher education funding shortchanges community colleges* [Issue brief]. New York: The Century Foundation.

Kaiser Family Foundation. (2018). *Opioid overdoes deaths by race/ethnicity.* Retrieved from https://www.kff.org/other/state-indicator/opioid-overdose-deaths-by-raceethnicity/?currentTimeframe=0&sortModel=%7B%22colId%22:%22Location%22,%22sort%22:%22asc%22%7D

Katznelson, I. (2005). *When affirmative action was white: An untold history of racial inequality in twentieth-century America.* New York: W. W. Norton.

Kruse, K. M. (2005). *White flight: Atlanta and the making of modern conservatism.* Princeton, NJ: Princeton University Press.

Lumina Foundation. (2018). *A stronger nation: Learning beyond high school builds American talent.* Indianapolis, IN: Lumina Foundation. Retrieved from http://strongernation.luminafoundation.org/report/2018/#nation

Ma, J., & Baum, S. (2016). *Trends in community colleges: Enrollment, prices, student debt, and completion* [Research brief]. New York: The College Board.

Martin, J. A., Hamilton, B. E., Osterman, M. J. K., Driscoll, A. K., & Mathews, T. J. (2017). *Births: Final data for 2015* (National Vital Statistics Reports, Vol. 66, No. 1). Hyattsville, MD: National Center for Health Statistics. Retrieved from https://www.cdc.gov/nchs/data/nvsr/nvsr66/nvsr66_01.pdf

McFarland, J., Hussar, B., Wang, X., Zhang, J., Wang, K., Rathbun, A., . . . Bullock Mann, F. (2018). *The condition of education 2018* (NCES 2018-144). Washington, DC: National Center for Education Statistics, Institute of Education Sciences, U.S. Department of Education. Retrieved from https://nces.ed.gov/pubsearch/pubsinfo.asp?pubid=2018144

Nichols, A. H., Eberle-Sudre, K., & Welch, M. (2016). *Rising tide II: Do black students benefit as grad rates increase?* Washington, DC: The Education Trust. Retrieved from https://1k9gl1yevnfp2lpq1dhrqe17-wpengine.netdna-ssl.com/wp-content/uploads/2014/09/RisingTide_II.pdf

Paul Quinn College (n.d.). Work Program. Retrieved from http://www.pqc.edu/nation-building/work-program/

Quinton, S. (2013, September 23). Georgia State improved its graduation rate by 22 points in 10 years. *The Atlantic.* Retrieved from https://www.theatlantic.com/education/archive/2013/09/georgia-state-improved-its-graduation-rate-by-22-points-in-10-years/279909/

Renick, T. (2017). *2017 Report, Georgia State University: Complete College Georgia.* Retrieved from https://success.gsu.edu/download/2017-status-report-georgia-state-university-complete-college-georgia/?wpdmdl=6471592&refresh=5b5612b054c761532367536

Rothstein, R. (2017). *The color of law: A forgotten history of how our government segregated America.* New York: W. W. Norton.

Scott-Clayton, J., Crosta, P. M., & Belfield, C. R. (2014). Improving the targeting of treatment: Evidence from college remediation. *Education Evaluation and Policy Analysis, 36*(3), 371–393.

Shapiro, D., Dundar, A., Huie, F., Wakhungu, P., Yuan, X., Nathan, A., & Hwang, Y. A. (2017, April). *A national view of student attainment rates by race and ethnicity—fall 2010 cohort* (Signature Report No. 12b). Herndon, VA: National Student Clearinghouse Research Center. Retrieved from https://nscresearchcenter.org/wp-content/uploads/Signature12-RaceEthnicity.pdf

Smith, A. B., Street, M. A., & Olivarez, A. (2002). Early, regular, and late registration and community college student success: A case study. *Community College Journal of Research and Practice, 26*(3), 261 –273.

Snyder, T. D., de Brey, C., & Dillow, S. A. (2018). *Digest of education statistics 2016* (NCES 2017-094). Washington, DC: National Center for Education Statistics, Institute of Education Sciences, US Department of Education.

Steele, C. M., & Aronson, J. (1995). Stereotype threat and the intellectual performance of African Americans. *Journal of Personality and Social Psychology, 69*(5), 797–811.

United States Department of Homeland Security. (2017). *Yearbook of immigration statistics: 2016.* Washington, DC: Office of Immigration Statistics, US Department of Homeland Security.

University of Maryland Baltimore County. (n.d.). Meyerhoff Scholars Program. Retrieved from https://meyerhoff.umbc.edu/

Walker, V. S. (1996). *Their highest potential: An African American school community in the segregated South.* Chapel Hill: University of North Carolina Press.

Williams, H. A. (2005). *Self-taught: African American education in slavery and freedom.* Chapel Hill: University of North Carolina Press.

Woodward, C. W. (1974). *The strange career of Jim Crow* (3rd ed.). Oxford: Oxford University Press.

Part III

Enabling Ideas

The final three ideas in this book are not so much national initiatives, established programs, or functions internal to community colleges as they are transforming forces that impact every aspect of the community college; in short, they enable colleges to implement initiatives and functions. Technology to support teaching and learning is ubiquitous in every community college in the nation. It is embedded in the veins and arteries that keep the heart of the institution pumping. Technology, because of its power and its promise, may be one the most effective forces that has transformed and will continue to transform the community college world.

It is our hope that the idea of transformational leadership will become as effective as technology in its impact on the community college. While most universities are stuck in traditional approaches to leadership, the community college is a rambunctious and dynamic new kind of institution that allows and encourages a more innovative kind of leadership. Some community colleges still operate under authoritarian leaders, but the effective community colleges have adapted concepts of transformational leadership (collaboration, participation, trust, equality, shared vision, culture of evidence, etc.) that tap into the strengths and values of all employees to create better-functioning environments in which more students can be successful.

In the past several decades community colleges have committed more and more to a "culture of evidence" as a foundation for making decisions and implementing innovations. In fact, a chapter on the "culture of evidence" could have been included in this book as one of the ideas that has been and is transforming the community college world. Fortunately, the importance of establishing a "culture of evidence" is threaded through many of these chapters.

In the last decade a totally new idea has emerged that has the potential for becoming one of the most transforming ideas in the community college world. Historically the trustees of a college have focused their attention on "buildings, budgets, and bonds" as Byron McClenney notes in the first sentence of his chapter in this book.

Today, in great part because of Byron's leadership, trustees across the nation are participating in training institutes to learn how to use data to monitor what matters. And what matters today is improving and expanding student success. When those in charge of selecting the president, governing the institution, and monitoring whether or not goals are being met begin to use data to determine success or the lack of success for students, that idea has great potential for transforming the community college world.

Chapter Eleven

Catching the Waves

Technology and the Community College

Mark Milliron and John O'Brien

The role of problem-solver is one that community colleges are well-equipped to play. Just over a century old, community colleges have been at the forefront of nearly every major development in higher education since their inception. To appreciate the role that community colleges can be expected to play in reforming higher education today, Americans would do well to consider their long history of innovation.
—Trainor (2015)

In 2000 the book *Taking a Big Picture Look at Technology, Learning, and the Community College* (Milliron, Miles, & League for Innovation, 2000) was released by the League for Innovation in the Community College. It was a collection of reflective essays, research reviews, and model program highlights showcasing the coming of age of technology in the bastion of educational access and innovation, the community college. As the research and case studies in the book illustrated, community colleges have a deep commitment to innovating around increasing access and opportunity in higher education. Moreover, when exploring new technology, the usual fear of change notwithstanding, they were more than willing to try, test, and share—more so than other sectors of education.

Little has changed, yet much has changed. Community colleges remain focused on access and innovation aimed at helping more, and more diverse, students be more successful on their higher education journeys. In addition, the mission and vision of these colleges attract innovative, deeply committed professionals who remain more than willing to try, to test, and to share.

What has changed, however, are the cultural dynamics, the funding levels, the policies, the political environment, the expectations, and crucially . . . the technology. With respect to the latter, the predicted "waves" of technology definitely came ashore, sometimes crashing, at other times rolling in more slowly. Indeed, higher education is swimming in more technology today than could have seriously been imagined in 2000. Remember, in the year 2000 GPS was still science fiction for most, smartphones did not exist, social media sites were years away, and the internet was dominated by technology devotees who spoke in a shorthand language most did not understand.

In the sections that follow the authors step back and take a hard look at the waves of technology that have washed over the community college shores during the last few decades. They also reflect on the core commitment to access coupled with the willingness to apply technology to new pressures, problems, and priorities. In addition, they look out to the horizon at some waves just crashing in and examine others on their way. All the waves, however, begin with access as the anchor, which to the seasoned community college observer is no surprise.

WAVE 1: ACCESS AND EFFICIENCY

The community college movement was inspired by an unwavering passion to expand access to higher education, and so it makes perfect sense that the first wave of technology adoption at community, technical, and comprehensive colleges was focused on access. Southern New Hampshire University (SNHU) president Paul LeBlanc writes in *EDUCAUSE Review* (2015) that technology implementations can be broken down into three levels:

1. Technology that allows us to do what we have been doing but to do it better.
2. Technology that allows us to do what we have been doing but to do it less expensively.
3. Technology that allows us to reinvent what we do.

This first wave of technology falls squarely in the foundational position of doing the work of the community college better. After all, while there is now a broader completion challenge, in the first decades of community college evolution, college—in very concrete ways—represented a ticket out of poverty, and *access* was interchangeable with *success*, not a separate milestone to be accomplished. While later waves of technology innovation focused on success, initial technology was more about building better, more convenient systems and less about dramatically changing the student experience or improving outcomes.

For example, until the 1990s, it was not uncommon to see deans building their course schedules using magnets on whiteboards to represent individual course sections. Finding ways to use spreadsheets or databases to accomplish this chore certainly improved the handling of this task, but it did not appreciably improve course offerings themselves, strategically adapt or expand course availability, or necessarily change a student's registration experience. Students who could register for courses by phone very much appreciated the convenience, but the deployment of this technology innovation was not a sea change when it came to course schedules or registration itself.

While these creative applications of existing technologies mattered, they were also very much in the style of Roosevelt's belief in "doing what we could with what we had." At this time, college information technology (IT) was very widely understood to be a utility, and this mind-set is apparent in the tools that were deployed. Utilities provide needed infrastructure, though they are typically not even visible until they break in one way or another.

Internet technologies and their applications were conceived of as water from a tap or electricity from a wall socket, as evident from the tendency in this first phase to put an "e" in front of everything under the sun: e-learning, e-tutoring, e-applications, and so on. More than once, people used "E" alone as shorthand to refer to the universe of technology innovation, and EDU-CAUSE even published a book noting the ubiquity of the E: The E Is for Everything: E-Commerce, E-Business, and E-Learning in Higher Education (Katz & Oblinger, 2000). Technology leaders became so e-happy in the first wave that one exasperated two-year college faculty group declared in a newsletter that they had, in fact, had "e-nough!"

This initial wave of changes was hardly transformational, but they provided incremental qualitative improvement. For example, spreadsheets were an existing tool, but in the 1990s faculty began to realize the power of deploying these standard office productivity tools to keep grades—making it possible to track student performance, discuss grades in process with students, and experiment with weighted gradings of assignments with ease. At the same time, faculty began to experiment with videos, though seldom breaking free of the standard "talking head" framework. Early WebCT systems even preserved the brick-and-mortar framework, creating discussion groups within the online course environment in traditional "classroom" configurations.

Nonetheless, a powerful, heady optimism prevailed as technology opened eyes to a future that was bright. In fact, this first wave brought a powerful sense that technology could solve countless challenges. Not enough revenue? E-learning enrollments! Not enough parking? E-learning! And the list went on and on. Two-year colleges, with a long history of open access and serving the underserved, swooned at the potential of new technologies to extend reach (while also promising to solve nearly every fiscal problem imaginable).

Those who feel that the massive open online course (MOOC) mania of a later decade was unprecedented clearly were not working at a community, technical, or comprehensive college in the late 1990s or early 2000s.

This initial surge of technology captured the imagination of academic leaders and faculty when it came to instructional technology and academic applications. Also in the 1990s, the enterprise resource planning (ERP) systems offered colleges an integrated approach to the business that supported institutions, working behind the scenes (the dreaded "back office") to manage financial transactions, human resources, student aid, housing, registration, and other crucial core business components. A good amount of this ERP energy was helped along by the Y2K panic: the pernicious fear that current enterprise systems were going to collapse because of their codes' inability to handle the switch from 1999 to the year 2000.

Similar systems began to bring powerful organizational savvy to resource management, including classroom scheduling. "E-fficiency" may have been a forbidden utterance in faculty circles during the first wave, with the exception of advancements like Scantrons, CFOs, and other enthusiastically launched systems that provided insights and efficiencies where they were very much needed ("Enterprise Vision," 1999). And the most forward-thinking colleges invested the money saved in the longer term through ERP systems back into the academic enterprise.

WAVE 2: ACCESS AND LEARNING

The first wave of technology at community colleges was all about access and about opening eyes to the enhancements and efficiencies technology made possible. The wave that followed (of course the metaphor simplifies the reality of concurrent waves) begins the rise of learning technologies, which has continued through the present time.

If the first wave relied on technology as a utility, this second wave could be understood as demonstrable evidence of technology making a difference beyond access alone into the realm of teaching and learning. Those involved in higher education technology initiatives at this time would find the often-cited context of "Web 2.0" helpful in capturing the meaning of this period. The build-out of the internet and growth in connectivity fueled initial technology deployments, while "Web 2.0" captured a shift to empowerment of the individual—in this case, the students and faculty—in the systems and tools that were being developed.

The rise of online learning was itself a story of empowerment and enablement—allowing faculty to build more creatively and extend access to diverse students. Beyond its ability to reach geographically dispersed students, community college educators soon found that the time-shifting capabilities of online learning leant themselves to the expansion of "asynchronous learning" options.

These online options that were not dependent on buildings and the synchronous attendance of teachers and learners led to new strategies to engage, involve, solicit feedback from, and improve the learning of striving students. Most important, this capability allowed community college educators to remove online learning from the sole purview of "distance learning." Time shifting was particularly important for working students. The Sloan Foundation, and its driving program officer, Frank Mayadas, were the real patrons of this work in the community college sector. The Sloan-C network—now theOnline Learning Consortium—became a major catalyst and support system to help ramp up these offerings.

Still, the credibility of pure-play online learning was a challenge. This challenge, along with the need to ready reluctant faculty, is one of the reasons the main use of learning management systems (LMS) in the early days was to create online resources for in-class experiences. This was a light version of blended learning, which was to become more and more the norm over the next ten years. Today most classes in community colleges are supported by an LMS, and a solid number of community college students (almost one in three) are also blending their learning journeys with some on-ground classes and some online. Interestingly, research is showing that these students are some of the most successful (Robinson, Kil, & Milliron, 2018), while EDUCAUSE's recent survey shows that both students and faculty prefer hybrid environments (EDUCAUSE, 2017).

Coincidental with the rapid expansion of online course and program development, these dynamic technologies allowed students to create content for instant worldwide consumption (blogging), collaborate, make social connections for learning, create mashups, and more; the idea of a static World Wide Web gave way to a dynamic, interactive web of connectivity, all of which lent itself to improved learning. For example, in *Practical Magic: On the Front Lines of Teaching Excellence*, Roueche, Roueche, and Milliron (2003) found that award-winning faculty were most likely to leverage technology for student-driven learning and engagement.

Reenergizing Teaching Materials

Community college faculty enjoyed a growing palette of possibilities that helped engage students in learning in both face-to-face and online environments. Early LMS systems with one-dimensional resources now offered the means to compile multimedia resources. With the appearance of YouTube in 2005, not only were instructional videos easier to find, but also the broad access to videos and their exponential growth exposed faculty to new ways to use video for learning beyond simply recording lectures. Michael Wesch's

2007 viral video *A Vision of Students Today* not only demonstrated new visually powerful ways to use video to make a compelling point but added a sense of urgency about updating teaching approaches to better reach these "digital native" students who are no longer content to learn passively.

Learning objects that offered illustrative images or interactive learning experiences were shared through web-based hubs like the Multimedia Education Resource for Learning and Online Teaching, better known as MERLOT. Interest in e-portfolios took off (Lorenzo & Ittelson, 2005), giving students a way to capture learning as they chose to define it—including learning artifacts and accomplishments at any age. In addition, new software tools encouraged and facilitated attention at the curricular level, with systems like WIDS (2016) making it considerably easier to document learning outcomes and align them to larger department or institutional academic goals.

Reimagining Learning Spaces

Technology tools provided new inspiration for community college faculty and the fledgling group of academic technology professionals supporting them, always on the prowl for new approaches to inspire the imagination of students. However, new learning materials were only part of the picture. At the same time, learning spaces enjoyed something of a renaissance.

Community and technical colleges were, from their inception, designed to be less tradition bound (e.g., the 1960s "classroom without walls" enjoyed some traction). Nonetheless, even at these institutions the vast majority of students lined up in rows facing a teaching stage. Technology dramatically changed the configuration of space in industries around the world, yet higher education held on tenaciously to the classical classroom.

During this second wave, the physical classroom began to change to unleash technology-enhanced learning. Horizontal rows could be moved into circular groupings around a laptop or smartboard, and colleges worked hard to increase the proportion of wired classrooms, multimedia classrooms, or whatever else classrooms were called at that time that were flexibly designed and technology ready. The broad range of excitement around advanced and flexible learning spaces is evident in the EDUCAUSE book *Learning Spaces* (Oblinger, 2006), which is replete with campus examples.

So, frequently struggling with finances, at many community colleges technology-ready classrooms often amounted to AV carts, with technology wheeled in and out as needed, until fully wired classrooms became more ubiquitous. As these classrooms became more commonplace, other technologies were developed to further engage students, most notably student response systems ("clickers") that fit in well with the active learning movement that saw a resurgence during this same period—perhaps as technology innovations created new possibilities for active engagement (EDUCAUSE, 2005).

Beyond the sea change in physical classrooms, surely one of the most exciting changes experienced during this period was the creation of virtual learning spaces (Brown, n.d.). As online enrollments continued to climb year after year at community colleges, more attention was focused on how to make virtual classrooms as engaging as or more engaging than traditional ones. In many respects, the reach clearly exceeded the grasp.

During this time the idea of games and simulations, as well as virtual worlds, was stimulating, though the actual experience was often less exciting than the idea itself. "Games for learning" and games for social good were inspiring, but early efforts were often clunky and more bolted-on than integrated into a given course.

Grant funding would spur development of simulations that were often not sustainable beyond the initial infusion of cash, and a standard development engine was not in place. In short, games and simulations were arguably ahead of their time. It is difficult to find a better example than virtual worlds used for learning spaces to make this point.

A. J. Kelton (2008) was hedging his bets when he said that the "outlook is good" in this area while acknowledging the uncertainty around platforms like Second Life. Alas, those who spent countless hours creating Second Life islands for their college, department, or course now find these sites barren and empty. Those who need to experience firsthand the downside of ed tech hype could certainly go on a cautionary tour of some of these abandoned locations (Hogan, 2015).

As IT staff and faculty wait to see how consumer virtual, augmented, and mixed reality products resolve into leading products and platforms, there is little doubt that what they thought might happen in the first decade of this century will happen in the years ahead. Recent EDUCAUSE research suggests that 40 percent of colleges and universities will have institution-wide deployments of augmented and virtual reality technologies in the next five years, and the flood of technology innovation anticipated a decade ago may well be fully realized now that AR and VR technology has advanced more fully.

Coinciding with these many layers of incremental and sometimes dynamic change, wave 2 was also a time of planting seeds. In many ways the conversations happening today related to potentially new models for higher education found their beginnings during this period—and were to some degree enabled by technology advances and applications. Broader creative reconfigurations of the semester may well be traced to Rio Salado College (AZ) in the Maricopa Community Colleges system, whose online offerings were far ahead of their time in allowing multiple start times throughout an academic year instead of a few fixed start dates. Similarly, this second wave of new technologies also encouraged broad interest at two-year colleges in credit for prior learning and competency-based education at scale with the creation and growing influence of Western Governors University.

Finally, an important spirit animating this period was the drive to more openness. This is not the flashy media story of later MOOCs (Mangan, 2012), which was really more of a rogue wave than anything else, but a comprehensive belief in openness of all kinds. Certainly the "O" in MOOCS is involved, but also the many other open initiatives during this time, including MIT's Open Courseware initiative (OCW), open source software and systems, Open Educational Resource Commons, creative commons, and more. The Hewlett Foundation was particularly important in expanding this work.

This interest in openness at community colleges was an important offsetting response to persistent concerns at this time related to a growing realization of the digital divide, whereby online access (and later broadband connectivity) was discouragingly linked to socioeconomic status and location. Naturally, community colleges were uniquely sensitive about issues of equity and focused on narrowing any digital divides. In some cases, local community colleges served literally as a connection hub not only for the college but for the greater community as well.

WAVE 3: ACCESS AND SUCCESS

Both access and efficiency and the access and learning waves put technology "on purpose" in their own ways. Put simply, once a need was identified, the available technology was applied to meet that need. Early on, the pressing need was to address access and efficiency, as the ever-scrappy community colleges were trying to do more with less in their work to bring more students into the fold. As the internet expanded and technology matured, it was clear that these tools also held the potential to bring the access and learning imperative to life.

However, in a presentation at the League for Innovation in the Community College's Conference on Information Technology in 1996, Terry O'Banion made a prescient and intentionally provocative observation: "The World Wide Web holds the horrible potential to make already terrible instruction that much more available." Indeed, many early online classes ended up being illegible overheads repurposed to stale web pages.

At the same time, the "learning paradigm" and "learning revolution" work began asking driving questions about how technology could be used to improve and expand learning significantly (Barr & Tagg, 1995; Boggs, 1995–1996; O'Banion, 1997). However, a follow-on question—a far less comfortable question—was also asked: How do we know? Specifically, if technology was used, how is it known if it improved or expanded learning? For that matter, even if technology was not used, how do we know if any innovation or initiative improved or expanded learning? Where are the data?

The how-do-we-know questions are both learning-moments questions and learning-journeys questions. As a result, technology tools emerged around learning outcomes mapped to learning journeys. Most notably, digital learning portfolios allowed for more expansive and accessible strategies to capture the results of capstone or project-based learning strategies. Then technology tools to capture in-class learning progression and mastery began taking shape.

Learning outcomes assessment became a tool set available to colleges that needed to map and document learning mastery for accreditation, licensure, and professional certification. As discussed in *Learning Outcomes for the 21st Century* (Wilson, Miles, Baker, & Schoenberger, 2000), leveraging technology to help answer the how-do-we-know questions at this level was vital if learning-centered innovation were to expand. However, these conversations were in some ways eclipsed as the completion agenda exploded on the scene in 2009–2010.

From Reporting on Access to Leveraging Analytics to Improve Completion

It could be argued that up until the latter part of the first decade of the twenty-first century, enrollment still ruled as *the* measure of a successful and healthy community college. While there had been clarion calls for an increased focus on other metrics (Roueche, Johnson, & Roueche, 1997), enrollment was the measure that mattered above all others in terms of public perception and fiscal stability. From diverse tuition strategies to the array of state and local funding models, operational sensitivity to enrollment was high. But the public perception and levers of funding were about to shift.

There is much more on this transition in chapter 2 in this volume. Suffice it to say that a confluence of federal, state, foundation, association, and intermediary initiatives, innovations, and research led to a clear understanding that access was simply not enough. For students, communities, and the nation to realize the potential of community college education, the completion of credentials had to be taken far more seriously. Therefore, data and information to help improve the learning journey became paramount.

However, given the long-standing focus on enrollment—particularly its close ties to funding models in most states and systems—getting enrollment data and high-stakes reports right still mattered. Technology had been and still was being deployed to meet this need. From sophisticated spreadsheets to advanced business intelligence systems anchored in data warehousing and reporting tools, the goal was to get good information to boards, state regulators, federal agencies, and accreditors. This work was at best required and at worst existentially threatening.

Institutional research (IR) departments took their work seriously—so much so that they were typically overwhelmed with requirements and particularly protective of their products and processes. Harvesting data from existing ERP systems was often difficult, made even more so by the need to bring together data from disparate systems outside of the purview of the student information system.

Still, through a variety of technology tools—and sometimes very creative work-arounds, innovations, and sleepless nights—progressive data-centric colleges collected key performance indicators (KPIs) and followed emerging continuous quality improvement (CQI) traditions. For example, the Continuous Quality Improvement Network (CQIN), an early and effective data-centered organization, featured colleges that won the Baldridge Award (e.g., Richland College, TX) in key publications and (e.g., Community College of Denver, CO, in *Embracing the Tiger*). These early leaders were shining examples of the courage to learn and guide organizational change with data.

As noted previously, over the last decade the field began to respond to emerging—and at times explosive—policy changes, practice pressures, and proactive leadership voices that made the case that enrollment and access were only part of the student success picture; progression and completion were core metrics that mattered as well (AACC, 2012). Responding, however, meant an expansion of what was expected in the reports more than it meant the move to advanced analytics and predictive modeling right away.

Indeed, the most pressing needs were technology tools that would better respond to increasing calls for more, and more nuanced, data demands by large-scale initiatives—for example, Achieving the Dream, Completion by Design, Complete College America, and the Aspen Prize—and newly motivated boards, state agencies, accreditors, and federal agencies. At the same time, leading voices at the Association of Community College Trustees (ACCT) began telling community college board members, "You may know your enrollment numbers, but if you don't know your institution's retention and completion rates, you're not able to effectively govern your college" (ACCTvideo, 2010). (See chapter 13 in this volume.)

As outlined in the white paper *Making the Most of a Healthy Change in Education* (Milliron, 2016), as early expanded data efforts gained steam, the higher education sector also began learning that an important innovation to help their students succeed at higher levels, and for the corresponding outcomes to improve, would involve putting data to work in new ways; in other words, they needed to explore advanced analytics. Much as electronic medical records and digital tools had created deeper and richer information streams in health care, the access and instruction wave that flooded across community colleges had created deeper and richer data pools from which to draw insight on learners and their success pathways.

Initiatives like the Action Analytics Symposiums at the Minnesota State Colleges and University system, the EDUCAUSE Next Generation Learning Challenge analytics challenges, and the Predictive Analytics Reporting (PAR) framework, and companies like Civitas Learning began showing how institutions could bring together the best of modern data science (e.g., predictive modeling, machine learning, and sentiment analysis) and creative design thinking to better understand and respond to student challenges and opportunities. From deeper intelligence to targeted mind-set nudging, a whole new suite of tools was now on the table.

The next step in this journey, however, involved developing tools, technologies, and apps that could be deployed directly to faculty, advisers, and students to enable them to make better decisions on their journeys. Researchers could "democratize the data" and involve more educators in student success innovation. The Integrated Planning and Advising for Student Success System (iPASS) work funded by the Bill & Melinda Gates Foundation arguably was one of the largest scale projects that attempted to explore the potential and impact of this work on student completion.

Focusing mainly on advising technology, iPASS explored a family of technologies—such as adviser case-management apps, early-warning systems, and career planning tools—coupled with process and policy change. What became clear from these efforts was that advanced analytics held the potential to move the needle on student success. However, new systems, processes, and even leadership strategies would need to be put in place to truly make the most of these efforts (CCRC, 2018). Moreover, there was culture work to be done to help institutions embrace new perspectives on data and governance to create organizational readiness, particularly around privacy and ethical uses of analytics (Ekowo & Palmer, 2017).

Embracing "How Do We Know?"

There is compelling work under way on exploring learning moments and journeys. For example, leaders at the Open Learning Initiative at Stanford University and the Link Research Lab at the University of Texas at Arlington are pushing the boundaries on linking learning technologies to learning science and affective response. Moreover, analytically powered systems are now available to leverage student and institutional data to more precisely understand which innovations are working, at what level, and for which students. Austin Community College (TX) has done some impressive work to explore the impact of its ACCelerator learning lab on developmental math leveraging these tools (Milliron, Kil, Malcolm, & Gee, 2017).

The student success matrix is a useful tool for conceptualizing the how-do-we-know anchoring question and its role in informing, improving, and shaping student success work (figure 11.1). It is a simple 2-by-2 that shows the potential of combining the power of technology-enabled systems with the change management work focused on helping more students learn well and finish strong.

On the X-axis of the matrix is the level of capacity an institution has in conceptualizing and implementing change in policy and practice around student success, such as supplemental instruction, learning labs, flipped classrooms, and so on. The Y-axis tracks the capacity of an institution to develop insight, often through reporting and advanced analytic technology tools and systems.

The resulting matrix provides a typology of community colleges and their ability to make the most of their student success work. Not surprisingly, there are low/low institutions that focus on data work because they are required to do so by accreditors and state agencies. Moreover, they are deeply uninterested in changing how they are doing things. Indeed, for them, a "culture of evidence" means they work to find evidence that what they are already doing is working. Then there are institutions that are high on insight, yet low on change capacity. In these institutions, the institutional research shops work hard to develop sophisticated reporting and analytic strategies and systems.

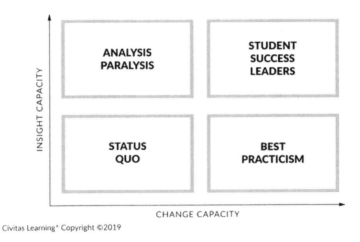

STUDENT SUCCESS TRANSFORMATION MATRIX
MOVING FROM CRISES TO CLEAR PATH

Civitas Learning® Copyright ©2019

Figure 11.1. Student Success Matrix

However, more often than not these data remain trapped in reports and or committees, confounded by analysis paralysis.

More common, however, are institutions that are doing hard work around change in the low-insight, high-change-capacity quadrant. They are adopting best practices that have worked at peer institutions, often a cornucopia of best practices. What they lack is the ability to use the data to try, test, and tune the possible practices based on *their* data. Far too often these institutions experience initiative fatigue as they continue to innovate but don't see substantial progress—or they cannot decide which of their initiatives are responsible for any progress they see, or do not see.

The good news is that the upper right quadrant is becoming more crowded as it becomes more common for student success leaders to expand and improve their capacity through advanced analytics and qualitative explorations. This insight is then coupled with skill and will in change management to measurably move the needle on student success work. Most exciting is that the deep work in this quadrant also holds the potential to bring more of the access, efficiency, learning, and success innovation together for students. Indeed, it may be the key to community colleges making the most of the next wave: access and transformation.

WAVE 4: ACCESS AND TRANSFORMATION

I never try to teach my students anything; I only try to create an environment in which they can learn.
—Albert Einstein

In the wave to come, the momentum will shift toward access and transformation—to afford more and more diverse students the opportunity to engage with a transformative college, do transformative learning work, and experience a learning journey that opens transformative pathways to possibilities for learning and work. Higher education is likely to see an explosion in digital curricular resources—both publisher and open community driven—that allow for instructors to flexibly enlighten and engage students and for independent learners to drive their own learning. Game-based learning, the efficacy of which Richard Van Eck (2015) calls "settled science," will continue to expand and refine its ability to bring learning to life in new and exciting ways. Virtual reality and augmented reality will bring learning context—for example, relevance, application, and utility—to learners in deeper and richer ways than ever thought possible.

While these tools will make for more engaging spaces for students to learn than ever before, the Internet of Things (IOT) will become more the norm, connecting a host of devices, appliances, clothing, health monitors, and more. Using data from IOT for improving the student experience, learning, and completion will become commonplace. As a result, privacy, governance processes, and security in data use will remain crucial topics. These challenges notwithstanding, students will press for far more personalized pathways and precise outreach to support their learning journeys.

All this means analytics will need to rise to the next level. IT staff and faculty will have to create optimization strategies that support efficiency, learning, student success outcomes, and transformative student experiences. The tools will be diverse, the data will be deep, and the expectations will be high.

An exciting time is at hand. Community college faculty are poised to have more tools, techniques, and technologies at their fingertips than ever before to help students access learning, succeed on their learning journeys, and ready themselves for productive careers and lives. Kash (2017) calls it the coming "golden age of learning," when key players are able to try, test, tune, and learn together all in a collective effort to watch students make the most of their time in the nation's community colleges.

Given the waves already here, not to mention those to come, community college leaders had all better collectively grab their boards, check their balance, and get ready to ride!

REFERENCES

AACC 21st Century Commission Report. (2012). Retrieved from http://www.aacc21stcenturycenter.org/wp-content/uploads/2014/03/21stCenturyReport.pdf

ACCTvideo. (2010, November 9). *College Completion Agenda Panel Discussion* (Part 2) [Video file]. Retrieved from https://www.youtube.com/watch?v=nU_Ft_TtwDw

Barr, R. B., & Tagg, J. (1995). *From Teaching to Learning: A New Paradigm for Undergraduate Education.* Retrieved from https://www.colorado.edu/ftep/sites/default/files/attachedfiles/barrandtaggfromteachingtolearning.pdf

Boggs, G. (1995–1996, December–January). The Learning Paradigm. *Community College Journal* 66, no. 3: 24–27. Retrieved from https://eric.ed.gov/?id=EJ516691

Brown, M. (n.d.) *Learning Spaces.* Retrieved from https://www.educause.edu/research-and-publications/books/educating-net-generation/learning-spaces

Community College Research Center (CCRC). (2018). *Evaluation of Integrated Planning and Advising for Student Success (iPASS).* Retrieved from https://ccrc.tc.columbia.edu/research-project/integrated-planning-and-advising-services.html

EDUCAUSE. (2005, May). *7 Things You Should Know about . . . Clickers.* Retrieved from https://library.educause.edu/~/media/files/library/2005/5/eli7002-pdf.pdf

EDUCAUSE. (2017). *EDUCAUSE Research Snapshot: Online Learning Attitudes.* Retrieved from https://library.educause.edu/~/media/files/library/2017/9/studentst2017infog.pdf

Ekowo, M., & Palmer, I. (2017, March). *Predictive Analytics in Higher Education. New America.* Retrieved from https://www.newamerica.org/education-policy/policy-papers/predictive-analytics-higher-education/

Enterprise Vision: Unleashing the Power of the Internet in the Education Enterprise. (1999, August 1). *THE Journal.* Retrieved from https://thejournal.com/articles/1999/08/01/enterprise-vision-unleashing-the-power-of-the-internet-in-the-education-enterprise.aspx

Hogan, P. (2015, August 13). We Took a Tour of the Abandoned College Campuses of Second Life. *Splinter News.* Retrieved from https://splinternews.com/we-took-a-tour-of-the-abandoned-college-campuses-of-sec-1793849944

Integrated Planning and Advising for Student Success (iPASS). (2017, June 14). Bill & Melinda Gates Foundation. Retrieved from https://postsecondary.gatesfoundation.org/areas-of-focus/innovation/technology-enabled-advising/technology/

Kash, W. (2017, March). Predictive Data Tools Suggest Dawn of "Golden Age of Learning" in Higher Ed. Retrieved from https://edscoop.com/predictive-data-tools-suggest-dawn-of-golden-age-of-learning-in-higher-ed/

Katz, R. N., & Oblinger, D. G. (2000). *The E is for Everything: E-commerce, E-business, and E-learning in Higher Education*. San Francisco, CA: Jossey-Bass.

Kelton, A. (2008, September 15). *Virtual Worlds? "Outlook Good."* Retrieved from https://er.educause.edu/articles/2008/9/virtual-worlds-outlook-good

LeBlanc, P. (2015, October). *Digital Game-Based Learning: Still Restless, After All These Years*. Retrieved from https://er.educause.edu/articles/2015/10/digital-game-based-learning-still-restless-after-all-these-years

List of Web 2.0 Applications. (n.d.). In EduTech Wiki. Retrieved from http://edutechwiki.unige.ch/en/List_of_web_2.0_applications

Lorenzo, G., & Ittelson, J. (2005, October). *An Overview of E-Portfolios*. Retrieved from https://library.educause.edu/resources/2005/1/an-overview-of-eportfolios

Mangan, K. (2012, October 1). Massive Excitement about Online Courses. *Chronicle of Higher Education*. Retrieved from https://www.chronicle.com/article/Massive-Excitement-About/134678

Milliron, M. D. (2016). *Making the Most of a Healthy Change in Education: The Emerging Student Success Intelligence Platform* (Civitas Learning white Paper). Retrieved from https://go.civitaslearning.com/student-success-platform-whitepaper

Milliron, M. D., Kil, D., Malcolm, L., & Gee, G. (2017, July–September). From Innovation to Impact: How Higher Education Can Evaluate Innovation's Impact and More Precisely Scale Student Support. *Planning for Higher Education* 45, no. 4. Retrieved from https://www.scup.org/page/phe/read/article?data_id=32006&view=article

Milliron, M. D., Miles, C. L., & League for Innovation in the Community College (U.S.). (2000). *Taking a Big Picture Look @ Technology, Learning, and the Community College*. Mission Viejo, CA: League for Innovation in the Community College.

O'Banion, T. (1997). *A Learning College for the 21st Century*. Washington, DC: American Council on Education and Oryx Press.

Oblinger, D. G., ed. (2006). *Learning Spaces*. Retrieved from https://www.educause.edu/research-and-publications/books/learning-spaces

Policy Studies Organization. (2017–2018, Fall–Winter). *Internet Learning*, 6, no. 2. Retrieved from http://www.ipsonet.org/publications/open-access/internet-learning/internet-learning-volume-6-number-2-fall-2017-winter-2018

Reclaiming the American Dream: Community Colleges and the Nation's Future. (2012). Retrieved from http://www.aacc21stcenturycenter.org/wp-content/uploads/2014/03/21stCenturyReport.pdf

Roueche, John E., et al. *Embracing the Tiger: the Effectiveness Debate and the Community College*. Community College Press, 1997.

Roueche, J. E., Roueche, S. D., & Milliron, M. D. (2003). *Practical Magic: On the Front Lines of Teaching Excellence*. Washington, DC: American Association of Community Colleges.

Trainor, S. (2015, October 20). How Community Colleges Changed the Whole Idea of Education in America. *Time*. Retrieved from http://time.com/4078143/community-college-history/

Van Eck, R. (2015, October). *Digital Game-Based Learning: Still Restless, After All These Years*. Retrieved from https://er.educause.edu/articles/2015/10/digital-game-based-learning-still-restless-after-all-these-years

Vardi, M. Y. (2012, November 1). *Will MOOCs Destroy Academia? Communications of the ACM*. Retrieved from https://cacm.acm.org/magazines/2012/11/156587-will-moocs-destroy-academia/fulltext

Wesch, M. (2007, October 12). *A Vision of Students Today* [Video file]. Retrieved from https://www.youtube.com/watch?v=dGCJ46vyR9o

WIDS Instructional Design Model. (2016, March 25). Retrieved from https://www.wids.org/Resources/Resource-Library/ArtMID/1668/ArticleID/27/WIDS-Instructional-Design-Model

Wilson, C. D., Miles, C. L., Baker, R. L., & Schoenberger, R. L. (2000, February). *Learning Outcomes for the 21st Century: Report of a Community College Study*. ERIC. Retrieved from https://eric.ed.gov/?id=ED439751

Chapter Twelve

Transformative Leadership Wanted

Making Good on the Promise of the Open Door

Margaretta B. Mathis and John E. Roueche

Higher education is no place for the complacent or faint of heart. College leaders must diligently—and unceasingly—stay focused on things that matter in the lives of their students and communities. They must anticipate constantly shifting needs—within the college, the state, and the nation—while crafting viable strategies to compete in the larger global community.

Upon considering the issues and strategic initiatives addressed in this book and the significant time and undertakings these endeavors represent, a fast spin down memory lane prompted reflections about familiar issues and the underpinnings of transformative leadership that have spawned over half a century of commitment to the well-being of community colleges and their expansive constituencies:

> In 1961, Edmund Gleazer, then of the American Association of (Junior and) Community Colleges, predicted the issues community colleges would face in the future—changing demographics, a global economy, and technological advancements. Today, colleges grapple with issues envisioned almost 50 (plus) years ago. . . . The pace and complexity of life create enormous challenges. As an economic futurist, Ed Barlow (2007) warned, "the key to success in the 21st century is alignment—staying in alignment with a world that will be characterized by complexity, diversity, and pace of change." (Roueche, Richardson, Neal, & Roueche, 2008, p. 1)

"In 1960, new community colleges were opening at the rate of 20 per year; by 1967, that figure was 50 per year" (*The Examiner*, 2016). A noted "Camelot moment," rapid expansion, and "access" were mantras among community college leaders serving returning veterans and baby boomers, as a new community college was being built each week.

In 1968 the publication of *Salvage, Redirection, or Custody: Remedial Education in the Community Junior College* compelled Gleazer to redirect the focus of the association toward a new and highly contentious issue among community and junior college leaders at that time:

> The comprehensive community college with nonselective admission policies attracts increasing numbers of students with educational deficiencies, especially in academic skills, which prevent success in typical college courses. However, while almost all community colleges agree with the open-door concept, only about half provide remedial instruction for low achievers. There is little agreement on objectives of remedial programs or on the means to reach their objectives. (Roueche, 1968, abstract 1)

Many of today's challenges were identified in the previous century—and illusive solutions du jour perpetuate as former initiatives are rolled out with new nomenclature and, perpetually, unsatisfactory outcomes. Fast-forward to the twenty-first century, when today's community college leaders continue to labor in the minefields of all-too-familiar and disruptive challenges such as continued open-door access, equity, *and* success; college closures and consolidations; free tuition; and declining enrollments—to name a few:

> With the aging baby boomer population comes the well-documented enrollment decline in many of our two- and four-year institutions of higher education. The rapid decrease in this major revenue source is compounded by the dramatic impact of state "disinvestments" (i.e., funding cuts) of community and technical college budgets across the United States. (Roueche & Mathis, 2018, p. 1)

This maelstrom exemplifies the convergence of opposing demands, calling for ingenuity and courage to lead transformation. "College leaders are expected to respond ever more quickly to meet emerging community and national needs" (Boggs, 2015, p. 14). Within the eye of this perfect storm, the community college landscape requires new and renewed leadership skills in the foreseeable future for colleges to stay afloat and effectively serve their respective constituencies.

What urgencies must be addressed while keeping a vigilant eye toward the horizon of an ever-changing future? *Toward what* are colleges leading? In their many deliberations, do leaders pause to consider, *"So what?"* before eliciting the many constituents in expensive and time-consuming propositions? What about the context makes an undertaking *ripe* for introduction and successful implementation? What is it about a vision that *propels* an institution (and country) forward, and what is the magic elixir that keeps stakeholders engaged and committed to the work while naysayers inevitably hover, preparing to pounce and provoke? Do community college leaders consider the *how* of introducing and fostering transformation as they look toward a desired and often illusive outcome?

What are the makings of transformative leaders who foster the requisite conviction and behavior to achieve desired goals on behalf of community colleges and the constituents they are designed to serve? To align with this century, community college leaders must adapt with creative solutions for an incongruous world. Following are insights and lessons, gleaned from observing successful leaders, about preparing and harnessing the power of individuals to work together toward common goals and nurturing human relationships to bring compelling visions to life.

LEADERSHIP DEVELOPMENT: EMBEDDING AND SUSTAINING THE DESIRED CULTURE

Unfortunately, too few colleges make crucial leadership development a strategic priority. Indeed, colleges can ill afford to vest the key to sustainable excellence in one or two people at the top. "Organizations must actively build the capacity and cultivate the behaviors necessary to take full advantage of enhanced productivity, innovation, and performance" (Norris, Baer, & Offerman, 2009, p. 1).

> Community colleges have finally been recognized by [U.S.] presidents, by legislators, by foundations, by policy centers, by business and industry as one of the most important democratic institutions in the world that is helping to improve our economy and meet the needs of citizens, said Terry O'Banion, chair of the graduate faculty for National American University. And at a time, we're finally recognized, we've failed to keep up with the preparation of leaders to take on the leadership role. . . . We're the leaders in the completion agenda and we're out there working and losing presidents left and right who would make this happen and make it work. (Smith, 2016, para. 4)

A joint publication by the American Association of Community Colleges (AACC) and the Association of Community College Trustees (ACCT) accentuates the vast turnover in community college leadership positions:

> The urgency attached to the board's role in selecting, supporting, and positioning their institution and new presidents to thrive and excel cannot be overstated. In 2016, more than 50% of the presidents of colleges that award associate degrees reported that they anticipated stepping down within the next five years, yet only 21.2% of these colleges report having a succession plan in place. (2018, p. 3)

According to AACC president and CEO Walter Bumphus, "It's not a wave of change we're experiencing; it's a tsunami. . . . And unless colleges prepare in advance for leadership transitions, there could be real and lasting consequences for the institution and the students it serves" (AACC Staff, 2018, pp. 8–9).

Community college executive team members and senior faculty are among those also predicted to soon retire. This "tsunami" comes during a time when community and technical colleges are in the national spotlight to deliver on the promise of an educated and skilled workforce. Simultaneously, many states are "disinvesting" and consolidating—thus putting additional pressures on college leaders to be innovative in keeping doors open for all students while delivering vital services to local businesses and communities.

Today's community college leaders are struck by the enormity and complexity of the issues with which they must grapple to be responsive to current needs. These seemingly tireless and nimble heroes must be strategic in preparing leaders-followers throughout the institution to address community and market needs and support students in their respective journeys for success:

> Clearly the magnitude of change required is substantial. The challenges are real. The risk in taking them on is not for the faint of heart. But the alternative is to continue to get the results we're getting. The longer we wait, the more students are lost. Now is a very good time to reach for the next level in our work. (McClenney, 2016, para. 27)

Incoming leaders must acquire an ability to foster crucial relationships while also being accountable to the very stakeholders who are dependent on the strength and vitality of the community college to deliver on the promise of America's future. They must take into account the "human factor" and lead with heart while navigating the unanticipated and preparing for the unfamiliar.

No one person can "do it all." It is the astute leader who involves internal and external institutional stakeholders in developing a culture that builds toward a desired future, rather than being mired in the many daily operational challenges that arise. A culture of excellence and execution requires that these noble men and women look beyond "self" and wisely prepare the next generation of leaders to foster an institutional culture that is responsive to economic and societal shifts.

Transformative leaders recognize the advantages of providing faculty and staff with experiences outside the comforts of their home institutions by going to see, upfront and personal, the successes of others in addressing similar challenges. Leaders are well-advised to create mentoring and coaching opportunities to prepare the next generation to face daunting challenges.

The need for leaders who are equipped to help students achieve career/ educational goals and to adapt and respond to change must be woven into the college's strategic plans. Effective practices include identifying and developing leaders—inclusive of faculty—throughout the institution to participate in internal leadership academies or institutes. These institutes can, and should, be tailored to reinforce the institution's mission, vision, and values—and to cultivate multidisciplinary and diverse leaders with the skills and wherewithal to work collaboratively and effectively to address complex and changing demands.

"Faculty and staff members who show leadership promise should be given opportunities to participate in leadership development activities sponsored by state and national organizations. They should be encouraged and even supported to get doctorates" (Boggs, 2015, p.14).

A MODEL COMMUNITY COLLEGE LEADERSHIP PROGRAM

Galvanized by the high projection of retirement among senior administrators and faculty, the demand for leadership development, and the declining number of doctoral programs in community college leadership offered by state universities across the country, leaders at the Roueche Graduate Center, National American University (NAU), set out to develop a Community College Leadership Program (CCLP) leading to a doctor of education (EdD). Led by John E. Roueche, president of NAU's Roueche Graduate Center, the university benefited from the wisdom and insights he had gained during his forty plus years of community college leadership development at the University of Texas at Austin.

In reimagining the CCLP, Roueche and his colleagues drew upon the well-established foundation of the former UT doctoral program as well as the extensive network of UT-CCLP alumni, friends, and other leader/colleagues across the United States to generate ideas for addressing twenty-first-century needs. They also benefited from the vigilant counsel of the university's National Community College Advisory Board—composed of nationally renowned community college scholars/leaders—and a dedicated and accomplished CCLP team, in developing a program that evolved into a radical innovation specifically designed for aspiring community college leaders, offered where they work.

The CCLP cohort model features over sixty nationally recognized community college faculty who believe that leadership development must include face-to-face interaction to hone the crucial leader and team skills required to be effective in today's environment. All fifteen doctoral courses were created by national experts with vast experience in the community college and are community college focused. The program draws upon an institution's data and needs as course projects and practicum experiences are designed:

> To encourage active and practical learning the local community college host-ing the cohort participates as a learning laboratory with real-life issues serving as some of the content. In this way, the cohorts will also serve as campus catalysts to explore and implement change and action.
> The program places high priority on recruiting women and minorities to ensure that future leaders reflect the demographics of community colleges. (Roueche & O'Banion, 2018, A New Model Section, paras. 5–7)

Roueche Graduate Center leaders met with community college and district leaders throughout the United States who were committed to leadership de-velopment to prepare the next generation for guiding their institutions.

Cuyahoga Community College (Tri-C) is notable as the oldest and largest community college in Ohio. The Mandel Leadership Development Program, established at Tri-C in 2008 under the leadership of President Emeritus Jerry Sue Thornton (*The Villager Newspaper*, 2013), has served as a platform for leadership development at the college. "Thornton . . . placed a high priority on a deep organizational culture of leadership and professional development" (Achieving the Dream, 2013, Emerging Leadership: Cuyahoga Community College Section, para. 1) Alex Johnson, the current Tri-C president, has built upon this foundation in advancing strategic leadership development as his legacy to the college.

Johnson became Tri-C's fourth president in July 2013. Shortly thereafter, he contacted John Roueche to inquire about starting a CCLP doctoral cohort. Johnson was successful in obtaining board approval to provide tuition assis-tance for twenty-eight employees, aspiring scholars/leaders at the college. By spring 2014 the first CCLP cohort was launched at Tri-C, reinforcing the vision, leadership, and development of a doctoral culture infused throughout the institution.

Strategic leadership development continues to be an institutional priority at Tri-C, exemplified by a second CCLP cohort that was launched in spring 2018 (the tenth of eleven CCLP cohorts under way or completing). Members of the first CCLP cohort of Tri-C employees, who participated in the inaugu-ral CCLP-EdD commencement in summer 2018, now serve as mentors to members of the new cohort.

When CCLP leaders were contacted by Kaye Walter, president emeritus of Bergen Community College (NJ), and Curtis Ivery, chancellor of Wayne County Community College District (MI), CCLP leaders were again re-minded that the key to sustainable excellence is in preparing the next genera-tion of leaders. Walter and Ivery are among the select leaders who are armed with an awareness of the varying environmental differences and demands future leaders must be equipped to tackle. They made leadership development a priority in their respective institutions—making a lasting imprint on fostering desired values, culture, and preparedness for navigating the future.

The CEOs at cohort colleges obtained the support of their respective boards to provide tuition assistance to employees who wanted to pursue a doctorate in community college leadership offered by NAU's Roueche Graduate Center, recognizing the benefits to their respective colleges. These leaders were purposeful in fostering values of access, success, equity, and completion, and in reinforcing expected norms, such as persistence, discipline, innovation, quality, and rigor. The multiplier effect of creating such a culture and developing leaders to sustain that culture can transform institutions:

> [C]ulture has the power to shape our identity. Over time and under the right circumstances, the norms and values of the group to which we belong become our own. We internalize them. We carry them with us. *The way we do things around here and why* eventually becomes *The way I do things and why.* (Duckworth, 2016, p. 247)

SHARED VISION, VALUES, AND INVOLVEMENT

In navigating the barrage of complex issues, CEOs must continuously hone cognitive as well as human skills of motivating and engaging others and consider the countless perspectives of stakeholders who are to be served by the college. While keeping student access, success, equity, and completion—and serving community needs—at the core of the mission, college leaders must be intentional about creating a shared vision and values and a culture of respect and involvement to keep crucial constituents engaged and at the table.

Today's community college leaders are both encouraged and compelled to reform institutions to better serve contemporary needs. *How* reform is introduced can elicit the desired evolution or provoke unintended mutiny and revolution. Leaders recognize that shared purposes, shared commitments, shared struggles, and "shared hearts" are a powerful combination for achieving shared values:

> Leaders who transform institutions into versions of their better selves are true artists. Those who have pitched their tents in higher education and in community colleges, in particular, work in one of the most human of all enterprises. Arguably, in this enterprise—more than in any other—these experiences involve individual faces and have strong ties to the human heart and spirit.
>
> It is the shared values—what one hopes and strives for, and what one believes the future should hold—that always must be tied inextricably to the engagement of human beings in the meaningful work that they should and can do together. Therefore, we argue that the art of leadership is all about vision,

about painting a face on the future, and, by exciting others to positive action, ultimately bringing that face to life. (Roueche & Roueche, 2008, paras. 1–2)

Not only must leaders have a clear vision of what their institutions can become, they must be able to see it within the confines of what already exists—rather, they must be able "to see what is not"—to look beyond the obvious, beyond what is known, beyond the reality of the present to the potential of the future.

At the beginning of the leadership development course and its weeklong residency, doctoral students in the CCLP take a leadership self-assessment (Roueche, Baker, & Mathis, 2014) and review leadership competencies developed by the AACC (2013) that are integrated into the CCLP learning outcomes. They are asked to share their individual purposes and values, noting that these may change throughout their lives. Prior to site visits, the doctoral students analyze community college case studies and speak with various stakeholders (e.g., accreditors, public policy analysts, media, board members, college presidents, and faculty) to consider varying internal and external contexts, needs, and perspectives in addressing current issues.

In NAU's CCLP, students are exposed to urban and rural institutions and state and national leaders during the course and residency. When visiting college campuses and speaking with college leaders, the doctoral students, many already holding leadership positions, are encouraged to watch and listen for artifacts and espoused beliefs (Schein, 2010) and compare them to the actual *lived* experiences at the colleges (i.e., "to see what is not"). How do actions vary from words? What is addressed, and what is missing, in conversations and actions? What is the tone, and how are constituents treated and engaged?

By comparing what is espoused with what is observed, students detect gaps that would benefit from leadership development for staff within the college or district. A final project is the identification of an issue and a viable solution that is informed by data and incorporates varying stakeholder inputs in developing a shared vision, solution, implementation process, and desired outcomes.

In a recent visit by the Wayne County Community College District (WCCCD) (MI) CCLP cohort to Lansing Community College (LCC) (MI), the doctoral students were exposed to the transformative leadership of Brent Knight, LCC president. During the site visit, Knight spoke frankly about the formidable issues confronting the college upon his arrival ten years earlier:

Lansing Community College was in dire straits when I was appointed president in 2008. In the several years preceding my appointment, the college had attempted to migrate to a new backbone operating system. The new operating system was unstable, and the college retreated to a prior system. In the interim, the college struggled with financial aid, payroll, and basic fiscal affairs. As a consequence, college finances were not auditable, senior management was depleted, there was discord among board members, and the college received considerable negative media coverage.

I was told by a prominent community leader that I had six months to turn the college around. Fundamentally, Lansing Community College had been one of Michigan's long-standing successful community colleges. I looked beyond the near-term issues, comforted by a vision of Lansing Community College as a leader college once again. (Knight, personal communication, June 14, 2018)

Leaders are biased toward action around shared values, problem solving, and problem seeking. They are not shy about seeking help and advice; neither are they shy about making the final, obviously more balanced decision. First and foremost, Knight used his network and recruited an expert CFO, a highly capable IT manager, and an expert college attorney to transition from "awful to award winning transparency"; soon the college was recognized as maintaining the highest audit standards. At the same time, Knight held tuition in check and improved the college fund balance:

Life requires unrelenting effort, a willingness to try, and contrary to a widely held conception, humans are well fitted for the effort. In humans the long process of evolution has produced a species of problem solvers, happiest when engaged in tasks that require not only physical effort but also the engagement of mind and heart. We are not only problem solvers but also problem seekers. If a suitable problem is not at hand, we invent one. Most games are invented problems. We are designed for the climb, not for taking our ease, either in the valley or at the summit. (Gardner, 1990, p. 195)

Strong leaders surround themselves with other individuals who represent the best of that special "species." These leaders tap into this human inclination to problem solve, and they strongly encourage problem seeking as a valuable contribution to colleges' efforts at mission accomplishment. This appears to lie in an institutional bias toward achieving a secure future for itself—that is, in a college's being bold enough to ask: "Are we the best college we can be, and if not, what must we do to be that college?" During the visit to LCC, the CCLP cohort witnessed the results of ten years of Knight's sharing his dreams, imagining with board members, and attempting to create a college like no other.

Although this is stressful, leaders are apt to put their careers at risk to position their respective institutions to sustain the current political and funding dynamics and engage stakeholders in building dreams they can support. Knight had a dream. "If we were able to turn that dream into reality, we could learn from that experience and repeat the process" (Knight, personal communication, June 14, 2018). "If we do not create the systems that will ensure the success of our students, the community college we know today may cease to exist, and the community college we dream of for the future may never come to be" (O'Banion, 2013, p. 3).

In the years that followed, LCC became a Bill & Melinda Gates Foundation guided pathways college and was able to focus on student success. Knight also transformed the campus and physical plant with his own dream of ambient learning. For example, the main classroom building has three hundred images, including Thurgood Marshall, John Glenn, James Meredith, Rosa Parks, and others; display cases, including one with slices of a human brain; an oil painting of a powwow; a writers' walk; and themed classrooms such as women's suffrage and the Underground Railroad. Knight and his colleagues also developed an inviting campus, a place where students want to be and enroll, with more than twenty outdoor sculptures, with the intent that LCC will become the pride of the community.

In January 2018 the LCC board of trustees adopted what may be a historic resolution. It is an effort to transform a traditional developmental/remedial program into a contemporary plan to help more students earn college credit as soon as possible and avoid running out of time and money with little to show for it. The resolution exemplifies the culmination of a shared vision, values, and involvement:

> In addition, the resolution acknowledges employees' "great commitment to achieving higher levels of student success" and directs the president to seek input from employees on how best to accomplish these core principles. It states the "Board intends to honor the President's commitment that implementation of the Six Core Principles be accomplished without causing loss of employment opportunities or reduction in pay rates for current faculty or staff." (Lansing Community College, 2018, para. 9)

COURAGE, CANDOR, AND COLLABORATION

Transformative leadership requires courage, candor, and collaboration. "Changing campus culture and student outcomes is a daunting task, requiring self-reflection, critical thinking and feedback, and significant, coordinated action across the institution" (Achieving the Dream, 2016, p. 2). Author Jon Meacham reminds us: "Churchill liked to quote Aristotle, who said that courage was the most important virtue, for it guaranteed all the others" (2018, p. 60).

In the early years of the transformational Achieving the Dream initiative, scalable intervention strategies were considered, with a laser focus on data and internal processes. The Achieving the Dream enterprise evolved to address institutional transformation. "The commitment and collaboration of the institution's leadership with respect to student success and the clarity of the vision for desired change" (Achieving the Dream, 2016, p. 1) are among the "essential capacities that must be in place for colleges to create the student-focused culture that promotes student success" (p. 2).

In scanning the community college horizon, El Paso Community College (EPCC) (TX), exemplifies the kind of courage, candor, and collaboration required to make changing culture possible:

> El Paso Community College received the Meyer Austin Institutional Student Leadership Award for simultaneously increasing student success and college access. With Achieving the Dream, the college instigated a college going culture in a metropolitan border area where 82 percent of residents are Hispanic, 27 percent are low-income, and 54 percent have a high school diploma or less education. (Achieving the Dream and Lumina Foundation, 2011, para. 2)

When the college reviewed its 2003–2004 data, staff members were astounded to learn about the large number of incoming students who required developmental education. "Of all the students taking the placement test for that 1-year period, 97 percent required remediation in math, approximately 70 percent required remediation in reading, and approximately 53 percent required remediation in writing" (Roueche et al., 2008, p. 100). Under the leadership of Richard Rhodes, then-EPCC president, a culture evolved of courageous conversations, candor about college data and effectiveness, and collaboration to change how the college operated as well as the expectations of college-going students and other community stakeholders.

Rhodes started by sharing disaggregated data with area school superintendents for students in their districts, which was the first time they had been presented with these data. Data were also shared in campus forums with staff and faculty and in a community advisory committee with local chambers of commerce, the local media, presidents and chief academic officers of area universities, and other college constituents.

To avoid finger pointing, laptops were made available for participants to take the placement test, which set the tone for an engaging dialogue in which all participants became learners in the courageous conversation. This use of data in an open and transparent conversation on the issue may have been one of the most important "tipping points" in the El Paso quest for making a difference in bridging the gap between high school exit competencies and college entrance requirements.

These forums were only the beginning of transformative undertakings. According to Rhodes, "Using data in our work towards the goals of Achieving the Dream helped us focus our efforts in a direction that would be more useful" (Roueche et al., 2008, p. 109).

Leaders understand the power of shared information, of everyone having a clear view of what needs to be and should be done—whether or not the way to do it is as clear—along with a heightened interest in getting it done. The message is that the "cards are on the table," and the atmosphere is open and direct, yet relaxed and flexible. The willingness to share information was one of the key discriminating characteristics of the ten most "excellent" colleges in one highly respected study of independent colleges nationwide:

> The sharing of information—and the sense of trust that permeates these institutions—fosters the respect for faculty. Detailed data and the complexities of institutional decisions are communicated in open forums. Faculty are heard on crucial issues and know the details when they debate with administrators or among themselves. This depth of faculty understanding mitigates against polarization. (Rice & Austin, 1988, p. 51)

College-wide climate assessments were also initiated at El Paso. Surveys of student perceptions of learning engagement were conducted, using the Community College Survey of Student Engagement (CCSSE) instrument, and the Noel-Levitz Student Satisfaction Inventory was administered to measure improvements in student perceptions, with outcomes shared with the entire college. Team and leadership development also took place, with EPCC employees contributing to recommendations for the concept of a leadership academy for EPCC to "grow its own":

> It is essential that solid understanding and leadership be cultivated throughout the institution, with an eye toward developing and sustaining a student success agenda.
>
> Regularly monitoring institutional progress and adopting policies that are based on data are important means of raising awareness and expectations that decisions made throughout the college are to be routinely informed by data. The active involvement of governance boards and CEOs is encouraged in asking the kinds of questions and modeling the kinds of behavior expected and encouraged throughout the institution to keep student success at the heart of the work.
>
> A shared vision can be adopted that is more likely to elicit broad ownership and reduce resistance by acknowledging the foundational work of current and previous boards, faculty, and administrative teams, and involving and regularly communicating with these crucial stakeholders. (McClenney & Mathis, 2011, pp. 31–33)

"Successful transformations require college leaders who can change the values and behaviors of others . . . focus the entire college on a vision of what it can become" (Roueche, Ely, & Roueche, 2001, p. 107).

COMMITMENT

Institutional transformation is, by necessity, incremental and evolutionary. Leaders must commit to achievement over the long haul. Research data confirm what leaders have always known intuitively: individuals really *are* hard-wired to resist change. Transformative leaders are resolute; they "have learned that the system will respond if they work at it long enough and hard enough; and if this fails to work, they have ideas about rejuvenating the system" (Burns & Sorenson, 1999, p. 330).

Irving McPhail, chancellor emeritus of the Community College of Baltimore County (CCBC) (MD), faced environmental challenges—internal and external—in response to a state legislative mandate that had been issued to consolidate three previously autonomous institutions "into a single college, multi-campus institution" (McPhail, Heacock, & Linck, 2001, p. 19). To fulfill the mandates of being accredited and achieving academic excellence, a learning-centered vision and mission were adopted by CCBC that were introduced by McPhail, which reinforced the foundational work of the three campuses.

It took years of planning, involvement, and professional development for the new campus representatives to begin to collaborate and coordinate efforts to develop system-wide goals and objectives in support of CCBC's vision and the changing needs of its diverse community. These efforts did not come easily. As a senior administrator from the college put it:

> The students' needs are probably the same in most cases. However, the students are different in some ways on each campus; they reflect the nature of the community from which we pull them. The staff and faculty often reflect what is going on in their community. What works for one campus may or may not work on the other campuses. The organizational culture, particularly the kind of psychological distance between people, sometimes got in the way of difficult decisions and difficult implementations. (Mathis, 2011, p. 75)

"Those who understand the challenge of culture change recognize that the task is enormous because it involves the creation of shared systems of meaning that are accepted, internalized, and acted on at every level of organization" (Hanson, 2003, p. 136).

CCBC leaders were committed to the alignment of academic and support services. They established councils and committees to provide professional development and planning around the analysis of data and the development of strategies to improve learning outcomes and implement change. Learning-centered principles were espoused in the college's strategic plan and supported by the board. They served as a vision-focused rallying point for the three campuses and for institutional transformation to achieve academic excellence and improve student success.

Effective systems and processes were established and evolved to provide data that informed an integrated approach to strategic planning, implementing, and evaluating. Councils, committees, and professional development days made a significant difference in developing awareness, building understanding and skills, and bridging the communication gap that existed among the campuses. Partnerships with public secondary schools, four-year institutions, and local businesses were fostered that contributed to the college achieving its goals.

As a result of these and other efforts, CCBC evolved into a national exemplar for improving student success and for reducing or eliminating the achievement gaps between African American and Caucasian students at CCBC.

LEADERS KNOW HOW TO GET IMPORTANT THINGS DONE

In today's environment, a college president/CEO must be prepared for the inevitable surprises that will hit and be adroit at forecasting, hiring, purchasing, partnering, bartering, measuring, and serving up the perfect blend of outcomes that will satisfy a myriad of stakeholder palates. The CEO and his or her leadership team must have a working knowledge of and be adept in "technical skills" such as governance and administration; union negotiations; school safety; public policy and affairs; organizational design, development, and reform; planning, finance, and resource development; and educational analytics, among others.

Leaders must also trust their own instincts and understand fully the depth and strength of their own passion. Strong leaders are self-actualizing individuals with a long history of setting high goals and achieving them and conveying with heightened credibility the confidence and the ability to get things done and make a difference.

Walter Bumphus, president and CEO of AACC, compiled ten leadership lessons that he shares with aspiring and sitting leaders. Reflecting on *Good to Great* by Jim Collins (2001), Bumphus notes that the book led him "to care more about 'we' and 'us' rather than 'me' and 'my.' Management is doing things right, but leadership is doing the right thing" (Bumphus, 2015).

With over thirty years' experience of teaching and leading, Bumphus provides observations and thoughts about personhood that have guided his community college leadership journey (see table 12.1). Research supports the crucial nature of *knowledge of self* in effective leadership—the importance of knowing one's strengths and being able to discern the fit between those strengths and the needs of the organization (Bennis & Nanus, 1985).

PERSISTENCE, PURPOSE, AND PEOPLE

Transforming a college's culture takes time, persistence, and fortitude. Culture change is apt to be fraught with resistance as stakeholders perceive that the traditional ways of doing things are changing. "A heightened sense of anxiety or fear may result as faculty and staff anticipate that additional con-

Leadership Lesson 1:
You have to know who you are as a leader and as a person.
"Leaders have to be humble. You have to think more of the organization than yourself. Have values to guide you."

Leadership Lesson 2:
Hire great people and support professional development.
"Hire people who are smarter than you."
"I cannot abdicate my responsibility. At the end of the day, I am responsible to make decisions. But surround yourself with greatness."

Leadership Lesson 3:
Develop your system of communications.
"Be transparent. Don't surprise the board. Communicate equitably across the board. Keep the board up to speed on all items. Develop a weekend memo. Get someone else to look at it. Be thoughtful of the tone. Once you hit 'Send,' it is over."

Leadership Lesson 4:
Inspect what you expect.
"You are responsible—be right, be effective. You never want to micromanage, but be on top of what is going on."

Leadership Lesson 5:
Continually tweak and refine your vision coupled with precise execution.
"We continue to redesign developmental education to get it right, now incorporating a laddered approach coupled with other courses and intrusive advising."

Leadership Lesson 6:
Minimize your enemies; develop, nurture, and respect relationships.
"Your friends will come and go, but your enemies will accumulate."
"You are in a relationship business. Be genuine and develop allies for the future."

Leadership Lesson 7:
Never let them see you sweat, and have an unrelenting work ethic. Getting the position is just the beginning.
"Don't act burdened. If you are working hard, people will notice. These performers will figure it out, they will."

Leadership Lesson 8:
Develop a passion for what you do.
"What is your legacy? When you are passionate you gain confidence in what you are doing. Confidence means the world. You can't tell someone with confidence what they cannot do."

Leadership Lesson 9:
What makes your talent and skills unique?
"Why should you stand out? Why should you be appointed to something? Work hard; be productive. How are you uniquely qualified to do the job?"

Leadership Lesson 10:
Keep a balanced life, have fun, and don't stay too long!
"Keep growing and moving forward. Make sure you take your vacations. Sometimes things work better without you. Focus on your health and being the best person you can be."

Table 12.1

tributions of time will be requested or perceive that their jobs and security could be jeopardized" (McClenney & Mathis, 2011, p. 30).

Transformative leaders are known for persisting in the face of daunting odds for quality, excellence, and accomplishment; they are exemplars of grit.

What is "grit," and why does it matter? How is it that some folks have "grit" and some folks don't? According to Angela Lee Duckworth, a psychologist:

> [N]o matter the domain, the highly successful had a kind of ferocious determination that played out in two ways. First, these exemplars were unusually resilient and hardworking. Second, they knew in a very, very deep way what it was they wanted. They not only had determination, they had *direction*.
>
> It was this combination of passion and perseverance that made high achievers special. In a word, they had grit. (2016, p. 8)

Transformative leaders model *purpose* and *moral imperative*. "The long days and evenings of toil, the setbacks and disappointments and struggle, the sacrifice—all this is worth it because, ultimately, their efforts pay dividends to other people" (Duckworth, 2016, pp. 144–145).

Long-term colleagues and friends Suanne Davis Roueche and Christine Johnson McPhail provide powerful examples of persistence, purpose, and care for people. Both women stand as sentinels with a shared calling for making a difference in the lives of community colleges and their students. Throughout their careers, these two professionals personified the existential definition of freedom, taking responsibility for what they did and what they made of themselves, moving beyond self-fulfillment to higher levels of contribution to the world and those around them. "Commitment is an act, not a word" (Jean-Paul Sartre, n.d.).

Suanne Roueche's contributions to community colleges were the inspiration for national awards: the John and Suanne Roueche Excellence Award, established by the League for Innovation in the Community College, and the Suanne Davis Roueche/NISOD Endowment at The University of Texas at Austin. At the heart of this remarkable woman was more than an award-winning scholar; she and John, married for more than forty years, established endowed scholarships at many colleges throughout the state of Texas and across the United States, including Austin Community College and The University of Texas at Austin. Even as her health was failing, Suanne dedicated her time and passion toward the causes she had supported throughout her life.

Christine McPhail, a leader whose example has inspired countless future leaders, further demonstrates a tireless commitment to the education of others and the advancement of community colleges. McPhail was the recipient of the 2010 AACC's National Leadership Award and the 2008 League for Innovation in the Community College's Terry O'Banion Leadership Award. Her inspiration and effectiveness gave rise to a national agenda focused on increasing the number of trained professionals for the community college leadership pipeline and a record-setting number of African Americans receiving doctoral degrees from her program at Morgan State in Maryland. McPhail models the purpose and moral imperative described in Duckworth's *Grit*.

Two such powerful, kindred spirits shared the propensity to rekindle a renewed dedication to a life of passion and purpose toward the betterment of students, colleges, and communities. Ultimately, a transformative leader's fundamental outlook is based on the importance of respect for people and the relationships that are fostered through continuous communication, collaboration, and sustenance in traversing toward shared vision, values, and goals:

> It is the power of a person to become a leader, armed with principles and rising above self-interest narrowly conceived, that invests that person with power and may ultimately transform both leaders and followers into persons who jointly adhere to moral values and end-values. A person, whether leader or follower, girded with moral purpose is a tiny principality of power. (Burns, 1978, p. 457)

The CCLP students are a passionate cadre of courageous, committed, and purposeful leaders. Not unlike community college students, doctoral students arrive with multiple commitments to family, friends, communities, and careers. And similarly, life events are apt to interrupt an already stress-filled undertaking when students are confronted by illnesses and unforeseen family member demands, as well as promotions and celebrations.

A good bit of the culture that is fostered within each NAU cohort includes trust and relationship building, developing stamina to weather personal and professional "storms," and rising above self-interest to address civic needs. The CCLP network of cohorts, faculty, and other colleagues is a vibrant part of the support team to answer questions; provide input on viable solutions; and reinforce support for celebrations, promotions, and challenging issues.

PERFORMANCE, PREPARATION, AND THE COURAGE TO LEAD

The power of vision is crucial to organizational achievement. However, authors Bossidy and Charan, in *Execution: The Discipline of Getting Things Done* (2002, 2009), remind us that effective implementation is a crucial component in differentiating great leaders from daydreamers. With this admonition in mind, leaders can ill afford to expect successful execution (or improved outcomes) if employees and other stakeholders are not knowledgeable or equipped to perform well, let alone as collaborative teams. In institutions of higher education, employed "eagles" are often incentivized to soar high and solo; unfortunately, teamwork is often sacrificed for individual pursuit of academic discipline, self-achievement, and individual recognition.

In consideration of these challenges, CCLP doctoral candidates participate in an Advanced Leadership Institute (ALI) as they progress toward the end of the program and dissertation completion. Under the instruction, coaching, and guidance of Donald W. Cameron, president emeritus, Guilford

Technical Community College (NC), this final convening of cohort members during the program is designed to further hone leadership skills and encourage leadership development for their respective institutions to increase understanding, involvement, and effective execution of goals.

The ALI includes a week of interviews and interaction with community college leaders; observations of, and discussions with, panelists on the importance of building strong partnerships to provide the appropriate services to business and industry; student-faculty-guest lecturer discussions about building a model for workforce and economic development; and corporate site visits. Cohort members round out the week by working in teams to develop leadership academies. In developing these institutes, the doctoral candidates are to demonstrate learning outcomes, including

- the ability to integrate knowledge of emerging issues, leadership, organizational development, and institutional transformation;
- an understanding of human relations issues, including employment, goal setting, evaluation, discipline, and professional development; and
- an understanding of team dynamics, how to build and develop effective leadership teams and elicit stakeholder involvement (Community College Leadership Program, 2018).

The team members analyze and address key aspects of leadership, including the courage and conviction to lead, and tailor the academies to include an analysis of the environment, strategic partners and needs, and internal/external stakeholders crucial to success. The teams create institutes that reinforce trust and relationship building, as well as strategic coaching, shadowing, professional development, and assessments to equip future leaders throughout the institution to build for the future. They present on the last day of the institute and discuss strategies for introducing the academies at their home institutions. Such leader-follower-team development is reinforced throughout the ALI as a crucial component in fostering a desired culture and values and achieving a shared vision and goals.

In *Rising to the Challenge: Lessons Learned from Guilford Technical Community College*, Roueche and Roueche state that the college, under the leadership of then president Cameron, "achieved its reputation (through) the unique collection of robust, well-thought-out practices being implemented—practices in leadership, stewardship, partnership, and teaching and learning (2012, p. 109). These practices thrive in a culture that consistently raises the bar for high performance and achievement standards.

PAINTING A FACE ON THE FUTURE

Key lessons have been shared in this chapter that were learned by successful leaders to engage stakeholders in transformation and organizational effectiveness. "Our experience tells us that the linkage—or partnership—between leaders and followers is only as strong as their shared beliefs about the importance of their work together" (Roueche, Ely, & Roueche, 2001, p. 109).

As evidenced in this book, purposeful and passionate leaders are unyielding in their pursuit of effective and sustainable solutions that will transform institutions—without overwhelming the very stakeholders who are needed to implement them. It is a compelling goal and remarkable achievement for any college leader to so transform the culture of his or her institution that when the college addresses its most challenging teaching and learning issues, the quality of the decisions can be judged by how closely they match up to its collective goals, hopes, and dreams.

As stakeholders grapple with the many challenges and changes their colleges face, leaders are reminded that colleges and communities are living in the future *we*—leaders and followers—create. Transformative leaders noted in this book are placing an indelible mark upon the community college movement by setting in place the research, relationships, and vision for a better tomorrow—founded on a knowledge of what it takes and *how* to lead in an ever-shifting terrain—*to make good on the promise of the open door.*

REFERENCES

Achieving the Dream. (2013, April 23). Awards of excellence. Silver Spring, MD: Author. Retrieved from http://www.achievingthedream.org/node?page=5

Achieving the Dream. (2016). Achieving the Dream's institutional capacity framework and institutional capacity assessment tool. Silver Spring, MD: Author.

Achieving the Dream and Lumina Foundation. (2011, February 8). Press release: El Paso Community College receives national award. Silver Spring, MD and Indianapolis, IN: Authors. Retrieved from http://www.achievingthedream.org/press_release/193/el-paso-community-college-receives-national-award

American Association of Community Colleges (AACC). (2013, August 9). *AACC competencies for community college leaders* (2nd ed.). Washington, DC: Author. Retrieved from http://www.aacc.nche.edu/newsevents/Events/leadershipsuite/Pages/competencies.aspx

American Association of Community Colleges (AACC) and Association of Community College Trustees (ACCT). (2018). *Executive leadership transitioning at community colleges.* Washington, DC: Authors. Retrieved from https://www.aacc.nche.edu/wp-content/uploads/2018/04/Exec-Leadership-Transitioning.pdf

American Association of Community Colleges (AACC) Staff. (2018, June–July). A focus on onboarding. *Community College Journal.* Retrieved from http://www.ccjournal-digital.com/ccjournal/20180607?pg=10#pg10

Bennis, W. G., & Nanus, B. (1985). *Leaders: Strategies for taking charge.* New York: Harper & Row.

Boggs, G. R. (2015). *Facing change in the community college: Leadership issues and challenges.* Austin, TX, and Phoenix, AZ: A joint publication of the Roueche Graduate Center, National American University, and the League for Innovation in the Community College.

Bossidy, L., & Charan, R. (2002, 2009). *Execution: The discipline of getting things done.* New York: Crown Publishing Group.

Bumphus, W. (2015, February 17). *Dr. Walter Bumphus: Leadership in the 21st century.* Speaker series. Austin: Longhorn Center for Academic Excellence, The University of Texas at Austin.

Burns, J. M. (1978). *Leadership.* New York: Harper & Row.

Burns, J. M., & Sorenson, G. J. (1999). *Dead center: Clinton-Gore leadership and the perils of moderation.* New York: A Lisa Drew Book, Simon & Schuster.

Collins, J. (2001). *Good to great.* New York: HarperCollins.

Community College Leadership Program. (2018). CCLP learning outcomes. Austin, TX: Roueche Graduate Center, National American University.

Duckworth, A. (2016). *Grit: The power of passion and perseverance.* New York: Scribner.

The Examiner. (2016, August 6). Obituaries: Edmund John Gleazer, 1916–2016. Retrieved from http://www.legacy.com/obituaries/examiner/obituary.aspx?pid=180988119

Gardner, J. W. (1990). *On leadership.* New York: The Free Press, a division of Simon & Schuster.

Hanson, E. M. (2003). *Educational administration and organizational behavior* (5th ed.). Boston: Allyn and Bacon.

Lansing Community College. (2018, January 25). Board of trustees passes resolution in support of developmental education redesign. Retrieved from http://lafayette.lcc.edu/employee-news/2018/01/25/board-of-trustees-passes-resolution-in-support-of-developmental-education-redesign/

Mathis, M. B. (2011). Case study—Staying the course in a perfect storm: Fostering and sustaining a student learning, equity, and success agenda. In B. N. McClenney & M. B. Mathis, *Making good on the promise of the open door: Effective governance and leadership to improve student equity, success, and completion* (pp. 73–83). Washington, DC: Association of Community College Trustees.

Meacham, J. (2018, May/June). Winston Churchill: Portrait of power. *Cigar Aficionado.*

McClenney, K. (2016, April 13). Point of view: Finding the path to student success. *Community College Week.* Retrieved from http://ccweek.com/article-5145-finding-the-path-to-student-success.html

McClenney, B. N., & Mathis, M. B. (2011). *Making good on the promise of the open door: Effective governance and leadership to improve student equity, success, and completion.* Washington, DC: Association of Community College Trustees.

McPhail, I. P., Heacock, R., & Linck, H. F. (2001). LearningFIRST: Creating and leading the learning college. *Community College Journal of Research and Practice, 25,* 17–28.

Norris, D., Baer, L., & Offerman, M. (2009, September 21–23). *Action analytics: A new imperative for higher education.* White paper from the National Symposium on Action Analytics. St. Paul, MN.

O'Banion, R. (2013). *Access, success, and completion: A primer for community college faculty, administrators, staff, and trustees.* Phoenix, AZ: League for Innovation in the Community College.

Rice, R. E., & Austin, A. E. (1988). High faculty morale: What exemplary colleges do right. *Change, 20*(2), 51–18.

Roueche, J. E. (1968). *Salvage, redirection, or custody—remedial education in the community junior college.* Los Angeles: ERIC Clearinghouse for Junior Colleges; Washington, DC: American Association of Junior Colleges. Retrieved from https://eric.ed.gov/?id=ED019077

Roueche, J. E., Baker, G. A., & Mathis, M. B. (2014, May). *Leadership competency assessment, revised.* Austin, TX: Roueche Graduate Center, National American University.

Roueche, J. E., Ely, E. E., & Roueche, S. D. (2001). *In pursuit of excellence: The Community College of Denver.* Washington, DC: Community College Press, American Association of Community Colleges.

Roueche, J. E., & Mathis, M. B. (2018, March). Foreword. In J. E. Roueche, G. Boggs, & M. B. Mathis (Eds.), *Facing the future: State funding of community colleges.* Austin, TX: Roueche Graduate Center, National American University.

Roueche, J. E. & O'Banion, T. U. (2018, May 26). Partnership scholarships can develop future leaders. *Community College Week.* Retrieved from http://ccweek.com/article-5867-partnership-scholarships-can-develop-future-leaders.html

Roueche, J. E., Richardson, M. M., Neal, P. W., & Roueche, S. D. (Eds.). (2008). *The creative community college: Leading change through innovation.* Washington, DC: Community College Press, American Association of Community Colleges.

Roueche, J. E., & Roueche, S. D. (2008, September 1). The art of visionary leadership: Painting a face on the future. *Celebrations.* Austin: National Institute for Staff and Organizational Development (NISOD), Community College Leadership Program, Department of Educational Administration, College of Education, The University of Texas at Austin. Retrieved from https://www.nisod.org/2008/09/01/art-visionary-leadership-painting-face-future/

Roueche, J. E., & Roueche, S. D. (Eds.). (2012). *Rising to the challenge: Lessons learned from Guilford Technical Community College.* Washington, DC: Community College Press.

Schein, E. H. (2010). *Organizational culture and leadership* (4th ed.). San Francisco, CA: Jossey-Bass.

Smith, A. A. (2016, May 20). Tension at the top. *Inside Higher Ed.* Retrieved from https://www.insidehighered.com/news/2016/05/20/many-community-college-presidencies-are-upheaval

The Villager Newspaper. (2013). Cuyahoga Community College Wins Award of Excellence from American Association of Community Colleges (AACC). Retrieved from http://www.thevillagernewspaper.com/2013/05/06/cuyahoga-community-college-wins-award-of-excellence-from-american-association-of-community-colleges-aacc/

Chapter Thirteen

Using Data to Monitor What Matters

A New Role for Trustees

Byron McClenney

AUTHOR'S NOTE

In many ways this chapter reflects my professional journey over two recent decades of work in the community college sector. I wrote one of seven chapters focused on community college work on accountability (Roueche, Johnson, Roueche, & Associates, 1997) and one of six chapters on colleges leading the learning revolution (O'Banion, 1997), both of which set the stage for significant transformation in the way governing boards monitor college activity.

I left the presidency after almost thirty-three years to codirect the Bridges to Opportunity national initiative, funded by the Ford Foundation, and to help found Achieving the Dream in 2003–2004 from a post in the Community College Leadership Program at The University of Texas at Austin (UT). While directing UT participation in Achieving the Dream, I served as the national director of leadership coaching for a decade. In 2007, with Houston Endowment and Greater Texas Foundation funding, I founded the Board of Trustees Institute for Texas community college boards, which held its twelfth annual event in 2018. Next came the California Leadership Alliance for Student Success (CLASS), which I codirected. Funded by Hewlett and Irvine foundations, it focused on work with CEOs and board members.

I led a UT partnership with the Association of Community College Trustees (ACCT) to create the Governance Institute for Student Success (GISS) with funding from the Bill & Melinda Gates Foundation. The first event was a 2010 statewide institute for Ohio community college boards, followed by events around the country over the next eight years. I have facilitated six to eight board retreats around the country each year since retiring from UT in 2014. This accumulated experience has provided insight into a new role for boards as they monitor what matters.

As with governing boards in other sectors of higher education, community college boards have historically been focused on buildings, budgets, and bonds. Much more attention has been focused on an annual financial audit than on a report from an accreditor. A pivotal point was reached in 1997 when conversations about institutional effectiveness and accountability reached a peak as regional accreditors, scholars, legislators, foundations, and others raised questions about outcomes. "The overarching issues of the effectiveness movement—ever-greater competition for funds; the press of legislative, board, and taxpayer attentions; increased scrutiny and public criticism—will surface again and again as we turn to college responses" (Roueche, Johnson, Roueche, & Associates, 1997, p. 19).

Roueche and Associates went on to say that "our survey responses indicate that colleges are not adopting, on any large scale, the basis of the conceptual frameworks most commonly advanced in the literature—that is, tying college mission to expected outcomes" (1997, p. 182).

During the same period a call was issued by Terry O'Banion (1997) for colleges to change their basic systems to focus on learning like never before. He suggested "trustees will need to participate in training sessions to begin to prepare for policy and resource changes related to philosophical and structural changes" (1997, p. 239). C. J. Smith reinforced the suggestion with a strong push for a shift in the role of a board. "Wise boards foster a climate that supports monitoring of institutional effectiveness" (2000, p. 158). Nine years later, she reflected on whether or not that shift had occurred: "While governing boards are accountable for institutional effectiveness, their accountability for student success is not well defined or performed" (2009, p. 29).

A strong foundation for change was forged through the push for accountability, institutional effectiveness, and the emerging learning revolution in the late 1990s. What emerged from all of the activity was a national agenda for student success and completion. Years later, O'Banion noted that anecdotal data about success were no longer enough. "With national initiatives such as Achieving the Dream and Completion by Design leading the way, community colleges have had to examine the evidence on student success nationally and in their own institutions" (2013, p. 9). The initiatives he mentioned began to form in 2004 and helped influence the concern about the role of boards in what was becoming transformational work.

Peter Ewell (2006) made a strong case for fundamental change in the way boards view their role. "Ensuring academic quality is a fiduciary responsibility; it is as much part of our role as board members as ensuring that the institution has sufficient resources and is spending them wisely" (2006, p. vii). He indicated the importance of evidence of quality outcomes and called directly for the monitoring of retention and graduation rates. He even went so far as to indicate that boards needed to be familiar with various student success programs, with evidence of effectiveness.

TRANSFORMATION FOR STUDENT SUCCESS

Chapter 1 in this volume, "The Learning Paradigm," describes a project by the League for Innovation in the Community College in which twelve vanguard learning colleges collaborated to become more learning centered. That effort, launched in early 2000, was a forerunner to a transformative effort by Lumina Foundation for Education undertaken during a planning year in 2003. The author was asked to prepare a paper focused on what a national initiative might include (McClenney, 2003). The paper called for all colleges to join the Lumina initiative to collect and update baseline data. The data would include the following:

- first-semester completion of first-time students;
- the proportion of students who enter remediation who successfully exit;
- performance in key subsequent college-level courses by those who exit remedial education;
- the number and percent of students who complete college algebra, English composition, anatomy and physiology, or other gatekeeping courses;
- retention (fall-to-spring and fall-to-fall);
- the graduation rate based on tracking of entering cohorts;
- the number and percent of students who transfer to four-year institutions; and
- disaggregation by group (race, ethnicity, gender) of all of the above.

The initiative Achieving the Dream was launched in 2004 after a planning year in which a group of national partners worked with Lumina Foundation to develop the approach. The data-informed approach was at the heart of the effort as twenty-seven colleges became the first cohort in 2004. Direct support was provided to the colleges by a leadership coach and a data coach.

All leadership coaches were recruited and supervised by Byron McClenney, who served as the national director of leadership coaching in his post at UT. The coaches, most of whom were former CEOs, wrote college visit reports, which were reviewed at UT for the purpose of learning about transformational change. Even though Achieving the Dream had decided not to focus on the board role, much was learned from the experience of coaches working with the colleges. This learning, accumulated over a decade of work, produced much insight about the importance of the board role. More than two hundred colleges were engaged in Achieving the Dream in its first decade.

Houston Endowment Inc. and its program officer, George Grainger, took an interest in the work and became a major funder of Achieving the Dream by funding the membership of all Gulf Coast community colleges. Grainger took a special interest in the role of boards, particularly as they either did or did not create the culture for transformative student success. The endowment provided a grant to UT with Byron McClenney as the director of what became the Board of Trustees Institute (BOTI). The Greater Texas Foundation later joined to help fund all Achieving the Dream colleges in Texas for participation in the BOTI.

The institute was launched in 2007 for all Texas community colleges involved in Achieving the Dream. Teams of trustees, along with the CEO, attended a multiday event in Santa Fe, New Mexico. The twelfth annual event was held in March 2018. Mining of Achieving the Dream coaching reports and the early work with boards in the BOTI led to creation of the characteristics of effective boards. The focus was on boards of colleges making progress on the transformative student success agenda. The description was utilized in BOTI events and in a later partnership with ACCT. The characteristics included the following:

1. Support a culture of inquiry, evidence, and accountability.
2. Approve a strategic plan with student success at the core.
3. Approve goals for student success and equity.
4. Expect to support a limited set of clear priorities (three to five) to improve student success.
5. Ask tough questions about progress on student success.
6. Create a culture within the college in which the CEO engages in courageous conversations with all constituencies.
7. Approve the allocation/reallocation of resources to support the student success agenda.
8. Expect a relentless focus on student success.
9. Consider evidence-based changes in policy affecting student success.

The "characteristics" were presented in plenary sessions at BOTI and influenced board conversations in breakout strategy sessions facilitated by resident faculty. Each institute included four such strategy sessions, culminating in an action plan to be shared with board members back home who were unable to attend BOTI or GISS sessions. Project staff conducted a follow-up study of eight colleges that had participated in BOTI for a number of years to identify what had changed as a result of BOTI participation.

Examples of actions taken by boards include the following:

- Approved a strategic plan titled "Focus on Student Success."
- Approved increased funding for student success initiatives.
- Received monthly reports on success initiatives.
- Included key performance indicators in the strategic plan.
- Conducted an annual retreat with the focus on student success.
- Conducted an annual review of board policies.
- Endorsed a developmental education improvement plan.
- Made a commitment to take promising practices to scale.
- Created annual "charges" to the CEO.
- Developed a monthly board agenda item focused on student success.

Most dramatically, the CEOs and their teams were enabled to take very significant steps internally to install high-impact practices.

Colleges utilized their planning and budgeting processes to take big steps such as eliminating late registration and requiring orientation for all first-time-ever-in-college students. Some colleges required a student success course for those same students, along with required advising leading to an educational plan. The boards in these colleges came to expect regular reports on the results achieved with the changes implemented. There was a growing synergy in the UT work coming from the BOTI activities and the follow-up with the annual gatherings of leadership coaches in Achieving the Dream to reflect on what was being learned about transformational change.

REASONS FOR PROGRESS IN TRANSFORMATIONAL CHANGE

The results of the leadership coach reflection process during a four-year period led to creation of a "Top Ten" list of the reasons for change, which then were used in BOTI events to further the conversations with Texas boards. An inventory was developed and utilized in several trustee institutes, including those developed in partnership with ACCT. The inventory was created with a five-point scale, from "Strongly Disagree" (1) to "Strongly Agree" (5), to allow trustees to respond to the elements. Items in the inventory were as follows:

- Create a sense of urgency for a student success agenda.
- Create a culture/climate within which the CEO can lead.
- Learn how to monitor student success outcomes.
- Understand the importance of institutional research.
- Approve goals for closing gaps in attainment.
- Approve a strategic plan with student success at the core.
- Approve annual priorities focused on student success.
- Ensure that priorities drive allocation or reallocation of resources.

- Approve a communications plan focused on student success.
- Encourage K–12 partnerships.

DEVELOPMENT OF THE GOVERNANCE INSTITUTE

Early results from the BOTI and five years of learning from reviewing leadership coaching reports from Achieving the Dream led to interest from the Bill & Melinda Gates Foundation in establishing a project to prepare more trustees in using data to monitor student success. Conversations with UT and ACCT led to the creation of the Governance Institute for Student Success (GISS).

Following extensive planning, the first statewide event was held in Ohio in 2010, clearly built on the BOTI experience at UT and the Governance Leadership Institute at ACCT. Evaluation of GISS events over the next three years (Suna Associates LLC, 2011, pp. 11–12) found results very similar to the results of the BOTI. Many boards held board retreats as a follow-up to the GISS, and the use of disaggregated data became common among the colleges with teams in attendance. The importance of professional development grew following GISS participation, and most boards began to include student success on each board agenda.

The evaluators described the key elements of the design model they say were embraced by the participants (Suna Associates LLC, 2011, p. 4):

- Participation by teams of typically four people (board and CEO) from an institution
- State-based outreach and dissemination strategies
- Self-assessments of board effectiveness
- Individual institutional and state student success data
- Expert resident faculty and carefully selected plenary speakers
- Case studies
- Guided review of policies and practices
- Commitments to action by each team

As a result of the early UT work and the collaborative work between UT and ACCT, the UT principals were asked by ACCT to prepare a publication on what had been learned in work with the boards (McClenney & Mathis, 2011) focused on student success. The resulting publication raised key questions for board consideration dealing with board roles, the use of data, creating a culture of inquiry and evidence, and the importance of leadership. In addition, case studies were provided on the experience of the Community College of Baltimore County (MD) and San Jacinto College (TX) to illustrate how colleges work in data-informed ways to improve student success.

McClenney and Mathis (2011) incorporated examples of board action following participation in one of the institutes that have been described. They mirror the examples previously provided and demonstrate how a board can support a CEO and a leadership team to implement big ideas to improve student success outcomes. To assist with follow-up at local institutions, Mathis (2011, pp. 63–67) compiled an extensive "Student Success Compendium," which reflected the research and writing about the emerging national agenda on student success and completion.

ACCT enhanced the deliberations by convening the 2011 Invitational Symposium on Student Success in Dallas. A result of the symposium was the Student Success Policy Action Agenda. Promotional materials from ACCT, such as "Bring Data-Informed Governance to Your State," based on participant feedback, were then utilized to spread what had been learned in work with the boards.

The elements of data-informed decision making, improving collaboration between boards and CEOs, allowing for board self-reflection, strengthening practices in support of student success and completion, and informing boards about promising strategies were becoming pervasive by 2012 in the states where trustees had been involved in the institutes. McClenney and Mathis (2011, p. 57), by examining the respective roles of the board and the CEO, posed some critical questions about how to further the work of the board and the CEO. Guiding questions for a local governing board and its CEO include the following:

1. How might our board meetings differ if our college were committed to a student success agenda?
2. How will our board and CEO create a climate that is conducive to holding honest conversations?
3. How can our board and CEO work together to build political will and move the student success agenda forward?

   a. In what ways will the role of our board differ from that of our CEO?
   b. Where are areas for collaboration?

4. What policies and practices can our board adopt to foster a climate to uphold academic quality and improve student equity, success, and completion?
5. In what ways can our board provide political cover for the CEO as he or she moves to operationalize student success policies?
6. What policies and practices would provide focus and support?

One of the important aspects of the institute model described here is that CEOs and board members have time for honest interaction during breakout sessions and table conversations following substantive plenary presentations. They also have time to examine their own data and then raise the "so what" questions together. For example, the first BOTI in 2007 presented data on students who had started their college experience in developmental math and followed them for two years to see what percent had completed a college credit math course. The shocking result was that most colleges saw single-digit percentages.

When those data are disaggregated the shock is even deeper, as trustees see gaps between groups on the basis of race, ethnicity, gender, and other characteristics. The organizing principle for the institutes moving forward was to always start with data on the individual colleges of the participating trustees. It was always important to disaggregate those data and to provide adequate time for the necessary conversations. Plenary sessions were designed to offer ways of thinking about solutions and to pose questions to be considered in breakout discussions.

PREPARING FOR THE FUTURE

The governance institutes continued beyond 2012 as the field began to deal with two transformational movements. The movements are carefully described in *Redesigning America's Community Colleges* by Thomas Bailey, Shanna Jaggars, and Davis Jenkins (2015). The authors describe the need to transform developmental education and provide numerous examples of early efforts to do that. They also call for development of guided pathways for students who have been limited to attending the traditional cafeteria college. As these movements began to develop, the subject matter of the institutes and the data shared began to change. Key performance indicators, scorecards, and dashboards were soon included in the board institutes.

The American Association of Community Colleges (AACC) has been active in working with national partners to advance the work identified by Bailey, Jaggars, and Jenkins (2015). As described in chapter 4 in this volume, the work on guided pathways has become a movement across the country. This work introduces an additional set of key metrics to monitor.

The same is true for work to accelerate progress through developmental education. An AACC Institute, Integrating Redesigned Developmental Education into Pathways, involved twenty-two college teams and provided a forum for national partners to share what they had learned. Further, chapter 7 in this volume describes the significant work of Complete College America to accelerate or eliminate what has been known as remedial or developmental education.

Byron McClenney endeavored to capture the changes in metrics called for due to changes in the approach to developmental education and the impact of work on guided pathways in a plenary presentation for the BOTI held in March 2018. The following questions were suggested:

- What percent of potential first-time-ever-in-college (FTEIC) students who take initial steps to enroll are actually enrolled on the census date?
- What percent of those enrolled on the census date actually earn no credits in the semester?
- What is the semester course completion rate (C or better) for the term?
- What is the fall-to-spring persistence rate for FTEIC students?
- What percent of FTEIC students successfully complete (C or better) English composition and the appropriate credit math course (algebra, statistics, or quantitative reasoning) in the first year?
- What percent of an entering cohort earn credits at the following levels in the first year (see table 13.1)?
- What is the fall-to-fall persistence rate for FTEIC students?
- What percent of FTEIC students successfully complete credits in a chosen major in the first year?
- What is the graduation rate (by entering cohort) after two years for certificate programs and after four years for associate programs?
- What percent of an entering cohort successfully transfers to a university after completing twenty-four credit hours? Thirty credit hours? General education core? AA/AS/AAS?

Additional monitoring might include the following questions:

- What percent of FTEIC students participate in a high-quality orientation?
- What percent enroll in a student success course (or freshman seminar, etc.) in the first term?
- What percent have an educational plan by the end of the first term? First year?
- What percent of FTEIC students have an assigned adviser or were assigned to an advising group by chosen major or pathway in the first year?

F-T	P-T
12+	6+
24+	12+
30+	18+

Table 13.1

Boards can monitor the suggested elements by creating an annual cycle of reporting of disaggregated data (race, ethnicity, gender, Pell status, and others) in order to see if the college is progressing on its agenda. By doing so, gaps in outcomes will become obvious and conversations can be held about plans to address the related issues and needed changes in policy and practice. The monitoring described here begins to fulfill the way Ewell (2006) defined the fiduciary responsibility of boards.

THE NEW BOARD ROLE

Moving well beyond the focus on buildings, budgets, and bonds, boards around the country are considering how to step up to the new role of monitoring what matters most in pursuit of student success and completion. They are seeing the importance of building a culture of inquiry, evidence, and accountability. Clearly the field has come a long way since 1997. Understanding of the importance of strategic thinking with student success at the core is now common.

There is a new realization of the importance of creating a climate within which a CEO can do courageous work with the people of an organization. When a review of student outcomes reveals gaps and raises questions around equity, there is a better chance for honest conversations. There is more openness to consideration of evidence-based changes in policy impacting student success.

Early in the work of Achieving the Dream, there was a tendency for colleges to attempt pilot projects with an eye to scaling if results were promising. There was also more interest in a focus on the "front door" of the college rather than on improving instruction to ensure students would exit the "back door" more successfully. That has changed in the last decade as a push for transformational change has gained ground.

Radically changing developmental education and implementation of guided pathways call for fundamental change in how a college delivers education. Boards need to be aware that change like that can cause disruption in institutional life. Being a party to the change and adopting appropriate ways to monitor progress can provide clarity for the institution. Monitoring data about student progression and tracking implementation of major program changes can be reassuring to a CEO and board members who are willing to undertake fundamental change.

Board members can anticipate significant help in monitoring what matters as associations at the regional, state, and national levels incorporate ideas in conferences and through publications. Many states are creating student success centers, and many foundations are supporting state efforts. A recent example is a grant from College Futures to AACC for the purpose of holding board retreats for California community colleges working on guided pathways. By working in a data-informed way, and with growing support from foundations and national organizations, boards will enable many more students to succeed in their institutions. It will be a satisfying journey for trustees and especially for students, who will benefit from new efforts by the board.

What started in the late 1990s as a movement toward accountability and a focus on learning as the primary outcome of education has created a foundation for transformational change in community colleges. These shifts have led to a new role and a set of new expectations for community college trustees that have the potential to transform the community college world.

REFERENCES

Bailey, T., Jaggers, S., & Jenkins, D. (2015). *Redesigning America's Community Colleges.* Cambridge, MA: Harvard University Press.

Ewell, P. (2006). *Making the Grade: How Boards Can Ensure Academic Quality.* Washington, DC: Association of Governing Boards of Universities and Colleges.

Mathis, M. (2011). "Student Success Compendium." In *Making Good on the Promise of the Open Door.* Washington, DC: Association of Community College Trustees.

McClenney, B. (2003). "Comments from Byron McClenney." Lumina Foundation for Education's Community College Initiative.

McClenney, B., & Mathis, M. (2011). *Making Good on the Promise of the Open Door: Effective Governance and Leadership to Improve Student Equity, Success, and Completion.* Washington, DC: Association of Community College Trustees.

O'Banion, T. (1997). *A Learning College for the 21st Century.* Phoenix, AZ: The Oryx Press.

O'Banion, T. (2013). *Access, Success, and Completion.* Chandler, AZ: League for Innovation in the Community College.

Roueche, J. E., Johnson, L., Roueche, S., & Associates. (1997). *Embracing the Tiger: The Effectiveness Debate & the Community College.* Washington, DC: Community College Press.

Smith, C. J. (2000). *Trusteeship in Community Colleges: A Guide for Effective Governance.* Washington, DC: Association of Community College Trustees.

Smith, C. J. (2009). "CLASS Evaluation Overview." Paper submitted to the William and Flora Hewlett Foundation, the James Irvine Foundation, and the Community College Leadership Program of The University of Texas at Austin.

Suna Associates LLC. (2011). "Summative Evaluation, Governance Institutes for Student Success." Paper submitted to the Association of Community College Trustees and Community College Leadership Program of The University of Texas at Austin.

Epilogue

The Missing Transformative Idea

Terry U. O'Banion

All of the thirteen ideas in this book have emerged from reform efforts to redesign the contemporary community college. [1]Each idea has its champions and advocates, support from national organizations, projects to field-test models or implement programs and practices, funding to support these efforts, and in many cases increased research to examine the value and veracity of the claims of its advocates.

In chapter 4 in this volume, Kay McClenney underscored the imperative to redesign the nation's community colleges. In *Reclaiming the American Dream: Community Colleges and the Nation's Future,* AACC's 21st Century Commission on the Future of Community Colleges (which McClenney cochaired) laid out the challenge:

> Despite these historic successes, and amidst serious contemporary challenges, community colleges need to be redesigned for new times. What we find today are student success rates that are unacceptably low, employment preparation that is inadequately connected to job market needs, and disconnects in transitions between high schools, community colleges, and baccalaureate institutions. (AACC, 2012, p. viii)

The commission acknowledged daunting financial challenges, including persistent underfunding of community colleges, but also pointed to evidence undergirding criticisms of community college performance, while at the same time affirming the institutions' crucial roles. It concluded: "The American Dream is at risk. Community colleges can help reclaim it. But stepping up to the challenge will require dramatic redesign of these institutions, their missions, and most crucially, students' educational experiences" (AACC, 2012, p. 1).

Reclaiming the American Dream stirred concerns and actions among national community college leaders and organizations about transforming the community college. A "tipping point" occurred with the publication of Bailey, Jaggars, and Jenkins's (2015) important book, *Redesigning America's Community Colleges: A Clearer Path to Student Success*. Based on research at the Community College Research Center—the most extensive research ever conducted on the community college—the authors prescribed a solution in the concept of the guided pathway (see chapter 4 in this volume). More than 250 colleges are now experimenting with implementing the guided pathway, and foundations have funded a number of projects that are embedding the idea into community college culture.

Data are beginning to come in on reform efforts related to the completion agenda, which has a goal of doubling, by the year 2020, the number of students who achieve a certificate or an associate degree, or who transfer to a university. According to *Policy Meets Pathways*, a report by Jobs for the Future: "A decade of interventions and improvements have fallen short" (Couturier, 2014, para. 1). In spite of ten years of interventions and student support initiatives, the nation's most disadvantaged adults and young people are not gaining traction toward degrees. In *Redesigning America's Community Colleges* (Bailey, Jaggars, & Jenkins, 2015), key leaders at the Community College Research Center note that "despite an expansive reform movement built on the dedicated participation of thousands of faculty, administrators, policymakers, state education officials, researchers, and others, there is little evidence that the nation is moving toward a widespread and significant improvement in the outcomes of community college students" (p. vii). Reform efforts are falling short, even though, in the history of the community college, (1) there has never been so much agreement or focus by all stakeholders on the importance of completion, which has become the overarching mission of the community college; (2) there has never been so much funding from foundations to implement programs and practices that support completion; (3) there has never been so much research on what works to achieve student success; and (4) there have never been so many institutes, policy centers, and special agencies created to recommend and guide policy, programs, and practices related to completion.

Stakeholders agree on many of the proposed solutions designed to transform their institutions into champions and producers of student success:

- Colleges should implement and bring to scale high-impact practices.
- Colleges should create structured, guided pathways for all students.
- Colleges should reduce the number of or eliminate remedial courses and enroll students in college-ready courses with specialized support.

- Programs should be created in which students attend full time and without costs.
- Academic advising should be redesigned and required of all students.
- Evidence must be organized and used to make decisions.
- Students and faculty should be more engaged.
- Leaders must involve faculty to ensure that change and transformation will take place substantively and permanently.

So, with all the agreement, funding, and action, what is missing in this panoply of solutions? One answer is that reformers forgot to transform the curriculum, perhaps because they have come to believe that "it is easier to move a cemetery than it is to change the curriculum. We get no help from the residents." In any case, except for new math pathways and an acceleration of developmental courses, an overhaul of the curriculum—especially of what colleges call general education these days—has been largely ignored.

WHY IS THE CURRICULUM SO IMPORTANT?

The curriculum is the collective wisdom and expertise of the faculty about what is important for students to learn. And that places the curriculum front and center in any reform effort. All other reform efforts are piecemeal practices and programs dancing around the heart of the educational enterprise: the curriculum. If the current curriculum is not reformed, all other reform efforts are little more than trimming the branches of a dying tree.

Historically, the curriculum was an organized body of knowledge required of all students. When Harvard University was founded in 1636, the curriculum was a body of knowledge ensconced in the trivium and the quadrivium, seven courses created in medieval times and passed down for centuries. The development of new knowledge and new specializations expanded the curriculum to the point that many leaders and reformers referred to the curriculum as fractured.

Over the last century there have been numerous attempts to define an integrated curriculum: a common body of knowledge that would benefit all students and society and that would better prepare students for specialization in a program of study. The creation of an integrated curriculum around the great books model and the creation of a general education common core in the 1950s, 1960s, and 1970s are vestiges of this last major effort to organize a common core of knowledge in American higher education.

Today, the curriculum is a food court, a cafeteria of courses, a smorgasbord of disconnected pieces of knowledge, an enticing buffet of tantalizing items to tickle the intellectual palate. (What is going on with these metaphors about knowledge and learning as something to be eaten, to be ingested?!)

The vivid metaphors do describe a current curriculum that is, if not fractured, at least unfocused and not integrated. The disintegration of the common curriculum idea may be a result of increasing specialization, of student demand for more vocational courses, or of the proliferation of courses to reflect the self-interests of faculty members.

Community colleges no longer talk about curriculum integrity, and with good reason. At Lorain County Community College in Ohio, students may choose from among forty-six different courses in the arts and humanities to meet a three-course general education requirement, from among thirty-six courses in the social sciences to meet a three-course requirement, and from among forty-eight courses in math and science to meet a three-course requirement.

At Orange Coast College in California, students have even more choices. For students who want an associate of arts general education degree, the college catalog offers three degree options. In one option, students must earn twenty-five units distributed among five different areas. In area C, arts and humanities, students choose a minimum of three semester units, to include one course from Group 1 and one course from Group 2. In Group 1 sixty-four courses are listed, but students may also select any literature course from A141 through A285 and any course numbered A160 through A285H. In Group 2 there are ninety-seven courses, from which students are required to select one.

This proliferation of courses to meet curricular requirements may stem from the best of intentions; faculty want to provide more choices for students regarding their careers and their future educational plans. However, recent research, reported by Judith Scott-Clayton (2011) from the Community College Research Center, points out that too many choices confuse students and lead to poor decisions and poor planning. Too many choices also present a challenge for academic advisers, who have to help students make meaning of all the choices and create a plan to navigate the many options of multiple programs and a plethora of courses.

A RETURN TO THE INTEGRATED CURRICULUM

There is some concern in community colleges about the cafeteria model of distributed courses. Some leaders are beginning to speak again about a cohesive, an integrated, or an intentional curriculum, once championed by the advocates of general education, harking back to McGrath's classic definition of general education as "a common core of learning for the common man." The emphasis on integration is reflected not just in courses, but in programs as well.

Queensborough Community College and Guttman Community College, both in New York, are often cited by researchers as productive models of curricular integration that lead to increased learning, retention, and completion. Queensborough requires all first-time, full-time students to choose one of five freshman academies in which to enroll. The academies are organized around business, STEM, health-related science, visual and performing arts, and liberal arts. At Guttman, all new students are required to enroll in a first-year experience program, which features a required common core of four courses. The new curricular initiatives at both colleges are much more complex than described here and are cited to make the point about a move away from the cafeteria models so prevalent today and toward a more integrated curriculum.

As more is learned about the limitations of current reform efforts, colleges will hopefully turn to a reexamination of the curriculum as one of the essential elements in meeting the goals of the completion/student success agenda. Queensborough and Guttman are models to watch. Portland Community College (OR) and Central Piedmont Community College (NC) have established faculty committees to explore and update their general education programs.

Dozens, perhaps hundreds, of community colleges may have created such committees or will be considering such reviews in the near future. Disenchantment with the cafeteria model and the evidence-based research coming from the Community College Research Center and other institutes and agencies about the need for guided pathways and fewer choices could prompt a robust return to the integrated curriculum as the missing element in current reform efforts.

REFORMERS SHOULD CONSIDER
AN ESSENTIAL EDUCATION FOR ALL

For those college leaders and foundations considering curricular revision or reform, there is a new curricular paradigm on the horizon that should be examined. The new paradigm is an attempt to create a framework for an integrated curriculum while helping to resolve the historical divide between liberal education and workforce education. The idea is that if colleges are going to reform the curriculum, why not address the problem of the divide between liberal education and workforce education at the same time.

For centuries there has been a division between those who advocate for a liberal education and those who advocate for workforce education or career and technical education. That historical division can be seen in clear relief today in national organizational structures such as the Association of American Colleges and Universities, which in 2019 celebrated its 104th year as the leading advocate of liberal education, and the Association for Career and Technical Education, which in 2019 celebrated its 93rd year as the leading advocate of workforce education. The division is quite visible in community colleges, where there are separate divisions, separate faculty groups, separate facilities, separate degrees, separate curricula, and separate funding. These differences between liberal education and workforce education are often referred to in the literature of higher education as the classic confrontation, historical dilemma, widening disconnect, or perennial collegiate argument.

Advocates of both positions often lament these divisions and call for a more integrated approach. Integration, however, usually means housing faculty from both sides in a common facility or teaching a course from workforce education and one from liberal education in a team approach. Contextual education, such as the I-BEST program in Washington State, is an experiment in teaming instruction around a technical course and a developmental studies course. Although these approaches to complementarity may be useful and a step in the right direction, they do not lead to an integrated or cohesive curriculum.

In *Bread and Roses: Helping Students Make a Good Living and Live a Good Life*, published by the League for Innovation in the Community College in 2016, the author proposes a new approach to the curriculum that will reflect the best of liberal education and the best of workforce education, in what is called an essential education for all students. An essential education is defined as an integrated core of learning that includes and connects the key components from liberal education and workforce education to ensure that *a student is equipped to earn a good living and live a good life*. It is a quality education essential to all students. An essential education is what some advocates have identified as a liberal career education or a practical liberal education.

In an essay calling for an end to the divide between liberal arts and practical education, the president of Northeastern University, Joseph Aoun (2015), calls for an essential education that he terms the "New Literacy":

> What the worn-out juxtaposition of the liberal arts versus the applied disciplines overlooks is that aspects of each are essential for living a full life, both professionally and personally.... Both domains have relevance, utility and beauty, and both contain crucial components of a new skill set—a new literacy—that students need if they're to flourish in modern life and the global economy. (para. 14)

Joseph Aoun echoes the same position Calvin M. Woodward took in 1879 when he established the first school-based job training program in the nation, the St. Louis Manual Training School of Washington University. When the first class of fifty boys began their studies on September 6, 1880, they were greeted by an inscription from Woodward over the entrance:

> Hail to the skillful cunning hand! Hail to the cultured mind!
> Contending for the World's command,
> Here let them be combined. (Barlow, 1976, p. 46)

Students today do not need a curriculum for the "skillful cunning hand" and another curriculum for the "cultured mind." What is needed is an integrated, cohesive, intentional curriculum that combines the best of both: a curriculum for an essential education that all students take as their first college experience.

And there are plenty of clues to the nature of that curriculum. Advocates of liberal education and of workforce education have been moving closer and closer to a curriculum that unifies the two sides. Most advocates from both sides will agree that all students need skills and knowledge in problem solving, critical thinking, teamwork and collaboration, and communications—cross-cutting skills necessary for making a good living and living a good life. Workforce educators have already identified these important skills as "soft skills." The next step is a brief leap to creating a core curriculum of these four key skills:

Problem Solving 101
Critical Thinking 101
Teamwork and Collaboration 101
Communications 101

Four three-hour credit courses as stand-alone courses or combined in a twelve-credit learning community is one model of an integrated curriculum. Some colleges will add core courses in diversity, global awareness, and information technology.

These key skill/knowledge areas have already been identified by some community colleges, but instead of creating specific courses they create learning outcomes for critical thinking or for problem solving and attempt to embed these lists of outcomes in all college courses or in a selected but long list of courses. In this way, college leaders believe they are addressing key skills for students, and while their documentation of intent may satisfy accreditation standards, there is no guarantee and little evidence that these elaborate and complex systems work.

Here is a view from a faculty member about assessing learning outcomes when they have been embedded across the curriculum:

> Having served as our campus' Student Learning Outcomes coordinator from 2007 to 2014, I've developed a fair amount of skepticism as to the benefits of outcomes assessment. Considering the tremendous resources (money, time, mental anguish, etc.) that we devote to the process, I find myself frequently

asking the question, "To what end?" . . . I have yet to see any compelling data that shows that students, programs, institutions, etc. really do "improve" in any meaningful way as a direct result of outcomes-based assessment. . . . I do not believe for one moment that any college or university would continue to assess outcomes were the process no longer mandated by the accrediting agencies. We ought to be honest with ourselves on this point: We assess because we are compelled to do so, not because it improves student learning. (Koutroulis, 2014)

Perhaps it is not the assessment that is the problem; it may be that colleges are trying to assess something that did not work in the first place. Faculty have become cynical and exasperated by making important that which is not important at all.

Consider the challenge of embedding a list of learning outcomes throughout the curriculum: How are students to meet all the learning outcomes if they are distributed across hundreds of courses or even a few dozen? How are outcomes distributed equally among courses; what if two or three of the outcomes make up half or more of the learning activities embedded in a handful of key courses? How do students aggregate an integrated core of learning if they specialize early in vocational or other courses that may not be subject to the inclusion of learning outcomes? How does the college track part-time students to ensure they have met all the learning outcome requirements? Can the college be sure that the learning outcomes, even though documented in the syllabus, are deeply embedded in the course and not just add-ons to meet requirements? Can colleges be sure that faculty understand how to teach for the outcomes in their courses—and are doing so? How does the college evaluate the faculty on how well they implement the outcomes? How does the college evaluate the extent to which the student has achieved an integrated core of learning based on the outcomes? If the learning outcomes are so important and include the core learning outcomes every student should achieve, then why don't colleges just create a required course for each of the outcomes to better ensure that students achieve them?

Core courses, of course, do not always work either, but they are more manageable for everyone, and they are easier to explain to students. If faculty from liberal education and from workforce education can agree on the common elements of core courses and construct content and teaching strategies that apply to the courses, colleges stand a better chance of creating an integrated curriculum that will help students make a good living and live a good life. It is an idea that could play a leading role in transforming the community college world.

NOTES

1. This chapter is adapted from T. O'Banion, "Curriculum: The Missing Element in Reform," *Learning Abstracts 18*, no. 9 (September 2015).

REFERENCES

American Association of Community Colleges (AACC). (2012). *Reclaiming the American dream: Community colleges and the nation's future.* Washington, DC: AACC.

Aoun, J. E. (2015, April 20). A complete education. *Inside Higher Ed.* Retrieved from http://www.insidehighered.com/views/2015/04/20/essay-calls-ending-divide-between-liberal-arts-and-practical-education

Bailey, T. R., Jaggars, S., & Jenkins, D. (2015). *Redesigning America's community colleges: A clearer path to student success.* Cambridge, MA: Harvard University Press.

Barlow, M. (1976, May). The vocational age emerges, 1876–1926. *American Vocational Education, 51*(5), 45–58.

Community College Research Center. (n.d.). Retrieved from http://ccrc.tc.columbia.edu/media/k2/attachments/shapeless-rive

Couturier, L. K. (2014). *Policy meets pathways: A state policy agenda for transformational change.* Boston: Jobs for the Future. Retrieved from https://www.jff.org/resources/policy-meets-pathways-state-policy-agenda-transformational-change/

Koutroulis, M. (2014, October 21). Re: Learning outcomes [Electronic mailing list message]. Retrieved from LearningOutcomes@listserv.cccnext.net

O'Banion, T. (2016). *Bread and roses: Helping students make a good living and live a good life.* Chandler, AZ: League for Innovation in the Community College.

Scott-Clayton, J. (2011). *The shapeless river: Does a lack of structure inhibit students' progress at community colleges?* CCRC Working Paper No. 25. New York:

Index

activities, 182–183; guided pathways, 185–186; history of community college concept, 168–169; importance of, 15–16, 179; partnerships, 172–178; philanthropic organizations and, 180; STEM focus, 184, 188; technology impacting, 170–171; training for displaced workers, 181; trends, 15–16,

186–188; as unique innovation, 167–168

workforce education *vs.* liberal education, 287–290

Worth, Jennifer, 16, 167–190

Worthen, Molly, 44

Youth Career Connect program, 198

About the Editor

President emeritus of the League for Innovation in the Community College, Terry U. O'Banion has worked in the field of community colleges for fifty-nine years. He has consulted at more than one thousand community colleges and authored sixteen books and over two hundred articles. Five national awards have been established in his name, including the Microsoft Student Champion Award and the Educational Testing Service O'Banion Prize for Teaching and Learning. He has been a dean at two Florida community colleges; a professor of higher education at Illinois, Berkeley, Texas, Toronto, Hawaii, and NOVA; and president of the League for Innovation in the Community College for twenty-three years. O'Banion earned a BA in English (with honors) and a master's degree in counseling from the University of Florida and a PhD in higher education administration-community colleges from Florida State University.

About the Contributors

Andra Armstrong is lead media outreach and strategic communications of the College Promise Campaign, serving as its first senior strategist. She holds a bachelor's degree in economics from the University of Massachusetts at Amherst and a master's degree in journalism and public affairs from the American University. Before joining the College Promise Campaign, she held a variety of reporting, editing, and production positions at *Congressional Quarterly*, Time-Life Books, C-SPAN, and NPR.

George R. Boggs is president and CEO emeritus of the American Association of Community Colleges and superintendent/president emeritus of Palomar College in San Marcos, California. He continues to be an active consultant, teacher, author, and speaker. He is the author of more than one hundred articles, books, and chapters on various aspects of higher education. He currently teaches classes in emerging higher education issues in doctoral programs at San Diego State University and National American University. Boggs holds a bachelor's degree in chemistry from The Ohio State University, a master's degree in chemistry from the University of California at Santa Barbara, and a PhD in educational administration from The University of Texas at Austin.

Walter Bumphus is president and CEO of the American Association of Community Colleges. He has served as a professor in the Community College Leadership Program and as chair of the Department of Educational Administration at The University of Texas at Austin, holding the A. M. Aikin Regents Endowed Chair in Junior and Community College Education Leadership. He has served as president of the Louisiana Community and Technical College System, chancellor of Baton Rouge Community College, president of Brookhaven College (TX), and president of the Higher Education Division of Voyager Expanded Learning. Bumphus has been recognized as a distinguished graduate from both Murray State University and The University of Texas at Austin and has received numerous awards for his national leadership in community colleges. He also has the distinction of having worked collaboratively with two presidential administrations and has served on some of the most important councils and commissions in the nation.

Michael Collins is vice president at Jobs for the Future, a national nonprofit working to transform the workforce and education systems to accelerate economic advancement for all. For over a decade he has led a multistate postsecondary reform network committed to increasing the success of students from low-income backgrounds through connecting colleges and state systems to evidence-based practices and policies and supporting the latter's implementation through nationally recognized initiatives such as Achieving the Dream, Completion by Design, and the Student Success Center Initiative. Collins serves on the board of the National Student Clearinghouse Research Center, National Center for Higher Education Management Systems, and Guttman Community College. He is a consulting editor for *Change Magazine* and a Pahara-Aspen fellow.

Nikki Edgecombe is a senior research scientist at the Community College Research Center at Teachers College, Columbia University, the nation's leading independent authority on public open-access, two-year colleges. Her scholarship focuses on education equity, developmental education, and teaching and learning in higher education. She also studies large-scale reform efforts and the translation of state policy to the institutional level. Edgecombe is the principal investigator for the Center for the Analysis of Postsecondary Readiness, a US Department of Education–funded research and development center jointly operated with MDRC. She is a graduate of Columbia University and the University of Pennsylvania.

Deborah L. Floyd is professor of higher education leadership, Florida Atlantic University, Boca Raton, Florida. Her career spans over forty-five years of academic service to community colleges and universities in Florida, Iowa, Kentucky, Texas, and Virginia, where she has served as a community college president, vice president and dean of students, assistant to a university chancellor, a professor, and a university graduate dean. She is a former member of the board of the American Association of Community Colleges and a past president of the Council for the Study of Community Colleges. She has published more than seventy-five articles, chapters, monographs, and books and is an active speaker and consultant. For eight years she has served as editor in chief of the *Community College Journal of Research & Practice*, which is published twelve times per year.

Barbara Gellman-Danley is president of the Higher Learning Commission. Prior to joining the commission, she was the president of the University of Rio Grande/Rio Grande Community College in Ohio. She previously served as vice chancellor of the Ohio Board of Regents, president at Antioch University McGregor, vice president at Monroe Community College, and vice chancellor at the Oklahoma State Regents for Higher Education.

She has held several board and commission memberships in her career and has consulted at more than thirty institutions on strategic planning, organizational reengineering, and technology. She holds a BS from Syracuse University, an MLS from Simmons College, an MBA from Oklahoma City University, and PhD in communication from the University of Oklahoma, with postgraduate work at New York University, Harvard University, and the University of Chicago. She holds three certifications: certified professional coach (CPC), associate certified coach (ACC/ICF), and social and emotional intelligence (SEI).

Ana Gutierrez is an associate director at Jobs for the Future, where she conducts research and provides capacity-building technical assistance for several regional place-based initiatives in California. Gutierrez has over ten years' experience in education, nonprofits, government, and politics. She has worked on projects including teacher preparation pathway development between regional K–14 systems and university teacher credentialing institutions; a study abroad program and scholarships for underrepresented, first-generation community college students; and inclusionary housing policies, land use management, and the creation of a seven-year community investment grant. She conducted a quantitative analysis for the US Department of Labor's apprenticeship program as part of an international research team. Gutierrez enjoyed a fourteen-year teaching career in California as an English teacher at Liberty High School in Brentwood and as a tenured English professor at Los Medanos College in Pittsburg, California. She has earned a BA from the University of California, Berkeley, and a master's degree from the Institute d'Etudes Politiques de Paris (SciencesPo).

Sarah Hooker is a senior program manager with Jobs for the Future (JFF), a national nonprofit that drives transformation in education and workforce systems to promote economic advancement for underserved populations. Based in JFF's California office, she leads program pilots; analyzes policy; and provides technical assistance related to high school improvement, college access, and dual enrollment. She has authored several publications on early college designs and high school to college transitions. Hooker also has substantial experience in the field of immigrant and English Language Learner education. She has worked with the Office of Civic Engagement and Immigrant Affairs in the City and County of San Francisco and the Migration Policy Institute in Washington, DC. Hooker holds a master's degree from the University of Chicago's School of Social Service Administration and a bachelor's degree from Pomona College.

James Jacobs was president of Macomb Community College (MI) from 2008 to 2017. Prior to his appointment he held many roles at the college, including director for the Center for Workforce Development and Policy. He also served as associate director, Community College Research Center, Teachers College, Columbia University, and currently serves as a research affiliate. Jacobs is a past president of the National Council for Workforce Education; a member of the Community College Advisory Panel to the Educational Testing Service; and a member of the executive board of the Global Corporate College, a network of US community colleges and universities. He currently serves as a senior adviser to the Ralph Wilson Foundation and lecturer at the University of Michigan School of Education. He also serves on local boards in Michigan, including the Center for Automotive Research, Metropolitan Affairs Council, Detroit Institute of Arts, and United Way for Southeastern Michigan.

Martha Kanter leads the College Promise Campaign, a national initiative to increase college access, affordability, quality, and completion in American higher education, starting in America's community colleges. She is also a senior fellow at New York University's Steinhardt Institute for Higher Education Policy. She specializes in policy efforts to identify and apply innovative, evidence-based education interventions, financing models, and behavioral incentives to raise America's high school and college graduation rates. From 2009 to 2013, Kanter served as the US under secretary of education, overseeing all federal postsecondary education programs. From 1993 to 2009, she was president of De Anza College and then chancellor of the Foothill-De Anza Community College District in Silicon Valley, California. She began her career as an alternative high school teacher in Lexington, Massachusetts. Kanter holds a BA degree in sociology from Brandeis University, an MEd from Harvard University, and an EdD from the University of San Francisco.

Eric V. Martin has served as vice president and chief of staff at the Higher Learning Commission since 2015. He understands the crucial importance of community colleges as a former community college student himself, later as an adjunct faculty member, and through other professional positions. He joined HLC in 2010 as a staff liaison and served 120 institutions, including numerous community colleges. Between 2012 and 2015 he also served as director of the Academic Quality Improvement Program (AQIP), an accreditation pathway with substantial community college presence. Before HLC, Martin worked closely with community colleges while at Governors State University, a then upper-division university partnered with community colleges throughout Chicago's south suburbs. His roles included director of writing across the curriculum, associate provost, and dean. Martin holds a doctor of arts degree in English from Illinois State University, and he recently completed the Institute for Educational Management at Harvard University.

Senior vice president, Roueche Graduate Center 2012–2018 and senior lecturer, The University of Texas at Austin, **Margaretta B. Mathis** has played significant roles in a number of recent national projects, including Achieving the Dream, Board of Trustees Institute, College and Career Transitions Initiative, Governance Institute for Student Success, Developmental Education Initiative, and Center for Community College Student Engagement's Survey of Entering Student Engagement. She is coauthor with Byron McClenney of *Making Good on the Promise of the Open Door* and is coeditor with John Roueche of the RGC columns "Community College Week" and "Diverse Issues in Higher Education." Mathis holds a BA from Ohio Wesleyan University, an executive MBA in international management from the Thunderbird School of Global Management, and a PhD in higher education administration from The University of Texas at Austin, where she was a distinguished graduate and senior Roueche fellow.

Byron McClenney serves as chair of the Colorado State Board for Community Colleges and Occupational Education. His career has included almost thirty-three years as a community college chief executive and a decade directing student success initiatives in the Community College Leadership Program at The University of Texas at Austin. He was a founder of Achieving the Dream and served for ten years as the national director of leadership coaching. Through a partnership with Association of Community College Trustees, he helped create the Governance Institute for Student Success and cofacilitated institutes around the country for eight years. Career highlights were receiving the AACC Leadership Award, the PBS O'Banion Prize, and the TIAA-CREF Hesburgh Award for work at the Community College of Denver. He has spent decades in consulting, research, writing, and speaking focused on developmental education, institutional effectiveness, institutional transformation, strategic planning, and leadership.

Kay McClenney is a partner in Mc^2 Consultants and serves as senior adviser to the president & CEO of the American Association of Community Colleges. She was founding director of the Center for Community College Student Engagement at The University of Texas at Austin, where she also served as a faculty member in the UT Program in Higher Education Leadership. McClenney has led an array of national projects focused on student success and equity; authored numerous publications; and received a number of national awards, including the national leadership award from the American Association of Community Colleges (2011) and the Diverse Champions Award (2017).

Mark David Milliron is an award-winning leader, author, speaker, and consultant, who has worked with community colleges, universities, K–12 schools, foundations, corporations, associations, and government agencies across the country and around the world. He is cofounder and chief learning officer of Civitas Learning. Outside of Civitas, Mark helps catalyze positive change in education through his service on the boards and advisory councils of leading education organizations, including the Trellis Foundation, the Global Online Academy, the Mastery Transcript Consortium, and ISKME/OER Commons. In previous roles, Mark served as the deputy director for postsecondary success with the Bill & Melinda Gates Foundation; founding chancellor of WGU Texas; endowed fellow and director of the National Institute of Staff and Organizational Development at The University of Texas at Austin; vice president for education and medical practice with SAS; and president and CEO of the League for Innovation in the Community College.

John O'Brien currently serves as the president and CEO of EDUCAUSE. Prior to this appointment he served as a faculty member, provost, and president of several community colleges in Minneapolis/St. Paul. He was associate vice chancellor for instructional technology, deputy CIO, and senior vice chancellor for academic and student affairs at Minnesota State Colleges and Universities, the fourth largest system of higher education in the United States, with thirty community and technical colleges, seven universities, and more than 375,000 students. He was a student at Augustana College (BA in English and education), Trinity College, Dublin (master's in Anglo-Irish literature), and the University of Minnesota (PhD, English).

John E. Roueche, president of the Roueche Graduate Center, 2012–2018, served as the Sid Richardson Regents Chair and as professor and director of the Community College Leadership Program at The University of Texas at Austin from 1971 to 2012. Since 1970 John Roueche has spoken at more than thirteen hundred colleges and universities on topics of teaching and leadership excellence. He is the author of 37 books and more than 175 articles and chapters focused on leadership, teaching, and learning. He has served as principal investigator for more than $40 million in projects funded by major American foundations during his years of service at The University of Texas. John Roueche has received forty national awards for distinguished service and leadership. More than two hundred of his doctoral graduates have become community college presidents.

Michael L. Skolnik is a professor emeritus in the Department of Leadership, Higher, and Adult Education at the University of Toronto, where he held the William G. Davis Chair in Community College Leadership and directed the PhD program in community college studies. He has published widely on community colleges and other topics in higher education and has been an adviser to numerous higher education agencies. In 1990 he was the first recipient of the Research & Scholarship Award of the Canadian Society for the Study of Higher Education. Skolnik's recent research has focused on international comparisons of community colleges and related types of post-secondary institutions, approaches to career education, and models for quality assurance in academic and vocational education.

Bruce Vandal serves as senior vice president and interim leadership at Complete College America (CCA), directing the corequisite remedial education reform strategy and providing key policy leadership on CCA's completion agenda. He directs several projects related to corequisite remedial education reform and math pathways, including the Scaling Corequisite Initiative, funded by the Lumina Foundation and the Michael and Susan Dell Foundation, and the Building Math Pathways into Programs of Study project, funded by the Lumina Foundation. Before CCA, Vandal was the vice president of development and outreach as well as the director of the Postsecondary Education and Workforce Development Institute at the Education Commission of the States, where he directed a number of national projects on developmental education. He earned his PhD in education policy and administration with an emphasis in higher education administration from the University of Minnesota.

Joel Vargas is a vice president at Jobs for the Future (JFF) and leads the work of JFF's west coast office in Oakland, California, as well as the national School & Learning Designs team. He also researches and advises on state policies to promote improved high school and postsecondary success for underserved students. He has helped policy makers and intermediary organizations develop state and federal policies that expand early college schools and other school designs incorporating college coursework into high school. Before JFF, Vargas was a teacher and directed, initiated, and studied a variety of middle and high school programs designed to help more underrepresented students get into and through postsecondary education. He received a bachelor's degree in journalism from Boston University and an EdD from the Harvard Graduate School of Education.

Suzanne Walsh is a deputy director on the postsecondary success team at the Bill & Melinda Gates Foundation, where she leads the foundation's institutional transformation strategy, which includes initiatives such as Completion by Design and the Frontier Set. Before joining Gates, Walsh worked at Lumina Foundation, where she managed the Making Opportunity Affordable initiative, and at the Heinz Endowments, where she focused on the innovation economy, including the role of community colleges and universities. Walsh started her work with community colleges as the coordinator of special projects at Cuyahoga Community College (OH). She has her juris doctorate and master's in social work from Case Western Reserve University, bachelor of science from Cornell University, and associate in applied science from Hudson Valley Community College (NY), where her father also taught. She was a member of the World Economic Forum's Future of the University Global Agenda Council and is a current member of the Global Learning Council. She is also a proud judge for Dance Your Ph.D.

Jennifer Worth is senior vice president, workforce and economic development, for the American Association of Community Colleges (AACC). She oversees projects that partner community colleges with workforce boards, economic development entities, labor market intermediaries, and other community organizations to drive workforce and economic opportunity. She interfaces with federal agencies and fosters relationships with foundations and industry partners to align talent pipelines from colleges. Worth also directs the annual Workforce Development Institute (WDI) for AACC, an annual event for workforce development professionals at community colleges. She has held positions at the National Center on Education and the Economy, the Academy for Educational Development, the Center for Post-Compulsory Education and Lifelong Learning, and the National Association of Workforce Boards. She serves on the board of SkillsUSA and the National Association for Community College Entrepreneurship. Her master of public policy and management degree was earned at the University of Melbourne in Australia.